Mattias Hamberg

Strategic Financial Decisions

Liber
•
Abstrakt

Strategic Financial Decisions

ISBN 91-47-06280-0

Redaktör: Ola Håkansson
Formgivare: Daniel Sjöfors
Sättning: LundaText AB

1:1

Printed in Sweden by
Daleke Grafiska AB, Malmö 2001

Liber Ekonomi, Baltzarsgatan 4, 205 10 Malmö
tfn 040-25 86 00, fax 040-97 05 50
http://www.liber.se
Kundtjänst tfn 08-690 93 30, fax 08-690 93 01

To Katarina
for all her Love and Support

Preface

Thank you for considering *Strategic Financial Decisions*. This book is about financial decisions in modern companies. When I look at corporate finance I see it as a research area within the social sciences. I see actors interacting in incomplete and uncertain markets. I see conflicts of interest and sometimes irrationality. I see human beings with all their faults and beauties. Within this chaos researchers must search for patterns; systematic relationships that enable us to understand the most important variables in financial decision-making better. This book is my description of corporate finance. Perhaps not everyone agrees with it at all occasions. But I do hope I stimulate a discussion among my readers, that I get you to think about why managers make certain decisions in certain ways, and that you question their motives. It does not matter if you fully agree with me, as long as you take a serious interest in the topic.

I started this project because I could not find a textbook that fully catered for the needs of my students. At that time ignorance was your bless. If I would have known the time and effort required to write this text, it would have been considerably less tempting to pursue the project. Over the years many people, in and out of academia, have inspired me and it is impossible to remember all of them. A particular gratitude goes to my friend, former colleague and mentor: Associate professor Mats Åkerblom of Uppsala University. His view of financial decision-making has shaped mine and many of the ideas presented in the text originate from his mind and his interpretation of the world.

My intention is that this book will be used in introductory and intermediary courses in corporate finance at Scandinavian universities. I personally think that it is beneficial to complement it with some research articles. In the end of each chapter I provide suggestions of suitable texts. An alternative is to use the book in conjunction with a more basic book covering the techniques of financial management. Then it would be possible to use it as the very first book the students read in corporate finance. In the end of each chapter there are a number of key concepts and key issues to discuss. I personally like to focus my teaching on these concepts and issues.

I am sure that there must be errors in a text as vast as this one. I applaud those of you smart enough to identify them. For the sake of all my other readers it would be neat if you could send me your corrections along with some comments on the text. I also welcome comments and suggestions for improvements in future editions. Please send these directly to me, or to the e-mail address: mattiashamberg@hotmail.com

Bergen in September 2001

Mattias Hamberg

Table of Content

Chapter 10

Company Valuation

Chapter 11

Corporate Objectives, Growth Strategies and Value

Chapter 1

The Fundamentals of Financial Theory

This chapter aims at:

- Describing the main objectives with the book you are holding in your hands, and discussing the motives for a behavioural approach to corporate finance.
- Providing a brief review of the origin of financial theory and explaining its relationship to economic theory.
- Outlining the major areas that financial theory can be separated into.
- Specifying the real-life problems that financial theory has helped us understand, and discussing to what extent managers can rely on financial theory when making decisions.

1.1 Introducing Strategic Financial Decisions

The purpose of the book you are holding in your hand is to explain in which ways financial theories can help managers when making strategic financial decisions in their corporations. Throughout the book there are innumerable examples of how decision-makers can be helped by the advances that have been made in corporate finance over the years, but there are just as many examples of situations where there are problems with applying the theories.

This book has been written because it is necessary to have a textbook that provides and emphasises a managerial perspective on corporate finance. In this book financial decisions are considered as they are made within organisations and by business managers. The perspective that is used is not a shareholder perspective, but a managerial perspective on financial decision-making. Management's view of financial issues is in many ways similar to that of the organisation's stakeholders (including shareholders), but in some ways it can differ. Management have to function as an intermediary both between stakeholders, and between product markets, where they make the investments, and capital markets, where they finance their investments. Most financial literature focuses on the economic consequences of financial decisions and tries to explain the optimal ones, based on the maximisation of shareholder wealth. While such behaviour might be what both shareholders and society in general are hoping for, it might not be what managers are actually doing. For me as an author this causes some problems. Should a textbook in corporate finance teach how managers ought to make financial decisions, or describe how they actually make their decisions in practise?

When having to choose between only these two alternatives I would also go for the more normative teaching of how decisions should be made in the light of economic theory. But in this book, these two perspectives are combined. The purpose is to show how managers ought to behave, but to continuously challenge this perspective by describing in what ways managers are likely to deviate from the suggested behaviour. In order to do this (without losing those readers who firmly believe in rational economic decision-making), I spend time explaining the origin, purpose and viewpoints of standard financial theory. The intention is never to tell the reader how to make "optimal" decisions (neither based on economic theory nor on any other theory), but to describe those factors that influence the decision-making. This can be individual-specific factors, company-specific factors, or situation-specific factors. To me, this is much more of a behavioural view of corporate finance than the one usually portrayed in other, more normative, textbooks.

Another objective of this text is to keep the discussion at a *strategic* level. Depending on whom you speak to, the term strategy can have different meanings. By keeping the discussion at a strategic level it is hereby meant that it is focused on general theories concerning major financial decisions in the corporation. In much of the text, practical technicalities dependent on time-specific matters are avoided. On purpose, the techniques used, for example, in the issuance of new equity, the design of leasing and factoring agreements, due diligence processes, and when hedging cash flows in foreign currencies are avoided. The reason for not incorporating these issues is that students benefits more from learning techniques, which can change over time, when they enter particular positions in their future business careers. Although the techniques that can be used to solve unique problems might vary, the economic problems and their underlying factors driving the choice of technique will remain the same.

There is one more issue that has encouraged the writing of this book. Financial decisions are very much affected by the environment in which managers act. Factors such as corporate culture, traditions within society, and legislation have a tremendous impact on managerial behaviours. There is no universal Financial Theory that provides objective truths to each and everyone. Somebody who wants to learn both what an "economically rational" decision is, and why actual decisions have been made need to understand the impact of the business context. Almost all textbooks within corporate finance are written by people who have an orientation towards Anglo-Saxon countries, and then primarily the United States. Also, most of the research within the area has been carried out by American researchers studying American corporations.

While referring to the abundant American research literature this book tries to provide a Scandinavian perspective. Because of this, the examples that are used throughout the text come from Swedish companies. The relationship between managers and shareholders is in general considerably different in Sweden compared to Anglo-Saxon countries. For students outside Anglo-Saxon countries it is extremely important to understand the differences and their implications on various financial decisions. Whenever it is possible that this specific context can have an impact, this is discussed.

As a university discipline corporate finance is relatively new, especially when considering the length of time that human beings have been involved in trade and commerce. But over the last forty years corporate finance has emerged from being an art performed by practitioners into a fully-fledged science involving thousands of researchers around the world. In fact, corporate finance is likely to be one of the fields within the social sciences that has changed the most over these last forty years. This is both for good and bad. With corporate finance being such an integrated part of all business activities, having a financial theory supporting companies' financial activities is generally speaking good. On the other hand, there is sometimes a tendency to take financial theory too seriously. Unlike physics or any other natural science, corporate finance is based on the interaction between individuals or groups of individuals. To find universal laws within such an interaction is not always feasible, in fact it is sometimes quite unlikely. Of all the things you learn from this text, I hope this is the one you remember the most.

1.2 The Development of Financial Theory

Humans have been engaged in various forms of business activities for thousands of years; enormous projects such as the pyramids were initiated and completed thousands of years ago, highly uncertain sea voyages around the world were being financed in the 15th century, and there is evidence of surprisingly advanced financial markets hundreds of years ago. If we are going to appreciate the importance of modern financial theory for and in support of decision-making, we must also ask ourselves how such projects, ventures and markets could take place so long ago? Did the people of those ages have any financial theories that could help them? If not, were they disadvantaged in comparison to the decision-makers of today, and if so, in which ways were they disadvantaged?

Not many people would dare to give more than tentative answers to such difficult questions. But we must at least raise them. Most certainly the issues mentioned above were addressed without the help of any financial theory, as we know it today. But people of these times had a gut feeling of how things could be done.[1] To take an example; the term "risk" stems from the ancient Greek term *rhiza*, which meant to sail around a certain cliff (Bernstein, 1995). This was a venture that was not certain and could

1 It is similarly interesting to think how people played games of chance before probability theory was developed. Gamblers in fact made several of the major developments within probability theory. Theoretical developments were probably established long after intuition had helped some gamblers to make themselves a fortune. See e.g. Bernstein (1996) for a discussion of the development of risk and probability theory.

have undesirable consequences. Risk might not be measurable, but decision-makers in these times were surely considering it. Moreover, in many times and eras of the past a lack of legal structure, public information, and even democracy caused very few problems. Emperors, kings, landlords and other autocratic leaders did not care about wages, interest, and the costs of raw materials. In their system they had free access or no access to resources. Financial theory might play a lesser role in such an environment.

Financial theory is an offspring from economic theory and so it must be within economic theory we look for its origin. It has been argued that the modern economic theory evolved as a response to the industrialisation that started in England in the 18th century. With industrialisation came an era, in which large private enterprises emerged in a relatively democratic environment. The great book by Adam Smith, *The Wealth of Nations*, from 1776 is usually recognised as the first systematic analysis of the business enterprise. The remarkable thing with *The Wealth of Nations* is however not that it was the first book to do so, the study was after all conducted at a time when the industrial revolution took place and somebody was bound to sooner or later make a comment on it, but the elegance with which it was made. Adam Smith took a particular interest in the organisation of the business enterprise and he was fascinated by, for example, the division of labour that the new factories were using. In many ways his descriptions and analyses are still today of greatest interest.

Adam Smith was not the only one who took an interest in the organisation and management of large private enterprises, and the societies they existed in. During the following century economic ideas were formulated and slowly a theory of economics emerged. During the first century after Adam Smith Economics was so closely connected to Politics that the whole area was known as political economy and it was not until the end of the 19th century that Economics became an area in itself. It has been argued that a separation of economic instruction and policy advice from political constraints gave the subject a more earnestly sought reputation as a science (Galbraith, 1987:266–267). The main textbook within this area at the time was *The Principles of Economics* written by John Marshall (1890). For decades this was the most used economic textbook and many of the core concepts of economic theory were discussed already then. With very few exceptions most of these economic ideas were developed and expressed by Anglo-Saxon researchers. Their dominance has not changed since these times. Today we refer to these economic ideas as (classical) micro-economic theory, and as the modern financial theory emerged it borrowed all its features from it. Classical economic theory is an equilibrium theory where the supply and demand for resources determine the price and volume that is traded. Economic theory also works at an aggregated level, explaining market equilibriums without getting enmeshed with the psychology of the individual market actors who instead are assumed to behave rationally.

By the end of the 19th century Wall Street in New York had emerged as the financial centre of the United States, whereas London was the prime capital centre of Europe. But beside them there was a much greater number of share markets than we have today. In Sweden, for example, several cities had their own share markets where local companies could be traded. Now with industrialisation, and large-scale projects, such as e.g. the building of railroads in the United States, the modern share markets, as we know them today, emerged. Without doubt the leading country in this development was the United States where the concentration of capital in the hands of a small group of people in combination with the creation of large production units with no strong owner shaped the governance system. In this environment the anonymisation of corporate ownership was one of the most significant characteristics. Already at the turn of the last century many of the largest American companies had no visible strong owner. To appreciate the merits of portfolio diversification, which we shall look more into in a later chapter, appears more sensible in such an environment.

In comparison, the situation in Sweden, and in much of continental Europe, differed. Here the ties between those who controlled corporate resources (management) and those who owned them (shareholders) were much closer. Institutional differences, which we will return to in Chapter Three, maintained these characteristics that to some extent still prevail. In the 1920s the role of the capital market in the United States increased dramatically. After the First World War, Europe had to be rebuilt and this led to a need for substantial investments. Economic activity was high and during the 1920s, and particularly its latter half, share prices increased like never before. This phenomenon was not at all an isolated American one, but was experienced in most developed countries. Speculators were drawn to the financial markets that often were seen as a gamble in which you could not loose. Well, in 1929 the bubble burst and for a long period of time many looked upon share markets with great scepticism (Galbraith, 1961). It took almost 25 years until the average American stock recovered to the value it had prior to the crash.

These developments are very important for us when trying to understand the development of financial theory, or rather the lack of development. Economic theory had been developed with great seriousness. The theories of how our economy worked were to be compared with the theories of natural sciences. Economic theories were based on rational behaviours, estimates of preferences and utilities, and markets where there were equilibriums between supplies and demands. If capital markets were not to be trusted, investors irrational and guided by hopes and fears, then finance did not fit the world of these economic scientists.

There were hardly any serious attempts to theorise around the activities taking place in financial markets, nor around the financial activities taking place in companies. Up until the 1950s we hardly find any contributions to modern financial theory. This does not mean people were not interested in financial matters. Early books in finance stressed financial techniques rather than financial theories. There were several guidebooks on how to make investments in capital markets that engendered great interest (e.g. Lefevre, 1923 and Graham and Dodd, 1934). But in the 1940s things started to change. Already in 1938 Williams had written a treatise on the valuation of securities, and in 1944 von Neumann and Morgenstern laid out a way of measuring utilities. These two contributions provided a ground for the coming mathematical analysis of individuals' choices, and thus their economic behaviours. Financial theory did, as an offspring of economic theory, focus on markets and assumed rationality at the individual investor level of analysis. Decisions in financial markets are therefore determined by preferences between risk and expected returns.

The works by both von Neumann and Morgenstern (1944), and Williams (1938) inspired the path-breaking contribution to financial theory developed by Harry Markowitz (1952; 1959). He created what is today known as *portfolio theory*. A giant-step forward in the development of financial theory and regarded by most people as the first contribution to

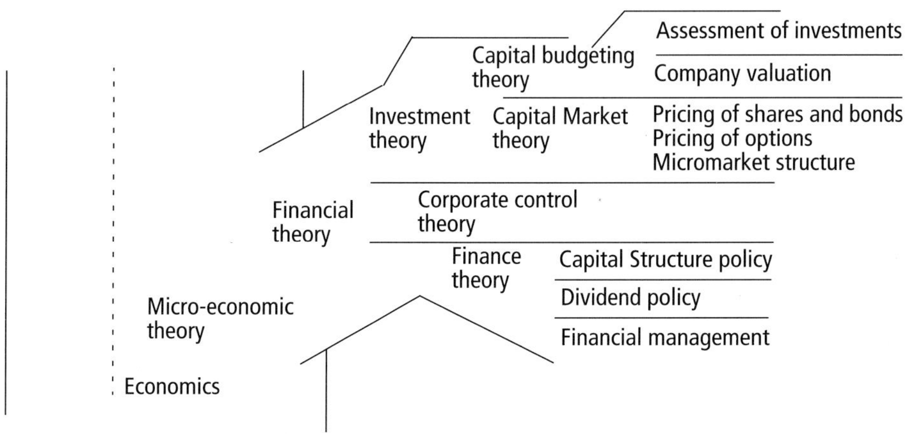

Figure 1.1 – The evolvement of financial theory.

modern financial theory. Markowitz created a theory in which risk is measured on the basis of historical security price volatility. Such volatility (risk) can be reduced if the investor holds more than one security and the securities have a correlation less than one. One of the ideas coming from Markowitz portfolio theory is that under the assumption that securities are correctly priced the optimal combination of securities is the market portfolio. When an investor holds the market portfolio all unnecessary security volatility vanishes. From now on, economists started to look at financial markets as a place where systematic analyses were possible.

Extensions to Markowitz's idea were made by several researchers. Tobin (1958) introduced the idea that investors had two options, either to invest in the optimal combination of risky securities (the market portfolio), or in a risk-free security. This eased the financial decision-making. In the early 1960s asset pricing models such as the *Capital Asset Pricing Model* (CAPM) were developed (Sharpe, 1964; Lintner, 1965; and Mossin, 1966). A great number of extensions to the CAPM have been developed over the years. There has also been suggested some alternative models, such as the *Arbitrage Pricing Theory* (Ross, 1976). Nonetheless, the capital market branch of financial theory is based on portfolios of assets where portfolio risk is the key determinant of return.

Capital market theory deals with the pricing of securities in financial markets. The efficiency of the market has always been a central part of economic theory, financial theory and capital market theory. When Markowitz developed portfolio theory, he, unlike e.g. Williams (1938), was not concerned with how investors had assigned securities their correct value. Markowitz just assumed investors chose between correctly valued securities. Because securities are always thought to be correctly priced, capital market theory is, just like economic theory is, an equilibrium theory. According to capital market theory, the supply and demand of capital resources are always in equilibrium and therefore it is impossible for an investor to systematically earn excessive returns. Whenever new information concerning the future appears the market processes this information and incorporates it into security prices. This calls for what today is known as *market efficiency*. It is in fact the market efficiency criterion, which forges the strong link between financial theory and economic theory. Without it, financial economists would have to look at the behaviours of individual investors and managers instead of focusing on the allocation of scarce resources at the market level.

Capital market theory is only one of the branches of financial theory. The area of corporate finance, which contains a wider perspective on the financing of investments within a company, also made tremendous leaps forward in the 1950s and early 1960s. In 1958 Miller and Modigliani published their widely acclaimed article in which they established that under the assumption of efficient capital markets, a company's value is not affected by *the choice of capital structure*. Three years later they took their analysis one step further and claimed that neither did *the choice of dividend policy* (Miller and Modigliani, 1961). Suddenly, the ideas stemming from economic theory could be shown to have direct consequences for decision-making within the business enterprise. This spurred a lot of research and had spillover effects on, for example, theories of working capital management. Ever since they published their analyses researchers have come to look for factors and situations where financial policies actually make sense. To find them one must look for market inefficiencies, of which the most common ones are taxation, information asymmetries and transaction costs.

Now these are financial theories, established on assumptions that were not always realistic. In the early days of modern financial theory researchers were more concerned with building theories, than they were with testing them. But in the mid-1960s, about the same time as these theoretical contributions were published, an important invention came about: the computer. With it came the ability to collect, store and analyse massive amounts of information. As before it was American universities that led this development. They were the ones which had not only the technology, but also the access to data. Now financial researchers could test whether their theories stood up to the challenges of real life. In this new era the University of Chicago soon played a dominant role. The Centre for Research in Security Prices (CRSP, pronounced "crisp") was, and still is, closely associated with the University and its databases, computer technology and financial support has helped finance take many steps forward towards the quantitative game it is today. Econometricians soon came to realise that capital markets form an excellent playground when developing and testing their statistical methods. Over the years, the academic community has been able to learn e.g. whether asset pricing models really function, whether value is created through financial policies, and whether the acquisition of another company adds value or not.

From the 1970s and onwards research within finance has been much more fragmented in its structure. Finance is now a field of research that is slowly maturing and with fewer path-breaking contributions (in comparison to those mentioned from the earlier years). But at least three major contributions occurring after 1970 must be mentioned. The first issue is option theory, which was developed by Black and Scholes (1973) and Merton (1973). *Option pricing theory* is the only major area within finance that is not explicitly dealt with in this book. Its application is primarily to be found in capital market theory. Among all developments made within finance and economics it is probably the theoretical concept that has had the most profound impact on practitioners. An option provides its bearer the right, but not the obligation, to buy or sell an asset in the future. Black, Scholes and Merton were able to show what the theoretically correct price of an option is (based on an asset traded in an efficient market). It is a remarkable contribution given that options had existed long before.

The next major development came in 1976 when Jensen acknowledged that managers might not behave as shareholders would want them to behave. There had been sporadic observations of potential conflicts of interest between shareholders and managers, but nothing that had engendered a great deal of attention within mainstream research (e.g. Berle and Means, 1932; Donaldson, 1961; 1969). With the help of Jensen, and others, *a theory of corporate control* now emerged. According to the principal-agent theory, these conflicts give rise to what is today known as agency costs. On the basis of this theory researchers and practitioners have learnt that incentive systems are necessary to control managers and enhance the creation of company value.

Finally, the issue of determining the value of an individual asset has had a renaissance during the 1990s. Investment theory (and the discounting of income streams) has its roots going back at least to the beginning of the 20th century. It is the idea Williams put forward in 1938 that a company's value is determined by the discounted value of future dividends that has been modified and taken a few steps further. Researchers and practitioners have recently learned to discount cash flows and integrate a multitude of financial aspects into their valuation models (Copeland, Koller and Murrin, 1994). This means that corporate finance is becoming increasingly interested in the activities of the individual investor. Lately, accounting researchers have entered the scene and challenged valuation models based on discounted cash flows, and argued instead for the discounting of residual earnings or other income streams.

This brief review of the history of finance has now taken us to the 21st century. As you have seen, the history of finance has been short but quite intensive. It has been formed by American researchers, looking at economic problems for American companies and using the research techniques that fit their empirical data well. Financial theory has its roots in economic theory and all major contributions have been made with this in mind. It is only until recently that the field has seriously opened up for ideas challenging the very roots of classical economic thinking.

1.3 Practical Implications

In the social sciences it is difficult to generate theories that will consistently explain behaviours. As the studied objects are human beings, capable of learning and changing their behaviours, stipulated relationships might change. There is thus a danger in believing too strongly in theories of the social sciences. Nevertheless, it is true researchers and practitioners have learnt a great deal over the last forty years of how financial markets function and how actors within the financial system can make better decisions. In this section we shall look at seven issues where financial theory has eased the practise of financial decision-making, or at least our understanding of financial decision-making. While none of the matters listed here provides a complete solution to a problem, they all provide general outlines.

1.3.1 Investment and financing decisions can be separated

When you first think about it, you might not realise the greatness of a separation of investment decisions and financing decisions. But when we as individuals need to make any investment we usually first think whether we can afford it or not. What financial theory teaches us is that if a corporation has access to capital markets, its management should not really have to worry about financial matters, at least not if those capital markets are efficient. Companies operate in product markets where they make their investments. Whenever they identify good investment opportunities they provide information about the projects to investors in the capital market who assess their risk and return, and allocate capital accordingly. This means that managers focus on investments in product markets while investors focus on investments in capital markets.

1.3.2 The market price is the best estimate managers have of value

Modern financial theory has likewise taught us that we should have faith in market prices. Fierce competition for information among investors forces share prices to trade as close to their right value as possible. Investors in the capital markets are reasonably rational profit-maximising individuals who try to interpret all relevant information about assets in terms of their risk and return. Whilst there are fluctuations in security prices (because there is a lot of uncertainty out there), we still have no *better* way of establishing the value of an asset than using the market price. It is in no buyer's interest to buy a security at a higher price than its correct value. At the same time it is in no seller's interest to sell a security at a lower price than its correct value. Market actors' constant struggle to estimate a security's correct value will ensure that well-functioning markets offer us the best possible estimate of assets' "true" economic value. Managers can and ought to take advantage of this.

1.3.3 Management should focus on investment decisions

Because of the fierce competition, financial markets represent some of the most efficient markets in the world. Thousands of buyers and sellers compete for homogeneous products, in a market whose sole idea is to reallocate resources in a frictionless mode. Information is released to the actors in as timely manner as possible and as they fight for the best interpretation of the information excessive returns are competed away. On the other hand, companies work on product markets that are far less efficient. Management is hired to take advantage of any opportunity there is to capitalise on product market inefficiencies. The corporation shall set up its strategy based on how it can use its competitive advantages in the most beneficial way and earn higher returns than normal.

A company's long term competitiveness, and hence its economic value, is based on its competitive advantages. Its assets, in terms of production capability, access to resources, and skills, have to be unique or difficult to replicate. Product markets allow companies to possess patents, property rights, and personnel with unique competences. Management's most important task should be to assess, choose the most profitable investment alternatives, and then manage them efficiently. It does this utilising its competitive advantages.

1.3.4 Management should not purposely engage in diversification activities

Risk is something both managers and investors have an aversion to. In a simplified manner we can define risk as the probability that the future will not turn out according to our expectations. As the prime concern of investors is return-on-investment, the risk they are running is the risk that they will not get the return they are expecting. The same goes for management. One of the best ways of handling this insecurity is to make multiple investments. Instead of placing 'all eggs in one basket', one spreads the risk and can thereby reduce the impact that individual investments have on total wealth.

Although there are some general advantages with diversified company activities, it is much better for shareholders if they, rather than managers, perform the diversification. First of all it is questionable whether management is capable of handling investments in multiple areas; dividing their time and effort into different issues. Secondly, a diversified company makes it more difficult for investors to understand company performance. And finally, with diversified companies investors have less opportunity to personally choose how to make their own diversification.

Investors acquire portfolios of assets in efficient markets. Compared to managers acting in the product markets, investors can easily and instantaneously diversify their portfolio and get rid of company-specific risk by owning shares in companies who are not affected by the same factors. What are left are the systematic economy-wide factors that affect all securities. Overall volatility will hence be reduced. This is beneficial for both the investor, who receives the same return as before but with a lower risk, and for the business enterprise, for which the cost of capital decreases and hence more investments become profitable. Everything else being equal, undiversified companies enjoy a higher value and lower capital costs.

1.3.5 Management's financing decisions are only value-relevant in inefficient markets

Given the competitiveness of modern financial markets, the opportunities to create wealth through clever financing strategies are strictly limited. Indeed, financial theory has taught us that if these markets are perfectly efficient no value whatsoever can be created there. The choice between different sources of capital and the choice of when to issue new equity and pay dividends therefore becomes irrelevant.

Despite this, companies do seem to follow certain patterns in their financing decisions. They are two reasons for this. One is that inefficiencies in the capital markets make financing decisions value-relevant. Corporate taxation and transaction costs are two examples of this. Management can therefore affect its value by deliberately affecting its financing. The second reason why patterns exist is that control over corporate resources plays an important role in financial decision-making. We shall return to this in a moment. While management finds financing decisions to be important, these decisions have a considerably lower importance than investment decisions. They are only value-relevant when financial managers understand how to capitalise on market inefficiencies.

1.3.6 Managers need incentives to behave as the owners want them to

As financial economists started to notice that the separation of ownership and control caused problems, they also tried to find remedies. Portfolio diversification has reduced the individual shareholders' ability and willingness to participate actively in the governing of the modern corporation. This increases management's interest in capitalising on asymmetric information. One of the suggestions coming from theorists has been to provide managers with better incentives to maximise company value, rather than something else.

In the best interest of shareholders, managers of modern corporations must feel and behave like shareholders. If they feel that they benefit when shareholders benefit, their goals will coincide with the shareholders. Over the last twenty years incentive schemes have been developed so that investors can reap the risk-reducing fruits from portfolio diversification, without suffering from potentially lower returns due to an inactive participation in the governing of their individual investments. It is in the best interest to implement value-related incentive schemes for top management.

1.3.7 Management often have different preferences than shareholders

Economists have built their theories around the simple notion that corporations are utility-maximising entities, only considering the risk and return of its business. Despite the obvious fact that management only run errands for shareholders economists often ignore the potential problems coming from the separation of ownership and control of corporate resources. Today researchers are not only seeing the problem and coming up with ways to handle it, but they are also taking an interest in the actual situation management is in. As we do this, we start to see financial decision-making in corporations differently.

Suddenly there are good chances management do not see investment and financing decisions as separate. There are reasons why management disbelieve the correctness of market prices. There are reasons why management do not just focus on the profitability of investments and why they in reality do, purposely, diversify their operations. The control aspect of finance provides reasons as to why certain capital structures and dividend policies are chosen. Now financial theory becomes more in touch with the real world. We now enable an amalgamation of financial theory and decision-making, and here is where this book takes off.

1.4 The disposition

The book is divided into eleven chapters. This chapter and the next one are introductory chapters. The first chapter deals with financial theory, its overall contributions and its limitations. Chapter Two deals with financial statements and the use of accounting information when interpreting the value and value-creation processes within companies: The foundation for understanding financial decisions.

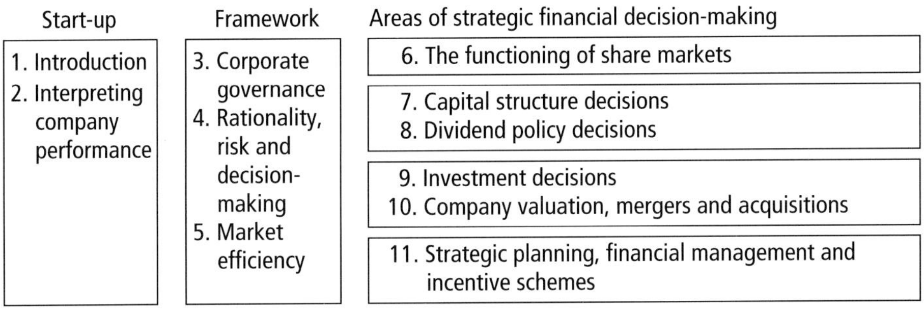

Figure 1.2 – Disposition of the book.

Chapters Three to Five cover some important general aspects of financial decision-making. Chapter Three brings up the issue of management's objectives when making financial decisions. A stakeholder model is introduced and conflicts between stakeholder interests are discussed. The obvious focus of this discussion is on conflicts between managerial and shareholder interests. The chapter ends with a discussion of corporate governance, and particularly the Swedish corporate governance system. Chapter Four targets the rationality aspect of financial decision-making and a large part of the chapter is spent debating the risk and uncertainty controversy. This boils down to the particular view of management and its decision-making ability that is kept throughout the rest of the book. Chapter Five is dedicated to the competitiveness of markets. This chapter brings up the efficiency (or competitiveness) of both the product market where companies make their investments, and the capital market, where companies finance their investments. Each section forms the basis for the upcoming chapters on capital market decisions, corporate finance decisions, and investment decisions.

Chapters Six to Eight deal with decisions related to capital markets and corporate finance. Chapter Six contains coverage of the main issues within capital market theory. The purpose is to show (a) how the cost of equity capital can be determined, (b) how investors can make use of diversification as an efficient tool to eliminate risk, (c) how investors view the operations of a company, and (d) the problems researchers still have to determine risk and risk premiums. Chapter Seven deals with the capital structure decision, or the question of how to finance an investment. The chapter starts out from a perfect world as described by economic theory, and then one-by-one factors are identified that drive real-world capital structure decisions. Chapter Eight follows the same structure as Chapter Seven, although here the focus is on dividend policy decisions. By starting out from a perfect world, individual factors driving dividend policy decisions are discussed. The chapter also contains a section on making share repurchases.

Chapters Nine and Ten are devoted to investment decisions. To start with in Chapter Nine the costs of capital are reviewed. Thereafter different investment models are presented and compared. A great deal of the chapter is spent discussing how managers actually use the models and which problems they encounter when relying on the models. Chapter Ten is a continuation of Chapter Nine. Instead of evaluating investment projects within the business enterprise, the same investment model is now used to value whole companies. As such, this chapter refers to the techniques investors implicitly use when buying and selling securities. The chapter ends with a lengthy discussion of mergers and acquisitions. Whereas techniques for valuing stand-alone companies are used primarily by investors, it is managers who primarily evaluate business combinations. The agency problem of mergers and acquisitions is discussed.

In the final chapter strategic financial management is related to corporate objectives. In the first part of the chapter the ideas of managerial welfare maximisation that were presented in Chapter Three are turned into a comprehensive strategic model that can be used to manage the company. This shows how different financial decisions need to be integrated in an internal financial system. In the second half of the chapter this issue is partly turned around, and a strategy for changing managerial behaviours is described. This calls for an incentive program where management can be assessed and rewarded based on their ability to create shareholder value. Here again the conflict between managers and shareholders arises. But now a way of handling it is provided.

Key Issues to Discuss

After reading the rest of the book it is possible for you to return to the seven statements made in this chapter. Explain each of them in greater detail than what has been made here.

1 Why can investment and financing decisions be separated?
2 Why is the market price the best estimate managers have of value?
3 Why should management focus on investment decisions?
4 Why should managers not pursue diversification strategies?
5 Why are financing decisions only value-relevant in inefficient markets?
6 Why do managers need incentives to behave as the owners want them to, and how can such incentive schemes be designed?
7 In which ways do financial decisions made by management differ from what is stipulated in financial theory?

Further readings:

Bernstein, P.L., 1992, *Capital Ideas*, New York: The Free Press.
Bernstein, P L., 1996, *Against the Gods*, New York: John Wiley & Sons.
Galbraith, J. K., 1987, *A History of Economics – The Past as the Present*, London: Penguin Books.

Chapter 2

An Introduction to Financial Statement Analysis

This chapter aims at:

- Providing a basic understanding of some of the more important accounting concepts that have an impact on our understanding of the financial decisions covered in the following chapters.
- Explaining for what purposes some of the most common financial ratios are used, and showing how these are calculated.
- Illustrating how financial ratios can be combined in order to better understand what drives company performance in terms of profitability and risk.

2.1 An Accounting-Based Model of Company Performance

2.1.1 The role of financial accounting

Chapter Two is devoted to an introduction to financial statement analysis. By only devoting one chapter to such a vast subject there is no chance of addressing all relevant topics. This review is instead conducted as coverage of the basics that you should have studied in a previous course in financial accounting. Nonetheless it is not possible to exclude financial statement analysis totally as accounting statements form the basis for understanding financial performance and financial decision-making. In most cases it is what comes out of these statements that we interpret as the outcome of financial decisions. Furthermore, shareholders as well as other external stakeholders consider accounting statements to be if not the only description of company performance, then at least the prime one. Our view of financial accounting will be that of the user of the information. We use the information to understand the performance of the business enterprise – today and tomorrow.

Financial accounting is a social phenomenon, existing because of human interaction and, similarly to all other phenomenon in the social sciences, it must therefore be a social construction. Financial accounting takes place on an aggregated level. The traditional role of accounting is to mirror an exterior real world, and not an interior subconscious state of mind. This causes accounting information to be strongly aggregated and limited in both its profundity and its scope. At the same time, there are many users of the information with heterogeneous information needs. The stakeholder model of the company, which we will discuss much further in Chapter Three, is one of the foundations for describing the users of financial accounting information.[1] Even though accounting regulators are well aware of the heterogeneous information needs different stakeholders have, they are aware that investors constitute the most prominent group of stakeholders. The International Accounting Standards Committee states:

> *"While all of the information needs of these users cannot be met by financial statements, there are needs which are common to all users. As investors are providers of risk capital to*

1 The main stakeholders are the: (1) owners, (2) debtholders, (3) customers, (4) suppliers, (5) employees, (6) managers, and (7) society.

the enterprise, the provision of financial statements that meet their needs will also meet most of the needs of other users that financial statements can satisfy." (IASC, 1989, §10)

In the social sciences there is no objective truth. Most supposed facts are simply arguments in a political debate filled with beliefs and values. There is little reason to believe that accounting information represents one true picture of company performance. It is more likely it reflects some individuals' perspective of the company. The motives that drive their views are diffuse and often internally inconsistent. As a user of financial accounting information it is thus important to apply a critical view of the information that is interpreted.

Although investors are seen as the prime user of accounting statements, it is not necessarily so that the information in the accounting statements fit their needs perfectly. To take a simple example; in Sweden accounting statements are used as a basis for corporate taxation. Investors need information they can use when forecasting the future – what the future cash flows will be. Tax authorities on the other hand need information that correctly reflects what has happened in the past. They do not tax corporations based on what will (is likely to) happen but on what actually has happened. When an analyst interested in the company's future performance uses the accounting information, that person has to be aware of the problems and possible biases that the multiple roles of financial reporting creates.

Accounting information is furthermore the most powerful instrument management has in its struggle with investors and other stakeholders. As producers of the information management has an information advantage and depending on their needs they can "bend and stretch" the information to fit their purposes. Far too often users of financial statements fail to recognise that accounting information is no objective and truthful picture of reality, but that it instead is a biased subjective tool used in the political process of governing complex organisations. The accounting information must be viewed with scepticism and one must allow oneself to recognise that producers of accounting information have strong incentives to distort our understanding of company performance, intentionally or unintentionally.

In the rest of this section some of the most fundamental features of financial reporting are covered. They are not described in detail and it is assumed that the reader has had an introduction to the subject in the past. The next section (2.2) deals with financial analysis based on accounting information. Many of the ratios covered there are used in various parts of the book. Thereafter Section 2.3 takes a closer look at profitability and risk. These two concepts are described and decomposed for us to understand the measurement of them somewhat better. As they are the main features of any financial theory they will be revisited many times later on in the book.

2.1.2 The income statement and the balance sheet

The *income statement* displays the company's performance during the last reporting period, usually a one-year period. According to accounting standards *income* is defined as revenues less expenses. *Revenues* come from the company's sale of products and services. *Expenses* of various kinds occur in the process of producing and selling a product. The income statement includes several sections. The operating section contains information on the revenues and expenses coming from operating activities, whereas the financial section contains information on the revenues and expenses coming from financial activities, such as the interest on loans, or dividends received from shares in other companies. Income taxes are stated after all contracted expenses have been deducted from income. The "bottom line", *net profit*, is what is left for the shareholders of this year's operations.[2] Based on this figure management suggests a certain level of dividend and the rest of the income is reinvested in the company and appears as a change in this year's equity value.

Although all reporting follows relatively strict regulations and norms, there are usually variations between different companies. Figure 2.1 shows the income statement of the Swedish industrial company SKF for the year 2000. This income statement has been slightly re-arranged to fit the model that is used throughout this book. On the right-hand side a number of abbreviations are written. These are used throughout the text whenever specific accounting definitions are needed. Please note the separation between core business and non-core business that has been made to support forecasts of future profits. *Core business* then represents what is generated from within the company's main operations. Revenues from non-core businesses can be generated from e.g. selling a building, whereas expenses from non-core businesses can be caused by e.g. restructurings.

One main difference exists between the format showed in Figure 2.1 and the one found in the reports of most Swedish companies. This is the separate reporting of the depreciation item. Instead of hiding it within cost of goods sold, *cogs*, or selling, general, and administrative expenses, *sgae*, it

2 In the rest of the book the terms profits and earnings are used interchangeably.

is given special attention. The reason for this will be explained later on in this section as it is not a real expense but an accrual.

Income statement	Full-year 2000	Full-year 1999	Abbreviation
Sales from core business	**39 848**	36 693	S
Cost of goods sold	**−28 722**	−27 177	cogs
Selling, general and administrative expenses	**−6 008**	−5 526	sgae
Gross profit	***5 118***	*3 990*	*GP*
Depreciation	**−1 633**	−1 873	depr
Operating profit	***3 485***	*2 117*	*OPc*
Non-core operating income and expenses	**189**	403	ncie
Total operating profit	***3 674***	*2 520*	*OPt*
Financial income, interest	**342**	254	Fi
(net lending income)	**332**	245	nlc
Financial expenses, interest	**−919**	−992	Fe
(net borrowing costs)	**−561**	−620	nbc
Other financial items	**−95**	−13	ofi
Profit after financial items	***3 002***	*1 769*	*Pfi*
Taxes	**−1 001**	−650	Ta
Minority interests	**−39**	−8	Mi
Net profit	***1 962***	*1 111*	*NP*
Dividends	**560**	228	Div
Retained earnings/profits	**1 402**	883	Re

Figure 2.1 – Income statement of SKF, year 2000 (in million SEK).

The *balance sheet* displays the value of a company's belongings at the end of a given reporting period. It states what the company owns and how it has financed its possessions. The accounting terms used to describe this balance are assets (A) and liabilities (L). The value of a company's assets is by definition equal to the value of its liabilities. To enable a fruitful discussion many textbooks make a simplification and say that a company's liabilities can be divided into two parts; debt (D) and shareholders' equity (EQ). Although this is correct, another division will be used in this chapter and this requires some rearrangement of the items in debt and equity.

The debt component is divided into *interest bearing debt* (IBD) and *non-interest bearing debt* (NIBD). An example of a non-interest bearing debt is a credit from a supplier. This liability bears a cost (in terms of a higher input price), but it is not financial. A typical interest bearing debt is the bank loan. Often the non-interest bearing debt is deducted from the sum of liabilities and the rest is referred to as *capital employed* (CE), or net assets. These are the assets that have been financed using external capital. We can define these relationships in the following way:

$$A_t = FA_t + CA_t = L_t = D_t + EQ_t \quad (2.1)$$

$$D_t = NIBD_t + IBD_t \quad (2.2)$$

$$CE_t = L_t - NIBD_t \quad (2.3)$$

Assets	**Full-year 2000**	**Full-year 1999**	
Fixed assets	**16 038**	16 017	FA
material assets	**13 089**	13 074	
goodwill	**717**	366	gw
other immaterial assets	**402**	578	
strategic financial investments	**328**		
non-strategic financial investments	**1 076**		Fafin
Current assets	**21 776**	18 806	CA
inventories	**9 262**	8 640	Inv
customer receivables	**7 091**	6 563	Cur
liquid assets used for operations			Laop
non-strategic financial investments	**5 423**	3 603	Cafin
other current assets			
Total assets (FA + CA)	**37 814**	34 823	A
Shareholders' equity	**13 594**	11 367	EQ
common equity	**11 632**	10 256	
retained earnings	**1 962**	1 111	
Minority interests	**467**	398	Mi
Interest bearing provisions and liabilities	**14 854**	14 105	IBD
debt contracts (bank loans, bonds, etc.)	**5 062**	4 832	dc
pension obligations	**6 746**	6 478	po
other deferrals	**3 046**	2 795	
Deferred taxes	**1 596**	1 509	Dt
Non-interest bearing provisions and liabilities	**7 303**	6 221	NIBD
supplier credits	**3 099**	2 785	sc
Total liabilities (EQ + Mi + Dt + IBD + NIBD)	**37 814**	34 823	L

Figure 2.2 – Balance sheet of SKF (in million SEK).

The association between the income statement and the balance sheet is part of what is usually referred to as a *clean surplus relationship*. According to the clean surplus, equity of year t is determined by (1) the beginning-of-period value of equity, (2) the period's net profit and (3) the transactions between shareholders and the company.

$$EQ_t = EQ_{t-1} + NP_t - Div_t = EQ_t + Re_t \quad (2.4)$$

Figure 2.2 shows the balance sheet of SKF and the main categories within a typical balance sheet. On the right hand side of the balance sheet abbreviations to be used later on, are included.

Total liabilities consists of interest bearing debt, non-interest bearing debt, minority interests, deferred taxes and shareholders' equity. Besides the two forms of debt (IBD and NIBD) the other three types of liabilities can be lumped together as *risk bearing capital* (RBC).

$$RBC = EQ + Dt(+Mi) \quad (2.5)$$

Total liabilities (used to finance total assets) can now be said to consist of non-interest bearing debt, interest bearing debt and risk bearing capital. The non-interest bearing debt bears a cost, but it is not a financial cost. The non-interest bearing debt is a debt that mainly comes automatically when one does business. The capital that is employed is instead the interest bearing debt and the risk bearing capital. We refer to these two capital sources as capital employed. Expression (2.6) is therefore similar to Expression (2.3).

$$CE_t = RBC_t + IBD_t = L_t - NIBD_t \quad (2.6)$$

In Chapters Ten and Eleven we will elaborate on different forms of investment models. In that discussion the *net operating assets* (NOA) form an important part. To define them we need to distinguish between the operating assets and the financial assets of a company. Operating assets are those that are invested in producing the products and services that make up the company's core business. *Financial assets* (FinA) consist of capital that has been invested in financial markets (in bonds, shares etc.) and is not used for operating activities. These are located both among fixed assets and current assets. Hence we can define financial assets and net operating assets as:

$$FinA = Fafin + Cafin \quad (2.7)$$

$$NOA = CE - FinA = RBC + IBD - Fafin - Cafin \quad (2.8)$$

Please note that in most of the book the terms D (as in debt) and EQ (as in equity) are used to describe the company's capital structure. Although this notation is different from what is suggested here it conforms to most other literature. In those chapters the idea is not to show correct accounting definitions, but to describe the factors behind financial decisions. The notation used here is instead primarily used in Chapters Ten and Eleven, where a precise notation is crucial.

In the notation used elsewhere EQ = EQ + Mi + Dt, and D = IBD + NIBD.

2.1.3 *Cash flows and earnings*

In Chapter One it was mentioned that the value of a company (or investment/project) is based on its ability to generate future cash flows. From a financial theory perspective cash flow is one of the most important items that can be found from financial statements. Cash flows are reported in a cash flow statement, but the issue is somewhat more complicated than just extracting (historical) figures from a certain statement. Cash flows represent all changes in liquid funds occurring during a certain period of time. It can be divided into cash flows from operations, changes in working capital, cash flows from investment and financial activities. As such it can be a rather blunt measure. But at the same time it is an objective measure – difficult to manipulate. The relevant measure of cash flow is one that is free after necessary investments have been made. We refer to this cash flow as *free cash flow*. Free cash flow can be defined in various ways depending on which party it is that has an interest in the cash flow. In Chapter Ten, where we learn how to value companies, we will discuss Free Cash Flow to Equity (FCFE), and Free Cash Flow to the Firm (FCFF). In general, a company's free cash flow is generated from managing past investments (operations), its investments in new operations (investment), and its financing of past and current investments (financing).

Cash from operations +/– cash from investment +/– cash from financing

A good measure of cash flow is one which can be used to forecast future cash flows. There is a continuous debate going on whether current earnings are good estimates of future cash flows or not. Numerous studies have been made and the bulk of these suggest that current earnings are better indicators of future cash flows than current cash flows are (see e.g. Neill, Schaefer, Banson and Bradbury, 1991). Does this sound surprising? It is in fact very logical. Accounting items are created using *accounting accruals*, such as for example depreciation. When a company makes a large investment it shows a large negative cash flow. The investment is made in order to generate positive cash flows in coming years. If one uses the cash flow statement to evaluate company performance in the year of the large investment we get a very distorted view of future cash flows. If, on the other hand, one uses accounting earnings the cost of making the investment has been spread out over the *economic life* of the investment. This depreciation period (the economic life-span of the project) has to be determined by management.

In Figure 2.3 the effect of depreciation is illustrated. The left-hand graph shows the estimated cash flows from an investment. The initial outlay is – 1000. Over five years the estimated cash flows are expected to be + 400 per year, which means that the total cash flows from the project sum up to + 1000.[3] The cash flows for the coming five years are thus thought to be: – 600, + 400, + 400, + 400, and + 400. When the initial cost is spread out over the coming five years the company's earnings will be: + 200, + 200, + 200, + 200, and + 200. Obviously the accounting earnings reported for period one is a much better indicator of future cash flows than the reported cash flow of period one.

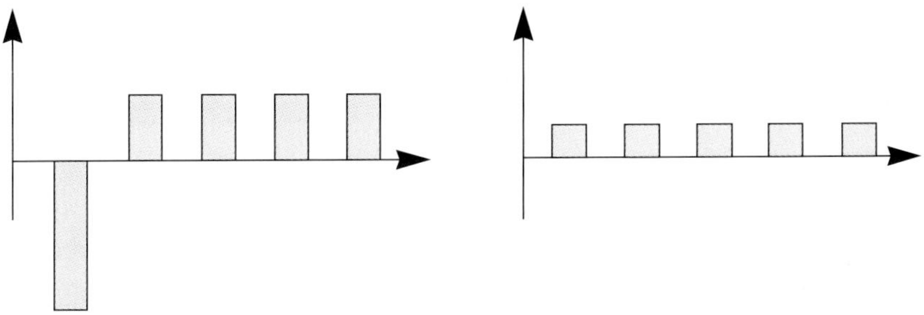

Period	1	2	3	4	5	Period	1	2	3	4	5
Operating CF	400	400	400	400	400	Revenues	400	400	400	400	400
Investment CF	–1000	0	0	0	0	Depreciation	–200	–200	–200	–200	–200
Financial CF	0	0	0	0	0	Fin. items	0	0	0	0	0
Result	**–600**	**400**	**400**	**400**	**400**	**Result**	**200**	**200**	**200**	**200**	**200**

Figure 2.3 – The effect of accounting accruals.

We need to establish an understanding of when cash flows are more useful than earnings, and what the positive and negative effects of each measure is. Current cash flow is a useful measure of future cash flows in mature companies where growth is continuous and steady. Current cash flow is a less useful measure of future cash flows for companies where large investments occur irregularly. On the other hand, cash flow information cannot

3 We are so far not considering any discounting of future values.

be manipulated to the same extent that accounting earnings can. It is also far from obvious to say that one should avoid using cash flows for newly started companies or companies in a high growth stage. For these companies it is immensely important to keep track of cash flows, but not in order to measure future cash flows, but to see whether management has enough cash to pay next month's bills. Finally, the validity of our accounting earnings measure is dependent on the choice of a correct depreciation plan. Accounting accruals, such as depreciation, are arbitrary.

2.1.4 Book values and market values

The purpose of having accounting statements is to portray the existing value of assets and the value-generating process in a company. In theory, optimal measures of this should approximate for what is referred to as the true economic value. But what is the value of a machine that a company owns? The price for which the machine once was acquired represents one estimate. But it is not the only one – after all, somebody sold the machine for that price which means they attributed a lower value to it than the sales price. What about changes in value of the machine between the time it was acquired and reported? If the machine has been used a lot then it might not be worth as much now as it was when acquired. If it has not been used, but its current price on the market is different than the historical price what happens then if it has to be repurchased? On the other hand, if the machine has been introduced to a sophisticated value-generating process within the company it might be worth much more today than it was worth when acquired. It seems as if the value of the machine can differ depending on the circumstances under which one evaluates it.

In this reasoning there are several valuation principles hidden. An asset, such as the machine mentioned above, can be valued at for example its historical cost (acquisition price), its historical cost reduced with an estimation of reduction in value (due to wear), its current market value, or as the present value of all future cash flows it will generate.

Accountants have been forced to make choices and decide how to establish the value of an asset. It is certainly not the purpose of this text to analyse accounting measurement theory, but instead to briefly introduce the problems users of accounting information have when interpreting financial decisions with the help of accounting information. In general, fixed assets, such as machines, are valued at their *historical cost* reduced with an aggregated annual reduction in value due to wear (called depreciation). The reason for this is the *conservative accounting* regime. Accounting principles are designed to protect against unrecognised increases in asset value. Unless an asset has been sold it should normally not be valued above its historical cost. Herein lies the discrepancy between reported book values and market values.

When we are interested in financial decision-making we are interested in the process of generating future cash flows. The historical price paid for a machine is of no value to us. There can be great discrepancies between the book value of a company's asset, and its market value. More so, the machine is likely to be used together with other machines, handled by people. This produces a unique chain of activities that generates cash flows. When one wants to understand future cash flows and financial decision-making, one has to observe this unique chain of activities, not single machines acquired in the past. The value of the company's unique chain of activities is reflected in the market value of the company.

In most cases the market value of a company's assets is much higher than the book value. The relationship between the cash flows a company generates and the book value of assets might be completely different from the relationship between cash flows and the market value of assets. This gives rise to the often forgotten truth that a good company might not be a good share to invest in. Although the company has performed well and will do so consistently in the future this performance is already incorporated (discounted) in the market value of the company.

We have so far looked at a few problems with using accounting information. As we move along in the book we will return to the use of accounting information, and its inherent and unavoidable problems.

2.2 Understanding Company Performance

2.2.1 Introduction to financial ratio analysis

Financial statement analysis is commonly based on *financial ratios*. Ratios measure the association between accounting items. *Financial ratio analysis* is used to make comparisons between companies. It is, for example, impossible to say whether company net earnings of SEK 5 Billion is a lot or a little if one does not compare it to another company's net earnings. But even when one does so, there can be problems as the other company might be of a different size. By relating a company's net earnings to, for example, capital employed we get a size-adjusted measure of the company's ability to generate profits. We call this particular financial ratio for profitability.

As you probably understand, comparability is immensely important in the analysis of a company's performance. The comparisons that ratio analysis can be used for are of three different kinds; (1) *comparisons between units*, such as for example between companies within the same industry, (2) *comparisons over time*, such as for example this year's earnings with last year's earnings, and (3) *comparisons with goals*, such as actual profitability versus the stated financial strategy. There is no rule saying that any financial ratio has to be of a certain value. A profitability of 100 percent is exceptionally good under some conditions, and less so under other conditions. All that matters is to make relevant and fair comparisons.

To enable a fair comparison, the figure in the financial ratio's numerator has to be logically related to the figure in the denominator. This is referred to as *the matching principle of ratio analysis*. The matching is particularly important when comparing measures of value from the balance sheet with measures of the value-creation process from the income statement. The information in the income statement displays what has happened during a period of time, while the information in the balance sheet displays what the financial position is at the end of the period. This problem is of particular importance when calculating the profitability.

It is common to divide financial ratios into five categories; (1) profitability ratios, (2) capital structure ratios, (3) liquidity ratios, (4) efficiency ratios, and (5) growth ratios. We will in the next sections briefly look at each of these categories, which will provide us with a toolbox for understanding company performance.

2.2.2 Profitability ratios

Profitability ratios provide various ways of measuring a company's ability to generate revenues in excess of expenses. The ability to generate a certain amount of profits differs for different companies and it is therefore useful to monitor differences in the companies' resource base. Profits are usually either related to the capital used to generate profits, or the total revenues the company generated. We refer to the first type of ratios as pure profitability ratios, and the second as profit margin ratios. The group of pure profitability ratios contains a wide variety of different measures. Below five of these are expressed:

Return on equity: $$ROE_t^{aT} = \frac{NP_t}{(EQ_{t-1} + EQ_t)/2} \qquad (2.9)$$

Alternatively: $$ROE_t^{aT} = \frac{NP_t}{EQ_{t-1}} \tag{2.10}$$

Return on risk-bearing capital: $$RRBC_t^{bT} = \frac{Pfi_t}{(RBC_{t-1} + RBC_t)/2} \tag{2.11}$$

Return on capital employed:

$$ROCE_t = \frac{Pfi_t + fe_t}{(IBD_{t-1} + IBD_t + RBC_{t-1} + RBC_t)/2} \tag{2.12}$$

Return on net operating
assets after taxes:

$$RNOA_t^{aT} = \frac{OPc_t - Ta_t}{(NOA_{t-1} + NOA_t)/2} \tag{2.13}$$

There are fewer profit margin ratios, as well as ways in which they can be estimated. Two of the most common profit margin ratios are:

Operating profit margin: $$OPM_t = \frac{OPc_t}{S_t} \tag{2.14}$$

Net profit margin: $$NPM_t^{bT} = \frac{Pfi_t}{S_t} \tag{2.15}$$

Profitability ratios are particularly important for financial decisions. For investors everything the company does comes down to earning money. Later on in the book we shall relate profitability ratios based on accounting information to the valuation of companies. What we learn here are just the right techniques to measure performance.

It is important to make use of the matching principle of ratio analysis here. When one compares the generation of resources portrayed in the income statement, which is a *flow concept*, with the value of the assets that have generated the resources, which is a *stock concept*, these have to be matched. The end-of-period value is not, necessarily, the same as the average amount of resources employed in the value-creating process during the period. If the resource base has changed considerably during the time-period the process covers, then the in-going or out-going stock of resources might be misleading. There is thus no matching between numerator and denominator and it is necessary for the analyst to look at the average amount of resources employed. In this context ratio (2.9) is slightly better than ratio (2.10).

It is also necessary to discuss a second issue related to the matching of numerator and denominator. It is unsatisfactory to compare profits with a capital base that has not been employed to generate the profits. Earnings after financial expenses are not comparable with total liabilities (used to finance total assets). In the earnings after financial expenses the interest cost has been deducted. It makes little sense to compare earnings *excluding* the benefits coming from borrowing (interest costs are deducted), when the capital base *includes* the borrowed capital. In ratios (2.9) to (2.13) the numerator is altered to match the denominator.

2.2.3 Capital structure ratios

Capital structure ratios provide insight into the extent to which non-equity capital is used to finance the company's operations (assets). These ratios are primarily used to assess the company's long term financial health and survival capability. We return to these ratios in Chapter Seven where we discuss capital structures, and the rationale behind choices of them.

Solvency:
$$Solv_t = \frac{EQ_t}{A_t} \tag{2.16}$$

Debt ratio:
$$d_t = \frac{IBD_t}{RBC_t}, \text{ alternatively } \frac{D_t}{EQ_t} \qquad (2.17, 2.18)$$

The cost of having interest bearing debt can be estimated in the following way.

Interest rate:
$$i_t = \frac{nbc_t}{(IBD_{t-1} + IBD_t - po_{t-1} - po_t)/2} \tag{2.19}$$

Alternatively:
$$i_t = \frac{fe_t}{(IBD_{t-1} + IBD_t)/2} \tag{2.20}$$

In ratios (2.19) and (2.20), it is extremely important that one gets a good match between the numerator and denominator. The main problem is that financial expenses are rarely specified with a sufficient degree of detail in annual reports. Pension obligations can cause problems, and also temporary financial expenses that are not borrowing costs but, for example, costs of issuing new equity.

When interest bearing debt is introduced in a company, this brings with it contractual costs. Depending on the variance in company revenue these fixed costs can cause not only negative cash flows but also a lack of cash and hence financial distress. The capital structure ratios are also useful when estimating how the return on investors' capital is leveraged by interest bearing debt. As long as the return on investment is higher than the interest cost it is profitable to finance operations with borrowed capital.

2.2.4 Liquidity ratios

If capital structure ratios are used to assess the long term financial health of the company, then *liquidity ratios* are used to assess the short term financial health, and particularly whether short term financial obligations can be met when they are due. Without adequate funds a company cannot sustain its business, and it might experience financial distress. A few ratios usable for this purpose are:

Current ratio:
$$cr_t = \frac{CA_t}{NIBD_t} \tag{2.21}$$

Cash position:
$$cp_t = \frac{Laop_t + Cafin_t}{CA_t} \tag{2.22}$$

Interest cover margin:
$$icm_t = \frac{OPt_t}{nbc_t} \tag{2.23}$$

The first two financial ratios are calculated using information of the stock of liquid assets the company has. For two reasons are these 'balance sheet' based ratios not always relevant. The first is that a company generates revenues over time and in the long run it is the process of generating funds that is more important than the stock. The second reason is connected to the first; even though the company has no stock of liquid assets it can, provided it has good possibilities to generate future funds, borrow capital (which means it extends the span of the balance sheet). The interest cover margin is partly a solvency ratio, and partly a liquidity ratio. It measures how many times the company can pay the costs of interest bearing debt with its operating profit. Liquidity ratios of various kinds are primarily used for cash management. In financial theory we are relatively unconcerned with the liquidity. As you will soon see in Chapter Three this is due to the shareholder perspective taken. If only an investment is profitable it will be financed. Liquidity is quite irrelevant.

2.2.5 *Efficiency ratios*

A high profitability might be the ultimate goal (at least for shareholders) but in order to understand what drives the performance of the company it becomes necessary to study the employment of resources. *Efficiency ratios* are used to observe how efficiently the company's resources are employed in the value-generating process.

Inventory turnover: $$InvT_t = \frac{(Inv_{t-1} + Inv_t)/2 \cdot 365}{S_t} \quad (2.24)$$

Customer receivables turnover: $$CrT_t = \frac{(Cur_{t-1} + Cur_t)/2 \cdot 365}{S_t} \quad (2.25)$$

Capital turnover: $$CT_t = \frac{S_t}{NOA_t}, \quad (2.26)$$

Alternatively $$\frac{S_t}{A_t} \quad (2.27)$$

Operating leverage: $$OpLev_t = \frac{OPc_t}{GP_t} \quad (2.28)$$

The inventory turnover and customer receivables turnover is measured here as the number of days a product is kept in stock and the number of days it takes until a customer pays. A lower ratio is thus more beneficial. But whereas inventory turnover is likely to be lowered over time (management gets little benefit from having capital tied up in inventories), having capital tied up in customer receivables is more acceptable. Customers often require a certain credit time and there is not necessarily a cost associated with having capital tied up in customer receivables. By charging a higher price for the product (or service) capital costs can be covered. As efficiency ratios have little to do with the company's strategic financial decisions we will not really consider these two in this book. The third ratio, capital turnover, is often used when a decomposition of profitability is made. This ratio shows the association between sales and the net operating assets that were employed to generate sales. We shall soon employ ratio (2.26) in the Dupont-formula, and ratios (2.27) and (2.28) in the extended Dupont-formula.

2.2.6 *Growth ratios*

Growth is an important aspect of a company's financial performance. As shown in Chapter Three 16 of 20 large Swedish companies perceive growth to be one of their main financial goals. Shareholders perceive growth in cash flows and earnings as positive. Management, on the other hand, can see growth in operations as beneficial. Growth (as well as company size) can be measured in a number of ways. The most common measure to use is sales revenue. Other measures can be relevant depending on what interest one has in the company. Shareholders are primarily interested in earnings (or cash flow) growth per share. Debt holders are interested in the amount of interest-bearing debt. Customers are perhaps interested in the number of products offered by the company. Employees are interested in the number of employees and the salaries offered to them. Managers are perhaps interested in several of these measures and the best approximation of all of them is likely to be *value added*. Value added is measured as sales revenue minus the cost of externally acquired resources.[4] It represents the additional value that has been generated by a company. In comparison sales revenue can be a biased measure.

(SEK)	Heel		Toe	
	1999	2000	1999	2000
Sales revenue	10,000	11,000	10,000	10,000
Externally acquired resources	4,000	4,000	4,000	2,000
Value added	6,000	7,000	6,000	8,000
Growth in Sales		10 %		0 %
Growth in VA		17 %		25 %

Figure 2.4 – Comparison between growth in sales and value added.

Consider the two shoe producers *Heel* and *Toe*, who are shown in Figure 2.4. Last year both companies had sales of SEK 10,000. This year *Heel* has increased its sales by 10 percent, to 11,000. *Toe* on the other hand experienced no sales growth. So far it seems as if *Heel* outperformed *Toe* in terms of sales growth. But *Heel* achieved its growth by acquiring one of its retailers. *Toe*, on the other hand, acquired one of its main suppliers. Although *Heel* had a higher growth in sales, it was actually *Toe* which expanded its operations the most. But the growth never showed up as growth in sales. In reality *Toe* had the highest growth and as long as profit margins are equal among retailers and suppliers *Toe's* profits will increase more.

4 Value added = Sales – (cogs + sgae + ncie + depr – total personnel costs). Personnel costs are found among the footnotes in Swedish annual reports.

2.3 Focusing on Profitability and Risk

2.3.1 Combining financial ratios

In this section some of the financial ratios from the previous section are combined to make a more detailed description of company performance. These combinations of course only provide further information about company performance if one understands the business itself. One has to understand which ratios are the key value drivers for any particular company in order to pick the right combination of ratios.

Financial ratios are interrelated for three reasons (White, Sondhi and Fried, 1994:231–232). *First* there are economic relationships that force ratios to move in tandem. When sales increases so do, for example, investments in working capital and operating cash flows. *Second*, many ratios are interrelated because they contain the same components. Inventory turnover is, for example, related to the net profit margin simply because sales revenue is a component in both ratios. In some instances the interrelationship is considerable whereas in others it is smaller, depending on whether the interrelated variable is the key driver or not.[5] *Third*, some ratios are composites of other ratios. These interrelationships are described below using the Dupont-formula and the leverage formula.

2.3.2 Decomposing profitability

From the investor's perspective profitability is all that matters. The prime reason for making any financial analysis is to determine the current level of profitability and how it will develop in the future. When making this analysis one of the best-known tools is the *Dupont-formula*. Its origin goes back to the American chemical company Dupont which used the formula in their internal control system in the 1930s. Its structure facilitates the analysis of company profitability and capital turnover. The general idea is that profitability is caused by a company's profit margin multiplied by its capital turnover.

$$\text{Profitability} = \text{Profit Margin} \cdot \text{Capital turnover} = \frac{\text{Profit}}{\text{Sales}} \cdot \frac{\text{Sales}}{\text{Capital}} \qquad (2.29)$$

In order to improve profitability management can either increase its profit margin, i.e., earn more money on every sale that is made, or increase its

5 Compare the importance of sales revenue in the interrelationship between inventory turnover and operating profit margin, with the importance of net profit in the interrelationship between net profit margin and return on equity.

capital turnover, i.e., sell more using the same amount of capital. Companies in different industries often show considerably different combinations of profit margins and capital turnover (see e.g. Nissim and Penman, 1999; Elling, et.al., 1998:69). Pharmaceutical companies, such as AstraZeneca and PharmaciaUpjohn, have very high profit margins, but with quite a lot of capital tied up in its operations. On the other hand, trading companies often have low profit margins, but the capital turnover is higher. These companies are relatively efficient in using their capital, but have lower value added in the products sold.

$$RNOA_t = \frac{OPc_t}{S_t} \cdot \frac{S_t}{(NOA_{t-1} + NOA_t)/2} \tag{2.30}$$

$$ROE_t = \frac{NP_t}{S_t} \cdot \frac{S_t}{(EQ_{t-1} + EQ_t)/2} \tag{2.31}$$

Figure 2.5 (on the next page) shows the composition of return on net operating assets (RNOA) for four Swedish industrial companies. The breakdown is made using Expression (2.30). Sales and operating profits are taken directly from the annual reports of each company, whereas the net operating assets are calculated using (the author's own) subjective judgement regarding financial assets and non-interest bearing debt. The figure shows different patterns for the four companies. Although Hennes & Mauritz have a profit margin equal to or lower than both Swedish Match and StoraEnso their capital turnover is considerably higher. This is what makes their RNOA so much higher. Volvo has a lower profit margin and a low capital turnover, and their RNOA is very different from that of the other companies. It is important to take industry differences into consideration when making these kinds of analyses. At first it looks as if Hennes & Mauritz does better because of the capital turnover, but when compared to its industry peers one can see that the profit margin is also much higher than average.

An even more extensive disaggregation of RNOA can be obtained with the formula in Expression (2.32). Return on net operating assets (RNOA) is now broken down into four components; (1) operating profit margin, (2) capital turnover, (3) financial leverage, and (4) operating leverage. For the sake of simplicity the average value of the stock components are not expressed in a mathematically correct way.

$$RNOA_t = \frac{GP_t}{S_t} \cdot \frac{S_t}{A_t} \cdot \frac{A_t}{NOA_t} \cdot \frac{OPc_t}{GP_t} \tag{2.32}$$

Company	2000 OPc	2000 Sales	2000 NOA	1999 OPc	1999 Sales	1999 NOA	1998 NOA
Swedish Match	1,886	11,553	11,133	1,689	9,420	8,518	6,444
StoraEnso	2,371	13,017	18,729	1,400	10,636	14,188	13,727
H&M	3,767	35,876	8,853	4,580	32,977	6,151	5,321
Volvo	6,154	130,070	163,433	6,726	125,019	147,879	156,078

Swedish Match

$$2000 \quad \frac{1,886}{11,553} \cdot \frac{11,553}{(11,133 + 8,518)/2} = 16.3\,\% \cdot 1.18 = 19.2\,\%$$

$$1999 \quad \frac{1,689}{9,420} \cdot \frac{9,420}{(8,518 + 6,444)/2} = 17.9\,\% \cdot 1.26 = 22.6\,\%$$

StoraEnso

$$2000 \quad \frac{2,371}{13,017} \cdot \frac{13,017}{(18,729 + 14,188)/2} = 18.2\,\% \cdot 0.79 = 14.4\,\%$$

$$1999 \quad \frac{1,400}{10,636} \cdot \frac{10,636}{(14,188 + 13,727)/2} = 13.2\,\% \cdot 0.76 = 10.0\,\%$$

H&M

$$2000 \quad \frac{3,767}{35,876} \cdot \frac{35,876}{(8,853 + 6,151)/2} = 10.5\,\% \cdot 4.78 = 50.2\,\%$$

$$1999 \quad \frac{4,580}{32,977} \cdot \frac{32,977}{(6,151 + 5,321)/2} = 13.9\,\% \cdot 5.75 = 79.8\,\%$$

Volvo

$$2000 \quad \frac{6,154}{130,070} \cdot \frac{130,070}{(163,433 + 147,879)/2} = 4.7\,\% \cdot 0.84 = 4.0\,\%$$

$$1999 \quad \frac{6,726}{125,019} \cdot \frac{125,019}{(147,879 + 156,078)/2} = 5.4\,\% \cdot 0.82 = 4.4\,\%$$

OPc = Operating profits from the core business, Sales = sales from the core business, and NOA = net operating assets. For Swedish Match the net sales is used. The figures for StoraEnso are expressed in Euros. The figures for Volvo exclude the car division.

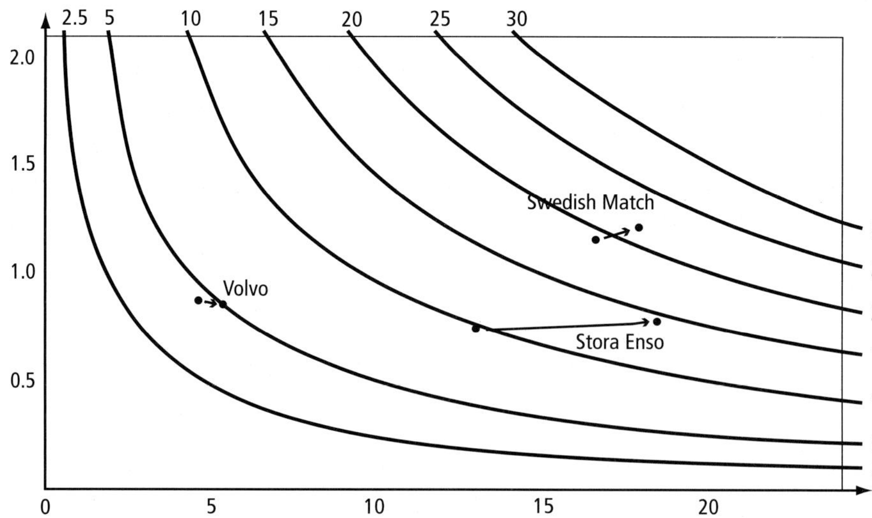

Figure 2.5 – Decomposing profitability using the Dupont formula. Note that the asset turnover of H&M is so great, its performance does not fit in the figure.

While this disaggregation is intuitively more difficult to appreciate because of its complex structure, it does give us an idea of how different aspects of a company's performance fit together and all contribute to the overall profitability. It is up to the decision-maker to determine what are the most important value drivers for an individual company. Based on this the right value drivers can be picked and used in a decomposition of profitability.

2.3.3 *The leverage formula, risk and variance in profitability*

The *financial leverage formula* is commonly used in financial analyses. It identifies the impact that the capital structure has on the return on equity. Possibly the first time the formula occurred in academia was in an article by Miller and Modigliani (1958) who used it when illustrating the cost of equity of a leveraged company. Most often this is referred to as the second proposition in the capital structure irrelevance theorem. It is extensively covered in Chapter Seven.

$$\text{RRBC} = \text{ROCE} + d \cdot (\text{ROCE} - i) \tag{2.33}$$

As long as ROCE is higher than the interest rate (i), an increase in financial leverage (d) will lead to an increased return on risk bearing capital (RRBC). Financial leverage is defined as (IBD/RBC). Thus from an investor point of view it might at first sight seem beneficial to increase financial leverage. But at the same time an increase in financial leverage will lead to higher fixed (financial) costs and since sales revenues vary over time, causing operating risk, the increase of cheap interest bearing capital also pushes more of the operating risk over to equity holders. In Chapter Seven it is shown how an increase in financial leverage shifts more of the business risk over to investors and that investors therefore increase their expectations on RRBC. The increased RRBC coming from increased leverage is therefore nothing but a compensation for the additional risk shareholders have to face. It is not possible to alter the value of a company simply by changing financing policy.[6]

The leverage formula is often combined with the Dupont formula in order to decompose profitability. When the Dupont formula (Expression

6 In coming chapters the leverage formula is expressed in terms of debt and equity. Hence it is then written as: ROE = ROCE + (D/EQ) · (ROCE – i), alternatively in Chapter Seven the same formula is written as $r_{EQ} = r_{WACC} + (D/EQ) \cdot (r_{WACC} - r_D)$. The reasons for these alterations will be returned to in these chapters.

2.30) is inserted in the leverage formula (Expression 2.33) the result looks like Expression (2.34). This might not give a clearer picture of actual company performance, but it does tell us of how well integrated financial ratios are.

$$RRBC = (PM \cdot CT) + d \cdot [(PM \cdot CT) - i] \qquad (2.34)$$

The variance in profitability

The leverage formula can be used as a starting point for analysing risk within a company (see Hamberg, 2000 for a much more thorough discussion). Accounting information is of a secondary kind and is used by a company's external stakeholders. They primarily use the accounting information to view the risk for financial distress, and the profitability risk. The main focus here is on profitability risk, but first a couple of words concerning the risk for financial distress. The *risk for financial distress* is the same as the probability that future cash flows are so low the company cannot manage its contractual agreements. In such a situation management is forced to take corrective action. It might lead to a default on a contract, and it might mean financial restructuring (involving either or both equity and debt holders). Usually financial distress forces management to take measures it would rather avoid. In the ultimate case it means bankruptcy.

The risk of financial distress is something stakeholders try to measure using accounting information. The great number of research studies conducted within the area has shown that a model combining financial ratios are relatively good at picking out future survivors and non-survivors. Companies with a low solvency, low liquidity and negative cash flows are more likely to run into financial distress than other companies. On the hand, a common problem these research studies have pointed at is the difficulty to pick out individual companies that will go bankrupt. This means that creditors have to complement their quantitative models by building personal contacts with clients.

The *profitability risk* refers to the probability that future profitability will deviate from expected profitability.[7] Profitability risk implies that the level of profitability in a company varies over time, and that the extent of this variability is not certain. Profitability risk is about future profitability, but it is estimated using historical profitability. The aim with the following

7 Profitability risk refers to those stakeholders having a residual relationship to the business firm, and risk of financial risk refers primarily to those stakeholders holding a contractual relationship to the business firm. Chapter Three contains a more thorough discussion of stakeholders, their differences, and their relationships to the business firm.

discussion is to introduce the two concepts of operating and financial risk and provide a brief understanding of how different components have an effect on the variance in company profitability. This kind of discussion is returned to in e.g. Chapters Seven and Eight. Profitability risk is determined by the operating and financial risks of a company. However when using the leverage formula to measure these two components they are integrated and so their individual impacts cannot be measured perfectly.

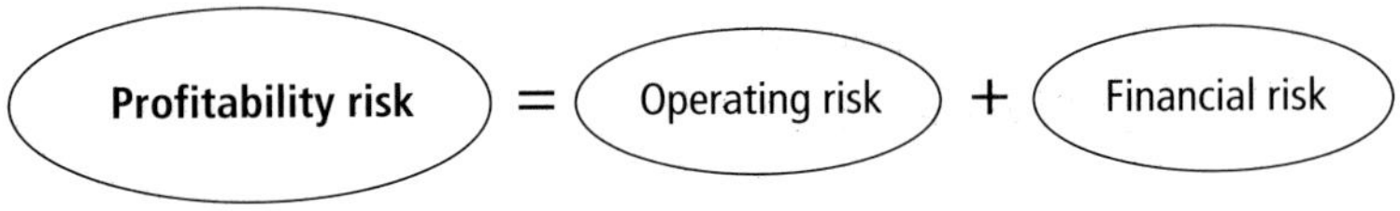

Figure 2.6 – Operating and financial risk.

With the help of the leverage formula we can identify the operating and the financial risk components. To do this, first imagine a company with no interest bearing debt, but only risk bearing capital. From a shareholder perspective, the before-tax return of this company is RRBC, which is defined as:

$$RRBC_t^{bT} = \frac{Pfi_t}{(RBC_{t-1} + RBC_t)/2} \quad (2.35)$$

Total profitability risk is then written measured as the variance in return on risk bearing capital; V(RRBC). For a company with no external debt the variance in RRBC is equal to the variance in return on capital employed (ROCE).

$$V(RRBC) = V(ROCE) \quad (2.36)$$

This company is only exposed to operating risk. Financial risk enters the scene once the company decides to acquire external debt. Let us first assume that the interest on these external debts is stable ($V(i) = 0$). In such a case the leverage formula can be transformed into Expression (2.37) and hence financial risk can be expressed as in Expression (2.38).

$$V(RRBC) = V(ROCE) \cdot (1 + d)^2 \quad (2.37)$$

$$(1 + d)^2 \quad (2.38)$$

Under the more realistic assumption that $V(i) \neq 0$, profitability risk can be expressed as:

$$V(RRBC) =$$
$$= V(ROCE) + V[d \cdot (ROCE - i)] + 2 \cdot Cov[ROCE, d \cdot (ROCE - i)] \quad (2.39)$$

From this expression we can see that operating risk is difficult to separate totally from financial risk as the two components interact. The third factor in Expression (2.39) shall be interpreted that two times the covariance between operating risk and financial risk is part of total profitability risk. A summary of the components of profitability risk is shown in Table 2.1. In Chapter Five there is some empirical evidence from Swedish companies regarding the profitability risk.

Table 2.1 – The components of profitability risk.

Concept	Abbreviation	Definition
Total profitability risk	PR	V(RRBC)
Operating risk component	OR	V(ROCE)
Financial risk component	FR	V[d × (ROCE – i)]
Residual risk component	RR	2 × Cov [ROCE, d × (ROCE – i)]

2.3.4 Operating and financial risk

Operating risk is here defined as that part of profitability risk that is related to the company's operating activities, which is reflected in the volatility in return on risk bearing capital. Operating risk is measured as the variance in return on capital employed. It is caused by four factors; (1) volume uncertainty, (2) price uncertainty, (3) volume sensitivity, and (4) price sensitivity.

1. *Volume uncertainty* means that one does not know the exact volume that is demanded by customers in the future. It is determined by factors of both internal and external character, such as, for example, competition within the industry, the extent of product substitutes, product life cycle. Fluctuations in produced volume also depend on the activities the company performs in, for example, marketing.
2. *Price uncertainty* is fairly similar to volume uncertainty. It means that one does not know the exact price per unit that produced goods can be sold for in the future. The price uncertainty is in general determined by the same kind of factors as volume uncertainty. In reality the volume and price uncertainty is measured conjointly as the historical variance in sales.

3 *Volume sensitivity* is dependent on having changes in production volume over time. When sales volume varies over time, earnings are affected differently depending on a company's production structure. Companies with a capital-intensive production function, have a larger degree of fixed costs, which makes them more sensitive to changes in sales volume. Production structures vary particularly between companies in different industries, but also to some extent between companies within the same industry. The production structure is often frequently referred to as the operating leverage.

4 *Price sensitivity* is dependent on having changes in sales price per unit over time. When the price of a sold good varies over time, different companies' profitability is affected differently. The effect of a change in output prices on profitability will depend on two factors: The ability to influence the price of input goods, and the productivity. If changes in sales price can be offset by changes in the input price then the company is less affected by price uncertainty. Also if improvements in productivity can be made, a company is less sensitive to price increases (see Hamberg, 2000).

Financial decisions will have to be made with operating risk taken into consideration. A company with high volume and price uncertainty might try to compensate this by reducing price sensitivity. When this is not possible management might have to change its financial policy and try to reduce financial risk. One good example of an industry where the operating risk is high would be the forest industry. Forest companies such as Rottneros, StoraEnso, and Assi-Domän are very much dependent on internationally determined prices on paper and pulp. At the same time they have made large investments in production facilities and therefore the proportion of fixed costs is high.

Financial risk is here defined as that part of profitability risk that is related to the company's financing activities, which is reflected in the volatility in return on risk bearing capital. Financial risk is most easily described as the extent to which debt financing magnifies operating risk. We define it as financial leverage multiplied with the difference between ROCE and the interest rate (i). It consists of two, or possibly three, components. These are (1) financial leverage, (2) covariance between interest rate and ROCE, and (3) the variance in interest rate.

1 *Financial leverage.* Debt financing introduces fixed costs into a company. This causes a leverage effect on company earnings. As long as the operating profits are larger than interest costs a positive effect is achieved. But in an opposite situation a negative effect occurs. Under the condition that profitability varies over time the financial leverage usually magnifies the variance in RRBC.
2 *Interest rate volatility.* A variance in the net borrowing cost has no direct effect on the financial risk, but a greater uncertainty regarding the interest rate makes it more difficult to do something about the sensitivity to interest rate volatility.
3 *Sensitivity to interest rate volatility.* A company can have a very high financial leverage without experiencing a great financial risk. It all depends on the covariance between ROCE and interest costs. A company for which the ROCE varies perfectly in accordance with its net borrowing cost will have no additional variance coming from a high financial leverage (see Hamberg, 2000 for a further discussion and examples).

According to some researchers there is a negative association between operating and financial risk (see e.g. Mandelker and Rhee, 1984). In a study of Swedish industrial companies it was shown that there is no statistically significant negative association between operating and financial risk, but one between financial leverage and operating risk (Hamberg, 2000). Financial leverage is a variable which management has better control over than interest rate volatility. A good visible example of the trade-off between financial leverage and operating risk is that of real estate companies which often have long term contracts and thus know what revenues they will earn. Although they have a lot of fixed costs (and a high volume sensitivity) they can increase their financial leverage.[8] A low operating risk is taken advantage of by increasing financial leverage.

2.4 Capital Market Oriented Financial Ratios

2.4.1 Introduction

The evaluation of companies listed on stock exchanges is often based on accounting information. Financial analysts usually estimate ratios in which

8 This is also partly due to the tangibility of the company's assets. In Chapter Seven this issue is elaborated further.

accounting numbers are related to market values. The purpose is, of course, to determine whether a company is over-, under-, or correctly valued. For a manager making financial decisions knowledge of this kind is of lesser importance. These ratios do however provide a bridge between accounting information, which is critical for our understanding of company performance and management's decisions, and the valuation of the company that the shareholders make. For this reason it would be an error to completely leave it out.

By using financial ratios when making investment decisions the investor engages in what is referred to as *fundamental analysis*. A fundamental analysis, as opposed to *technical analysis*, looks at the relationship between an asset's value and some underlying factor related to what has caused the value. Decisions to buy and sell a security is made on the basis of the relationship between share prices and accounting measures of value and value-creation. In technical analysis, the analyst is not interested in the actual operations of a company, what the cash flows are, the profit margin, or the profitability. All that matters is historical prices, trends in share prices and the volume of shares traded in the market. To us the fundamental analysis is of more importance than technical analysis. In Chapter Five it is in fact shown that technical analysis might be a waste of time. In this section we pay attention to four common financial ratios linking company performance (measured with accounting information) to security pricing.

2.4.2 *Profitability oriented ratios*

Price-to-earnings (P/E) ratio

The price-to-earnings ratio is a measure, which states the relationship between the value of a company and its current (or forecasted) periodic ability to contribute to the value. Under the assumption that the earnings component is a correct measure of the periodic value creation, the normal price-to-earnings ratio is determined by a company's cost of equity (investors' required rate of return). The higher the cost of equity is the lower the P/E ratio should be. The cost of equity is determined by the risk that equity holders face; higher risk means higher cost of capital. Therefore a higher risk for investors implies that the P/E ratio is lower.[9]

9 To take a simple example of how to estimate the "normal" P/E ratio let's assume you have put SEK 1000 in a savings account and earn 10 percent in fixed interest. The cost of equity is then 10 percent. At the end of the first year you have earned SEK 100 and the account's balance is SEK 1100. The P/E ratio is then (1000 + 100)/100, which is equal to 11. Alternatively we can solve the following equation: $(1 + r_{EQ})/r_{EQ}$, where r_{EQ} is the cost of equity.

When calculating a company's P/E ratio this can differ substantially from what is normal using the cost of equity method described above. This is either because the measure of earnings based on accounting information is misleading, or that investors expect future earnings to be substantially higher than current earnings. Without going into the details here, investors expect future earnings to grow at a rate higher than the cost of capital that leads to a creation of value. This kind of reasoning is continued in Chapters Ten and Eleven.

Price-to-cashflow (P/CF) ratio

The price-to-cash flow ratio is a measure that is similar to the P/E ratio. Its purpose is more or less the same; to identify the relationship between value and periodic value creation, but here a cruder measure of value creation is used. The P/CF can be substantially lower than the P/E ratio if the company has made considerable investments in the past. The measure has serious problems if one compares two companies with different investment policies, and particularly if one does not take into account the expected return on current investments.

2.4.3 Other ratios

Price-to-book (P/B) ratio

The price-to-book value is a measure of the difference between the market value of a company, and its reported book value. If accounting were "perfect" from a shareholder point of view, this ratio would always be one (1). Because of the difficulties of measuring the value of assets, and the conservatism of the accounting system this ratio is most often greater than one. In Chapter Six we shall learn that there seems to be an association between this ratio and security return.

Dividend payout ratio

In Chapter Eight in this book we will deal particularly with the dividend policy of a corporation. For some investors dividends can be an important aspect when choosing between different securities. The dividend payout ratio is estimated as dividends per share divided by share price.

In some industries, where cash flows are high and growth opportunities are low, the dividend payout ratio is relatively large. It can in fact be considerably higher than interest received in banks, and that is attractive to certain kinds of investors. This will be discussed in greater depth in subsequent chapters.

Key Concepts

> Income statement
> Income
> Revenue
> Expense
> Net profit
> Core business
> Balance sheet
> Clean surplus relationship
> Interest bearing debt
> Non-interest bearing debt
> Risk bearing capital
> Capital employed
> Net operating assets
> Financial assets
> Free cash flow
> Accounting accruals
> Economic life
> Historical cost
> Conservative accounting
> Financial ratio
> Financial ratio analysis
> Profitability ratio
> Capital structure ratio
> Liquidity ratio
> Efficiency ratio
> Value added
> Dupont-formula
> Financial leverage formula
> Risk for financial distress
> Profitability risk
> Fundamental analysis
> Technical analysis
> The matching principle of ratio analysis

Key Issues to Discuss

1. Discuss the role of financial accounting and the different needs of stakeholders that accounting information has to fulfil.
2. Financial theorists are primarily concerned with cash flows. Why are accounting earnings an issue to pay attention to? Exemplify the consequences that accounting accruals can have on 'bottom-line' profits (vs. cash flows from operations).
3. It has been argued that accounting-based measures of company performance need to be valid and reliable. Discuss how biases in the comparison of companies can be caused by violations of the matching principle.
4. Estimate the performance of SKF (Figure 2.1 and 2.2) using the financial ratios described in Section 2.2.
5. Discuss the problems with using the information gathered in Question Four in terms of; (a) comparability, and (b) validity.
6. Use the Dupont-formula to decompose SKF's profitability (RNOA) and make comparisons with the companies illustrated in Figure 2.5.
7. Explain thoroughly why a company with a very high proportion of fixed operating costs face, ceteris paribus, a higher operating risk. It may help to use a graph when answering the question.
8. Explain how come a company with a very high financial leverage still might face no financial risk, as described in Chapter Two. It may help to use a graph when answering the question.
9. Give some practical examples of companies for which the association between operating and financial risk ought to be strongly negative. Motivate why this is the case.

Further readings:

Hamberg, M., 2000, *Risk, Uncertainty & Profitability – An Accounting-Based Study of Industrial Firms' Performance*, Department of Business Studies, Uppsala University.

Penman, 2001, *Financial Statement Analysis and Security Valuation*, New York: McGraw-Hill.

Chapter 3

Corporate Governance

This chapter aims at:

- Explaining the differences between management's and the shareholders' financial objectives.
- Providing a view of financial decision-making in which management's main priority is not always profit-maximisation.
- Showing how shareholders can control managers and make them perform more in the interests of shareholders.
- Describing the issue of corporate governance in Swedish industrial companies and pointing out some of its major features.

3.1 Conflicts of Interest Between Management and Shareholders

3.1.1 The stakeholder model

Do managers always act in the best interests of the owners of a company? Naturally, if the answer to such a question were to be yes, there would be little point in continuing with the rest of this chapter. But in which issues do managers and shareholders think differently, to what extent do they do so, and how can one overcome the problems? The essence of this chapter is to go against traditional financial theory and provide the theoretical framework for an alternative view of financial decision-making. It is referred to as an alternative as most academicians still teach how management ought to behave rather than give reasons as to why management behave in certain ways.

In Chapter One the foundations of classic financial theory were introduced. The main assumption behind classic financial theory is that the company consists of rational profit maximisers, who consistently try to maximise the value of the company. While doing so they only have one thing in mind: making profitable investments where the risk is matched with incoming cash flows. This picture is considerably more idealistic than realistic. In this chapter it is argued that rational behaviour from management's side will lead to different behaviours than those desired from shareholders. This is referred to as goal incongruence.

All companies have a multitude of stakeholders and each of them have their own specific interests in the company, and thus also in its performance and management's decisions. The main stakeholder in the company is the group of shareholders, or investors. In economic theory their interests are proposed as the company's main priority – we refer to it as *shareholder wealth maximisation*. But in order to do business, management have to engage a number of parties. They are referred to as the company's stakeholders as they all hold some stake in the company's operations. Figure 3.1 contains a *stakeholder model* of the company, in which the company is viewed as a nexus of contracts between the various stakeholders (cf. Jensen and Meckling, 1976). The stakeholders are divided into internal and external stakeholders depending on whether they have a direct influence on the decision-making or not.

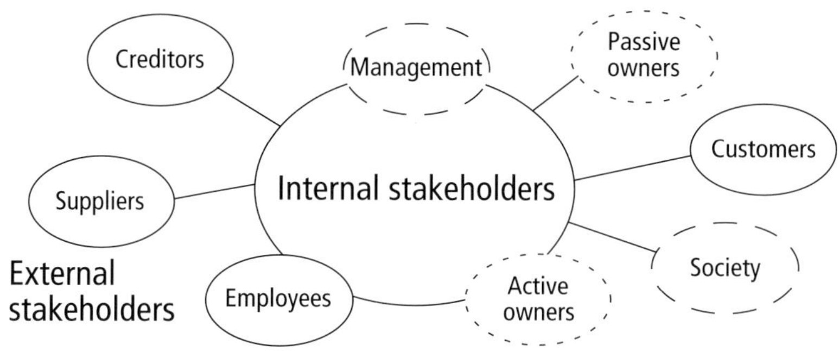

Figure 3.1 – External and internal stakeholders of a company.[1]

Most stakeholders hold a *contractual relationship* to the company. This means that they are hired to perform certain duties and that they receive a pre-determined reward for doing so. For example, companies hire employees to perform certain tasks. The employees receive a monetary reward for doing so. Companies need raw materials, which they buy from other companies. These suppliers receive a monetary reward for supplying the material. Companies sell their finished products to customers, to whom they deliver the product and receive a monetary reward for doing so. These are all examples of contracts between the company and its stakeholders. The monetary reward is laid down in the contract. The risk that the stakeholders bear is the risk that the company cannot fulfil its part of the contract. In such a case the contract will be broken. For all the stakeholders with a contractual relationship to the firm risk is only related to negative consequences.

In contrast to these stakeholders the shareholders have a *residual relationship* to the company. The term residual relationship refers to the residual value that is left after stakeholders with a contractual relationship have received their contracted reward. Shareholders expect a certain residual value (return on their investment) depending on the inherent risk of the investment, but they are never guaranteed that return. The risk these stakeholders bear is the risk that the actual residual value is not the same as the expected residual value. Investors might have invested 1000 in a company. Risk is defined as the probability that the actual value differs from expected value, in *either* a negative or positive way. Due to the risk involved investors do, in this case, demand a return of ten percent, which then equals 100. We shall learn about how to determine risk and return in several of the following chapters of the book.

1 The idea of illustrating stakeholder relationships in this manner comes from Elling (1995:23).

Although shareholders form the ultimate stakeholder group with a residual relationship to the company, there are others. Tax authorities also have a somewhat residual relationship to companies. Indeed they receive a defined percentage of earnings in taxes, but the tax is based on the residual value, that is, the value left after all other stakeholders have received their contractual reward and the amount will therefore vary depending on company performance. Management of most companies are nowadays remunerated in relation to performance. When the company performs well they are paid well, whereas bad performance gives them a lower compensation. With such an arrangement management has greater incentives to take profit-maximising actions. One of the main ways of handling the goal incongruence is by giving management a residual relationship to the company.

3.1.2 Stakeholder demands

All stakeholder groups put pressure on the company. Their interests have to be coordinated by management – this is what it has been hired for.[2] On behalf of the shareholders, management has to make sure the company earns a sufficient return. A return that corresponds to the level of risk involved. But management cannot ignore the other stakeholders. They have to invest capital to develop the products that customers want. They have to create a working environment in which employees will perform their tasks well. Set up a working environment that can attract and retain skilled people. They have to create an organisation producing socially acceptable products, such as, for example, products that are not hazardous to the environment.

Stakeholders who are dissatisfied with management's actions are likely to punish it severely. The ultimate punishment must always come from shareholders who have the right to fire management or reduce its remuneration. But all other stakeholders also have demands management takes into consideration. Figure 3.2 shows some examples of such demands. Of course demands vary over time, between companies, and between industries.

2 This is true (in our society), even though the owners, who are the primary stakeholder group with a residual relationship to the company, have the ultimate responsibility for managing the relationships to other stakeholders and bear the consequences of such relationships.

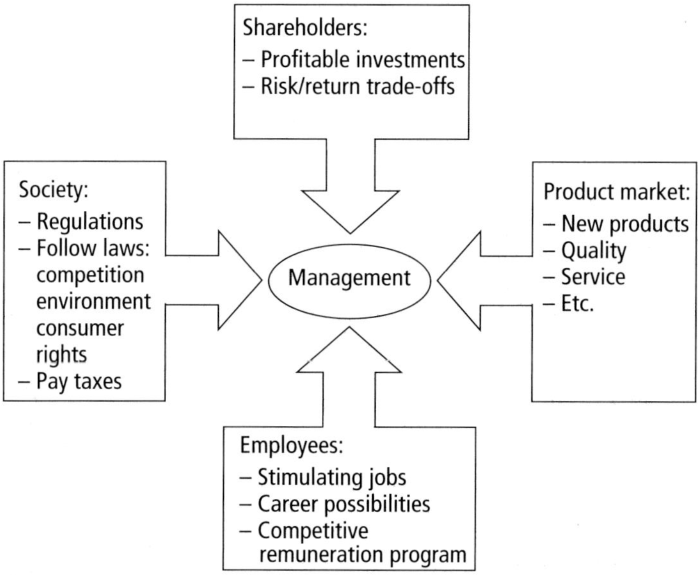

Figure 3.2 – Stakeholder demands.

Shareholders' demands will be focused on the inherent ability of company operations to generate profits using the existing resources. The product market's demands will be focused on new products and services that satisfy existing needs better and better. In competition with its competitors, the company will have to find an optimal mix of core product and supporting services which fulfil the needs of targeted customers. Society sets rules and regulations, which companies have to follow. These include for example environmental concerns (such as pollution restrictions) and taxation. Finally, the organisation itself is an important stakeholder. Employees require stimulating jobs, where they can be rewarded according to performance. They want career opportunities and competitive remuneration programs. Negligence of any stakeholder demand will surely be a threat to company survival and management success.

The clash between management and shareholders is caused by goal incongruence. Shareholders constitute the most prominent stakeholder group, but management most often view their interest in the company's operations as one among several. Management realise that they should maximise the value of the company, but while doing so they need to handle the pressures coming from other stakeholders. In the next section we examine management's role and its strategies to handle the pressures of different stakeholder groups.

3.1.3 The role of management

The relative importance of different stakeholder groups can vary over time. Although shareholders have always played a prominent role in the governing of companies, their role has changed. In comparison to twenty years ago, modern companies are to a greater extent owned by professional investors who have to report increases in shareholder value. They force management to maximise shareholder value. We will return to this later in the section on corporate governance in Swedish companies. Even if it is stressed here that many stakeholders are important, no management team completely overlooks the interests of shareholders.

Despite this, a managerial perspective of financial decision-making will be somewhat different from that of the shareholders. It is important for us to recognise these differences and interpret situations, involving financial decision-making, on the basis of both perspectives. In 1974 Findlay and Whitmore were amongst the first to recognise the existence of a managerial perspective of corporate finance. In so doing they distinguished between *Shareholder Wealth Maximisation* (SWM), and *Managerial Welfare Maximisation* (MWM). The MWM perspective comes from management feeling a responsibility to more than one stakeholder. The main differences between the two perspectives are identified in Table 3.1.

Table 3.1 – Potential differences between shareholder and managerial interests.

	Shareholders	**Management**
Overall goal	Shareholder Wealth Maximisation.	Managerial Welfare Maximisation.
Motto	Profitability above all else.	Shareholder satisfaction is enough.
Capital structure	Find the lowest average cost of capital.	Follow the norms of the industry.
Investment policy	Accept all proposals meeting the required return.	None. Investments are seen as a residual.
Dividend policy	None. Dividends are seen as a residual.	Keep shareholders satisfied.
Attitude towards company growth	Grow when profitable investments are available.	Grow whenever you can. Restraints: management need to satisfy shareholders, and have financial slack.
Attitude towards risk	Shareholders have a portfolio perspective. Only systematic risk matters. Risk is related to return.	Management are subject to unique risk. Managers face uncertainty. Uncertainty is not clearly related to return. Risk of insolvency, risk of takeovers.
Reporting policy	Objective reporting required. Accurate information should be provided to investors as soon as possible.	Report information that benefits management.

Source: Findlay and Whitmore (1974).

Throughout this book all of the issues mentioned in Table 3.1 above will be discussed in much greater depth. For a reader with little pre-knowledge of finance and investment some of the terms in Table 3.1 might be confusing. The fundamental difference between management and shareholder interests is the emphasis on either growth or profitability. While shareholders want a return on investment that is as high as possible (given the intrinsic risk) this is not necessarily management's primary objective. We will soon provide the theoretical reasons why management view growth to be of at least equal importance to profitability. Management want to satisfy shareholders but not maximise their interests. Thus management perceive investments as a residual; they want to invest as much of the company's capital as possible in reasonable investments. They choose a capital structure and a dividend policy, which shareholders are satisfied with. Management are afraid of risk, primarily because diversification is difficult for them to achieve. In Chapter Four it is therefore argued that managers do not face risk, but they manage uncertainty. Companies that manage uncertainty well will perform better than other companies, but in order to do better than others, management do not want to reveal exactly how well they are doing, or what exactly they are doing. Management wants to report the information they find suitable. Investors on the other hand can diversify away risk so they do not care if one company within an industry is better than the others; they hold shares in all the companies. Investors want to have as much information as possible to assess the current performance and future possibilities for each company. That there is a conflict here is evident, as management and shareholders have different views of finance and investment decisions. The next step in the analysis is to understand management's role as the intermediary between all the other stakeholders. Hence we adopt the MWM perspective, and recognise its differences to SWM, as we continue our analysis.

3.1.4 Managing corporate wealth

Donaldson (1984) performed a substantial research project on strategic financial decision-making. He analysed the overall objectives of management's decisions from quite a theoretical perspective. Donaldson's description of financial decision-making is similar to that of Findlay and Whitmore, but he then goes further by providing four motives that underlie management's behaviour. The most important of these motives is survival. The three other motives Donaldson refer to are independence, self-sufficiency and self-fulfilment, and they support the ability to survive. A summary of these motives is given below.

Survival	Managers do not explicitly talk about the survival of their company. Such talk would carry too much of a negative overtone. Instead, the survival motive is found implicitly in everything the managers do. The preservation and enhancement of the company's future are the essence of planning. In practical terms, organizational survival means that management must always command sufficient corporate purchasing power to support the company's vital functions. To not survive is the ultimate managerial failure.
Independence	The independence motive is closely related to survival. Management strives for the freedom to make decisions and take actions without having to consult external parties to the enterprise. Freedom can never be complete, but must be seen as relative. In planning as well as decision-making management takes independence into consideration. This can include independence from government regulators, potential acquirers, lenders negotiating contracts, customers putting pressure on product development, etc.
Self-sufficiency	This third motive follows naturally on from the first two; management recognise that they exist in a hostile and highly competitive world and thus they are reluctant to be financially dependent on other, equally self-interested external parties for their vital needs. To ask for capital is to give up some independence. Self-sufficiency often leads to a desire to finance projects with internal rather than external funds.
Self-fulfilment	Within the highly competitive world management have to act, they look for specific visible measures of achievement; personal or organisational. Financial goals inevitably play a major role in fulfilling management's expectations and making them satisfied with their performance. Self-fulfilment is achieved when financial goals are obtained, goals which ultimately enable the company to survive.

Source: Donaldson (1984).

In his in-depth study of financial managers, Donaldson came to the conclusion that the motives described above make management focus on their *corporate wealth*. Corporate wealth should not be confused with company value, as it is quite different. Donaldson (1984:3) defines it as the wealth "...that management can use at its discretion to implement decisions involving the control of goods and services.". This is wealth vital to the organisation's survival; wealth which deals with actual cash flows and realisable values in management's possession. By such a definition corporate wealth is more immediate, certain, and meaningful to corporate management. Management desire corporate wealth as it can give relief in situations where stakeholders put sudden pressure on them. It is a "shield" providing them with more control and flexibility. From an SWM perspective corporate wealth is basically equal to *financial slack*, a term often used by financial economists. Financial slack is capital that is currently not used in an optimal way (not earning a return corresponding to the investment's intrinsic risk). On such grounds shareholders ought to dislike corporate wealth.

In order to make the theoretical contributions of Donaldson usable in practise Åkerblom (1996) has divided corporate wealth into four measurable components. To determine the value of each component for individual companies is a very subjective and difficult task. A structure for such an analysis is, however, provided here.

1. Free cash flow for the planning horizon

Corporate wealth deals with management's planning horizon. As such the free cash flow coming from existing operations during this period of time form part of corporate wealth. Cash flows in the near future are more certain than cash flows further away and are therefore preferred. Management need to be sure cash comes in and can be used either as management have intended in their plans, or alternatively as a "financial buffer" in case of unexpected stakeholder pressures. Obviously not all free cash flows can be used, particularly not as a financial buffer. A minimum investment requirement is that free cash flow is used to cover investments for a preserved competitive position (or at least maintained capacity). Shareholders will also ask management to prove that excess cash is reasonably well invested. If not cash should be returned to shareholders.

2. Possible reductions of current assets without disturbing operations

Financial slack can be kept, intentionally or unintentionally, in many places within a large organisation. Excessive cash might be sitting in the company's bank account and then it is easy to detect. But it can also be hidden among other reported current assets. The turnover of customer receivables might be lower than what is needed to maintain a satisfactory level of sales. The turnover of inventories might also be lower than it is today without disturbing customer relationships. If management know this, they can easily reduce customer receivables and inventories whenever needed and thereby make capital available for their own welfare maximisation.

3. Possible sales of fixed assets without disturbing corporate strategy
Financial slack can also be kept among the fixed assets. To alter the company's composition of fixed assets can have long term strategic effects. But all realisations of assets that can be made without impairing the company's long term strategic position can potentially be made in order to free corporate wealth. Management can, for example, sell and lease back a manufacturing plant, sell off shares in non-strategic companies or move into a less expensive office building in order to make corporate wealth available. The market value of a company's assets is often much higher than the reported book value and therefore corporate wealth can be well hidden in large companies.

4. New loans not impairing management control, and not substantially increasing risk
Some companies have a very slim balance sheet, with very little visible financial slack. Does this mean that they have no opportunity to make use of corporate wealth? The answer is no, because corporations with high solvency and sound business operations generating stable cash flows have little problem raising their debt ratio and borrowing capital from creditors. As long as the debt ratio is on a par with the industry average (i.e., companies with equal risk) stakeholders are likely to accept new loans. On the other hand, new loans are quite easily detected and they draw attention to management's actions. Most managers are therefore likely to prefer corporate wealth that is under their direct control.

The four components are of different natures. The second, third, and fourth component concern the corporate wealth that management currently have at their disposal. These components are measured with information on existing values in the company. The first component is future-oriented, that is, its size varies depending on the company's creation of value in the future and the time frame.[3]

3 To use the terminology of Chapter Two, the first component is a *flow concept*, whereas the others are *stock concepts*.

It is important to understand that although management view corporate wealth as something positive, we cannot expect them to maximise it, but merely to try to reach a satisfactory level of it. The optimal level of corporate wealth is determined in symbiosis with the external stakeholders. Therefore managers *manage* corporate wealth. Too much corporate wealth is likely to have dear consequences, as the shareholders then take action. Particularly when we calculate future free cash flows we have to bear in mind that pressure from shareholders will increase with too high free cash flows not reinvested in projects earning an adequate return.

3.1.5 Using growth as an explicit financial goal

Most companies use financial goals in order to direct their organisation's attention to certain problems, or to evaluate its progress based on some key success factors. Financial goals are mainly used internally, but often they are openly expressed in the annual reports. Such information from twenty of the largest Swedish industrial companies is analysed below.[4] The results are shown in Table 3.2. Amongst these companies one does not find any goals related directly to corporate wealth. This is hardly surprising as a corporate wealth goal would be controversial to external stakeholders. Donaldson (1984) argues that such goals are neither found within organisations, as they are also difficult to communicate and measure.

Table 3.2 – Financial goals of 20 large Swedish industrial companies.

	Number of companies	Typical example
Any financial goal	17	
Growth	10 (16)	15 %, or growth higher than industry average
Profit margin	5	Operating margin: 10 %
Profitability	10 (17)	Return on equity: 15 %
Dividends	9	33 % of net earnings
Solvency	6	D/E: 10 %
Other	4	Capital investments lower than depreciation

Source: Annual reports from twenty Swedish companies in 1999.

4 All twenty companies are highly internationalised with a majority of their sales coming from abroad.

When Donaldson (1984) did his study he found one goal that almost all companies had clearly expressed, and that same goal is just as common among Swedish companies. Managers want their organisation to expand. A high growth strategy is in general seen as beneficial. Among the Swedish companies 10 out of 20 companies had an explicit growth target, usually expressed as growth in sales of between 10 and 25 percent. Another six companies clearly said that growth was one of their main goals (but they did not say how fast they wanted to grow). Of the four companies with no growth target one is an investment company and three work in considerably mature industries where organic growth is very low. Perhaps surprisingly, just as many companies which have growth targets (10 and 17) also have profitability targets. It is interesting to note that only half of the companies say something about the share performance and only one company expresses a financial goal in relation to shares (Securitas wants a growth in Earnings-Per-Share of 25 percent[5]). According to this survey, as well as Donaldson's study, growth seems to be just as important as profitability.

But what is the reason for this? Donaldson argues that growth in fact is a proxy for corporate wealth. Becoming a larger company provides increased control and flexibility for management. The relationships to stakeholders become easier to manage in a large and growing organisation. As the organisation expands, it can achieve economies-of-scale and earn higher profit margins. It can attract new employees and provide good career paths for them. It also receives more publicity, which makes it easier for it to achieve good credit ratings, and hence cheaper capital. As the company grows, it is easier to become a market leader and invest relatively more than its competitors in R&D. If these are potential benefits stemming from being a large organisation then setting a growth target is understandable. Growth both satisfies all stakeholders and provides management with good opportunities to increase corporate wealth. Moreover, growth is based on the fundamental need for survival, independence, self-sufficiency,

Figure 3.3 – Connections between theoretical reasons and management's goal.

5 Indeed this hardly qualifies as a capital market oriented target, but is really a profitability target.

and self-fulfilment. Figure 3.3 illustrates the connections between the theoretical arguments of Donaldson and the explicit goal in terms of corporate growth. Growth facilitates a more undisturbed *management* of corporate wealth. Managers need to have corporate wealth, control and flexibility in order to handle the constant pressures coming from the stakeholders.

Corporate wealth, control and flexibility might be what management are after, but it has to be manifested within the organisation. Therefore growth is portrayed as the ultimate goal. But financial resources restrain the ability to grow. If the company's financial performance cannot sustain a high growth strategy then the stakeholders will show their dissatisfaction. High growth through increased borrowing and investing in bad projects is unsustainable – at least in the long run. Managing corporate wealth is the same as having a balanced growth strategy, where management balance the interests of different stakeholders. These ideas are implemented in practical terms in Chapter Eleven, where an internal financial system is introduced and analysed.

3.1.6 The shareholders' view of corporate wealth

The discussion held above does not completely contradict classic financial theory. Shareholders are important, but they are not the only important stakeholder group. From a shareholder perspective it can, however, be seen as if maximising corporate wealth is a behaviour which inhibits maximising shareholder wealth. Donaldson argues that slack is being built into the organisation. Slack which can be used at management's discretion, whenever they deem it necessary to do so.

Financial slack refers to capital, which is not deployed to earn a sufficient return. So from a financial theory perspective this capital is misused, and should be either invested in profitable projects, or returned to shareholders who can allocate the capital to other, profitable, projects. As we will learn in coming chapters, shareholders should be diversified and if so they do not care much about individual companies/investments. Financial slack protects the company from bankruptcy, unusual production disturbances and suchlike. To take bankruptcy as an example, it is costly for shareholders but if they only invest a small portion of their fortune in a single company then they are insensitive to unsystematic negative events (or positive for that matter). Furthermore, managers know more about future cash flows from projects than shareholders do. Theoretical arguments (which are further discussed in Chapter Seven) have been made that financial slack increases company value when management know that profitable investment opportunities exist, while shareholders have great suspicion.

Although it is correct to argue that financial slack is mainly negative to shareholders, it is highly unrealistic that it can ever be fully removed. It is in the nature of humans to maximise their own interests and as long as the interests of managers and shareholders are different there must be a *goal incongruence*; management does not want the same things as shareholders. Financial slack is acceptable also for shareholders if management systematically have access to better information than shareholders and if bankruptcies are costly. The costs of having goal incongruence can be reduced, and from a shareholder perspective we will now look at means to reducing the problems with the separation of ownership and control over corporate resources.

3.2 Principal-Agent Theory

In the very first systematic analysis of a modern industrial company Adam Smith made the following observation:

> *"The directors of such [joint-stock] companies, however, being the managers rather of other people's money than of their own, it can not well be expected, that they should watch over it with the same anxious vigilance with which the partners in a private copartnery frequently watch over their own. Like the stewards of a rich man, they are apt to consider attention to small matters as not for their master's honour, and very easily give themselves a dispensation from having it. Negligence and profusion, therefore, must always prevail, more or less, in the management of the affairs of such a company."*
> *(Adam Smith: The Wealth of Nations, 1776:700)*

The essence is obvious: Smith identified that management might not always behave in the best interests of shareholders. Despite this recognition, it took another 200 years until financial theorists started to model the problems of having a separation of those who control corporate resources from those who own them (Jensen and Meckling, 1976; Fama and Jensen, 1983). In 1976 Michael Jensen laid the foundation for what is now known as the *Principal-Agent theory*.[6] Management is hereby seen as agents to shareholders who are the principals. The focus of Jensen's analysis is on the creation of shareholder wealth. Because of goal incongruence the separation of ownership and control of corporate resources causes an agency problem. In the Principal-Agent literature the difference between the interests of shareholders and managers creates agency costs. The *agency cost* occurs to shareholders and it reduces the value of the company. The difference in interest between managers and shareholders is analysed in this literature stream from an economic perspective, and not a behavioural one. Hence the idea is to minimise agency costs and not to accept them as they are. Agency costs are not observable, or measurable, because we do not know the economic value of investments/companies. We can, however, define agency costs as:

$$\text{Agency cost} = \begin{array}{l}\text{Value of the company}\\ \text{if completely run in the}\\ \text{interests of shareholders}\end{array} - \text{Current value}$$

Shareholders hire managers to perform certain duties in the hope that they can do so better than shareholders themselves can. As the owners of corporate resources give away the control to somebody else they also lose insight into the activities performed by the company. Because of the delegation of decision-making authority management will always know better than shareholders which projects are available to the company and they usually possess more information to judge the prospects of these projects. But the problem with hiring somebody with different interests is magnified as managers have an information advantage. The less owners know about management's decisions, the more likely it is that managers will maximise their own interests (under the assumption that the managers know how much/little the owners know).

When two parties engaged in a contract have different information we say that information is asymmetrically distributed. *Asymmetric information* is one of the most important issues to consider in modern financial the-

6 The agency problem is an essential element of the "contractual view" of the company. Well ahead of time, Coase (1937) made significant contributions to the area. Jensen and Meckling (1976) contained the first modern analysis of agency problems. For a comprehensive summary one should read for example Shleifer and Vishny (1998). While it is possible to see the "stakeholder model" (in Section 3.1) and the "Principal-Agent model" as alternatives within the corporate governance literature, this is not the case here. They are looked upon as complements.

ory and we shall frequently indulge in its implications throughout the book. Without asymmetrically distributed information the goal incongruence would be unproblematic. The problem of asymmetric information is analysed in two ways depending on whether the agent uses his/her information advantage before or after a contract is signed. An *adverse selection* problem occurs when a contract is about to be signed but where the principal does not have access to all information. A classical problem within a corporate setting is the issuance of new equity. Is the information management give to shareholders correct or is it just provided so that shareholders invest the amount of capital that management want? An *moral hazard* problem on the other hand occurs after a contract has been signed. If management have borrowed capital from a bank in order to finance a certain investment the conditions of the loan (in terms of interest rate and amortizations) are dependent on the actual investment. But what if management in reality use the capital for something else without letting the bank know what is happening? The problems coming from asymmetrically distributed information are often solved by the use of *debt covenants*; restraints in the written contract. In the case of the bank loan discussed above, it is likely that the creditor would write that a condition for receiving the loan is that the company possesses certain assets (connected to the investment). When these assets are no longer in the company's possession, the contract has to be renegotiated.

Agency costs can be analysed in terms of *monitoring activities* and *bonding activities*. If there is simply a separation of ownership and control of corporate resources and absolutely no action is taken by shareholders to ensure that management act in their interests then all agency costs will be *residual agency costs*. These are caused by the goal incongruence and the magnifying effect that asymmetric information has. The principals, i.e., shareholders, can then reduce both the effect of goal incongruence and the effect of asymmetric information. To reduce the effect of asymmetric information shareholders have to monitor management activities, and they have to make sure management know they are being monitored. The most obvious of such monitoring devices is the construction of the annual report and the auditing process. Without it small shareholders would know very little about companies' activities. Other monitoring devices are e.g. the annual meeting and the board of directors. Although these two devices give owners a better understanding of the business operations they also function as a means to take action whenever something needs to be changed. Within the principal-agent setting one should choose the most efficient combination of monitoring devices. Theoretically speaking the *monitoring cost* has to be weighted against the reduction in agency cost it entails.[7] For companies with low agency costs (where e.g. the main shareholder is also the CEO) it makes little sense to spend an unnecessarily large amount of capital on information.[8]

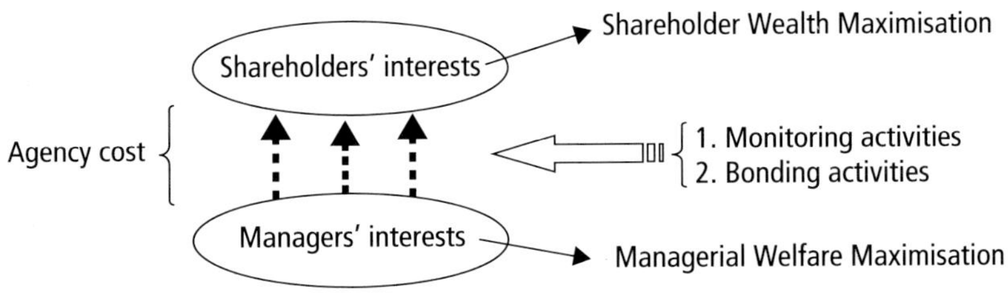

Figure 3.4 – Difference between shareholder and manager interests.

To monitor managerial behaviour is not the only activity shareholders can engage in. They can also try to bond management's interests with their own. In theory bonding activities can work without making reductions in the information asymmetry, but in practise it is extremely important that shareholders can understand the implications on company value that come from management's decisions. The essence is to find the cheapest possible way to make managers focus on shareholder wealth. Shareholders also have to make sure that it is a true creation of wealth that management have contributed to and not one in which value is based on false expectations of future cash flows. Therefore bonding activities have to be supported by monitoring activities.

The idea of making management more focused on shareholder wealth became increasingly popular in the 1990s. The easiest way to accomplish the task is to give managers shares in the company they manage. In reality shares require quite a large capital investment and can, therefore, be impractical. Convertible debenture contracts, options and other derivatives are often better tools. Bonding activities also cause *bonding costs* to shareholders. To take on an additional (residual) risk, management demand compensation. Management cannot diversify themselves and they there-

7 As agency costs are merely a theoretical construct and cannot be objectively calculated this is easier said than done. Also, we have to remember that there is not always great room for individual solutions to the principal-agent problem as institutional settings (such as company law, accounting rules and culture) have great influence.

8 If it is a public company, however, the interests of minority shareholders can then be in danger. The agency conflict then changes to one between majority and minority shareholders. We shall discuss the matter later on in this chapter.

fore take on a greater risk than shareholders. As said above, bonding also requires additional monitoring activities, which add to the total cost.

The increased emphasis on the principal-agent problem in corporate finance has enabled financial researchers to understand and prevent difficult situations in the corporate control of the modern business enterprise. With the rise of modern finance we have seen an increased diversification among investors. This was briefly mentioned in Chapter One, and will be extensively discussed in Chapter Six. There are clear benefits for investors to spread the risks and invest in shares with less than perfect correlation. But increased diversification also leads to a situation where each shareholder holds a smaller proportion of each individual company. The power of the average principal is thus, ceteris paribus, decreasing. The overall cost for shareholders to take action is, however, the same. In the economic literature this is referred to as a *collective action problem*. While it is in the best interests of the group of diversified shareholders to take action (monitor and discipline management) no rational individual shareholder wants to do their job. All shareholders hope somebody else, other than he or herself, will act so they can take a free ride. Meanwhile the opportunity for non-value maximising managerial behaviour increases. With this development we see an increased shareholder interest in corporate control devices that do not require any substantial engagement from individual shareholders. Such a focus has led to attempts from the investor group to align managerial interests with their own interests. Incentive schemes filled with options and suchlike are examples of these attempts. In order to handle the increasing agency problems that come from the shareholders' greater use of portfolio diversification an interesting financial tool called Economic Value Added (EVA), has been developed.

Economic Value Added is a concept originally developed by the American consulting firm Stern Stewart in the late 1980s/early 1990s. It is most correctly viewed as a response to the widened distance between shareholders and managers that occurred during the 1980s. The EVA system has two equally important components: the monitoring and the bonding of corporate management. The monitoring component is a sophisticated method to estimate the value creation process within a company during an observed period of time. The bonding component is a method in which the remuneration of top management is based on the estimate of value creation.

Economic Value Added is the additional value a business unit generates during an evaluation period (usually one year). It is measured as the operating earnings after depreciation and taxes reduced by the appropriate costs of all sources of capital – both interest bearing debt and risk bearing capital. Different adjustments of operating earnings are usually made (in relation to, for example, goodwill, R&D, and sale and write-downs of fixed assets). The cost of capital is calculated using current market-based measures. Proponents of the EVA-system say that it provides a better measure of corporate performance and it can, therefore, be better used to evaluate and compensate management. In Chapter Eleven we shall look at the EVA-system as a tool for shareholders to direct management activities towards shareholder wealth enhancement.

3.3 Corporate Governance Systems

3.3.1 Differences in governance systems

Corporate governance is a complex phenomenon spanning several different areas of business research and practice. When talking about corporate governance we usually mean the structures, processes, cultures and systems that make up an organisation. In a more practical sense, corporate governance can be seen as the power distribution within an organisation. It certainly revolves around the structure of relationships, and the reciprocal responsibilities, that exist among the majority and minority shareholders, the board of directors and top management as they determine a company's objectives and strategies. In this section we shall learn to appreciate the importance of understanding how different companies are governed.

Different countries and different companies have different *corporate governance systems*. A corporate governance system is the context within which individual companies are governed and as such they are highly influenced by country-specific institutional factors such as culture, standards and laws. As one examines these systems closer, one finds that they consist of substantial differences (see e.g. Kaplan, 1997; Shleifer and Vishny, 1998). In no way can this short outline give a full picture of the complexity and richness of all corporate governance systems, but we can highlight some of the substantial differences between systems and also distinguish between the situation Swedish companies are in, and the one that Anglo-Saxon companies are in.

The Anglo-Saxon corporate governance system is generally characterised as a "market-oriented" system, and as such, it is dependent on free and active markets. There is a tradition in Great Britain and the United States to ensure that changes in the corporate sector are promoted through active capital markets. In these governance systems the ownership of both shares in the company and corporate debt is diverse and frequent. Capital markets are comparatively liquid and have more actors. Dispersed ownership has been, and still is, much more common in the US than in most of Europe, including Sweden. Trading on the US stock exchanges is still much more driven by professional investors than trading on, for example, the Stockholm Stock Exchange (SSE).

The governance system in continental Europe (e.g. Germany) is, on the other hand, a much more closed and "bank-oriented" system. In a bank-oriented corporate governance system the corporation usually has strong ties with individual owners and financiers. These ties have been developed over long periods of time. Banks and other financial institutions often provide a majority of the externally needed capital. There is usually a strong owner, who often participates actively in the control of operations. An external market for corporate control is small and for practical reasons less frequently used. Matters are dealt with through stable relationships between parties who have known each other for a long time. Table 3.3 shows some of the main differences between the two systems.

Table 3.3 – Differences between financial governance systems.

Type of financial system ⇒	**Bank-oriented system**	**Market-oriented system**
General characteristics of financial markets and financial institutions		
Depth and width of financial markets	Low	High
Ratio of financial assets held by banks to total assets held by financial institutions	High	Low
Overall capital structure		
Degree of internal finance	Low	High
Debt/equity ratios	High	Low
Creditor structure		
Ratio of bank credits to total liabilities	High	Low
Importance of bond financing	Low	High
Degree of concentration	High	Low
Turnover	Low	High
Shareholder structure		
Degree of concentration	High	Low
Commercial banks shareholdings	Significant	Insignificant
Interfirm shareholdings	Widespread	Less common
Turnover of controlling blocks	Slow	Faster

Though it is less common that a company functioning in a bank-oriented system is quoted on a stock exchange, it is not uncommon. It is rare, however, that they source capital publicly. The main shareholders often hold a substantial proportion of their funds in individual corporations and are unable to exploit the benefits of diversification. This can also make external equity financing troublesome. Instead the bank or an affiliate is likely to be a prime source for capital. With a high degree of ownership concentration, the turnover of controlling blocks is very slow, perhaps non-existant. Management of such a company have to manage a single relationship to a main owner. In a bank-oriented system agency costs are likely to be lower, which might mean that management have less flexibility in its decision-making, and also less ability to withhold corporate wealth. On the other hand, corporate wealth might not be all that necessary as information is less asymmetrically distributed and owners are more willing to take responsibility in troublesome situations.

Managers of companies acting in a market-oriented system are much more dependent on financial markets. Shareholders are dispersed and will often "vote with their feet", which means that they rather sell shares in the company than take action on its daily operations. As diversified shareholders are less willing to take action, a market-oriented governance system is highly dependent on a functioning market for corporate control that can discipline badly performing companies. Managers have to use more formal information channels as almost all external financing will be through, anonymous, equity and debt markets. It is likely that managers in such a system rather rely on internal financing, which enables them to retain control, than external financing.

These are only two, stereotyped, forms of governance systems. In some countries industry-groups play an important role – primarily in Asia. When Japanese companies have started to expand internationally, westerners have learned to appreciate the impact that *Keiretsus* have on Japanese business life. Keiretsus are large alliances between industrial, marketing and banking companies that seek to control all aspects of the sourcing, production and retail distribution. Even though individual companies are listed on stock exchanges "outside owners" have little or no ability to affect decisions within the keiretsus. Yet in other economies governments might play a central role in most business activities. Whereas the market-based governance system provides owners with great opportunities to diversify away risk it usually lacks the decisiveness, flexibility and unity of will that many other systems have. It would be wrong to say that one system is superior to any other (at least when it comes to systems within highly developed countries). Having said this, it does indeed look like global capitalism is opening up previously closed systems and makes them more market-oriented.[9]

3.3.2 Corporate governance in Sweden

In Sweden, as in many other countries, the 1980s and 1990s have been characterised by dramatic changes in corporate ownership. At the same time a gradual shift can be identified, a shift which goes away from a closed bank-oriented system towards a more open market-oriented system. The intention with this section is not only to give a picture of how Swedish companies are governed but also to point out certain characteristics that distinguish the Swedish governance system from that of other countries.

The shares of most major Swedish corporations are listed on the SSE. Today, there are a few smaller share markets, but they most often serve companies with either special needs or, as is most often the case, those who cannot meet the criteria established by the official stock exchange. With the emergence of the Internet and the simplicity of making computer-based trading these competing markets are likely to remain serious, although small, competitors to the regular exchange. As of today approximately 250 companies are listed on the SSE. A bigger "threat" to the SSE is instead that large international corporations choose to list themselves abroad rather than in Sweden. Currently about 30 Swedish corporations are cross-listed (listed on the SSE and on, at least, one other stock exchange). Large international mergers have caused the main trading of companies such as Astra-Zeneca, Pharmacia and ABB to move abroad. By no means has this caused the overall development of the SSE to be negative. The growth in value of the listed companies during 1980–99 was among the highest in the world. The value of traded shares has increased from 29 Billion Swedish crowns in 1982 to 2,609 Billion Swedish crowns in 1999. More important is the fact that market value turnover has increased.[10] In 1990 it was 15 percent, whereas in 1999 it was 94 percent.

9 There is a discussion among both practitioners and academicians as to whether corporate governance systems are being harmonised or not. Although some have a somewhat different opinion (see e.g. Shleifer and Vishny, 1998) it is the author's personal opinion that global capitalism is forcing more and more countries to switch towards a more market-oriented governance system. The abandoning of differential voting rights in Sweden and other countries, as well as Germany's current attempt to get rid of cross-ownership, or Japan's "forced" opening of its product markets are vivid examples of the harmonisation.

10 Defined as the value of companies in relation to the traded volume.

In this section we will focus on the general characteristics of the whole governance system. Like in many other countries there is a growing institutionalised ownership, although financial institutions are not yet as influential as they are in Anglo-Saxon countries. Many of the companies dominating Swedish industry today have their origins in entrepreneurial companies established about a century ago. Most of them were already then family-controlled, and many of them still are. When they listed on the stock exchange they did so because of a need for capital infusions, and not because the control of the company needed to be changed. Swedish companies instead, through their owners, established close affiliations with banks, usually regional banks standing close to the companies' founders. Long term relationships with banks ensured survival and because of this, the liquidity on the SSE was very low for many years.

At the end of the 1980s and the beginning of the 1990s a pattern became clear: more and more people invested in funds and gradually institutional investors (such as mutual funds, insurance companies, and investment companies) became more influential. They have slowly started to place greater demands on company management and the controlling owners, although their increased pressure is probably lower than one could expect given their relative rise in capital ownership. Their entrance has been supported by several factors, particularly the globalisation of financial markets. Restrictions on international investors were removed at this point in time and particularly American investment funds started to search for international diversification opportunities. Also, the Swedish parliament had approved tax relieves on savings in mutual funds in the late 1970s. In the 1990s new pension reforms have redirected savings to the share market. These are all small steps towards a much greater emphasis on the share market today, compared with 30 years ago. In 1999 approximately 40 percent of the value of Swedish companies was owned by foreigners (both funds and individuals), as can be seen in Figure 3.5. Also, the proportion of foreigners engaged in the trading of shares in large Swedish companies is great. Currently about one quarter of all trading on the SSE is done directly by foreign investors. Institutional investors, both Swedish and international, make up almost all of the trading in the larger corporations.

This leads to a situation where individual ownership has been replaced by institutional ownership. Financial institutions have no controlling owners behind them, but are to a large extent owned by a diffuse group of private persons, with a sole interest in the maximisation of short term returns. Considering the dramatic changes in ownership that have occurred since the beginning of the 1980s it is appalling that control over most Swedish

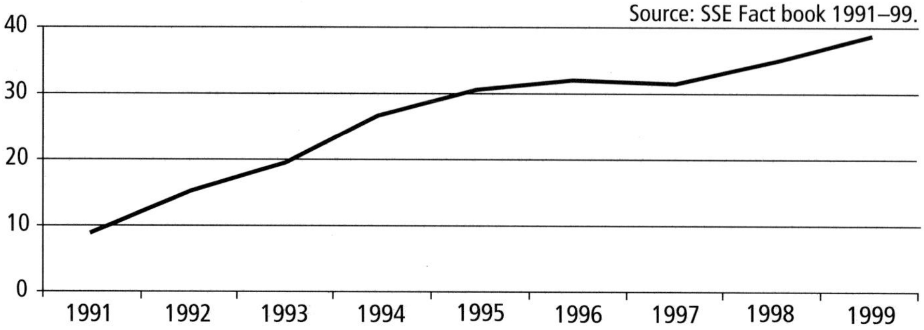

Figure 3.5 – Foreign ownership of Swedish companies listed at the SSE.

industrial companies still remains in but a few persons' hands. Ownership concentration in individual Swedish companies is high by international standards. There are reasons for this, reasons that go beyond the unwillingness of institutional investors to take an operating responsibility in the companies they own. To understand the situation one must look at the characteristics of the Swedish governance system. These are characteristics that have recently been severely criticised by, particularly international, investors. The main reason why control has been retained by a small group of owners is due to *differentiated voting rights*.

The Swedish Companies Act allows Swedish companies to issue shares with different voting rights. An owner's percentage of votes may therefore differ substantially from his/her percentage of the company's equity. This difference is much more profound in some of the old well-established companies. The current Swedish Company Act allows shares with ten times difference in voting power. However, through grandfathering, some companies have inherited a governance structure where there is up to a one thousand times difference in voting power. These companies may continue to issue new shares with these voting rights. The current pressure from institutional investors is however likely to prevent such behaviour. But even the ten times difference in voting power has a substantial control bias, where one person, typically the founder or heirs of the founder, can retain control with little capital. In comparison, differentiated voting rights are not allowed in, for example, the American governance system. Shareholders of Swedish companies have until recently shown little interest in removing the differentiation. It seems to be accepted, even though there is an obvious risk that majority shareholders may take advantage of minority shareholders. The risk of this happening is likely to drive down the actual

Table 3.4 – Differentiated voting rights in Swedish companies.

	1992		1999	
	number	**%**	**number**	**%**
1:1000	3	1,5 %	1	0,3 %
1:100	1	0,5 %	1	0,3 %
1:10	165	81,7 %	182	55,8 %
1:2, 1:4, 1:5, 1:6, 1:8	6	3,0 %	10	3,1 %
No differential	27	13,4 %	132	40,5 %
Total	202	100 %	326	100 %

value of such companies below their intrinsic value.[11] Capital costs are increased as investors add a *control premium* to shares with less voting power.[12] The value of a company is thereby not only determined by the intrinsic risk of its investments but also by its ownership structure.

In 1992 almost 90 percent of all listed companies on the SSE had differentiated voting rights. Institutional investors are, however, starting to raise the issue more frequently and by 1999 the number of companies with differentiated voting rights has decreased to 60 percent. Both Electrolux and SKF have removed the 1:1000 differentiations and currently it is only Ericsson that maintains a differentiation where an A-share is worth 1000 times more than a B-share. In 2001 when Ericsson reported massive operating losses their differentiation of voting rights were, again, criticised. It is probably only a matter of time until the two controlling parties, the Handelsbanken sphere and the Wallenberg family, are forced to abandon it.

The overall reduction in voting right differentiation shown in Table 3.4 stems from the entry of many newly started companies. The old traditional industrial companies still maintain a differentiation. One has to bear in mind that removing the differentiation will have to lead to substantial changes in the governance system. It would also require institutional inves-

11 A study by Harris and Raviv (1988) shows that differentiated voting rights constitute a non-optimal corporate governance rule. Instead they, hardly surprisingly, argue that the American system of one share-one vote is a socially more optimal corporate governance rule.

12 A similar thing can happen to companies in which there is a majority shareholder influencing business activity, but not in a SWM way. Rebates are often given to investment companies (such as Investor, Industrivärden and Ratos) because of their control ambitions, which might lead to, e.g., an unwillingness to take measures in a necessary restructuring of industries.

tors to take a much more active role in controlling the operating activities of Swedish companies.

Besides the differentiation of voting rights, which is the major difference between the Swedish governance system and most others, there are a few other characteristics worth mentioning. One measure with which management of Swedish companies protect themselves from undesired changes in ownership structure is *cross-ownership*. Cross-ownership refers to a situation where two companies hold shares in each other. As long as Company A owns less than 50 percent of the votes in Company B, and vice versa there is no parent-subsidiary relationship between the two. By indirectly owning shares in themselves Companies A and B can influence the decision-making at their own shareholders' meetings. As shown in Figure 3.6 cross-ownership can also exist between more than two companies, then often referred to as circular ownership. The principle is however the same. Within the Handelsbanken sphere cross-ownership and differentiated voting rights are frequent. Handelsbanken, SCA and Industrivärden all hold substantial shares in each other. With, more or less, the same people in all boards of directors it is very hard for external investors to influence decision-making.

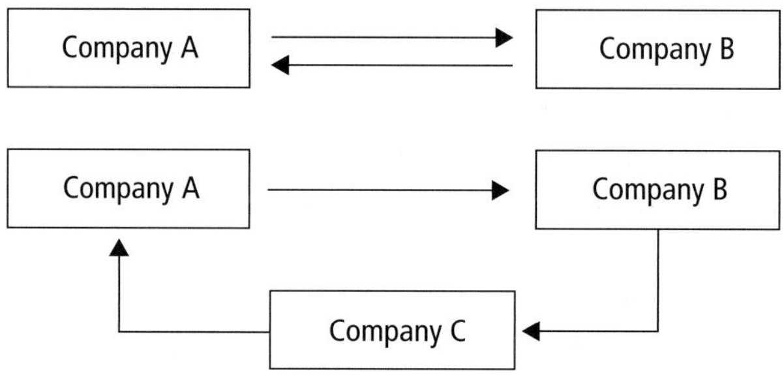

Figure 3.6 – Cross-ownership and circular ownership between three companies.

A third feature of the Swedish corporate governance system is the ability to create *pyramid structures* in the ownership of companies. This is eased by the existence of differentiated voting rights and cross-ownership. A pyramid structure is illustrated in Figure 3.7. Investor A has a capital of 100 with which she controls the votes in Company B which is worth 1,000. The assets in Company B consist of shares in Company C. Company C is worth 10,000 and Company B controls the votes in Company C. By using differentiated voting rights and a pyramid structure Investor A holds a firm grip over a company which is worth 100 times more than the capital owned by investor A. The fantastic leverage provided by the combination of differentiated voting rights and a pyramid structure comes on behalf of

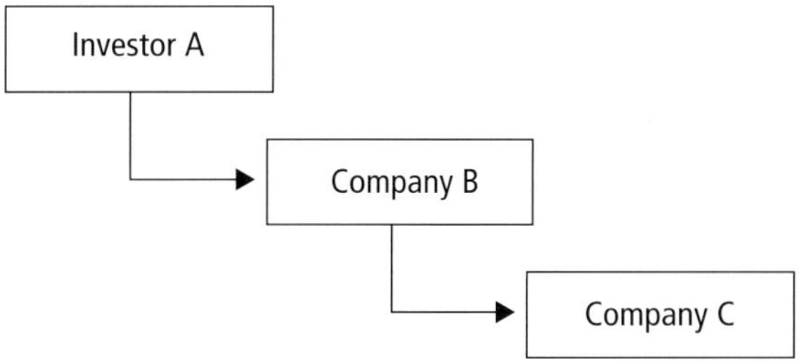

Figure 3.7 – Pyramid structures in companies.

other shareholders in company B and C. They have invested 90 percent of the capital but have no control over operations. As mentioned before, it is likely that such a company would trade at a rebate because investors add a control premium to its capital cost. The best example of how the pyramid structure can be combined with differentiated voting rights in order to exercise control over a company is the Wallenberg family's control over a company such as Ericsson. Through foundations the family owns 21 percent of Investor's share capital, which gives them control over 44 percent of Investor. Investor in turn owns 3 percent of Ericsson's share capital and 22 percent of its voting rights. The picture is somewhat complicated as the Wallenberg foundations also have a direct ownership in Ericsson. In total, however, Wallenberg has invested capital (related to Ericsson) worth less than 30 Billion Swedish crowns but still exercises considerable control over a company worth at least 15 times more.[13]

Hostile takeovers are rare among large Swedish companies, which obviously is a reflection of the governance system already described. A hostile takeover is typically one where an acquiring company makes an official bid for another company without having a prior acceptance from the main owners or management. Such a bid is usually substantially higher than the current share price. In Chapter Ten we shall discuss the issue of mergers and acquisitions more thoroughly and will then return to this subject.

Despite the fact that hostile takeovers are rare, mergers and acquisitions are just as common in Sweden as they have been elsewhere over the last twenty years. In fact, differentiated voting rights can facilitate corporate takeovers, as a buyer only has to find and convince a limited number of sellers. Many of the Swedish companies are large multinational companies with operations in many countries. As such they take part in the consoli-

13 Wallenberg control about 40 percent of Ericsson's voting rights and the Handelsbanken sphere controls approximately the same. Together they hold all the chairs on Ericsson's board of directors.

dation and globalisation processes that have been sweeping over most industries over recent decades. Foreign ownership of shares with high voting power was restricted until the beginning of the 1990s, which could be one reason why foreign ownership was limited for such a long time. Swedish companies have, however, been expanding their operations abroad by acquiring competitors for many years. During the 1990s a large number of Swedish companies have received new foreign owners, a trend which has attracted the attention of the media. Whether it is good or bad that foreign companies acquire Swedish companies is quite an irrelevant question, and instead one should ask whether the Swedish governance system is good enough to compete with the governance systems of other countries.

As said before, there is a transformation of the Swedish governance system towards a more open market-oriented system. If the Swedish governance system makes it harder to reform mature industries and develop new ones there is a problem. As of today with the growth of the information technology (IT) sector this seems not to be the case. Clearly there are some problems with mechanisms such as, for example, differentiated voting rights, which did not matter as much in a more closed bank-oriented financial governance system. In the more open market-oriented financial governance system these mechanisms become controversial. Newly created companies, primarily in high growth sectors such as biotech, information technology (IT) and mobile tele-communications, usually have a different, and more market-oriented, governance structure.

For various reasons Sweden emerged in the late 1990s as one of the leading countries when it comes to IT and mobile telecommunications. Between 1996 and 2000 more than 130 new companies were listed on the SSE. Most of them relate to the IT sector. These companies stand in very sharp contrast to the companies previously described. They consist of young people building their businesses on new ideas about the future. Organisation structures are flat. Many of the founders are still the main owners and usually sit in the top management. Agency costs are not a problem, at least not between management and the main owner. Remuneration schemes, typically based on share options, are not just common but typical. With the emergence of these new companies there has been a surge in individual ownership on the SSE, or at least a halt in the long term decreasing trend of individual ownership. A personal opinion regarding the governance of these companies is that the problem for institutional investors is no longer whether management maximise shareholder wealth, but if they maximise their own personal shareholder wealth or all shareholders' wealth. If too much of the value of such companies lies in human capital, the value can disappear in no time. The situation between company stakeholders of these companies is likely to be considerably different from the older and more traditional industrial companies. Nevertheless, the conflicts and the control issues will not disappear but only change shape.

3.3.3 Summary

Currently it is fair to say that the Swedish corporate governance system lies somewhere between a market-oriented system and a bank-oriented system. Over the last decade we have seen changes in the system, and of these changes the most notable ones are:

A. An increased proportion of international investors/owners
Because of, for example, deregulation and the willingness of international investors to both diversify their portfolios and take advantage of prospects in international markets, the number of investors has increased on the SSE. Also the number of international acquisitions of Swedish companies has increased. The increase in trading volume on the SSE is to a large degree driven by international investors.

B. An increased proportion of professional investors
More and more of the trading on the SSE is conducted by professional investors, both Swedish and foreign. This is because of, for example, changes in savings patterns and pension systems, but also because larger investors can better take advantage of diversification opportunities and economies-of-scale in trading and information gathering. One of the clear effects coming from the increased proportion of professional investors is that ownership tends to become more and more dispersed.

C. A greater focus on shareholder wealth
Professional investors place short term share returns higher on their priority list than traditional owners did in the past. Although investors can be euphorically optimistic about companies with negative cash flows in the short term (remember the IT boom in 1999–2000) they are harsh in a medium time frame and most of them are hopelessly pessimistic in the long term.

D. Increased use of incentive schemes
As the group of investors becomes more focused on short term share returns and they become at the same time more diversified, the implementa-

tion of incentive schemes in corporations is on the increase. It is rare to find large public companies where top management do not hold stock options, convertibles or suchlike. Several have implemented massive remuneration programs based on Economic Value Added or similar measures.

E. More information is made public faster than in the past
With the help of primarily information technology, today's professional investors are able to gain access to considerably more information. Annual reports are becoming thicker and more informative, quarterly reports likewise, press conferences are shown live over the Internet, analysts' earnings forecasts are compelled and publicly announced, et cetera.

F. Fewer companies have differentiated voting rights
Professional, and particularly international, investors, openly criticise those companies not using a one-share-one-vote system. So far it is primarily companies with an enormous difference in voting power that have made changes. Newly started companies often have the entrepreneurs as owners and there is no reason then to differentiate between shares. This is a very slow process indeed.

G. There is less cross-ownership
Professional investors also dislike cross-ownership as it enables managers to create financial slack. Step-by-step cross-ownership has been dismantled. In the Handelsbanken sphere it still exists.

H. Increased amount of restructuring through mergers and acquisitions
The number of international (as well as national) mergers and acquisitions has increased dramatically. A particular integration between the Nordic companies has been seen over the last decade. Within the banking, construction and forestry industries this has been particularly prominent. Nevertheless, hostile takeovers are rare. A great number of restructurings occur through venture capitalists, who acquire shares in both newly started companies and older companies needing to be restructured.

It is difficult to judge the benefits and drawbacks of a governance system. A couple of points concerning the Swedish system are certainly worth mentioning. For further discussions of different corporate governance systems please see the survey macarried out by Shleifer and Vishny (1998).

1. Low agency costs between main owners and management
In most large Swedish industrial companies there is a relatively close co-operation between the main owners and management. When the main owners want to make changes in, for example, a strategic plan it is relatively easy to do so. Benefits of EVA systems are likely to be lower in the Swedish governance system. Differentiated voting rights enable this close co-operation without forcing main shareholders to invest all of their capital in just one investment.

2. Higher agency costs between main owners and minority owners
The fact that the main owners often have considerable power and influence over operations with little capital means that there is a group of shareholders with little real power. The agency cost between them and the main owners is high. The effect of this should be a reduced value of shares with low voting power.

3. Control premium might inhibit issues of new equity at competitive prices
One of the drawbacks of having differential voting rights is the control premium that is usually added to the shares with low voting power. If these shares make up a large proportion of the total number of shares new equity might have to be issued at a low price. Equity thus becomes unnecessarily expensive. The other option is for the main owner to decide that new equity with high voting power will be issued, but that will decrease the power of the current main owner. It is likely this situation will lead to a higher degree of internal financing and reliance on external debt.

4. Different market for takeovers
Generally speaking it is common in Sweden for the acquirer to discuss in private with prospective sellers before releasing an official bid. When an offer is made it is therefore quite common for current shareholders to accept it. Such a market has only one real drawback, namely that minority shareholders holding shares with low voting power can be forced to accept bids that are unfavourable to them.

3.4 Some Final Comments

In this chapter it has been provided a view of companies' financial decisions not often found in financial literature. It is believed that management will not act solely in the interests of shareholders, not because they find their goals irrelevant, but because they have to balance the goals of all stakeholders. To do so is not an easy task, management constantly confront uncertainty and to maintain control they often tend to pursue a growth strategy that can provide financial slack. Financial slack is more or less the same as corporate wealth; capital which is at management's discretion. It is, however, not management's intention to maximise corporate wealth, but to use it to moderate the constant pressures from stakeholders.

Shareholders do in general view financial slack as negative. The main reason for this is that they can diversify away all unpleasant effects of single investments. A reduction of agency costs serves in the best interest of shareholders. Shareholders try to change the behaviours of management as efficiently as possible. Therefore they monitor and bond management's interests with theirs. The situation in Sweden is slightly different from that in many other countries. Because of some characteristics of the governance system the agency costs between shareholders and managers are not as large as elsewhere. There are nonetheless problems, particularly related to minority shareholders and differentiated voting rights.

In the section on corporate governance we have seen a system that currently seems to be changing. Professional investors are pushing for higher share returns and a greater focus on short termshort term profitability. Does this mean that management does not care about financial slack any longer? –No, but it does mean that management are likely to be paying greater respect to the demands of the shareholder group. It also means that as incentive schemes grow more popular, the goal incongruence might decrease a little. We have seen that information about company activity has become more plentiful for investors in recent years, but that does not mean investors know more about what goes on within the organisations they own shares in, as companies tend to grow larger, more complex and have operations in more countries. Take Electrolux as an example. Its annual report contains less than 80 pages but within it operations generating sales of more than 120 Billion Swedish crowns are described. 90,000 employees work in a company selling products in 155 countries and producing them in more than 30 countries. In November 2000 Electrolux acquired the household appliance unit of Email, an Australian company with sales of five Billion Swedish crowns, 4,800 employees and a market share of 60 percent in Australia and New Zealand. In the future the information to be given about this sizeable company will be filtered down to sales revenue and operating profit. There is very little shareholders in Electrolux know about what goes on in this unit on the other side of the world. The potential for financial slack increases as companies become larger, more complex and spread their operations internationally. It is not so sure that top management can and will eliminate slack in their subunits. Agency costs can arise everywhere within the organisation. Not least within business areas and "small" units such as, e.g., the mentioned Australian unit of Electrolux.

Key Concepts

- Shareholder wealth maximisation
- Managerial welfare maximisation
- Stakeholder model
- Contractual relationship
- Residual relationship
- Corporate wealth
- Financial slack
- Goal incongruence
- Principal-Agent theory
- Agency cost
- Asymmetric information
- Adverse selection
- Moral hazard
- Debt covenant
- Monitoring activity
- Bonding activity
- Residual agency cost
- Monitoring cost
- Bonding cost
- Collective action problem
- Economic Value Added
- Corporate governance
- Corporate governance system
- Differentiated voting rights
- Control premium
- Cross-ownership
- Pyramid structures
- Hostile takeovers

Key Issues to Discuss

1. What are the main differences between holding a contractual relationship to a company and holding a residual relationship? Is one preferable to the other?
2. Give examples of differences between stakeholders holding contractual relationships to the company (such as e.g. between creditors and customers). Think of situations where they have substantially different information needs. Also give examples of differences between stakeholders holding residual relationships to the company. In what ways could information needs vary between them?
3. Are stakeholder demands always the same? Pick a company (such as e.g. Vattenfall, AstraZeneca or Volvo) and explain how there can be differences in stakeholder demands between the companies.
4. Explain the main differences between the Shareholder Wealth Maximisation perspective and the Managerial Welfare Maximisation perspective.
5. What are the differences between the two concepts *corporate wealth* and *financial slack*?
6. Pick a company of your own and estimate its corporate wealth in accordance with the definition in the text. Do you believe most of its corporate wealth has already been created? Given the planning horizon you have chosen, how much corporate wealth do you believe will be created?
7. Discuss the problems for management to use all of the future free cash flows as corporate wealth. What can happen if they do so?
8. It was argued in the text that the goal incongruence between management and its stakeholders is leveraged by the existence of *asymmetrically distributed information*. What do we mean with this and how can the stakeholders handle the problem (according to the principal-agent theory)?

9 Discuss broadly the impact a corporate governance system has on the management/ shareholder relationship. Exemplify by comparing a *market-oriented governance system* with a *bank-oriented governance system.*

10 Make sure you understand the major features of the Swedish corporate governance system. Discuss why corporate ownership still is rather concentrated in Swedish companies.

11 Does the Swedish corporate governance system inhibit structural changes to take place (relative to the bank-oriented or the market-oriented system)? Motivate your answer.

Further Readings:

Donaldson, G., 1984, *Managing Corporate Wealth*, Westport: Praeger.

Findlay, M. C., & Whitmore, G. A., 1974, "Beyond Shareholder Wealth", *Financial Management*, pp. 39–55.

Shleifer, A., & Vishny R. W., 1998, "A Survey of Corporate Governance", *Journal of Finance*, pp. 737–775.

Chapter 4

Managing Risk and Uncertainty

This chapter aims at:

- Introducing the basic ideas of rationality that underlie economic theories, and challenging it using theories of economic psychology.
- Discussing the measurement of risk in society and the differences between risk and uncertainty.
- Providing a conceptual theoretical model of how uncertainty/risk can be managed in organisations.
- Discussing management's perception of and attitudes towards risk.

4.1 Introduction

4.1.1 Risk and uncertainty

As argued already in the first chapter, financial theory is in essence very simple: it involves only two variables, risk and expected return, and their association is positive. But arguing that financial theory is simple is not the same as saying that it is easy to understand and apply its concepts. To do so, we have to find valid and reliable measures of risk and expected return and we have to make sure there is nothing that blurs or inhibits their positive association.

Later on in this chapter we shall spend some time discussing managers' perceptions and attitudes towards risk. We shall then see that what humans in daily terms call risk is something different from risk according to economic theory. In order to reach an understanding of what these differences are, and why they are there, we need to address a number of theoretical issues. These concern a distinction between risk and uncertainty, alternative views of risk and managerial attitudes towards risk, and finally some notes on risk management.

The essence of the chapter is to portray risk differently than what corporate finance textbooks usually do. I want to show that "risk" is indeed a concept to which managers pay a lot of attention, but they most often do it differently than economic theory expects them to. The reason will soon be obvious to you: there is confusion between risk and uncertainty.

All of us use the term risk in our vocabulary on a daily basis. Risk is used to describe all situations where the future is not absolutely certain. When asking people why they believe a situation is risky they often answer that they do not possess all the necessary information to understand what is about to happen or that they do not have the ability to understand the information they possess, or a combination of the two. An economist should find this confusing and in fact even partly contradictory to the theory he/she has learnt. According to economic theory individuals confront risk when they have all the information and know how to use it, otherwise they are faced with uncertainty. One of the purposes of this chapter is to compare and distinguish between risk and uncertainty. While doing so we move from a market-oriented analytical perspective to an individual-oriented analytical perspective. We end up with a more appropriate description of financial decision-making. But let's start at the other end, with some notes on how economic theory views utilities, economic rationality and risk attitudes.

4.1.2 Rationality in financial economics

For sure, no other concept has been as successfully exported to other social sciences from economics as the concept of rationality. For decades economists and other social scientists have proposed and argued for the idea that people behave rationally. But assumptions of rationality are indeed not just important for economics and finance, but also within sociological, psychological and political studies. What distinguishes economists from researchers in these other fields is the special form of it: the rationality of the utility-maximiser (Simon, 1978). In this section the ideas behind rationality, utility, and risk-aversion are explained. We will however not go into great detail with all the work that has been done in the area partly because there is no room for it, and partly because we have little use for it.

From a financial economist's point of view, rationality can be defined as an assumption that generates norms for economic behaviour, indicating what is to be expected if well-informed economic agents seek to maximise their gains. To distinguish it from later definitions of rationality we refer to it as *economic rationality*. How do individuals then behave when making their rational decisions? We can describe the economic agents' behaviour using four *axioms of rational choice* under uncertainty (Savage, 1954).

1 Comparability.	The individual can rank and choose among all possible alternatives/outcomes.
2 Transitivity.	If Alternative *A* is preferred to Alternative *B*, and Alternative *B* to Alternative *C*, then *A* is also preferred to *C*.
3 Strong independence.	The individual does not differentiate between two alternatives with the same risk.
4 Certainty equivalent.	For every risky alternative the individual is able to determine an exactly equivalent alternative that is equally preferred but involves a certain return.

Economic theory discusses the rationality of the utility-maximiser. *Utility* can be defined as the subjective value an individual attributes to a certain number of products, services or characteristics. In the eyes of the financial economist utility can usually be measured in monetary terms, and a *utility-maximiser* is therefore a person who desires as much profit as possible given the circumstances. As people are assumed to always prefer more wealth to less wealth the marginal utility of wealth is positive, i.e., every additional unit of wealth increases our utility. The utility an individual attributes to a product is in reality hard to determine. It is based on his/her preferences.

Given the four axioms of rational behaviour and the assumption that the marginal utility of wealth is always positive, one can conclude that *individuals will always seek to maximise their expected utility of wealth.* To put this into practice what will happen is that the individual will consider all possible alternatives, calculate their utility (based on the individual's preferences) and then choose that alternative that maximises the expected utility of wealth. In the case of an investor that would be the alternative that provides the highest return (given the inherent risk). This is all one needs to know when establishing a utility function, which is representative for the individual decision-maker, and when determining the individual's choice and attitude towards risk. We shall refrain from giving detailed descriptions of how to calculate these functions, but the curious reader can turn to for example Fama and Miller (1972) or Copeland and Weston (1992).

4.1.3 Preferences to risk

So far we have established a number of axioms under which we assume individuals will make their decisions. We have also established the idea that decisions are taken so that the decision-maker's utility is maximised. Keep in mind here that utilities are unique and that no two individuals can be expected to have the exact same utility functions. We can now establish the individual's preference for risk given his/her utility function. We do so with the help of Expression (4.1), which tells us that the expected outcome is determined by the probability of one alternative multiplied by its outcome plus the probability of the other alternative multiplied by its outcome.

$$E(W) = (\alpha_A \cdot U(W_A)) + ((1 - \alpha_A) \cdot U(W_B)) \qquad (4.1)$$

Let's apply this formula to a numerical example. Say that you have the chance of playing a game for which there are two possible outcomes. There is a 20 percent chance you will win SEK 500, and an 80 percent chance you will gain nothing. Expression (4.1) then tells you that the expected value of the game is SEK 100.

$$E(W) = (20\,\% \cdot 500) + ((1 - 20\,\%) \cdot 0) = 100$$

Although there is an 80 percent probability you will gain nothing if you play the game only once, you will very quickly realise that on average the game is favourable to you; its average outcome is SEK 100. This is the expected value of the game. Now let's say you are offered an alternative. A certain amount that you receive instead of playing the game. We refer to this as the *certainty equivalent* of playing the game. The question is; what is the lowest amount that you would be willing to accept in order not to play the game? Most people would settle for an amount lower than 100. Perhaps 85 or 90 is enough for you.

If you, as most other people, think that the certainty equivalent is lower than the expected value of the game then you have an aversion to risk. You would rather accept a lower certain amount than a higher uncertain amount. If you, on the other hand, said that the certainty equivalent is higher than 100 then you could be referred to as a risk lover. Obviously it is possible that some people would rather play the game than take a certain amount of 100. The game does offer a 20 percent chance to win 500. Finally, if your certainty equivalent is 100 you are risk neutral, i.e., it does not matter to you whether you take the risk or not.

These attitudes towards risk can be illustrated using, stereotyped, utility functions. All of them are based on (a) that utilities are generated by converting an individual's preferences using the axioms of rational choice, and (b) that more wealth is preferred to less wealth. The second assumption is what makes the functions slope upwards from left to right. The situation in Figure 4.1a means that for every additional unit of wealth the utility of the game increases more. The situation in Figure 4.1b means that the utility of the game increases proportionately to the increase in wealth. Finally, Figure 4.1c displays a situation where an increase in wealth is followed by a disproportionate increase in utility from the game.

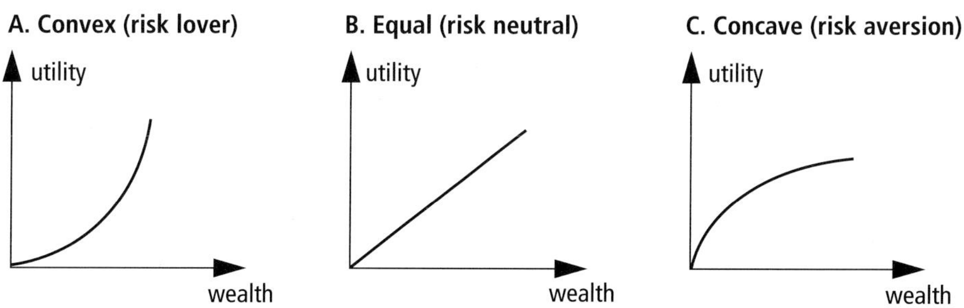

Figure 4.1 – Utility functions.

The utility function shown in Figure 4.1a is that of a *risk lover*. To this person the utility of playing the game is greater than the expected wealth of the game. The utility function displayed in Figure 4.1b is that of somebody who is *risk neutral*. Speaking in terms of utility, this person is indifferent between playing the game and accepting the certain amount. Finally, the utility function shown in Figure 4.1c is that of a person with *risk aversion*. He or she would rather choose a lower certain amount than the expected value of an uncertain game.

Given the rationality of the investor, and the utility-maximising behaviour one generally finds that the utility function is concave to its origin. Investors are on average risk averse and thus they prefer less risk to more risk. If the utility function were not convex (a decreasing marginal utility) this would lead to some strange behaviours, as individuals would never do anything else but things that maximised their utility. Addiction would be the ruling norm in society. But in real life, as we get more of those things that maximise our utility the additional benefit from them decreases – we start doing other things.

4.1.4 Risk measurement

As risk deals with the future, risk measurement is intimately connected to the art of forecasting, and the desire to understand and control the future. In this section, risk is defined as the probability that a future outcome of a situation is not the same as the expected outcome. To estimate such a probability we need information from the past about similar situations. The future, as we all know, has yet not happened! But the past contains information that can guide us when we try to estimate future happenings.

Risk measurement must deal with a past that resembles the future and all risk judgements must be based on extrapolations of past happenings. When we talk of risk as a probability concept we see it as a deviation from a most likely situation. But how can you say that there is a ten percent chance that a man/woman will walk on the surface of planet Mars before 2010? It has never happened before so you cannot know. The technical problems involved with this kind of space exploration are still not known. What might happen is that experts try to judge information on e.g. differences between sending a space shuttle to the moon and Mars. With no past situations at all resembling the future forecasting is doomed to fail. But if we are asked to estimate the profitability of Ericsson next year, we can look at past figures. To make the estimates we would ask questions such as: How did Ericsson perform over the last ten years? What is its competitive situation today in comparison with yesterday? Are there any indications of what is going to happen next year? In the case of Ericsson, past events are much more likely to resemble future events than in the case of space exploration.

As risk is only about the future, risk measurement is about extrapolating past events in a future-resembling way. The only way of estimating the probability of deviations is (usually) to have a multitude of deviations from a similar expectation in the past. Figure 4.2 show an accumulation of such events. The left-hand side is a normal distribution of events and in such a situation 68 percent of the observations are within one standard deviation from the mean, 95 percent of the observations are within two standard deviations from the mean, and more than 99 percent of the observations are within three standard deviations from the mean. The right-hand side of Figure 4.2 shows a skewed distribution of events.

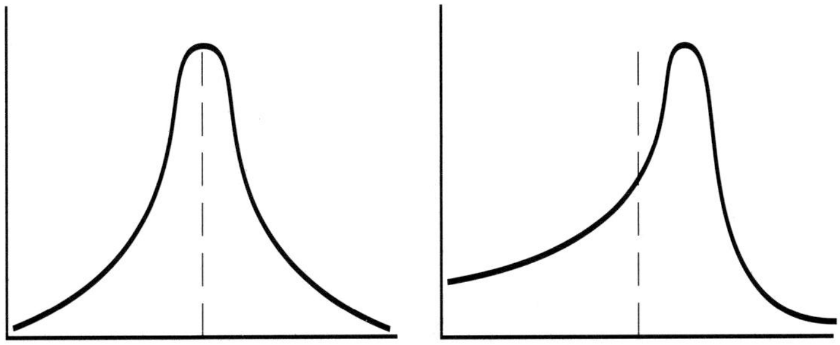

Figure 4.2 – Normal distribution and skewed normal distribution.

The term risk is very often used in situations involving contractual relationships. In a contractual relationship the exchange of resources is regulated through a contract. All involved parties should know what to expect according to the contract. Contracts reduce uncertainty and provide safety to all parties. But there is also a risk involved with setting up a contract; the risk that the opposite party cannot fulfil his obligations.

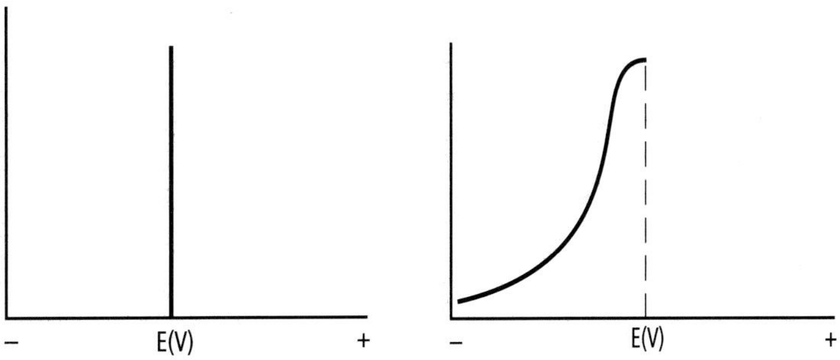

Figure 4.3 – Certainty and semi-variance.

Given the assumption that all parties are maximising their utility, there is no reason to believe a party that has engaged in a contract will give away more than absolutely necessary. Suppose you borrow money from a bank. You then engage in a contractual relationship where you receive financial means during a period of time and in exchange you are expected to pay rent on a periodical basis to the bank. The bank takes a risk. You may default and be unable to repay the money you borrowed. This uncertainty the bank faces is purely negative as you will never pay more than what is regulated in the contract. A rational utility-maximising borrower who is obliged to pay 10 percent in interest, will never pay 15 percent. The right-hand side of Figure 4.3 shows the so-called *semi-variance*, which is a useful measure of risk. Imagine a bank sitting with 100,000 contractual agreements with its customers. Some of these will be broken (the other party will run into financial distress). The distribution shows the probability of losses for the bank. As there can be no outcomes better than those the contract stipulates, the distribution only shows negative aspects of risk.

4.1.5 A few final comments

From this discussion you should have a better understanding of what risk is about. The essential point is that risk is dependent on the estimation of future outcomes and the probability that they will occur. Herein lies a great difficulty, which we now address.

The important thing to remember is that all investors are assumed to be economically rational and utility maximising. The axioms of rational behaviour are immensely important for financial theory to work. If economic man cannot rank alternatives, or chooses inconsequently between them, then we have serious problems. In financial theory utility functions are usually assumed to be constant over time and between situations. Later on in this chapter this idea will be challenged. The utility theory's final implications concern the risk-return relationship. As investors are risk-averse they expect a compensation for bearing risk: higher return. This is the foundation of modern financial theory, to which we will return many times in the continuation of the book.

Although the ideas put forward here are quite unrealistic, some financial theorists believe that in markets where many boundedly rational actors come together the aggregated behaviour (of all the representative investors or economic men) will be close to that stipulated above. If this is the case, then decision-making under uncertainty will follow the rules set out here. Rubinstein (2001) contains an enlightening discussion on rationality in financial economics.

There are however two potential problems. The first occurs if there are systematic biases affecting actors in the market. This can be that information is provided in a biased fashion to all actors in a market.[1] The second occurs when applying the ideas to the situation of individuals or to unique situations. Those of us interested in human behaviours and decision-making in real-life are likely to have some objections at this point, but in order to appreciate the neatness of utility theory one needs to understand its purpose and background. Economics is primarily the study of how people and societies allocate scarce resources and distribute wealth amongst one another and over time. Economics thus works on an aggregate level, trying to predict aggregate behaviours, using aggregated figures. Economists have a certain view of the world, which is not necessarily similar to that of other researchers in the social sciences. This view enables certain kinds of analyses while it leaves out others.

4.2 Risk and Uncertainty

4.2.1 The distinction between risk and uncertainty

In economic theory there is a distinction between risk and uncertainty. This distinction was established by Frank Knight (1921), but has been used by numerous researchers and practitioners over the years. Knight's distinction between risk and uncertainty is important when trying to understand financial theory and its application within organisations. His risk/uncertainty distinction relies on the separation of (1) knowing possible future outcomes, and (2) knowing the probability that a certain future outcome will occur. Both of these two elements have to be estimated in any risk analysis. Table 4.1 is based on this separation. The following discussion centres on the information in this table.

Table 4.1 – Different forms of risk and uncertainty.

Level of uncertainty	Characteristics	Examples
None	Outcomes are known	Physical laws, natural science
Economic risk (*Objective* uncertainty)	Outcomes are identified and probabilities known	Card games, coin tossing
Economic uncertainty (*Subjective* uncertainty)	Outcomes are identified but probabilities are unknown	Fire, earthquake, accidents
Irreducible uncertainty	Outcomes are not fully identified and probabilities are unknown	Space exploration

1 In Chapter Six we deal with some of these when discussing "behavioural finance".

Economic risk prevails only in those situations where uncertainty can be determined in an objective manner. We can define an objective situation as one where everyone has the same information and understanding of a situation. When speaking about pure economic risk it is assumed that all actors, current and potential, know both the possible outcomes and the probabilities of these possible outcomes of future situations. When do these situations occur? The easiest answer to give is that they hardly ever do. Knight (1921) referred primarily to card games and the tossing of coins. Games are fairly uncomplicated, have given rules, and are not influenced by the skill of the participants. But even these games are not always influenced by economic risk. Take the game of chess as an example. Chess provides two players with a game that has set rules. The only problem is that the game is so complex the players cannot foresee every possible move at all times. The complexity of the game forces the players to rely on the management of the uncertain: their skill. And if you think the next move in a game of chess is hard to foresee, then think about real life. Because of social interaction between humans it is nearly impossible to find universal laws.

Knight actually stated an alternative situation in which economically risky situations can be achieved. The first one, which we have just described, is based on deductive reasoning: When rolling a dice or flipping a coin it is possible to mathematically derive the probabilities of receiving a certain outcome. But Knight also thought that if the same kind of event occurs a large number of times, and it will happen again in the future then we can empirically forecast it. An example of this is the probability with which we can estimate that a baby is able to walk when he/she is 11 months old. There are no universal laws telling us when they can walk, but from empirical observations we know very well when it usually happens. Although Knight classified this as economic risk, it is doubtful whether it is a pure economic risk, as individuals still can, and will, have heterogeneous expectations. There is a fine line between economic risk and economic uncertainty.

It is reasonable to assume that hardly any real life situations are characterised by pure economic risk and instead humans are confronted with *economic uncertainty*. In such situations we know pretty much what the possible outcomes are (or the range of outcomes), but we do not know the probabilities. Individuals might have their own interpretation of the situation (a subjective view) but no general agreement is likely to exist. This is what most situations in real life look like.

But situations with economic uncertainty are very much different from one another. While some situations are characterised by subjective opinions of future outcomes and probabilities, there might be many individuals who try to estimate the same economic uncertainty. The valuation of a quoted company is a good example of such a subjective situation. For some companies there are thousands of investors analysing the company, and trying to estimate its value. Some currently hold shares in the company, while others do not. In the marketplace all their subjective opinions about the future are aggregated so that a market price is formed. The market price is the best possible estimate of the company's value, provided that outcomes and probabilities are not objectively known. This situation can be referred to as *"marked-based" economic uncertainty*. The more value-relevant information and the more skilled actors you have in the market, the better the market's predictions of the future will be.

Compare such a situation to one where the management of a company are about to launch a new product in a new market. In this case there is only one management team judging a unique situation. This is a highly subjective situation involving nothing but economic uncertainty. The ability to rely on an aggregated uncertainty estimate does not exist. This situation can be referred to as *"expert-based" economic uncertainty.* Please note that it is not argued that any situation is preferable to the other, although, a priori, a market-based situation seems to have better qualifications. But a market full of foolish sheep is certainly not better than one single knowledgeable expert.

Finally it is worth mentioning the unmentionable: *irreducible uncertainty*. These involve situations about which we currently have no idea. It might be a space invasion or anything else that has never happened before, or it might be something that was not calculated. If a Swedish company makes an investment in Denmark this year, it is certainly not estimating that there is a chance it will be expropriated by the Danish government (and thus its value would be reduced to nil). But it can still happen.

4.2.2 Rational choice and uncertainty

How does this distinction between risk and uncertainty relate to the axioms of rational behaviour and the risk aversion we pointed out earlier, you might ask. Decisions under economic uncertainty basically conform to the same axioms of rational choice as decisions under risk. The problem is that economic uncertainty brings subjectivity into the decision. Subjectivity takes the form of individuals having different sets of information and different opinions about future events. In the "market-based" form of economic uncertainty, an efficient market, where all actors are given the same information at the same time, distributes information randomly amongst its actors. In such an environment the aggregated behaviour of the market is likely to follow the axioms of rational choice. But whenever individuals do not have access to the same information it might be so that some have better chances of reaching a good decision. This does not mean individuals are not rational and averse to risk, but it makes cross-sectional comparisons difficult. An asymmetric distribution of information, skills and resources sets the positive risk-return relationship aside. This is where the role of the business enterprise comes in.

4.2.3 The role of the business enterprise

In situations where all actors in a competitive market know the probabilities of future events there is little room for a business enterprise. Competition will then quickly make sure that it is impossible to earn excessive returns, i.e., profits that are above the level that everyone else (objectivity) taking the same risk, earns. Ericsson, or any other company, would never develop new products if ten other companies can do exactly the same, because competition would drive down the profit margin. Luckily (for Ericsson), economic uncertainty enables companies to possess (at least in the short term) competitive advantages. The whole of Chapter Five is devoted to this subject.

Companies exist because the future is uncertain and without economic uncertainty there would be no opportunities to generate profits. In fact, Knight (1921) argues that economic uncertainty is the real cause of profits, not economic risk. If economic uncertainty prevails it causes an asymmetric distribution of information in society. Companies survive by knowing something that others do not know or performing in a way that others cannot mimic. In essence, this is where financial theory and corporate strategy theory collides. Corporate strategies are based on a superior position relative to competitors, i.e., that a company can (at least for some time) perform better than other companies.

We can rephrase what we said in the last paragraph: the company consists of an aggregate of uncertain events that have to be managed. When that is done successfully, the company creates competitive advantages that lead to the generation of profits. If one is to found a theory on economic risk, one has to believe that subjectivity can be substituted by objectivity. But, at least according to the definitions we have provided here, we only substitute expert-based economic uncertainty for market-based economic uncertainty. If market-based economic uncertainty is a sufficiently valid representation of economic risk, we do not know, but it is the best we can find. With efficient markets it seems as if we do get reasonably close. In economic theory the market has all the information and knows how to handle it and hence there is little room for the company. But in reality it evidently exists and it is indisputable that it handles economic uncertainty.

Risk management, which is an art many modern companies perform, is nothing but a management of economic uncertainty. When companies reduce their economic uncertainty they do so by utilising skills that are unique to them. Less economic uncertainty does not mean less expected return – in fact it is quite the contrary. Companies that are good at reducing the uncertainty that surrounds them are often companies that prosper.

4.3 Managerial Perceptions and Attitudes Towards Risk

4.3.1 Bounded rationality

This book is just as much about how managers actually make decisions, as it is about how they ought to make decisions. So far it has been shown that economic risk and economic uncertainty are two quite different things. In this section we shall make a few comments on a vast subject; management's actual behaviour in decision-making. Our object is to relate it to previous discussions of the assumptions within economic theory, and while doing so particularly emphasise risk/uncertainty.

We have learned that economics deal little with the behaviours of individuals, but that there are implicit assumptions regarding economic man. He, or she, is supposed to gather all possible information concerning potential decisions and their outcomes and then choose between them in a coherent way. His/her behaviour is aimed at utility-maximisation. Because of this, there are three particular areas that one can separate and discuss individually. The *first* one is if economic man really can get hold of all information, or if there are any potential biases in his search process and gathering of information. The *second* concerns whether economic man can really make unbiased and consistent assessments of the information that has been gathered. And the *third* one is whether the economic man's definition of utility is consistent over time and if it corresponds to the utility of the shareholder.

Economists are not really concerned with individual behaviours, and therein lies a danger of applying the implications of economic theory to individuals. In the first section of this chapter we learned to appreciate the concept of rationality and its high expectations on us humans. But if we cannot live up to such high standards does this mean that in reality we have to abandon the idea of rational choice? Both yes and no. Yes, because we cannot say any individual behaves in an economically rational way, but on the other hand, not many of us would admit we are constantly making irrational decisions. To be irrational is to be wrong, mistaken, weak, and perhaps even a failure. Most people believe they act in their own best interests, given their current situation.

In financial economics the concept of rationality is seen in quite a strict manner. Because financial economics deals with the allocation of resources in financial markets it avoids studying human thought-processes. Simon (1978) has adequately referred to economic rationality as a *product-of-thought rationality*, as opposed to a *process-of-thought rationality*. A product-of-thought view of rationality ignores the mental processes underlying the rational decision. It just assumes that overall an individual should come up with a certain decision in a certain situation given the preferences he/she has shown and the information which is given. Actual human thought-processes are of no interest, but only the final outcome is.

A process-of-thought view of rationality, on the other hand, acknowledges human thought-processes, both when it comes to the search for information and the interpretation of information. An individual using a rational decision-making process would turn out irrational if the input information was wrong, even though he/she did everything else correctly. To take a practical example: suppose a car hit you while you were crossing a street. Unless you actually like getting hit by cars, the end-result of your actions was irrational, as a rational human being should not have crossed the street at that time. But would you really make a decision if you knew beforehand that it was going to be irrational? When crossing the street, you probably did not look too carefully and hence you thought, given the information you had, that crossing the street at that moment was safe. In this way, not many decisions are actually irrational. When examining them *ex post* they might look so, but it is merely an effect of having incomplete information and a limited decision-making ability. Humans are only boundedly rational.

4.3.2 Some notes on the decision-making process

As we adopt a process-of-thought view of rationality in financial decision-making, it is possible to disaggregate the actual process individual investors go through when making their decisions. This process can, for the sake of simplicity, be divided into two parts; (1) the process of gathering information, and (2) the process of interpreting the gathered information. This separation is a simplification, as decision-making is an on-going process and the two parts constantly interact. As new information is gathered, your thought-processes are altered and you search for new information.

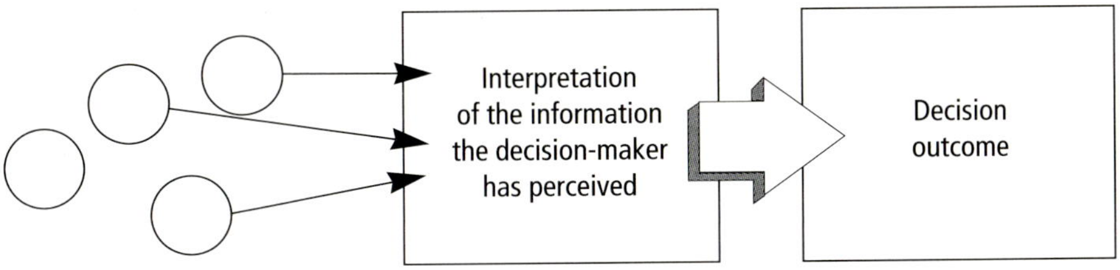

Figure 4.4 – A tentative model of decision-making.

Figure 4.4 illustrates this basic model where some pieces of information enters the decision-making process, gets interpreted, and ends up as a decision. According to capital market theory investors are assumed to search for and interpret all available relevant information. In reality people's ability to receive information is limited. All information about what is happening around us must come through our senses. But the capacity to receive information through them is limited. Nobody can absorb all information and hence there must be some kind of selection of information. Furthermore, information is *per se* complex and we can hence only see parts of it (or some aspects of it). In fact, two people with considerably different backgrounds might interpret the same kind of information in two completely different ways. To deal with the complexity (and information capacity) humans try to bundle the information to get more, and better, information through the information channels. In real life human attention is scarce; we never consider all information and all alternatives. We limit ourselves, both intentionally and unintentionally.

To deal with these problems it has also been argued and documented that individuals do not try to maximise their expected return, but that they seek a satisficing level (see e.g. March, 1994). Humans search for information that maximises their utility, but stop searching when they have enough information to feel comfortable and are sure they will do reasonably well. In a world with too much complex information, such a behaviour is what prevents people from the madness of going through all information before making a decision.

The issues that arise from this are; (1) what information do we pay attention to and select, (2) when do we stop searching and processing information and (3) does everyone behave the same or can there be systematic behaviours in the search for and the interpretation of information? Unfortunately it is not possible to provide straight-forward answers to such difficult questions. Often, though far from always, targets are set in accordance to the social interaction. Humans tend to stop searching if they do better than what they believe is expected of them. Usually that means to do better than their peers. In the rest of this section we deal with ways of simplifying the gathering and interpretation of information. Such simplifications are referred to as *heuristics.*

One of the heuristics that is frequently identified is the *availability of information heuristic.* People tend to choose information that is easily accessed rather than information that is more difficult to retrieve. Speaking in terms of investments in financial markets it is common to speak of a 'home bias' in equity portfolios (see e.g. Cooper and Kaplanis (1995)). Swedish investors usually consider investments in Swedish companies whereas Italian investors tend to consider investments in Italy, even though transaction costs are negligible. Another observed behaviour is referred to as an *imitating heuristic.* People tend to choose information that many others choose at the moment. It has been proven that we do so even though we know that the others have no better ability to pick the right information. By imitating others one can at least be satisfied knowing one is not worse off than the others.

Often those controlling major information channels imitate each other and thereby the flow of information becomes more homogeneous. This can have extraordinary consequences on how individuals perceive information. Three examples are given here. After the ship Estonia sank in 1994, the media focused all their attention on the safety of sea travelling. Immediately after the catastrophe there was a considerable drop in the number of ferry passengers in Sweden. Obviously it was not more unsafe to travel by sea after the incident, but substantial attention was drawn to the danger. This attention was undoubtedly increased by media attention. Our second example refers to the scandals related to Swedish politicians using their positions for various private benefits in the mid-1990s. After one scandal had been identified, it drew attention to the matter and soon another twenty cases had been found. Once the "hunt" for this kind of news stories had started it could not be stopped. It is unlikely that first there were no scandals and then suddenly almost each and every politician was corrupt. Instead the media, again, increased society's attention. Finally, as IT and telecommunication companies increased their market values rapidly in years 1999 and 2000, the media started to focus more and more on these particular sectors. At this time the placards of Swedish evening papers promised certain returns in safe investments such as e.g. Framfab.[2] Probably many small investors made biased investment decisions because of all the uncritically positive "analyses" circulating in the media. The role of the media in stock market crashes is one that has received attention in research (see e.g. Shiller, 2000). Investor self-confidence thrives on homogeneous information.

There are even more heuristics connected to the process of interpreting the gathered information. To employ these heuristics is not irrational, but they exemplify the cognitive biases that humans have. We shall look into four of these heuristics; (1) framing, (2) representativeness, (3) overconfidence and (4) imitating behaviour.[3]

The *framing heuristic* deals with how we view the information that is known. When the Central Bank decreases interest rates, it can be interpreted as both good information (lower interest rates) and bad information (signs of a slower economy). What determines the interpretation is the point of reference held by people (in this case the investor community). A framing effect thus affects the very formulation of a problem. The framing effect is furthermore often linked to a phenomenon known as *mental accounting* (Statman, 1995); people divide their financial resources into separate mental accounts and treat them individually when making financial decisions. This can explain 'irrational' decisions such as saving on a savings account earning 5 % annually, while paying 8 % on a loan on the house. The mental accounting idea has been used to explain for example dividend behaviours (Shefrin and Statman, 1984).

The *representativeness heuristic* is closely related to the framing heuristic. When framing a situation people must relate to things they have experienced or perceived in the past. We seek to identify patterns enabling us to

2 Shiller (2000:50) compares such contemporary placards with those in 1929 in the US. Shortly before the crash the *Ladies Home Journal* then had an article entitled "Everybody Ought to Be Rich", which discussed the unlimited prospects of the stock market and how society can help all individuals capitalise on it. See Galbraith (1961) for a more detailed description of this article and other spectacular events surrounding the crash of 1929. In August 2001 Framfab has lost 99 % of its value in March 2000.

3 Antonides (1996) contains considerably more information on these and other heuristics used in decision-making.

grasp more information quicker. Sometimes these patterns really exist, while sometimes they are just preconceived ideas and stereotypes. Ask yourself if it always rains in Great Britain, all Swedes are blond, librarians are always shy, and if immigrants have a low level of education? To relate current information to past information through representative frames of reference is of course a sound way to interpret situations, the problem occurs when the representativeness is biased.

Overconfidence is arguably not a heuristic, but a common trait among humans. Many studies have documented how people often put a greater trust in themselves than they ought to. They gather information and after they have made up their mind, they avoid seeing things differently. Physicians, engineers, entrepreneurs and financial analysts have all been shown to possess overconfident behaviour (see Odean, 1998; Daniel and Titman, 1999). Research has also shown that people who believe they are expected to know more than others tend to have greater overconfidence. Obviously overconfidence is related to the satisficing decision-making behaviours previously mentioned. By being confident a decision-maker will worry less about not having all information and not knowing everything. The accuracy of previously gathered information is instead exaggerated, which makes it easier to sleep at night.

Also in the interpretation of gathered information it is common to find that decision-makers imitate other decision-makers. This behaviour has been proven particularly strong when there is much uncertainty and decision-makers cannot trust the quality of existing information. To imitate others is to do something socially acceptable. If all the kids in pre-school say that Djurgården is the best Swedish ice-hockey team, then it is easier to say the same than to argue with them. The same goes with dividend policy choices, management theories and even company valuation. Imitation can be both conscious and unconscious. Regardless of which, it will lead to trends and fads. If the imitation is taken too far, it might even be followed by an opposite behaviour. This reversal is sometimes referred to as a reversion to the mean.

In several of the coming chapters we will see how the kind of heuristics described here can have an effect on the financial decision-making. In particular when we come to Chapter Six and behaviours in capital markets we shall return to heuristics.

4.3.3 Prospect theory

According to economic theory rational human beings would rather have a certain than an uncertain return. This aversion towards risk is best illustrated by comparing two investments with the same expected value, but with known probabilities that are different. This is the kind of example that was given at the beginning of the chapter. Contemporary research has shown that the perception of risk depends on the situation the decision-maker is in. This important contribution to our understanding actual decision-making was provided by prospect theory (Kahneman and Tversky, 1979).

Its prime feature is called the *value function*, which stands in contrast to the utility function mentioned earlier. The value function has three distinct features. *First* it is defined in terms of gains and losses rather than in terms of wealth (the possession of assets). By not focusing on the terminal wealth, the value function reflects the observation that individuals determine gains and losses in relation to a reference point. Obviously the utility function never deals with losses, as people people never can lose the wealth they do not possess. The *second* feature of the value function is that it is concave above the reference point and convex below. The consequence of this is that individuals are more sensitive to gains and losses near the reference point. The first 100,000 you make is the most attractive, or alternatively, the first 100,000 you lose is the most unattractive. The *third* feature of the value function is its asymmetrical shape.

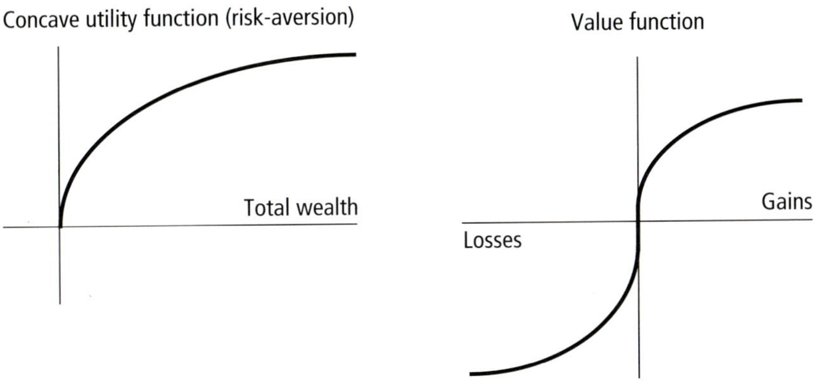

Figure 4.5 – The value function in comparison to the utility function.

The loss curve is steeper than the gain curve. This implies that losses are relatively more unattractive than gains are attractive. People are averse to losses, a characteristic that has been labelled loss aversion (Bell, 1983). People exhibit inconsistent attitudes towards risk. The consequence of the value function is that most people are risk-averse in gains and risk seeking in losses. We prefer a sure gain of 1,000 rather than a 50–50 chance of making 2,000 or nothing. But many of us prefer a 50–50 chance of losing 2,000 or nothing, rather than to accept a sure loss of 1,000.[4]

Prospect theory challenges the traditional thinking in economic theory. Whether the value function truly contains a more valid description of economic decision-making than the utility function is not known as of today. If it does, then a great deal of financial thinking might have to be redone, or at least empirical studies might have to be replicated and commented upon.[5]

4.3.4 Managerial decisions and risk-taking

Our next task is to consider management's outspoken attitudes towards "risk". There have been a couple of studies where financial decision-making has been surveyed (for example Donaldson, 1984; MacCrimmon and Wehrung, 1986; Shapira, 1995). It must, however, be emphasised that researchers know much more about how managers ought to act than they know about how they actually act. We have divided this commentary into three sections. These are (1) management's definition of risk, (2) management's attitude towards risk, and (3) the ways management deal with risk.

Management's definition of risk

The definition of risk that business managers use, is surely less precise than that in economic theory. In contrast to the views found within economic theory, risk is not seen as a variance in a probability distribution.[6] Several

4 Alternatively, think about going to the racetracks. You go there primarily to enjoy yourself. Let's assume your objective is to return home with an unchanged monetary wealth (of course we know that the average player will have a negative change in wealth when going home, but expectations differ from reality sometimes). In your wallet you brought SEK 3,000. In the first nine races you loose SEK 250 in each race, totalling a change in wealth of SEK –2,250. The last race of the day is by far the trickiest race for you to guess, as you have never heard of any of the horses in the race. Still you decide to bet all of the SEK 750 that you have left. As you place your bet with the bookmaker you probably say to yourself that it cannot get worse than this anyway...

5 This matter is of course highly controversial. The point has, however, been raised both by researchers deeply rooted in the field of "behavioural finance" (such as e.g. Thaler, 1999) and by researchers in "traditional finance" (e.g. Copeland and Weston, 1992).

6 Similar definitions have actually also been found among investors (DeBondt, 1998). When asked concerning their beliefs about risk and return only 18 percent of the questioned professional investors said that risk depends on whether a share price moves with or against the market (covariance).

traits are evident. *First* of all managers do not see risk as associated with a positive deviance from expected value. Risk is only about losing; it refers to a hazard or a danger. There is a risk that profitability may fall below the target, but it is not perceived risky to pursue a strategy which might perform much better than expected. In general, people tend to treat positive deviances from expected value as attributable to their own superiority, not luck.

A *second* trait is that managers do not view risk as a probability concept. March and Shapira (1987) found that several managers rather saw the volume put at risk as more important than the probability. One manager they interviewed expressed this in the following manner; "A gamble of one million dollars in terms of success in a project is risk; however a gamble of half a dollar is not a risk". Most managers interviewed by Shapira (1995) asked for estimates of the "worst outcome" or the "maximum loss". Such a key value, connected to volume at risk, is more important than standard summary statistics grounded in ideas of probability. Obviously liquidity affects managerial financial decision-making.

A *third* trait is that managers do not try to reduce all different aspects of risk into a single quantifiable measure. When MacCrimmon and Wehrung (1986) asked managers to rank a number of investment alternatives, only one out of ten managers did so in accordance with expected value. Instead of expected investment return, a number of other criteria where used for the ranking, such as the break-even point, minimising major loss, or minimising variation. These results are similar to other studies (Donaldson, 1984; Segelod, 1986). There is support for this also in Shapira (1995), whose respondents noted comments such as: "No one is interested in getting quantified measures" and "You don't quantify the risk, but you have to be able to feel it". The results found in these studies are interesting considering the current movement towards measuring and managing risk within large organisations. Past research indicates that individuals' ideas of risk can be radically different from those the risk management techniques were intended to be used for.

Management's attitude to risk

According to classic economic theory managers should, like all other individuals, be averse to risk. When faced with two alternatives having the same expected value they should choose the one with the least risk. Given the previous definition of risk as variance in outcome, managers should require a compensation for an increased volatility. In accordance with economic theory an increased variability is followed by expectations of a higher return. It is not certain managers perceive risk and return to be positively correlated. A considerable amount of accounting-based research shows that the level of return in companies and industries is negatively correlated to the variability in return (e.g. Bowman, 1980; Miller and Bromiley, 1996; Hamberg, 2000).

Risk attitudes have been shown to vary, even for the same individual having the same information, depending on the perceptions of the individual. Kahneman and Tversky (1979) argue that when an individual is above his/her expectations then a more risk-averse behaviour can be expected than when the individual is below expectations. In a situation far below expectations a normally risk-averse individual can be desperately risk-seeking. Recently, researchers have begun to incorporate other factors that influence individuals' attitudes to risk. Personality is a rather stable feature, but also mood, feelings and motivation affect how willing people are to take risks. It appears as if some managers are more risk-averse than others, or at least it seems as if they are thought to be so. It is yet not clear whether different attitudes towards risk depend on personal traits, organisational traits or if they do just vary randomly. The managers Shapira (1986) interviewed thought that the attitude towards risk depended more on incentives than personal traits. Lower level managers perceived higher level managers to be more positive to risk taking than themselves, whereas higher level managers thought it was important to educate lower level managers in risk management.

Dealing with risk

In accordance with economic theory empirical research has shown that managers try to avoid risk as much as possible, rather than just accept it. But most research shows that managers do not usually try to anticipate future events, but instead they act, or react, in the short-run to current events. Contracting is a convenient method of reducing risk/uncertainty. Within an organisation it is likely that the delegation and delay of decisions is a way for individual managers to avoid risk (MacCrimmon and Wehrung, 1986). If you cannot avoid risk what do you do then, considering risk aversion?

According to research it is common for managers to try to control risk. Obviously this is contrary to economic theory where risk is something one faces, as it is exogenously determined and uncontrollable. Three out of four managers interviewed by Shapira (1995) see risk as controllable. They do not accept the odds, but they try to change them by using both skills and information. Only when they have been working on the presumed dangers and modified the situation can they be confident enough to accept the risk. They then feel more sure of success.[7]

The research presented here does not only stand in sharp contrast to decision theory, but it also forces us to challenge the view of risk we have learnt so far. Are managers facing risks that are conceptually different from the risks we talk about in economic theory, or are they substantially misinterpreting the situation? I would argue that the reason for all the surprising results illustrated in this section is the distinction between risk and uncertainty (or rather the lack of distinction). When we talk of risk in economic theory we talk of an objective situation where decision-makers have all information and skills necessary to make rational decisions. In the case they do not have that there is at least no asymmetrically distributed information between market actors. But managers face uncertainty, not risk. Managers do not have all the information, and skills are unequally distributed between companies and managers. Decision-making is subjective and managers remove uncertainty by controlling it. Do they always succeed? Probably not, but at least we know they behave so when facing uncertainty. It makes it easier for us to understand financial decision-making.

4.4 Managing Economic Uncertainty

Based on what has been said so far, we can say that economic risk is something managers confront, but economic uncertainty they manage. When risk management is discussed in academic literature or among business consultants it is seen as a deliberate choice made by management. It is usually seen as something that will benefit the organisation and improve its profitability (see e.g. Hamilton, 1996). Risk management activities include identifying risks in the organisation, implementing loss control programs in operations, and providing training and education on safety-related issues (Williams, Smith and Young, 1995). Such activities can hardly be said to contain "objectivity", but only a subjective removal of uncertainty.

Management is constantly exposed to uncertainty: When it provides a

7 DeBondt (1998) found that investors think more or less the same. 89 percent of the questioned professional investors thought that it was better to invest in a small amount of companies whose operations they knew well, instead of a large amount of companies they knew little about. Risk can be reduced through active participation in the market.

credit to a particular customer, when it chooses a certain inventory level, and when it chooses to sell a certain product to a certain customer. Doing business involves a voluntary exposure to some uncertain situations, but it must be recognised that no engagement in business also brings with it an exposure to uncertainty. In fact, not giving credit to the customer, choosing another inventory level, and not selling that certain product to that certain customer creates a similar exposure to uncertainty (but of a different kind). Whether we like it or not we will always expose ourselves to uncertainty of some kind.

Economic risk refers to an objective view of the future where humans can make rational decisions. But economic uncertainty, as Knight describes it, is subjective and can often be dealt with.[8] As it is found everywhere all decision-makers within the organisation must handle it. Both economic risk and economic uncertainty have to do with expectations of the future, and hence they are handled by forecasting future events. Any forecast relies on the available information (about the past) and the decision-maker's knowledge about how to use that available information.

The way to determine the probability distribution for a future event is to study past events of similar character and estimate to what extent history will repeat itself. Consider for example a printing-workshop that wants to expand. It faces much less uncertainty when investing in a new printing press than in a new department handling information solely on the Internet. The overall profit margin might be higher for the Internet publishing industry, but for this unique company it is more profitable to install a new printing press because it has been done before. Internet publishing involves many more unknown variables than the new printing press. What is within the company's own domain is often felt to be more controllable than what is outside.[9] Therefore, setting up a new printing press can (on an individual level) be more profitable than starting up an Internet department (even though the opposite relationship would exist at the industry level). Information and knowledge of how to handle information form important components in the handling of economic uncertainty. Indirectly, this example

8 A slight complication is that it is not uncertainty, as defined by economists, that companies (or common people) try to avoid, but instead the negative consequences of the uncertain event. Positive consequences are often seen as being the results of skill rather than being a fortuitous outcome (March and Shapira, 1987).

9 Asymmetrically distributed information and skills work to the advantage of the company.

also shows how a company can reduce some of the uncertainty by taking action; increased information or knowledge of how to handle information leads to a reduced level of economic uncertainty. A well-implemented information system might not just reduce uncertainty (or "risk" as management tend to call it) but also improve profitability.

What happens if a company is exposed to a future event where it does not have all the information or the knowledge required to understand what would happen? Can the economic consequences of an uncertain event then be avoided, and if so how? Actually, the main alternative might be to do nothing. If an uncertain situation turns out negatively, but brings no *severe* economic damage to the company and if similar uncertain situations will occur again over an acceptable period of time, a *natural hedge* against the uncertainty is created. Think of a Swedish company selling regularly to Japan. Each month the company signs a contract where the price is determined in Yen. Delivery, and final settlement, occur three months later. The value of the Japanese Yen might go up or down during the time period and thus cause the actual profit margin of the sale to differ. But why try to hedge each sale? Within five years the company has been exposed to the same source of uncertainty 60 times. Sometimes it makes gains, and sometimes it makes losses. As time goes by, the expected cumulative effect is likely to be zero. Naturally, this last example can also be used in order to illustrate when it is necessary to handle the uncertainty. Uncertainty is only necessary to handle when it is possible that the future will have a vast impact on the company and/or a certain event occurs infrequently. More frequent occurrences create a spread of risks that we call an *inter-temporal diversification effect.*

An alternative strategy is often used when the economic consequences are exceptionally large, and/or the occurrences are rare. Then the consequences might be transferred to another party who is able to gather them from many similar events, which have a low correlation. Hence a diversification effect similar to the one described above is achieved. If there is an active market for the risk/uncertainty management can pay a price to get rid of it. This is what happens when one hedges a future exchange rate exposure. A *hedging activity* is used when a future exposure to uncertainty (usually price volatility) is offset by paying for some kind of insurance.

There is some uncertainty management can do little about. A fully unanticipated earthquake, or a revolutionary technological breakthrough are events characterised by irreducible uncertainty. The only two ways a company can reduce its effect is to either engage in *contracting activities* or by lowering its exposure to a certain source of uncertainty through *diversifi-*

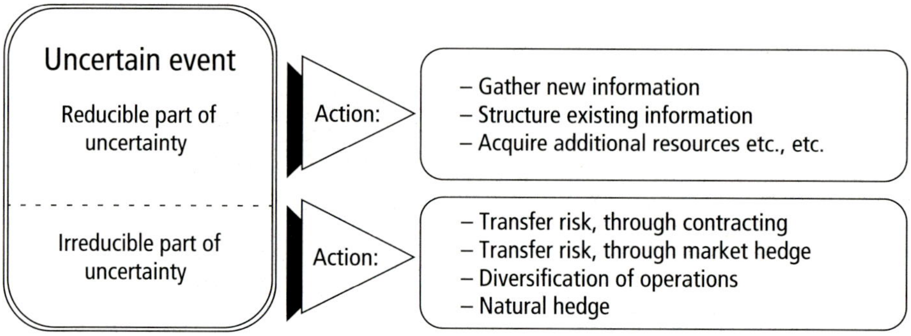

Figure 4.6 – Risk management in a risk/uncertainty framework.

cation activities. A contract reduces the number of uncertain parameters and as long as the other party fulfils its obligations the future is somewhat more certain. The uncertainty of not having skilled workers who can produce a particular product when a sales order comes can be handled by engaging in a contract with workers. Entering an insurance contract can reduce the economic impact of a sudden fire in a factory. Diversification strategies can be used for handling sudden supply and demand shifts in different resource markets. A car manufacturer might manufacture both cars and trucks as they are rather similar products but with different users whose needs are not perfectly correlated. When car sales are down, truck sales might be reasonable. At the same time a car manufacturer might seek more than one supplier in order to reduce the probability of being dependent on only one source of input goods. Figure 4.6 shows some conceptually different ways of managing uncertainty within the company that has been described here. Obviously, the alternatives depend on the character of the uncertain event. But management do manage economic uncertainty.

It must be emphasised that if the future situation is not characterised by economic risk but economic uncertainty, then individuals will hold different opinions about the future and they will tend to act differently. Just as this is a theoretical explanation about why companies exist, it is also a potential theoretical explanation as to why there is no perfect correlation between risk and return. With merely uncertainty around one has to rely on subjective decision-making and bounded rationality. Uncertainty can be reduced if more information or knowledge is added to the decision-making parties within the organisation. But reducing uncertainty then goes hand in hand with improving performance. If you practise golf you will, with time, develop a more consistent swing and thereby reduce the ex post variance in performance, but you will also hit further, aim better and so on, and thus improve your level of performance.[10] It is the same for companies; if one is better than one's competitors at earning a high rate of return, one can also be consistently better at earning a higher return.

It is important to stress that from an economic theory perspective "risky" situations are usually just economically uncertain situations. Uncertainty affects all the company's activities. But in competitive markets where aggregated samples can be used, market-based economic uncertainty substitutes expert-based economic uncertainty. Often efficient markets provide better estimates of the future.

Key Concepts

> Rationality
> Axioms of rational choice
> Utility
> Utility-maximiser
> Risk-lover
> Risk-neutrality
> Risk aversion
> Risk measurement
> Certainty equivalent
> Semi-variance
> Economic risk
> Economic uncertainty
> Market-based economic uncertainty
> Expert-based economic uncertainty
> Irreducible uncertainty
> Bounded rationality
> Product-of-thought rationality
> Process-of-thought rationality
> Heuristics
> Availability of information heuristic
> Imitating heuristic
> Framing heuristic
> Mental accounting
> Representativeness heuristic
> Overconfidence
> Prospect theory
> Value function
> Loss aversion
> Natural hedge
> Inter-temporal diversification effect
> Hedging activity
> Contracting activity
> Diversification activity

Key Issues to Discuss:

1. In your own words, describe the main differences between most people's definition of risk, and that used in financial economics.
2. Discuss the consequences of the four axioms of rational choice, i.e., what happens if we do follow them?
3. What does it mean that the utility function of somebody with an aversion to risk has a concave utility function? Explain using a numerical example.
4. Explain the differences between (a) economic risk, (b) market-based economic uncertainty, and (c) expert-based economic uncertainty. Is it in reality always possible to distinguish between them? Motivate your answer.

10 Assuming that the environment is about the same over time, i.e. the average standard of golf play (at the market level) is not really altered.

5 Frank Knight (1921) argued that the real reason for having companies in an economy is because of economic uncertainty. Explain what is meant by this.
6 In what ways does the concept of bounded rationality differ from economic rationality and what consequences does this have?
7 Try to come up with your examples of the mentioned heuristics that people often use. Perhaps you can relate to your own personal experiences.
8 It is in the text argued that biases caused by heuristics only matter for financial economics if they are systematic. What is meant by this?
9 Prospect theory is an important contribution to our understanding of economic decision-making behaviour. Describe and discuss the value function's three main features, and compare it to the utility function.
10 Discuss the reasons why management defined risk as they did. Can you understand why it to them differed from the definition given in financial economics?
11 Distinguish between the reducible and the irreducible part of economic uncertainty. Give examples of how management can handle each of them.

Further Readings:

Antonides, G., 1996, *Psychology in Economics and Business*, 2nd Ed., Dordrecht: Kluwer Academic Publishers.

Copeland, T. E., & Weston, J. F., 1992, *Financial Theory and Corporate Policy*, Reading, Massachusetts: Addison-Wesley. Chapters Four and Five.

Hamberg, M., 2000, *Risk, Uncertainty & Profitability – An Accounting-Based Study of Industrial Firms' Performance*, Department of Business Studies, Uppsala University.

Shapira, Z., 1995, *Risk Taking: A Managerial Perspective*, New York: Russell Sage Foundation.

Chapter 5

Competition and Market Efficiency

This chapter aims at:

- Revealing the necessary requirements of an efficient market.
- Discussing to what extent product markets are efficient, and determining what implications the current degree of efficiency has on the company's activities.
- Discussing to what extent capital markets are efficient, and determining what implications the current degree of efficiency has on investors' activities.

5.1 The Idea of Having Efficient Markets

Competition is a very important term when it comes to understanding financial theory and strategic decisions within companies. This chapter reveals some of the most fundamental ideas needed for economic theory to function. The consequences of these ideas are then studied for both *product markets*, where companies make investments, and *capital markets*, where companies finance their investments. The main point is to show the degree of competition there is in and between these two markets.

Competition is a concept very closely connected to market efficiency. A market is efficient when it allows fierce competition between actors in the market. Fierce competition makes it difficult to earn an *excessive return*, i.e., a return higher than what other market actors, faced with the same risk, earn. When it comes to capital markets there is a very strong belief in the importance of market efficiency. Regulators do everything they can to enable fierce competition. Modern capital markets are some of the most efficient markets one can think of. The reason why regulators put so much effort into maintaining a high level of efficiency is found within economic theory. An issue that is explained in this chapter.

Product markets are usually far less competitive than capital markets. Most countries have competition authorities that monitor the level of competition in industries and, whenever needed, take measures against situations where the level of competition is too low. But product markets are, and always will be, affected by human beings. Humans have different needs and desires and hence there is less interest for individual products and services, which means fewer buyers and sellers in each market. Humans do not have access to the same information, nor do they have ability, or interest in, interpreting information in the same way, and hence resources are more heterogeneously distributed. Also, humans do not have the ability to respond instantly to the activities of other market participants, and therefore product markets cannot return immediately to their equilibrium. In the real world buyers and sellers are not solely *price-takers*, but they have the ability to influence the market prices.

There are considerable differences between product and capital markets, differences that no legislator ever can or wants to remove. Product markets must be allowed to not be perfectly competitive. Many entrepreneurs take great risks and invest a lot of capital for which they do not see the benefits until years later. No pharmaceutical company would want to invest billions of SEK without knowing that if or when they develop a good product, they have the sole right to that particular product (a patent) for years to come. In many cases less competition must be allowed in order to encourage product development.

Corporations thrive on market inefficiencies. We need to remember that all corporate strategies ultimately are based on having inefficient product markets. Because of asymmetric information and heterogeneously distributed resources competitive advantages can be exploited. Profitable investments are based on successful corporate strategies and hence on the exploitation of inefficient product markets. This is a major difference between the competitive situation in product markets and that in capital markets. In the following text, several more (although smaller) differences will be identified. Differences that help us understand the decisions managers make in both of these markets. Most contribution to value is made through investment decisions: activities in the product market. Because of the efficiency of capital markets, managers should not be able to contribute much value through financing decisions.

5.2 Product Market Efficiency

5.2.1 Introduction

In the summer of 2000 the consortium of Swedish banks which jointly owned Bankgirot, the unit which handles a large portion of all giro transactions in Sweden, announced that they were acquiring Postgirot. Postgirot is owned by the Swedish post office which is government controlled. Together Bankgirot and Postgirot have control over almost the whole Swedish market for giro transactions.[1] The Swedish competition authority (Konkurrensverket) has as its main duty to investigate the degree of competition there is in different product markets. After a closer look at the deal their verdict stood clear: The merger could not be allowed since the market power of the combined unit would be too great. The Swedish competition authority feared that Bankgirot and Postgirot would dominate the market, take advantage of their position, and that customers would have no alternative if dissatisfied.

This is just one of many cases in which competition authorities rule that companies cannot behave in a certain manner because they are thereby threatening competition. This does not only happen in Sweden, but also in

1 That amounted to SEK 8,169 Billion only in 1999.

the rest of Europe and elsewhere. In 2000, the Swedish bus and truck producer Volvo had to take back its bid on Scania because the competition authority of the European Union feared it would achieve a too dominant position in Scandinavia. In other cases merging companies have been forced to sell off parts of their business in order to not have a too dominating position in particular segments. The American company Microsoft was recently required to split its business into smaller units because of a too dominant position. The court ruled that Microsoft had exploited its dominant position for the *Windows* operating system, in order to, unfairly, outcompete Netscape and its *Netscape Navigator* web browser. As of this writing, the case is in appeal.

Obviously there is a global belief that companies may not be too dominating in a market. Most developed societies try to hinder *monopoly*, where one company has total control over a product, service or resource that has no close substitutes. But herein lies a paradox as companies strive to earn as much money as possible. The absolutely best way to earn abnormally high returns is by being the sole provider of something that is highly attractive. A good corporate strategy is one in which competitors are outsmarted and high stable long term profit margins are established. In the area of marketing students learn how to segment a market and position a product within the segment. One has to find competitive advantages of each product, characteristics that makes them unique. But a fully unique product is one that has a monopoly position; no other product/service can satisfy a need as well as this product/service. In short, management of a company only applauds legislation that hinders monopoly, when they are not affected themselves. All companies try, whether they like to admit it or not, to earn excessive returns.

The idea of having fair competition is not totally new. In economic theory (all the way back to Adam Smith in the 18th century) competition has been seen as beneficial. But throughout history legislators have not always followed the idea. An interesting Swedish example is from the 1920s and early 1930s when the Swedish businessman Ivar Kreuger built a, short-lived, business empire around the idea of having a global monopoly on the production of matches.[2] Kreuger managed to convince governments around Europe and elsewhere that they ought to give him a monopoly in return for various forms of international loans. His empire was never fully attained, but this was more due to the collapse of global financial markets

2 See e.g. Thunholm (1995) for an excellent coverage of Kreuger both as an industrialist and a global financier.

in 1929 than a lack of interest from governments to form monopolies in the industry.

5.2.2 Models of market competition

In a world characterised by perfect competition no company can earn a risk-adjusted return higher than its competitors. As soon as one company introduces an exceptionally profitable product competitors will do likewise and hence price competition will reduce profit margins and excessive returns. But in reality we do have companies which earn more money than their competitors. Some companies might do this randomly and over shorter periods of time, whereas others seem to do it more systematically and more persistently. This is a phenomenon, which has spurred much research over the years, and in this section we will look at it briefly.

Excessive returns are in fact a special case of *abnormal returns*. An abnormal return is a return that differs from what other market actors, facing the same risk, earn. The abnormal can be either higher or lower than normal. Although most researchers do recognise short term abnormal returns there is more disagreement as to how soon they disappear, and to which resources competitive advantages are connected.

There are several alternative models to the classical definition of market competition. These allow, to some extent, for abnormal performance at the company level. One model was proposed by Chamberlin (1933), who reacted against the strong assumptions of the classical model and particularly the assumption that products and companies have to be homogeneous. His view was instead that they are heterogeneous. Competition thus goes on between companies with different, although overlapping, resources and characteristics. Perhaps the heterogeneity can give rise to abnormal performance. Chamberlin's view is that companies can have a monopoly on

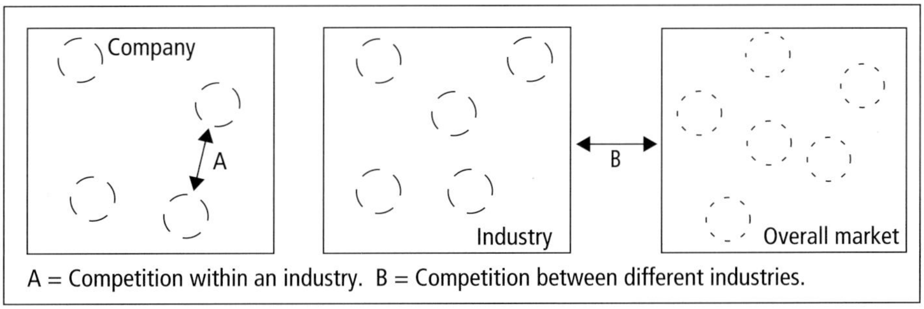

Figure 5.1 – Competition within and between industries.

individual products, but because of close substitutes, industries are characterised by *monopolistic competition*, which drives down excessive returns.

Monopolistic competition allows for differences between companies in the short term but because of the relatively near substitutes long term competition is secured. Chamberlin's view of competition is related to that within industrial organisation. Several of the empirical studies that will be mentioned take the industrial organisation school of thought as their origin. Their model of competition was originally developed to assist policy makers in formulating sound economic policies and, as such, it examines the characteristics and structure of different industries and how they affect the behaviour and performance of companies. The performance of individual companies is however of no interest and their characteristics are thought to be random. The only company-specific factor that they pay real attention to is size. For them returns within different industries can be different in the short term, but never in eternity.

In the 1950s and 1960s researchers began to take an empirical interest in differences in profitability. One of the most interesting discoveries they made was that industry profitability differed, and that the differences sometimes did remain over time.[3] Researchers argued that the reason for this is due to the *industrial organisation* (the structure of the industry). A great deal of the theoretical developments within corporate strategy has been based on the idea that industrial differences can persist for some time. One of the best-known of these developments is Porter's model of industrial structures, or the 'five-forces'. In his analysis Porter (1980) argues that profitability within an industry is determined by (1) the supplier's bargaining power, (2) the customer's bargaining power, (3) entry barriers to the industry, (4) near substitutes, and (5) competition within the industry. The five forces are illustrated in Figure 5.2 and in the following text we shall look at each of them briefly.

The *Competition within the industry* is primarily a short term factor to consider as it deals with the current competitive situation. This is rivalry between established competitors. In some industries performance is depen-

3 Some of the more influential early studies were carried out by Bain (1956), Stigler (1964) and Mann (1966). According to this school of thought, business profitability is determined by the structure of the industry within which the company finds itself. This idea is often referred to as the "Structure-Conduct-Performance" framework. The structure of the industry determines company conduct, which ultimately drives performance.

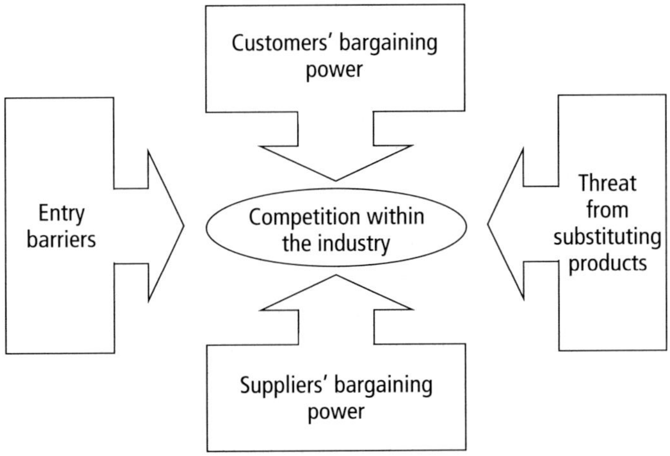

Figure 5.2 – Porter's model of industrial structure.

dent on *price competition* that drives down production margins, whereas in other industries it is dependent on advertisement, innovation or other "non-price" dimensions. Price competition usually means considerably lower margins and more fierce competition. Factors playing an important role in the rivalry between established competitors is the concentration rate, diversity of competitors, scale economies, excess capacity and exit barriers, as well as the uniqueness of products and services sold.

Companies also have to look at other industries and potential *Threats from near substitutes*. The ability to earn profits is given by the maximum price a customer is willing to pay for a product or service. If a similar product, or a very near substitute, exists on the market, customers will be more price sensitive. If customers have a propensity to shift between similar products, profit margins are likely to go down. The travel and communication industry might be tempting to split into bus, train and air transportation businesses. But as conditions and customer preferences change, train transport might be competing with air transport, or bus transport. As technology and preferences change these "industries" start competing with each other.

A third factor Porter discusses is *Entry barriers*. If one company, or a few companies, earn substantial excessive returns there is always a possibility that other companies will recognise the profitability, be tempted by it and try to enter the market. This is what has happened to the mobile phone business, where several "traditional" consumer product companies such as Alcatel, Panasonic and Sony have tried to capture a part of an industry that initially was dominated by Ericsson and Nokia. The nature of an entry barrier can vary. It can depend on large investments in industry-specific assets, and although current industry profitability is high, entry is too costly for companies not already in the market. A capital-intensive production also creates economies of scale, which large established companies have better chances to capture. This is the case of a special steel company like Sandvik. An entry barrier can also depend on product awareness among customers: Although Coca-Cola is highly profitable it is not sure competitors can earn the same returns as they are based on a supreme market position that is hard to copy. Finally large investments can be protected through patents and/or copyrights. It is hard to enter a profitable segment of the pharmaceutical industry because of the patents companies hold. AstraZeneca's patent on Losec is a good example of how one company can earn excessive returns for a long period of time.

The fourth and fifth factors concern *Suppliers' bargaining power* and *Customers' bargaining power*, respectively. With power Porter means the relative strength of the supplier/buyer in relationship to the other companies within the industry. An important role here is played by the size of the supplier/buyer. Those buyers and suppliers who are larger often have a better bargaining position. Product uniqueness also plays a role. Large automobile producers, such as Volvo, Saab and Scania have wanted and been able to lower their procurement costs. To deal with squeezed profit margins the considerably smaller sub-contractors have been forced to either differentiate their products or to become larger. This is transforming the whole auto-supplier industry. Some suppliers who have made large investments are locked into an industry with no exit possibility. Profit margins become depressed and consolidation is the only option. For companies such as Haldex and Finnveden, consolidation has become a major part of doing business. Another issue to consider here, and particularly for end-consumers, is price sensitivity. Research shows that people are more sensitive to price changes when a product's cost makes up a greater portion of their total expenses. It has also been shown that if a product is of importance for the quality of the buyers' products or services they tend to be less price sensitive. For end-consumers of e.g. petrol there are several companies offering the same core product. Government and industry standards make competition fierce and it has put old-fashioned petrol stations out of business. Price sensitive customers with a lot of bargaining power cause fierce competition within the industry. Today petrol stations are transforming into 'service stations', providing their customers with supplementary products and services where they can differentiate and earn higher margins. In the 'service station' one usually finds both a small assortment of groceries and fast food.[4] For petrol stations, which already have access to a large group of customers, these industries are relatively easy to enter. This is just one example of how an industry can be transformed, reducing customers' power and increasing industry returns.

5.2.3 The chances of earning excessive returns

In the early studies it was often argued that profitability within industries averaged out and was of little interest (Bain, 1956; Brozen, 1970). More recent research has shown that this is not necessarily correct. As researchers have become more familiar with the problem, data has become more abundant, and the ability to handle large quantities of data has increased, we have learned that there are differences both between industries and within industries. In a large international study it was shown that throughout seven different countries the level of profitability varied between companies (Mueller, 1990). Swedish companies were also involved in the study. In the larger samples it could be shown that these differences persist over long periods of time. Contemporary Swedish research also indicates that abnormal returns do exist for some time before they fade away (Landström, 2001).

Today researchers recognise that there are abnormal returns both within industries and between industries. These 'company-specific' abnormal returns and 'industry-specific' abnormal returns rely on different things. What we do know is that most abnormal returns disappear as time goes by. This process is called mean reversion, i.e., the performance of individual observations does over time reverse towards the mean of comparable observations. We can distinguish between a *company-specific mean reversion* process (where the abnormal returns of individual companies disappear), and an *industry-specific mean reversion* process (where the abnormal returns of individual industries disappear).

4 There are signs that supermarkets and petrol stations are joining together, which makes sense particularly in small communities. The post office has started to work together with e.g. petrol stations (and grocery stores) so that customers can pick up packages there.

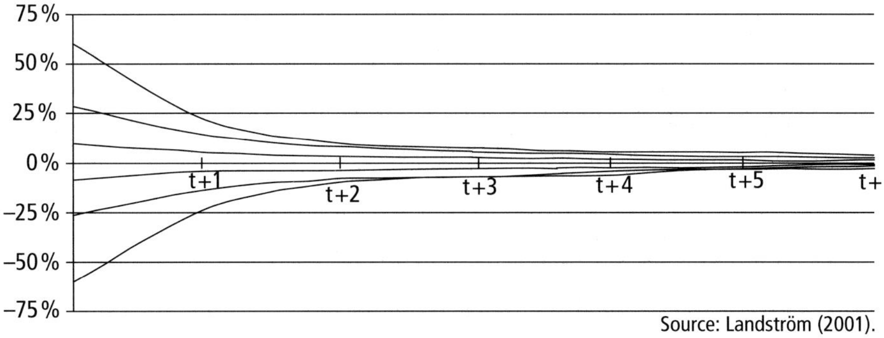

Figure 5.3 – Mean reversion in profitability of Swedish companies, 1978–96.

Mean reversion processes naturally vary from industry to industry. Figure 5.3 is taken from a current study of 1,500 Swedish industrial companies between 1978 and 1996 (Landström, 2001). Companies have been grouped into six portfolios based on their pre-tax RRBC and then monitored over the following six years. Already after two years most of the differences have disappeared. In general, the company-specific mean reversion process is believed to be quicker as there are fewer barriers within an industry than between two different ones. If an industry is defined with the system used by Porter (the five-forces model of industry competition), rivalry within an industry is generally speaking fierce. Many of the early researchers of industrial organisation therefore thought of company-specific abnormal returns as a matter of luck. But even if it is primarily a matter of luck (or coincidences which are not possible to successfully replicate) it is a fact that some companies perform better than others. It seems unlikely that abnormal company-specific returns in industries with fierce competition remain for more than a business cycle. It also seems unlikely that abnormal industry-specific returns remain for more than eight to ten years.[5]

The Swedish company Hennes & Mauritz is an excellent example showing that companies can have a persistent excessive return. H&M is in a highly competitive and mature industry and while it continuously enters new markets it has been able to retain a high profit margin. Not many of Porter's ideas on industry competition can be used to explain such superior company-specific performances. It is also hard to distinguish between com-

5 These are only rules of thumb. Please notice that risk is not considered here. We shall learn later that risk means that investors, companies and industries will require and earn different returns. Many studies do however take risk into account and still find substantial abnormal returns.

petition within and between industries. Are airlines and trains in the same industry? Petrol stations and convenience stores? Cinemas and video stores? Also, companies in the same industry might be protected by e.g. entry barriers. A pharmaceutical company holds patents that protect its new products for some time. Because of such difficulties it is not always easy to detect abnormal returns.

If it was possible to do consistently much better than everybody else there would be one company dominating its industry completely. There is hardly any industry where this is the case though. Both researchers and practitioners spend considerable time searching for the Holy Grail: eternal market dominance. Fortunately they never seem to find it and in the long run companies have to settle with normal returns. The question should rather be how one can hang on to an excessive return a little bit longer.

5.2.4 The risk-return paradox

In 1980 an interesting empirical finding was presented. Companies which have a higher historical accounting return also enjoy a more stable one over time (Bowman, 1980). This is indeed paradoxical as economic theory suggests that one has to accept higher risk when desiring a higher return. Since most researchers have defined risk as the *ex post* volatility in return (or profitability) the negative association between the level of return and the variance in return became known as a *risk-return paradox*. This association has proven to be strong across industries and countries (see Hamberg, 2000, for Swedish evidence).

To understand the phenomenon, take a look at Table 5.4 below. The graph shows the profitability (RRBC) over time for four Swedish companies during the time-period 1982 to 1996. The pharmaceutical company Astra had an average profitability of 36.6 percent. OEM, which is a trading company in electronics, had an average profitability of 32.7 percent. The steel manufacturer Avesta had an average profitability of 11.8 percent, and Kabe, which produces caravans, had an average profitability of 7.2 percent. It is interesting to look at the four companies' variance in profitability over time. Astra has a very stable high profitability. Over fifteen years it never goes below 30 percent! OEM also has a high profitability and during these fifteen years it is never lower than 17.2 percent. The average profitability for Swedish industrial companies during these fifteen years is 17.1 percent (Hamberg, 2000).

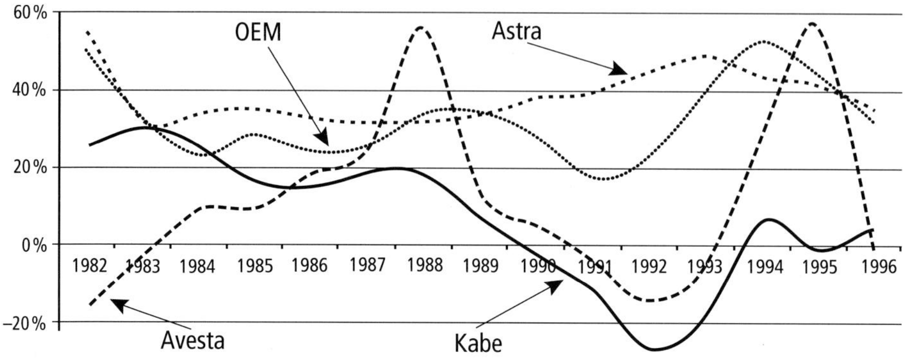

	1982	1983	1984	1985	1986	1987	1988	1989	1990	1991	1992	1993	1994	1995	1996
OEM	50.0%	32.8%	23.3%	28.1%	24.4%	25.7%	34.0%	34.3%	28.5%	17.2%	22.8%	39.6%	52.8%	44.2%	32.0%
Astra	55.1%	32.2%	33.7%	35.4%	33.0%	32.0%	32.1%	33.6%	38.0%	39.8%	44.8%	49.2%	44.0%	41.4%	35.5%
Kabe	25.4%	30.3%	25.6%	16.3%	14.9%	18.6%	18.2%	7.3%	−2.5%	−11.2%	−26.5%	−18.4%	6.2%	−0.9%	4.5%
Avesta	−16.1%	−3.1%	9.1%	9.4%	18.1%	24.3%	55.8%	13.5%	5.0%	−3.7%	−14.0%	−6.0%	29.1%	56.5%	−1.4%

Figure 5.4 – Variance in profitability for four Swedish industrial companies.

When looking at Avesta and Kabe the situation is completely different. Avesta is situated in an industry heavily influenced by business cycles and externally determined steel prices. Twice it earned negative returns and twice it earned returns higher than 50 percent. The variance in profitability is remarkable. Kabe is much less dependent on business cycles and its profitability follows a very different pattern. Nonetheless it varies from +30 percent to −27 percent. These companies are perhaps stereotypes, but they represent a pattern that is obvious in all of these studies of the risk-return paradox. Many companies with a high average profitability also have a stable one, and many companies with a low average profitability have one that varies substantially over time.

As researchers have studied the risk-return paradox closer they have found that it is bad performers (low profitability companies) that primarily cause the negative association. In fact, among high profitability companies the relationship is often positive or neutral. Furthermore, it is in recessions that bad performers deviate from normal. High profitability companies are then much more able to maintain their past level of profitability.

These findings are indeed interesting. If product markets are reasonably efficient companies which launch successful strategies should not be able to sustain a superior position forever. This group of studies thus supports the inefficiency of product markets showed in the previous section. But they also indicate that the variance in profitability is different. In inefficient product markets decisions are characterised by uncertainty. High profitability companies have had the ability to remove uncertainty better and hence they generate both high accounting returns, and stable ones over time.

5.2.5 Some final comments on product market efficiency

Fierce competition is believed to be an important part of well-functioning market economies. In general, most product markets are poor replications of microeconomic theory. Companies always try to have unique products and business concepts, and dominate the market or market segment they operate in. Uniqueness leads to a monopoly situation, meaning that no other company satisfies certain needs in exactly the same manner. Domination means that the company's position can give rise to excessive returns. But the overlap between products and business areas enable reasonably fierce competition, and the avoidance of pure monopoly situations. Many industries are dominated by a small number of companies. Even though fierce competition is important, so are incentives to stimulate the development of new products and services.

Although this discussion leaves us with more unanswered questions than we had to start with, it does teach us some very valuable lessons. The *first* is that product markets are not as efficient as the markets we read about in economic textbooks. Regulators have to make product markets reasonably efficient so that there is competition which drives down prices and stimulates product development. On the other hand competition cannot be too fierce, because that would also give fewer incentives for doing business. Entrepreneurs need to feel that they are able to earn excessive returns. Companies have to be given the incentives to do research and hence we allow patents, copyrights and trademarks.

The *second* lesson regards returns in product markets. The main role of the business manager is to make and manage investments that earn a return above their cost. As managers desire excessive returns and as our society, to some extent, allows them to earn such returns, they can be seen for some periods of time. The problem is that there is no way we can say for how long an excessive (or abnormal) return will last, and which company it is who will earn it. To believe that any company can earn excessive returns into infinity, without a reversion to the mean, is nonsense.

The *third* lesson relates to the pattern by which returns revert to the mean. Researchers have found that there are differences between industries and within industries. Most of the time the mean reversion within industries is stronger than that between industries. The reason for this is likely to be the more permanent inefficiencies that are to be found at the industry level. High barriers to entry are a prime example of this. For companies to earn abnormal returns within industries is likely to be more random. This is not to say that abnormal returns cannot persist over longer periods of time. Just that we cannot predict when and where this will happen, and that it is more likely it will not occur, than that it will occur.

5.3 Capital Market Efficiency

5.3.1 Are capital markets more efficient than product markets?

This part of the chapter introuces the general theories behind our view of how capital markets function. It tries to provide an understanding of how investors can make use of capital markets and how they expect companies to function. Before the 1950s, there were hardly any theories regarding how capital markets function or how they ought to function. When a number of financial "discoveries" enabled such a theory to emerge, one of its most prominent features was named the *efficient market hypothesis* (EMH).[6] According to this hypothesis an efficient market is one in which share prices fully reflect all available value-relevant information. As soon as new relevant information that can have an effect on the share price of a company is released, investors use that information to trade on. This new information can be information about a new product the company has developed or new markets it is about to enter. It can be information about competing companies, the global economy, interest rates in Sweden or the trade deficit in the US. When investors trade, value-relevant information is incorporated into the share price.

In the language of economics one says that investors' reactions to new information drives the value of the asset to a new equilibrium where supply meets demand. The efficient market hypothesis tells us that as long as financial markets are efficient they will be in equilibrium. Market efficiency is one of the assumptions behind the whole idea of capital market theory.

6 This term was established in 1970 in an article by Eugene Fama. There had been several studies before then based on the same idea or which pointed at the phenomenon. Bacheliere (1900), Working (1934) and Kendall (1953) are empirical works by statisticians. Roberts (1959), Samuelson (1965) and Fama (1965) are some of the first works by economists elaborating on the idea.

The efficient market hypothesis has several implications for both investors and management. The important *lesson for investors* to learn is that because information is immediately incorporated into share prices they cannot expect to earn more than a normal return. If information reveals that investors can earn a higher return by holding another security with the same risk, they will instantly sell the one they are currently holding and buy the cheap security. Such behaviour is called *arbitrage.* Arbitrage activities drive down the price of the overpriced security, and drive up the price of the cheaper security. In this way, share prices adjust before the average investor has time to trade on it.

The important *lesson for management* is that they will receive the proper value for the securities they issue in an efficient market. In an efficient market companies cannot fool investors and obtain a too cheap financing. From this idea one can understand that financing decisions made by management should not contribute to the value of the company. If product market decisions are to be value-relevant product market efficiency has to be set out of place, and if capital market decisions are to be value-relevant capital market efficiency has to be set out of place.

5.3.2 Criteria for market efficiency

In order to have an efficient capital market several criteria have to be fulfilled. Above all, capital market theory assumes rational behaviour from market actors. Investors are profit-maximisers who follow the axioms outlined in Chapter Four. In one of the most influential contributions to this research area, Fama (1970) laid out the three pillars upon which the theory relies. These are that investors have access to the relevant information, that they have the ability to understand the (monetary) consequences of the information, and that financial markets enable 'frictionless' trading. We shall look at each of these three components in more detail.

1) Access to information

All value-relevant information has to be readily and timely available to both current and potential investors. When for example Ericsson releases its quarterly report it must be done in such a way that it quickly reaches all investors, and that the monetary consequences of Ericsson's operations are interpretable. To uphold a high degree of market efficiency regulators want as much relevant information as possible to reach as many investors at the same time. Individual market actors, however, want as much information as possible but they want it before the other market actors. Only with advantageous information asymmetry can they earn an excessive return.

2) Knowledge of how to handle the information

This assumption is interconnected with the assumption of rational behaviour. For us to have efficient capital markets we need to have skilled people making investment decisions. They need to know how to interpret general information about a company, the industry it is competing in, and the effects the global economy has on the industry and company. Furthermore they need to be able to transform such information into estimates of company value. Investors need to possess theoretical and practical skills in e.g. finance, accounting, and economics. They also need to know the business of the company they analyse. Only when an individual investor is better than the average investor can he/she earn an excessive return. It is this constant desire to be better than others that drives improvements in personal skills, and which pushes financial markets towards efficiency.

3) Market frictions

With no market frictions investors are able to make changes in their investment portfolios without incurring losses in time or capital. Trading should involve low *transaction costs* (e.g. brokerage fees), low *information costs*, and short delays in time when buying or selling a security. Generally speaking the more active a financial market is, the less problem one has with market frictions. Both transaction costs and information costs, which are basically fixed costs, can then be split between more deals. Large market frictions might lead to investors being reluctant to act on certain information.

In financial markets competition has to be as fair as possible. All actors should play under more or less the same rules, meaning that they should have access to the same information at the same time. The cost of accessing information should be low so that there are virtually no entry barriers to the market. If there were segments of the market that constantly gained access to more valid and reliable information, obtained the information before others or obtained the information substantially cheaper than other segments, there would be a distortion to efficiency. This might not have a negative effect on efficiency in the short term, but would in the long term discourage the misfortunate from trading and undermine the general trust in the market as a fair game. Clearly it is in every individual actor's interest not just to get hold of information nobody else has, or be better at interpreting the information than everybody else, but also to use the system to one's advantage.

5.3.3 Categories of market efficiency

In the previous section the general criteria for market efficiency were outlined. There are differences concerning the degree to which share markets in different countries are efficient. One of the main reasons for these differences is the orientation and efficiency of a country's corporate governance system. Share markets in Anglo-Saxon countries have, at least in the past, been considered to be more efficient. This is only natural as the governance systems of these countries primarily rely on active trading. Free and active share markets are a requirement for market efficiency, but are also a requirement for well-functioning market-oriented governance systems. It is important to note that different segments of a share market can vary substantially in efficiency. The market for the largest companies is usually considerably more efficient than the market for smaller companies. The reason is that more analysts follow large companies than small companies.[7]

In the previously mentioned article by Fama (1970), he defined and discussed three levels of market efficiency. They are referred to here as categories of market efficiency and they are determined by the kind of information actors in the market have access to, and trade on. If only information concerning past share prices is incorporated into the current share price then there is a *weak form of market efficiency*. If all publicly

7 For a brokerage firm (and individual investors) there are fixed costs involved in analysing a company and turn over (buy and sell) its shares. Let us assume that (1) the cost of analysing a company is independent of the risk of the company, and that (2) the return for a certain company in a given risk class is 10 percent. With fixed costs of e.g. 500,000 for analysing the company the investor would have to have at least five million invested to break-even. That can be a substantial amount of the free float in some companies. The problem becomes even clearer when considering that investors have other alternatives. Even though you know that it is more profitable to invest in a smaller company the comparative return for a large company in the same risk class might be only two to three percentage points lower. If fixed costs are 500,000, then the investor needs to possess shares worth 20–25 million to break-even. The costs of turning over a position in such a company might be higher than the improved profitability (when considering the fixed costs of analysing the company). Even if the value of the small company is 500 million, the free float might only be 100 million. The low liquidity in the share causes costs that offset the comparatively higher returns of many smaller companies.

available information is incorporated in the current share price then there is a *semi-strong form of market efficiency*. Finally, if all current information (public and private) is incorporated in the share price there is a *strong form of market efficiency*. We shall now go through each category separately.

Weak form of market efficiency

The weak form of market efficiency is really a question of whether trends can exist in share markets. Ask yourself: If the price of a share has increased three days in a row, is it more likely it will increase than decrease on the fourth day? Or similarly; if the price of a share has decreased three days in a row, is it more likely it will decrease than increase on the fourth day? A strategy based on extrapolation of patterns in historical share returns will be unable to generate profits above normal if a *weak* form of market efficiency holds. The reason we call it a weak form of market efficiency is that it is based on the easiest set of information one can obtain as an investor; previous share prices. The argument used in support of this form of efficiency is that the information is so easy to obtain and interpret that anyone can do it, and any profit would disappear in that process. Hence investors will have to make use of more sophisticated methods to beat the market.

To illustrate how competition has an effect on share prices let's assume that there is, for some reason, a cyclical pattern in the market for a certain share. Perhaps this is because accounting profits move in accordance with a predictable business cycle. Figure 5.5 shows how the actual value of this company has moved in the past and how it is thereby assumed to move in the future. We also see the "true" value of the company, expressed as the solid line.[8] But if actors in the market can interpret historical information correctly they would understand how the actual share price moves in a predictable way (around the "true" value) instead of being random. Any rational profit-maximiser would then trade on the pattern. If you were an investor standing at $t = 0$ and you could see this pattern in the market, what would you do? Of course you would buy the share at the B^1 position and then sell it when it reaches the T^1 position. But if you and many other investors buy at B^1 your action will drive the price at that time upwards, towards its "true" value. Similarly, if you sell at T^1 your action will drive the

8 This value increases in accordance to the risk of the company. More about this issue in Chapter Six.

price at that time downwards, again towards its "true" value. The information on past share performance will be incorporated into the current price.

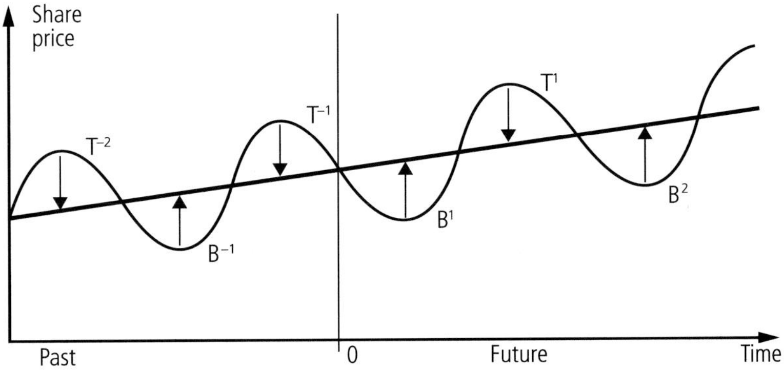

Figure 5.5 – Systematic volatility in the share prices.

Since investors are thought to act in this way, the weak form of market efficiency forces share prices to move in an unpredictable way, or according to a *random walk*. The random walk model runs parallel with the market efficiency assumption. Although it is a consequence coming from having efficient markets, the concept was actually outlined before the efficient market hypothesis (e.g. Kendall, 1953; Roberts, 1959).

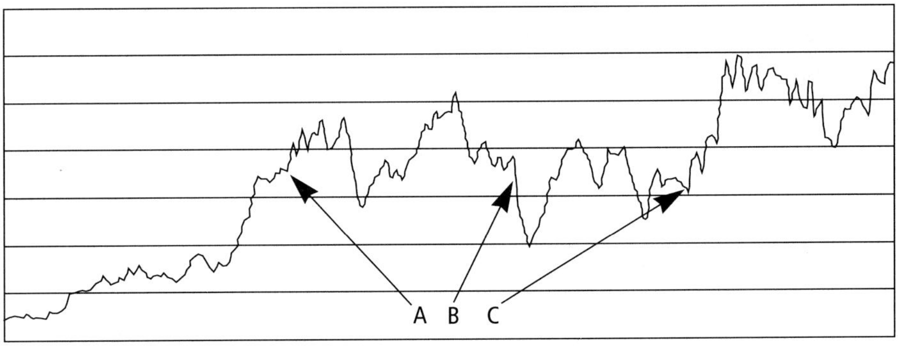

Figure 5.6 – Share price movement on the stock exchange.

Figure 5.6 illustrates the value of one of the larger Swedish companies quoted on the Stockholm Stock Exchange on a monthly basis. The essence of the random walk model is that one cannot on the basis of historical share prices say in which direction the next market movement will be. Neither at time A, B, or C in Figure 5.6 do we know where the market is heading. The value of the company changes randomly, but with an upward trend, as we move along from the past (left) to the future (right).

We will in the section on behavioural finance in Chapter Six discuss irrationalities in human decision-making that perhaps can cause trends in financial markets. But clearly there are good theoretical reasons to believe one cannot make consistent abnormal profits by trading on historical share prices.

Empirical assessments of security return predictability

Before the 1950s it was generally believed that patterns occurred in stock market prices. A number of researchers did however show that share prices are more or less uncorrelated over time (Kendall, 1953; Roberts, 1959; Fama, 1965). Buying winners and short-selling losers then turned out to be an unprofitable investment strategy. Early tests also employed so-called *filter rules*, such as for example "buy a stock when it has increased by x percent, and keep it until date y, unless it decreases by z percent" (Fama and Blume, 1966). Also this form of investment strategy was condemned by the very first empirical studies of capital market efficiency and the formation of share prices – this particularly when researchers took trading costs in account.

Empirical research over recent decades has however revealed patterns in stock market returns that believers in classical financial theory find difficult to accept. Predictability in both the short and long term seems to be possible. These results will only be briefly discussed here. Lo and MacKinlay (1988) developed a method of testing serial correlation in share returns by exploiting the fact that the variance of returns should increase in direct proportion to the sampling interval. With this approach they found strong evidence that weekly returns are positively correlated. In fact the correlation coefficient between two immediately preceding weeks (called first-order autocorrelation) is as high as 30 percent. This strongly rejects the random walk hypothesis and the weak form of market efficiency. In studies of the long term performance the results are almost as disappointing for believers in market efficiency. Several studies have documented the fact that the positive autocorrelation found in the short term turns into a negative autocorrelation when researchers look further into the future (see e.g. Fama and French, 1988; Poterba and Summers, 1988). Believers in market efficiency have responded to these studies and in particular they have attacked the research methodologies. The debate is still far from solved as behavioural finance has come up recently with potential explanations as to why we obtain these empirical results. There have also been a few studies of the Stockholm Stock Exchange. Frennberg and Hansson (1993) obtained results in line with the previously mentioned studies. On the other hand, Berg and Lyhagen (1998) found no long term effects and while there was some short term dependence it was hardly enough to cover transaction costs. Their results were thus more in line with the weak form of market efficiency.

Return predictability is often connected to company-specific factors such as the size of the company, market-to-book value and earnings. Companies with certain characteristics perform better/worse than other companies (see e.g. Fama, 1991). We come back to some of these factors in the section on behavioural finance in the next chapter. In that section we shall supply some theoretical underpinnings to the negative long-run dependence found in some studies. Researchers then argue that investors extrapolate positive past returns too far, and that the negative autocorrelation is a mean reversion process, due to an overreaction. Based on these patterns so-called contrarian investment strategies can be built.

Another topic researchers are debating is seasonal effects such as e.g. the January effect. Security returns seem to be systematically higher, particularly for small firms, in the month of January (Keim, 1983, 1988; Roll, 1983). Researchers are still debating why this pattern persists. Rational investors who know about this phenomenon should trade on it and buy small stocks, particularly those which have declined in value and are more likely to be candidates for tax-loss selling, in late December and resell them at the end of January (Schwert, 1983).

Semi-strong form of market efficiency

Most researchers believe that in general modern share markets are best described as semi-efficient. With this they mean that investors quickly respond to new public information so that share prices constantly incorporate all available and value-relevant public information. This is a step further than just saying that current share prices reflect movements in historical share prices. Instead the value of a traded company reflects all information there is about the company's future prospects. Earnings from the last quarter, inflation figures from Japan, and industry growth expectations are all immediately incorporated into the price when announced to the public.

Much of the research on whether this is true or not has been done with the use of the *event study methodology*, which has been proved to be one of the most significant methodological developments within capital market theory (Fama, Fischer, Jensen and Roll, 1969). Its significance lies in its

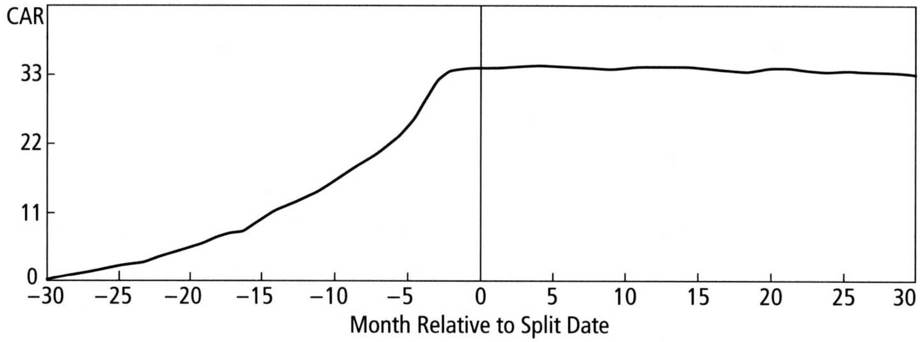

Figure 5.7 – Event study methodology applied to stock splits.

simplicity. When interested in how investors evaluate a certain company-specific event, such as for example a stock-split[9], the researcher observes many companies that have been exposed to the same event and investigates the market's aggregated response. The day of the split is regarded as day zero for all observations and the actual return of the shares is then compared with the expected (and sometimes risk- and size-adjusted) return before and after the event occurred. The difference is referred to as abnormal return, and when several days' abnormal returns are summoned the result is referred to as a cumulative abnormal return (CAR).[10] CAR is the measure used to investigate the market's aggregated response to new public information.[11]

To illustrate how these studies are conducted. Figure 5.7 contains some results from the very first application of the event study methodology. Fama, Fischer, Jensen and Roll (1969) then studied a large number of companies involved in stock splits. As you can see the share price of these companies increased substantially more than the share price of other companies (a risk-adjusted comparison with the market index) prior to the split. This is of course the reason why the split was made in the first place. When the split was announced however there was no reaction from the

9 A stock split means that the number of shares increase but with no issuing of new equity. Obviously such an arrangement has no effect on a company's operations. If each shareholder gets two new shares for each old share (2:1) that should only imply that there are twice as many shares each worth half as much.

10 The term *abnormal return* refers to a return different from normal. The concept is similar to that explained in Section 5.2 when talking about companies abnormal returns in product markets.

11 The event study methodology is described in Fama, Fischer, Jensen, and Roll (1969). McWilliams and Siegel (1997) provide a comprehensive and superb coverage of methodological issues as well as its empirical applicability within the field of management research.

market. Nothing happened in the company's operations that merited a different valuation, it was simply the number of outstanding shares that changed. The split occurred because of prior rises in share price and not because of changes in the expectations of future share price.

Event studies are without doubt one of the most substantial methodological contributions made during the last thirty years. The results of most early event studies were interpreted in support of the semi-strong form of market efficiency. Prices react almost instantaneously and in an unbiased way to announcements of company-specific information. In studies of investors' responses to new, value-relevant information the event studies often show small changes in share price before the announcement (due to either insider trading or expectations from market actors that certain information will soon be announced) and then a quick correction in the share price after the announcement. There have been a great number of studies showing that after the correction, little (if any) additional abnormal return can be expected (i.e., CAR does not increase/decrease further). But as always, there is a continuous questioning of established theories. Recent studies have therefore questioned the efficient market hypothesis. We return to them in the end of the next chapter when discussing behavioural finance, and delays in the market's response to new information.

An alternative way of examining the semi-strong form of market efficiency is to test the rationality of investors' information processing. Studies of American share markets show that the per-hour variance in trading is much higher during weekdays than weekends (72 times to be precise). Obviously this indicates that the market moves more when there is information to process, than when there is no information (French and Roll, 1986). Other researchers have investigated whether share prices respond to unanticipated information (of various kinds). Empirical results provided by, for example, Brown, Harlow and Tinic (1988) support the semi-strong form of market efficiency as both expected return and risk changes systematically when market- and company-specific information is announced.[12] Finally it is worth mentioning some studies testing whether rumours are value relevant. Again these studies have been primarily based on American data, where a common source is the column "Heard on the Street" in the Wall

12 They also find that investors react more strongly to bad news than good news, which can be interpreted as an overreaction to bad news and underreaction to good news. They do, however, argue that this is only rational given the risk-aversion of investors. The finding is however interesting to compare with behavioural finance findings like, for example, the study by DeBondt and Thaler (1985), which is reviewed in the next chapter.

Street Journal. When establishing a trading strategy based on buying shares of companies regarded to be likely takeover targets, no abnormal return is obtained (Pound and Zeckhauser, 1990). The only plausible explanation must be that the information is already incorporated into the share price.

Based on a massive amount of research one can conclude that the share markets respond relatively quickly to new information. Probably the response to new information is not complete as there is evidence of under- and overreactions, but most researchers agree that when new information is released investors do, on average, a fairly good job evaluating it. Hence they support the semi-strong form of market efficiency.

Strong form of market efficiency

A capital market has a strong form of market efficiency when all information is incorporated into the share price. In a review article of market efficiency Fama (1991) referred to strong market efficiency as a test for *private information*. Fama did so, because most of the studies within the area examine whether there are actors in the share market who earn excessive returns by trading on information not available to the public. Most tests of market efficiency have concerned the weak and the semi-strong form of market efficiency, and not the strong form. The ultimate rejection of the strong form of market efficiency is to find somebody infinitely rich, without having violated capital market regulations.

Generally speaking it is hard to find evidence that there are investors who consistently outperform the market. At the same time, American market regulators (SEC) bring several cases every year to the courts and people are being convicted for insider trading. This signals that markets are not completely efficient in a strong form.[13] In the following analysis we shall focus on two forms of trade on private information. The first is when corporate insiders trade in their own company's shares to earn excessive returns. The second is when outsiders gain non-public information to earn excessive returns.

Early studies revealed that corporate insiders earn excessive returns by buying shares in their own company (e.g. Jaffe, 1974). Some of this trading is illegal – we refer to it as inside trading based on *material information*, which can be e.g. undisclosed earnings information, or information of a value-relevant acquisition before the deal has been announced. As long as material undisclosed information exists there cannot be a strong form of

13 Seyhun (1998) and Jeng, Metrick and Zeckhauser (1999) have provided new evidence that insiders can earn excessive returns even when they trade completely legally.

efficiency. The next step to take is to ask whether insider trading based on *non-material information* can earn excessive returns. Management and members of the board of directors are allowed to buy shares in their own company. Often they buy shares because they expect the company to be worth more than its current value. They then expect other investors to realise the same thing later on. There are studies also within this area that show that insiders can earn excessive returns in this fashion (Seyhun, 1986). Insiders have better access to information, but they are at the same time biased to think that their company is better than it actually is, or that the prospects for the future are gloomier than they look. The results of these studies contradict the strong form of market efficiency. But one should keep in mind that at least trading on material information is illegal.

The next question is whether investors can mimic insiders (trading legally on non-material information) and thereby earn an excessive return. As people potentially sitting on insider information have to report their trading, the "information-value" that their behaviour has should be quickly incorporated into the share price. This question is yet not fully solved as empirical results contradict each other.[14] In general researchers tend to think that trading strategies based on information about insider trading is not value enhancing; markets are too quick to incorporate this public information.

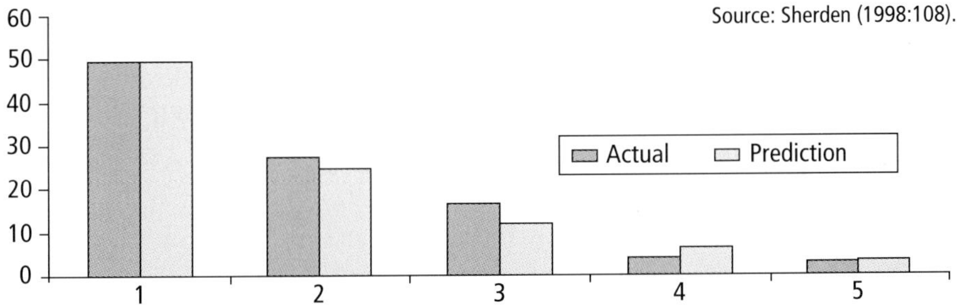

Figure 5.8 – Sustained investment performance by mutual funds.

For investors without *access* to material information, and who are investing in large companies active on liquid markets the only way to beat the market index is to be better at *processing* existing information. There is little evidence that some investors can systematically outperform the market in this way. Surely some do, but that can very well be attributed to luck. To illustrate this, we again use American data. Figure 5.8 displays the per-

14 While Jaffe (1974) argued that it is not possible to earn abnormal returns on mimicking insiders, a study by Seyhun (1986) shows the opposite.

centage of mutual funds that remain in the top half in investment performance for one to five consecutive years at the beginning of the 1990s.

Next to the actual figures you find the expected value if this was a completely random process. Think of it as flipping a coin. For the first year there is a 50 percent chance of being in top half (1/2), for two years in a row it is a 25 percent chance (1/4), for three years in a row it is a 12.5 percent chance (1/8), et cetera. The actual figures follow this pattern almost precisely, which indicates that even though there are some mutual funds, or some investors, who do better than the rest, this is not falsifying the efficient market hypothesis.[15] Actually, pure luck can explain the excessive returns.

One of the most important tasks market regulators have to do is to make sure investors have as little opportunity as possible to trade on private information. Earning excess returns on private information is, arguably, not robbery. It is a trade between anonymous investors who voluntarily decide to buy/sell the share. From a market efficiency perspective insider trading certainly has a positive short term effect as it forces the price of the share towards its correct value. But trades on private information are thought to have a demoralising effect on other market actors. Given the merits of market efficiency regulators strive to create an environment where all value-relevant information is provided to all investors as quickly as possible. If regulators allow information to be asymmetrically distributed, and even unrightfully withheld from some participants, it is easy to see a scenario in which no public information is released, or no information is value-relevant when it is released and that will most likely quickly undermine the market morale, increase capital costs and reduce the total wealth of society.

There is a fuzzy line between what is and what is not insider trading. In most large public companies the top management is rewarded based on the share performance. As discussed in Chapter Three information is asymmetrically distributed between managers and investors. But if management own shares in their own company how can we prevent them from trading these shares on the market, and how can we know if/when they buy or sell based on private or public information? This is a problematic issue for market regulators. In order to handle it managers are allowed to trade

15 Another issue is that low performers rarely stay in the market for a long period of time. As not many people want to invest in a mutual fund with a terrible track record, these funds are often replaced with others investing in more or less the same shares but without the below-average track record. Good performers stay in the market whereas bad performers exit and re-enter.

shares, but market regulators monitor and publicly announce their trading. Investigations are often carried out if the returns look suspicious. All potential insiders are therefore required to announce what transactions they have been engaged in. This gives other investors the opportunity to mimic insider trading, and regulators the chance to take measures when regulations are broken. It should be mentioned that during the 1990s only two individuals were convicted for insider trading in Sweden. The situation is similar in the rest of Europe. Abnormal returns remain a questionable issue within capital markets.

5.3.4 Some final comments on capital market efficiency

To put it simply; the reason why we have efficient capital markets is greed. Investors trade in capital markets only because they want to earn as much money as possible. In order to have efficient markets in a capitalist society one must provide an opportunity for people to earn a substantial amount of money through their skills at interpreting what happens in the economy. Market regulators provide this opportunity simply because they believe efficient markets enable the best possible way of forecasting the future and allocating resources within society. But at the same time they offer this opportunity to investors, they try to accomplish an environment with as fierce competition as possible. Competition leads to market efficiency where excessive returns are close to impossible to achieve. Greed at the individual investor level forces him/her to search for more relevant information and it implies that only the best interpreters of the information can stay in the business.

Table 5.1 – Degrees of market efficiency.

Degree		**Criteria**	**Investor strategy**
No market efficiency		Markets are predictable.	Investors can earn money just by following patterns in past prices.
Weak market efficiency		Historical information is incorporated in share prices.	Investors can use public information to earn excessive returns.
Semi-strong market efficiency		Public information is quickly incorporated into share prices.	Investors can use non-public information to earn excessive returns.
Strong market efficiency	Non-material information	Private information is incorporated into share prices.	Investors must use material private information to earn excessive returns.
	Material information	All private information is incorporated into share prices.	Investors cannot systematically earn excessive returns.

In general modern researchers within finance have a solid base in economic theory and thus hold a strong belief in market efficiency and rational behaviour. But perfect market efficiency is an unobtainable goal of market regulators. It is unobtainable not only because there is so much uncertainty and asymmetrically distributed information in society, but also because no trades would occur if investors could not once in a while earn more than others.

Some people tend to think that share prices move even though there is no information provided to the market that day. This is not necessarily true, as it is impossible to determine in which way information affects prices. Information regarding the industry or competitors also affects the share price of a company. Moreover, that it takes a while for information to be understood is rather a proof that financial markets are not perfectly efficient, than a proof that they are inefficient.

Of course actors trading on share markets can never know everything about what is going to happen in the future. Market efficiency is instead a question of how fast and correctly they can interpret new information about the future. If all actors had the same interpretation of new information there would hardly be any trades. Different interpretations of the same information are therefore good for the functioning of the market. If the market was perfectly efficient no market actors could earn an excessive return and hence they would lose the incentive to search for and interpret new information. It is the movements towards and away from the equilibrium price that drive the market. But at the same time this makes capital markets fully reactive to sudden events.

Finally, some people tend to think that it is good to have efficient capital markets and therefore one should take away taxes, liquidity constraints and much of the regulation. This is most likely the wrong way to go. Financial markets need to be monitored and regulated if they are to function well. Those share markets we tend to see as the best functioning ones, are also without doubt the most regulated markets. Regulations are needed to ensure that competition is not set out of place. Without regulations market actors would surely come up with excellent strategies aimed at maximising their own benefits at the expense of others. Too much uncontrolled greed is not compatible with either economic theory or a democratic society.

Key Concepts

- Product market
- Capital market
- Excessive return
- Abnormal return
- Price-takers
- Monopoly
- Monopolistic competition
- Industrial organisation
- Price competition
- Company-specific mean reversion
- Industry-specific mean reversion
- Risk-return paradox
- Efficient market hypothesis
- Arbitrage
- Transaction cost
- Information cost
- Weak form of market efficiency
- Semi-strong form of market efficiency
- Strong form of market efficiency
- Random walk
- Filter rule
- Event study methodology
- Post-earnings announcement drift
- Private information
- Material information
- Non-material information

Key Issues to Discuss

1. Explain how (and why) competition in markets is affected by the following issues:
   a) The number of buyers and sellers in the market.
   b) The homogeneity of products and services traded in the market.
   c) The buyers' and sellers' ability to influence the price of products and services traded.
   d) Market frictions (inefficiencies).
2. Discuss why societies dislike monopolies whereas companies like them.
3. What attitude towards monopolies in product markets do investors hold? Do they like or dislike them? Be careful with your answer!
4. Does Porter's model of industrial structure allow for abnormal returns? Is there a difference between the short and the long-run?
5. Give reasons as to why there might be some possibilities to earn company-specific and industry-specific excessive returns.
6. Explain the main idea behind the risk-return paradox. Why is it a paradox that companies earning a high return have a more stable return over time?
7. Could the risk-return paradox be explained by accounting accruals (discussed in Chapter Two)? In order to answer the question it helps if you discuss what risk is and how it is measured using accounting information.
8. In Chapter Four systematic biases in individuals' decision-making capability were discussed. Could these have an impact on capital market efficiency? Discuss and motivate your answer.
9. Discuss if share price fluctuations can be evidence of capital market inefficiency.
10. Is it reasonable that share markets ever become fully efficient?
11. How do regulators at the Stockholm Stock Exchange try to avoid insider trading? Find information on the Internet (or elsewhere) concerning recent cases of insider trading. What happened?
12. Should capital markets be as liberal and unregulated as possible? Discuss the merits and drawbacks of such markets.

Further Readings:

Ball, R., 1995, "The Theory of Stock Market Efficiency: Accomplishments and Limitations", *Journal of Applied Corporate Finance*, pp. 4–17.

Fama, E. F., 1970, "Efficient Capital Markets: A Review of Theory and Empirical Work", *Journal of Finance*, pp. 383–417.

Fama, E. F., 1991, "Efficient Capital Markets: II", *Journal of Finance*, pp. 1575–1617.

Hamberg, M., 2000, *Risk, Uncertainty & Profitability – An Accounting-Based Study of Industrial Firms' Performance*, Department of Business Studies, Uppsala University.

Chapter 6

The Relationship Between Risk and Return in Financial Markets

This chapter aims at:

- Explaining how management can determine the cost of equity, using risk and return in financial markets.
- Providing an understanding of the merits of portfolio diversification as well as its potential pitfalls.
- Illustrating how to use asset-pricing models and discussing their ability to explain security returns.
- Introducing the concept of behavioural finance and thereby explaining some of the 'anomalies' found within empirical capital market research.

6.1 Security Pricing

6.1.1 Defining risk and return in a financial market

This chapter explains how investors price securities traded in financial markets. Its particular focus is on the share market. There are many books concerning the issue of security pricing and this chapter only provides a brief introduction to the topic. From a management perspective it is nonetheless important to understand how investors determine the cost of equity. Management might not explicitly be affected by the investors' activities on a day-by-day basis but, at least according to economic theory, they ought to know and use the appropriate capital costs when evaluating investment projects. To understand the demands shareholders place on management, it is necessary for them to understand how shareholders price securities.

All investors have one thing on their mind: to earn returns. By making investments they forego consumption and they need compensation for this. Obviously they hope that the return will be as high as possible, but it needs to be at least as high as the returns from alternative investments with the same risk. A *security return* is defined as the periodic change in asset value.[1] We distinguish between *realised, ex post, returns*, and *expected, ex ante, returns*. The returns that we observe in capital markets are realised returns, i.e., the actual changes in the value of assets. When looking into the future investors have expectations of future returns. In the efficient market these expectations change in respect to the information provided. Changes in expectations are made so that the security value reflects the underlying risk, making the investment's return comparable to other investments with a similar risk structure.

As you probably understand, the key to an appropriate estimate of returns lies in a continuous valuation of the asset the investor holds, or is considering to hold. *Security value* is determined by the investment's future cash flows and intrinsic risk. In the previous chapter on market efficiency as well as in this chapter we are not too concerned about the functioning of this process. We simply assume that there is no better way of finding an 'objectively' set price on a security than to let a bunch of anonymous price-takers eager to earn money, trade on as much information as possible. Financial markets have a semi-strong form of efficiency (Fama, 1970). In Chapter Ten we will however explore the issue in more depth and those

1 In this chapter we use the terms asset and security interchangeably.

particularly interested in the matter are suggested to read that chapter in conjunction with this one. The realised security return is estimated using a straightforward measure, as described in Expression (6.1).

$$R_i = \frac{[Div_1 + (V_1 - V_0)]}{V_0} = \frac{[dps_1 + (v_1 - v_0)]}{v_0} \tag{6.1}$$

where R_i = the asset's return
Div_1 = cash dividends for the period
V_1 = Asset's market value (end-of-period)
V_0 = Asset's market value (beginning-of-period)
dps_1 = dividend-per-share for the period
v_1 = share price (end-of-period)
v_0 = share price (beginning-of-period)

The share price of Electrolux on the 1st of January 1999 was SEK 139.50 and the year-end share price was SEK 214. Dividends for the period were 3.50. The realised return on holding Electrolux shares during 1999 can therefore be calculated as:

$$R_{Elux} = \frac{[3.50 + (214 - 139.50)]}{139.50} = \frac{78}{139.50} = 55.9\ \%$$

In the long run, the asset's return should be equal to the investor's required rate of return on that asset. In the short term, there are a number of other factors influencing the return for a single asset during a single period. The actual return reflects changes in realised future cash flows as well as changes in expectations regarding non-realised future cash flows. The semi-strong form of market efficiency ensures that all relevant information is quickly incorporated into the share price. But as new information is constantly entering the market, the change in share price takes both new information regarding cash flows and risk into consideration. It is therefore not likely that investors expect the long-run annual return for a company with the same risk as Electrolux to be 55.9 percent.

The return defined in the example above is only a one-period realised, *ex post*, return. But when the investor makes an investment he/she does not know with certainty what the return is going to be, but he/she has formed an expectation of the future. This is what we refer to as the expected return: $E(R_i)$, which is illustrated in Expression (6.2).[2]

2 Similarly, the realised return in Expression 6.1 can be re-written as expected returns: $[E(Div_1) + E(V_1) - V_0]/V_0$

$$E(R_i) = \sum_{j=1}^{n} (R_j \times \alpha_j) \tag{6.2}$$

where R_j = the return for situation j
α_j = the probability of situation j

Below follows an example using two investments (A and B) for which there are three possible future scenarios, each providing a particular return, and each having a particular probability. As you probably realise, very few situations in real life involve only three alternative scenarios, and even fewer situations involve objectively known probability distributions. Nevertheless, these two investment alternatives show how we can derive expected returns from investments mathematically. In this case both investments are expected to earn a return of ten percent.

Investment A:
$E(R_A) = [(8\,\% \times 0.25) + (10\,\% \times 0.50) + (12\,\% \times 0.25)] = 10\,\%$
Investment B:
$E(R_B) = [(2\,\% \times 0.25) + (10\,\% \times 0.50) + (18\,\% \times 0.25)] = 10\,\%$

In reality one would have to develop the probability function expressed in Expression (6.2) into a continuous format. Figure 6.1 illustrates such a format, and we are now basically back to the discussion in Chapter Four. To believe that individual investors can estimate the returns and probabilities for all future scenarios is naive. But as we aggregate more and more views of the future and finally end up with the value contributed to an investment through all actors in efficient markets we are as close as we can get. We have then ended up with market-based economic uncertainty, as described in Chapter Four.

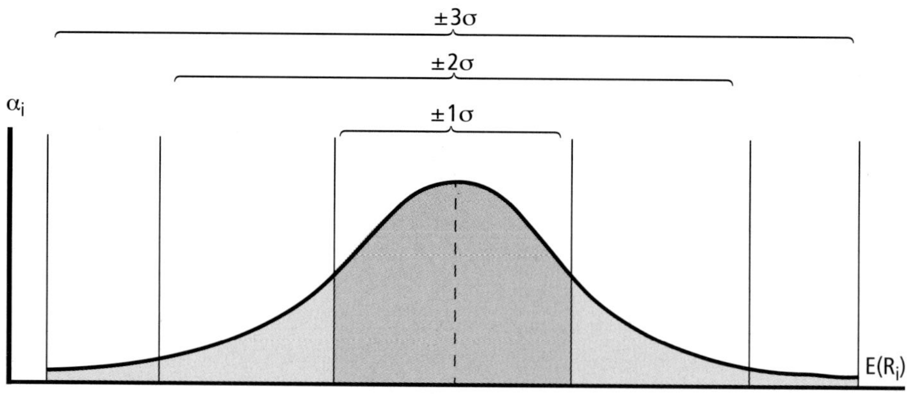

Figure 6.1 – Continuous probability distribution for a security return.

Given that the financial market quickly incorporates all value-relevant information, the risk of an asset can be measured as its historical, *ex post*, volatility. This volatility then represents the probability that the future realised return will deviate from the expected return. The most common statistical indicator of risk is the *standard deviation* of expected return, $\sigma(R_i)$, which measures the dispersion around the expected value. We illustrate this in Expression (6.3).

$$\sigma(R_j) = \sqrt{\sum_{j=1}^{n} [R_j - E(R_j)] \times \alpha_j} \tag{6.3}$$

Although we will soon be more specific in our definitions of risk, one can still say that in general the higher the standard deviation, the greater the risk. Between risk and (expected) return there is a positive relationship, the higher the past variation in security value, the higher expectations investors have on its future return. Let us now calculate the standard deviation for Investments A and B mentioned above.

$$\sigma(R_A) =$$

$$\sqrt{[(8\% - 10\%)^2 \times 0.25] + [(10\% - 10\%)^2 \times 0.50] + [(12\% - 10\%)^2 \times 0.25]}$$
$$= 1.41\ \%$$

$$\sigma(R_B) =$$

$$\sqrt{[(2\% - 10\%)^2 \times 0.25] + [(10\% - 10\%)^2 \times 0.50] + [(18\% - 10\%)^2 \times 0.25]}$$
$$= 5.66\ \%$$

It is sometimes preferable to measure the asset's dispersion as a *variance*, $Var(R_i)$, which is the squared standard deviation. Because of the close mathematical connection between standard deviation and variance it is understandable that the higher an asset's variance is, the greater is its risk.

$$Var(R_j) = \sigma(R_j) = \sum_{j=1}^{n} [R_j - E(R_j)]^2 \times \alpha_j \tag{6.4}$$

We can see that although Investments A and B provide the same level of expected return, the variance in return differs between them. Obviously an investor averse to risk would rather choose the more secure return of 10 % (Investment A) than the more insecure return of 10 % (Investment B). When risk is measured as variance, a person with a *risk aversion* will always choose the investment with the lowest variance. An investor who is indifferent between two investments having equal return but different variances is said to be *risk neutral.* Finally, a *risk-taking* person would prefer the investment with higher variance, when choosing between two investments with equal pay-off. As we learned in Chapter Four most individuals are assumed to be averse to risk and they would hence prefer Investment A.

It is worth mentioning a few words about the assumptions behind the definition of risk as a probability distribution. A normal probability distribution always resemble a "bell-shaped" curve (as in Figure 6.1). On both sides of the mean the curve's extensions are mirror images of each other. In this sense the distribution is symmetrical. In a normally distributed probability function, as mentioned in Chapter Four, approximately 68 % of the outcomes will lie between ±1 standard deviation from the expected value, approximately 95 % of the outcomes will lie between ± 2 standard deviations from the expected value, and almost all observations will lie between ± 3 standard deviations from the expected value. This normal distribution has the advantage of being describable using only the mean and the variance, and in security analyses it is often referred to as a *mean-variance analysis*. A mean-variance analysis of risk works as long as; (1) security returns are normally distributed and (2) investors are risk-averse and hence choose between investments on the basis of return (mean) and risk (variance). In such cases one can describe, and use, the important interactions between securities and observe how they perform together. Now let's introduce two more statistical measures used to understand the interaction between securities: covariance and correlation.

Covariance is a statistical measure used to express the tendency of two random variables to move together. If they move in the same direction they have a positive covariance and if they move in opposite directions they have a negative covariance. The size of the covariance is dependent on the size (and magnitude) of the studied variables, and thus it is necessary to scale the covariance. This is done by converting it into a *correlation coefficient* (ρ), which value lies between – 1 and 1.

$$\mathrm{Cov}(R_i R_j) = \sum_{j=1}^{n} \{[R_i - E(R_i)] \times [R_j - E(R_j)]\} \times \alpha_j \tag{6.5}$$

$$\rho_{ij} = \frac{\mathrm{Cov}(R_i, R_j)}{\sigma_i \sigma_j} \tag{6.6}$$

The concepts covered above form the statistical foundation for the coming portfolio analysis of security pricing. Covariance and correlation are two extremely important concepts in modern security analysis. To understand the differences between correlation coefficients take a look at Figures 6.2. In the first figure, two series of numbers have a correlation of one, meaning that they move perfectly in tandem. In the second figure, the two series of numbers have a correlation coefficient of zero, meaning that their movements are random in relation to each other. Finally in the third figure, the two series have a correlation of minus one, meaning that they move perfectly in tandem – but in opposite directions.

a) Perfect positive correlation ($\rho = -1$)

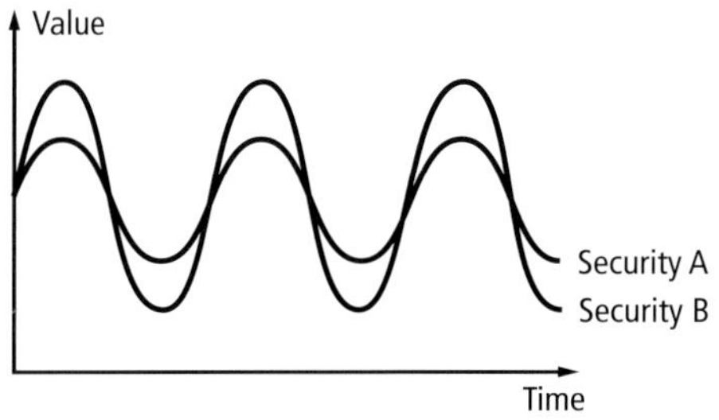

b) No correlation ($\rho = 0$)

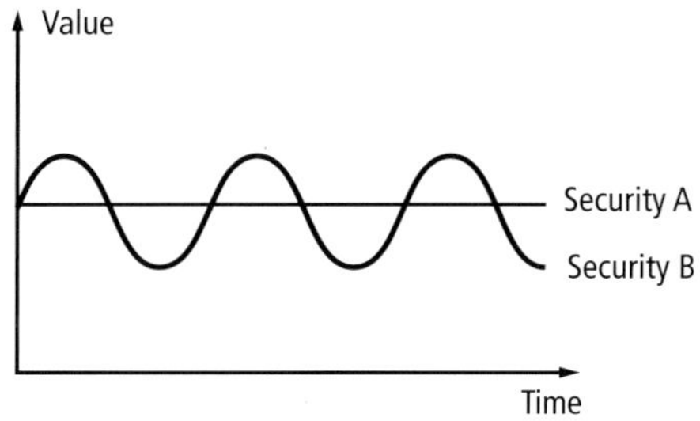

c) Perfect negative correlation ($\rho = -1$)

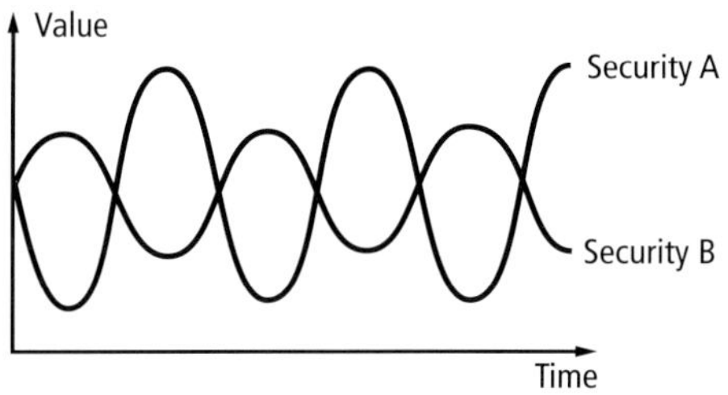

Figure 6.2 – Correlations between securities.

By assuming efficient markets and rational behaviour, we can pursue our mean-variance analysis and investigate how securities interact. As we will soon discover, there is much more to return and risk than just the mean and variance of individual securities. The correlation between securities greatly affects the overall risk.

6.1.2 Portfolio risk and return

In 1952 Harry Markowitz was 25 years old. At this age he published an article in the Journal of Finance which did not just stand in sharp contrast to previous mainstream finance research, but which also, in time, revolutionised the way academicians view the activities taking place in financial markets. In just 13 pages he was able to prove statistically that by focusing on *combinations* of securities instead of *individual* securities, investors can achieve a more efficient combination of risk and return. Suddenly researchers and practitioners started to observe the correlation between securities, and, as we will soon see, they went on to develop asset-pricing models based on the same technique. We will, however, start from the very beginning.

Portfolio return is a weighted average of the returns on the individual assets of which the portfolio is formed. Let's say we are investors who consider only two shares, denoted a and b. Let w_a be the proportion of the portfolio we assign to share a, and let w_b, where $w_b = (1 - w_a)$, be the proportion of the portfolio we assign to share b. The expected return on this portfolio is described in Expression (6.7).

$$E(R_p) = w_a \cdot E(R_a) + w_b \cdot E(R_b) \tag{6.7}$$

Of course this weighted average calculation is the same regardless of the amount of assets included in the portfolio. What Markowitz observed, however, was that the same linearity feature does not exist for portfolio variance. By adding more securities to the portfolio, risk (measured as variance) is reduced without causing any impact on portfolio return. Let us examine this more closely.

The variance of a portfolio's return is defined as:

$$Var(R_p) = E[R_p - E(R_p)]^2 \tag{6.8}$$

For a two-asset portfolio, like the one described above, this can be broken down into:

$$\begin{aligned} Var(R_p) &= w_a^2 \cdot Var(R_a) + w_b^2 \cdot Var(R_b) + \\ &+ 2 \cdot w_a \cdot w_b \cdot E\{[R_a - E(R_a)] \cdot [R_b - E(R_b)]\} \end{aligned} \tag{6.9}$$

The last part of Expression (6.9) is the same as Expression (6.5).

$$Cov(R_a R_b) = E\{[R_a - E(R_a)] \cdot [R_b - E(R_b)]\} \tag{6.5}$$

Hence Expression (6.9) can be written as:

$$\mathrm{Var}(R_p) = w_a^2 \cdot \mathrm{Var}(R_a) + w_b^2 \cdot \mathrm{Var}(R_b) + 2 \cdot w_a \cdot w_b \cdot \mathrm{Cov}(R_a R_b) \tag{6.10}$$

At the same time we can re-write Expression (6.6) as:

$$\rho_{ij} = \frac{\mathrm{Cov}(R_i, R_j)}{\sigma_i \cdot \sigma_j} \Rightarrow \mathrm{Cov}(R_i, R_j) = \rho_{ij} \cdot \sigma_i \cdot \sigma_j \tag{6.11}$$

By inserting Expression (6.11) into Expression (6.10), we obtain Expression (6.12):

$$\mathrm{Var}(R_p) = w_a^2 \cdot \mathrm{Var}(R_a) + w_b^2 \cdot \mathrm{Var}(R_b) + 2 \cdot w_a \cdot w_b \cdot \rho_{ab} \cdot \sigma_a \cdot \sigma_b \tag{6.12}$$

The essence of portfolio diversification does not become clear until Expression (6.12) is generalised to portfolios with many more assets. As more assets are included more covariance terms must be accounted for and hence the equation becomes more complex. The number of covariance terms increases exponentially. If we are to analyse a market consisting of 100 securities, we will have 100 standard deviations and 4950 covariance terms to consider. However, as we do this, we see that the contribution from individual assets' variance to total portfolio variance decreases rapidly.

Let's start with a two-asset portfolio (share a and b) and assume that $w_a = w_b = 0.50$, i.e., that the two shares are equally weighted. In this case the variance of the portfolio includes just 25 % of a's variance: $w_a^2 \cdot \mathrm{Var}(R_a) = (0.5)^2 \cdot \mathrm{Var}(R_a) = 0.25 \cdot \mathrm{Var}(R_a)$, and an equal amount of b's variance. But this portfolio contains only two shares. If we extend the portfolio so that it includes ten shares of equal weight ($w_a = w_b = \ldots = w_n = 0.10$) then it contains only 1 % of a's variance: $w_a^2 \cdot \mathrm{Var}(R_a) = (0.1)^2 \cdot \mathrm{Var}(R_a) = 0.01 \cdot \mathrm{Var}(R_a)$. The variance of the portfolio becomes more and more dependent on the correlation between individual assets. If there is no systematic bias in the distribution of returns in the chosen portfolio we will be able to reduce the contribution of individual assets to portfolio variance to almost nothing by including 15–20 (uncorrelated) shares.

When investors make use of *portfolio diversification* they have little interest in the variance of the individual security, as it contributes virtually nothing to portfolio variance. Instead they become interested in the individual security's covariance with all other securities included in the portfolio. It is the selected combination that generates total risk.

We have approached the path-breaking idea of portfolio theory from a rather statistical perspective but let's put this reasoning into a more practical framework. Investors holding portfolios of assets are only interested in the covariance between an individual asset and the market return. But what does this covariance represent? Think of any quoted company that you know of. Then assume that it is traded on a reasonably efficient share market, which means that all relevant information about this company is quickly and accurately incorporated into its share price. Then think of what events can change the value of the company. Information about a new patent the market previously did not know of will perhaps change its value. A change in the Swedish interest rate is likely to change its value. Perhaps even inflation figures from the US can have an effect on the share price of the company you are thinking of. Some events are more or less unique for the individual company (although it sometimes has an effect on its competitors), other events are similar for companies in an industry, a national economy, or even the world economy. Then think of a second company. Is this second company affected by exactly the same factors in exactly the same way?

By including more companies in a portfolio the portfolio will be exposed to more and more factors. The investor will, for example, hold some securities which are insensitive to Swedish consumption figures, and some which are extremely sensitive to them. She might hold securities that are inversely affected by some news (good news for one company might be bad news for its competitor). The efficient market drives security prices up and down depending on good and bad unanticipated news affecting company value. But with more securities in the portfolio the investor will have a more stable return, simply because no two securities can ever react exactly the same to all information. By studying the historical covariance between securities we get an idea whether or not the securities are likely to react to the same information. Figure 6.3 shows how the average volatility of a portfolio is reduced when additional securities are included. The reduction in volatility depends on the lack of perfect correlation between an individual security and all other securities in the portfolio.

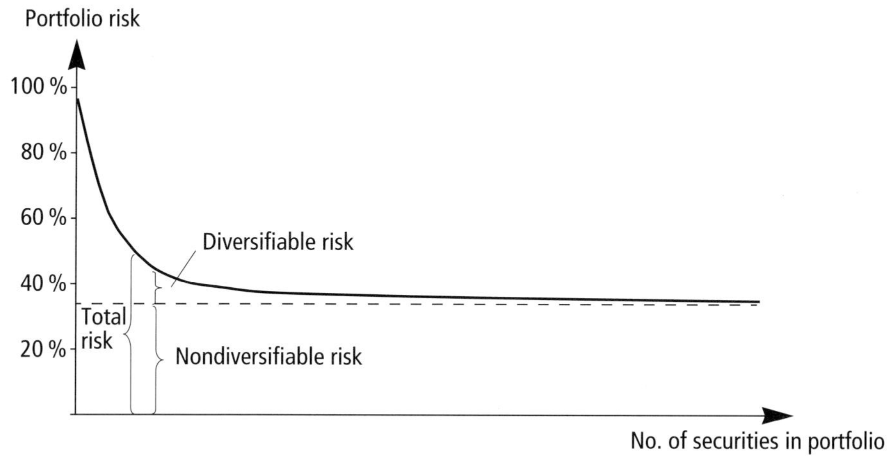

Figure 6.3 – The effect of adding more securities to a portfolio.

To sum this up we can say that there are some factors which will systematically affect securities, and other factors which will unsystematically affect them. That part of the volatility which does not go away when the investor adds more securities to his/her portfolio (diversifies) is referred to as *nondiversifiable risk* (or *market risk* or *systematic risk*), i.e., covariance with the market portfolio. The other part (that disappears with diversification) is the *diversifiable risk* (or *unique risk* or *unsystematic risk*). We say that:

Total risk = Diversifiable risk + Nondiversifiable risk

The section on the Arbitrage Pricing Theory contains a further discussion on different systematic components of risk.

Problems associated with portfolio diversification

The main problem with portfolio theory is that it is so dependent on *uncorrelated* security returns, and the existence of correlated returns has a vast impact on the efficiency of portfolio diversification. Let's illustrate the impact with an example taken from Markowitz (1959). If we assume that all securities have the same variance V_s and that all pairs of securities have the same correlation coefficient ρ. Then the average covariance would be $\rho \cdot V_S$. Portfolio variance would approach $\rho \cdot V_S$, and because of this portfolio standard deviation quickly approaches $\sqrt{\rho} \cdot \sigma_s$. If we compare three hypothetical two-asset portfolios where Portfolio A has no correlation, Portfolio B has a correlation of 0.10, and Portfolio C has a correlation of 0.30 between the individual securities, we find significant differences between the efficiency of portfolio diversification. As the number of securities included in the portfolios increase, Portfolio A will soon have a zero standard deviation, whereas Portfolio B would approach 32 % of average standard deviation ($\sqrt{0.10}$), and Portfolio C would approach 55 % of average standard deviation ($\sqrt{0.30}$). Obviously there is a difference in the efficiency of portfolio diversification, which is dependent on the covariance of the included securities. Higher covariance between securities means fewer benefits from diversification for individual investors.

Research studies clearly show that equity markets around the world are becoming more and more integrated. Multinational corporations are basically portfolios of investments in all major economies. Capital flows freely between capital markets and investors evaluate companies more and more on a global basis. The correlation between securities seems to be particularly high in bear markets[3] with high volatility (Lin, Engle and Ito, 1994; Longin and Solnik, 1995). The increased globalisation of equity markets has come together with an increasing covariance between financial markets. When investors diversify their portfolios and when companies engage in more and more global activities (direct foreign investments) this does not mean the general uncertainty in the world decreases. But the effect might be (still not empirically proven) that markets contain a larger and larger portion of the nondiversifiable risk component.

6.1.3 The efficient frontier

If we assume an efficient market and the existence of investors who want to have as high a return as possible given the volatility of the combination of assets they hold, then we can create a *minimum variance portfolio*. We call this an efficient portfolio, as it provides investors with the best achievable combination of risk (volatility) and return.

If we think of modern equity markets, they consist of a great number of assets and the possible combinations of these assets are almost endless. But of course there is only a small subset of these asset combinations (portfolios) that are efficient. One can find this combination for each portfolio return by combining those assets that together have the lowest possible variance. Figure 6.4 represents all possible asset combinations in a graph where expected portfolio return (y-axis) is combined with the standard deviation of the portfolio (x-axis). The shaded area represents all possible

3 This is the Anglo-Saxon term for a market with decreasing share prices, as opposed to a bull market, which is a market with increasing share prices.

combinations of assets. A rational investor would according to portfolio theory only choose an asset combination which lies on the *efficient frontier*, in other words, a portfolio where you get the highest possible return given the variance of the portfolio.

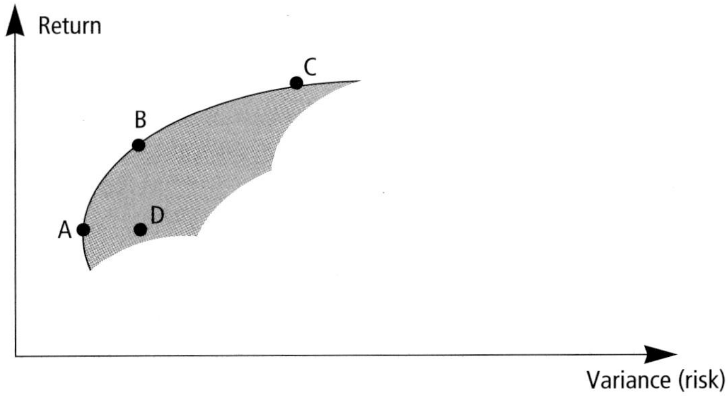

Figure 6.4 – The efficient frontier.

In a mean-variance analysis, the asset combinations marked with an A, B and C in Figure 6.4 are much better than D. Instead of choosing portfolio D an investor can choose portfolio A, which provides an equal return but with lower risk, or alternatively portfolio B that provides a higher return with equal risk. The choice between efficient portfolios is determined by the investor's preferences for risk.

Although Markowitz's contribution ended here with the establishment of the efficient frontier, we continue somewhat further. According to Markowitz, investors should choose a portfolio of investments that is on the frontier. But assume that you also have the opportunity to invest in a risk-free security (no-variance alternative), offering a certain return. Such a situation changes the set of opportunities for the investor. The risk-free alternative is included in Figure 6.5. The line from R_f to B we refer to as the *capital market line* and it illustrates the possible combinations of the risk-free security and the most efficient risky security (or portfolio of risky securities).[4] Investors are able to earn a higher return, given the level of risk (volatility) on this line than is attainable on the frontier alone (in other words, in just the risky asset portfolio).

4 The most efficient portfolio of risky assets is dependent on the preferences of the individual investor. It is sometimes referred to as the tangency portfolio, i.e., the point on the efficient frontier where the capital market line touches the efficient frontier.

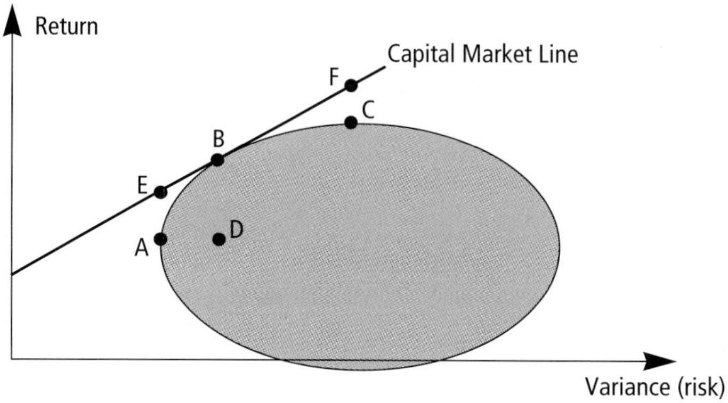

Figure 6.5 – The capital market line.

With only the risky portfolio investors had the opportunity of investing in the asset combinations of A, B, and C. But just as portfolio D was inefficient in Markowitz's example, portfolio A and C are inefficient here. Instead of investing in portfolio A an investor can choose portfolio E, and instead of portfolio C an investor can choose portfolio F. Tobin (1958) is the person who extended the thoughts of Markowitz (1952). He showed that if you have efficient markets and investors can obtain a risk-free security the optimal decision is to invest in a combination of the tangency portfolio (B) and the risk-free security. The tangency portfolio contains the best possible diversification opportunity. It is the asset combination with the lowest variance.

Investors should choose their combination of the risky-asset portfolio and the risk-free asset on the basis of their personal risk preferences. If they want less risk than portfolio B offers, they should include some long term government bonds in the portfolio. If investors want more risk, they should borrow money on the shares in their portfolio and leverage their position. By introducing a risk-free asset to the system investors no longer have to just choose an optimal combination of securities. The Capital Market Line denores all efficient investment combinations the investor can choose among.

6.2 The Capital Asset Pricing Model (CAPM)

6.2.1 Portfolio risk

The first versions of the CAPM were provided by Sharpe (1964), Lintner (1965), and Mossin (1966). Their work was built on portfolio theory developed by Markowitz (1952, 1959) and the extension made by Tobin (1958). The reason for its success is that it provides both researchers and practitioners with a model that generates testable predictions about the risk and return characteristics of individual assets by specifying how they co-vary with the market portfolio of all risky assets.

Investment decisions are solely based on the asset's risk and expected return, and these two concepts are measurable in the financial market. An asset's risk is determined by how the asset impacts on the variability of returns of a well-diversified portfolio if an investor chooses to purchase the asset for inclusion in his or her portfolio. As shown in the previous section the unique (unsystematic) risk can be diversified away and thus the investor is left with the market (systematic) risk. This leads us to the definition of (portfolio) risk according to CAPM. Risk is defined as an asset's *beta* (β):

$$\beta_i = \frac{Cov(R_i, R_m)}{\sigma^2(R_m)} \tag{6.13}$$

where the covariance between the return of an individual asset (R_i) and the market return (R_m) is scaled by the variance of the market return.[5] The beta therefore has a value that is distributed around 1. An asset that has a beta-value of –1 has a perfect negative correlation with the market portfolio. When the whole market goes down, this share goes up, and vice versa. An asset that has a beta-value of 0 has no association with the movements of the market portfolio. An asset with a beta-value of 1 moves perfectly with the market portfolio. An asset that has a beta-value higher than 1 moves with the market, but with a greater magnitude. Given risk aversion it would be beneficial for investors to find securities with negative betas, however empirical research show that such securities are extremely rare. Most securities have a beta-value between 0.7 and 1.3, i.e., they move more or less with the market.

The beta-value is a straightforward measure of the degree of co-movement between an asset's return and the return on the market portfolio. Given the assumption that all assets are correctly priced, investors will only be willing to purchase assets with systematic risks if these investments offer a corresponding return. Investors expect investments with a high systematic risk to be associated with high systematic returns, but they can accept

5 By assuming that investors have homogeneous expectations, the market portfolio becomes the tangency portfolio.

investments yielding low returns as they have a lower systematic risk and hence reduce the risk of the portfolio. It all comes down to the investor's preferences and thus their risk aversion.

But we are now only halfway to the Capital Asset Pricing Model. Investors do not have to invest in the market portfolio, but they also have the alternative of investing in a risk-free asset. We now let point B in Figure 6.5 refer to the market portfolio (where all assets are held according to their market weight), which then has the most optimal mean-variance combination. Rational risk-averse investors choose between holding this optimal risky portfolio and the risk-free asset. Their choice depends on their risk preference. As shown in Figure 6.3, most unique (unsystematic) risk disappears already when 15–20 *uncorrelated* securities are included in the portfolio. For a large diversified investor the *Capital Asset Pricing Model* can represent the expected return of an individual security:

$$E(R_i) = R_f + \beta_i[E(R_m) - R_f] \tag{6.14}$$

In this model, $[E(R_m) - R_f]$ is the *market risk premium*, and β_i is the systematic risk for the individual security. An investor can therefore compose his/her own portfolio of securities (instead of buying the market portfolio). The beta-value for an individual portfolio is determined as:

$$\beta_{port} = w_a \cdot \beta_a + w_b \cdot \beta_b + \ldots + w_n \cdot \beta_n \tag{6.15}$$

The expected return of their portfolio $E(R_{port})$, is equal to the risk-free return plus the portfolio risk multiplied by the market risk premium. Alternatively, we can write the risk-premium of a portfolio as:

$$E(R_{port}) - R_f = \beta_{port}[E(R_m) - R_f] \tag{6.16}$$

6.2.2 Estimating the components of CAPM

You probably feel this has been an easy journey so far. Well, we now need to find estimates of the components we use in the capital asset pricing model. We need an estimate of (1) beta, (2) the risk-free return and (3) the expected return on the market portfolio. In reality none of these theoretical components are easy to find and measure.

Beta

To estimate the beta-value (β_i) of a stock is a pretty straightforward procedure.[6] Beta is calculated using historical data during a determined estimation period. Often researchers and practitioners choose monthly observation from 3 to 5 years (equalling 36 to 60 observations). In the following example we use 12 (fictitious) monthly observations for the returns of a share (A) and the market portfolio (MP). Security return is defined as in Expression (6.1).

Table 6.1 – The calculation of security beta.

Observation	Share A	Market Portfolio	Deviation, share A	Deviation, MP	Deviation for both A and MP
1	3 %	−1 %	−0.92 %	−2.92 %	0.00027
2	7 %	3 %	3.08 %	1.08 %	0.00033
3	15 %	4 %	11.08 %	2.08 %	0.00231
4	12 %	6 %	8.08 %	4.08 %	0.00330
5	−2 %	0 %	−5.92 %	−1.92 %	0.00113
6	3 %	7 %	−0.92 %	5.08 %	−0.00047
7	−4 %	−2 %	−7.92 %	−3.92 %	0.00310
8	9 %	8 %	5.08 %	6.08 %	0.00309
9	2 %	−2 %	−1.92 %	−3.92 %	0.00075
10	5 %	0 %	1.08 %	−1.92 %	−0.00021
11	4 %	3 %	0.08 %	1.08 %	0.00009
12	−7 %	−3 %	−10.92 %	−4.92 %	0.00537
Average	3.92 %	1.92 %			
Variance/covariance			0.0041	0.0014	0.0017
Standard deviation			0.0637	0.0378	
Correlation					0.72
Beta-value					1.21

Alternatively, we can describe the determination of beta using a *time-series regression model.*[7] The ratio of covariance-to-variance (β) is a slope coefficient that can be easily obtained from a linear regression. Expression

6 The beta-values of Swedish quoted companies can frequently be found in newspapers and business magazines, such as e.g. Affärsvärlden.

7 A time-series regression is a statistical analysis where each observation corresponds to a date in time. For security analyses one uses for example the return of Volvo in February 1997. A much more thorough description of time-series regression models can be found in e.g. Gujarati (1995).

(6.17) illustrates such a regression for which R_{jt} is the return in month t for security j, α_j is the regression's intercept, β_j is the regression's slope coefficient, R_{mt} is the return in month t for the stock market index, and finally ε_{jt} is the regression error in month t for security j.

$$R_{jt} = \alpha_j + \beta_j \cdot R_{mt} + \varepsilon_{jt} \tag{6.17}$$

The regression's slope coefficient is the covariance-to-variance ratio and hence also the security's beta-value. We can illustrate the line of best fit among the observations from Table 6.1 as in Figure 6.6.

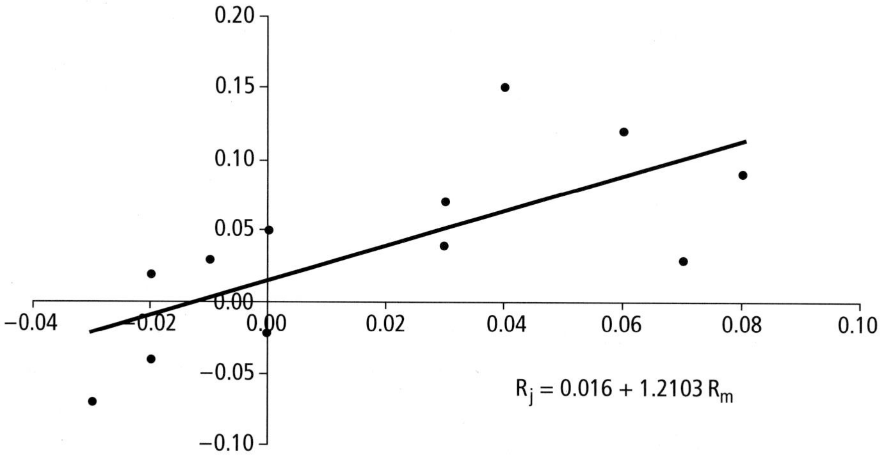

Figure 6.6 – Estimating the beta-value using regression analysis.

Empirical problems associated with the beta-value relate to its explanatory power and whether β is inter-temporally stable, i.e., if beta in the past represent beta in the future. Beta-values are relatively easy to estimate but much empirical research shows that these measures are not very stable over time.

Risk-free return

A *risk-free return* (R_f) is a return where the holder of the asset is certain that the expected return is the same as the actual return. There can thus be no default risk, which essentially rules out any security issued by a private company. The only securities that might have a chance being called "risk-free" are government securities (not because they are better run than companies but because governments print the currency[8]). Moreover, there can

8 Note that we talk about return in nominal terms and without the impact of exchange rates.

be no *reinvestment risk*, which means that you have to be able to match the length of your exposure with the expiration date of the risk-free security. If your time-perspective is three years and you acquire treasury bills expiring in six months, these have to be reinvested at rates that cannot be predicted with certainty today. For long term (and infinite) investments a ten-year government bond can approximate for the risk-free interest rate. But if the length of the exposure is certain one should choose the government issued security that matches this length of time the best.

Identifying the market portfolio

The market portfolio should consist of all risky securities available to investors. For the CAPM to function appropriately one has to identify all of these securities and determine their weights in the market portfolio. This is, of course, not possible, and the market portfolio identified and used can, therefore, only serve as a proxy for the true market portfolio. When beta is estimated in e.g. Affärsvärlden, the 'generalindex' serves as the proxy for the true market portfolio.

Expected return on the market portfolio

A relatively high market risk premium causes a lower valuation of the security.[9] If the market premium changes, so does the value of all companies. Several American studies within this field document the difficulty of determining the expected return on the market portfolio ($E(R_m)$). It has been found to vary as much as between three and eight percent (Claus and Thomas, 2000). The expected market return is usually estimated using historical returns (although researchers increasingly start to work with the implied cost of capital derived using, for example, accounting information[10]). As shown by Damodaran (2000) the standard error of any risk premium estimate is so high it is almost useless to use less than twenty years of observations to estimate the return.

The average return on the Stockholm Stock Exchange since 1950 has been approximately 13 percent and at the same time the standard deviation has been 21 percentage points. This gives us a standard error of approximately 3 percentage points.[11] Currently the ten-year government bond is

9 This is explained in detail in Chapters Nine and Ten.

10 See e.g. Gebhardt, Lee and Swaminathan (1999).

11 As Damodaran (2000) argues this standard error is probably understated because it is based on the assumption that returns are uncorrelated over time. There is substantial empirical evidence that stock returns are inter-temporally correlated, which would make the standard error much larger.

approximately 5.3 percent, which would give us a risk premium of 7.7 percent.[12] In a recent Swedish study actors at the SSE were asked which risk premium they used in their daily financial decision-making (Klevby and Liljeberg-Svensson, 1999). It turned out this risk-premium is much lower than 7.7 percent. On average the 15 interviewed actors used a risk-premium of 3.95 percent. A guess is that the risk premium is approximately five to six percent, considerably lower than the average security returns of the last seven years.[13]

6.2.3 Methodological issues

The original version of the CAPM is relatively easy to understand, but in order for it to function empirically a number of assumptions have to be made. As a reader of this book you are merely introduced to the existing problems. Many of them still are being debated and giving them their rightful attention here takes up too much time.

- All investors are single period, risk-averse, utility-of-terminal-wealth maximisers who choose among portfolios solely on the basis of their mean and variance of expected returns. This implies that risk is never viewed in any other way than using a mean-variance approach. Empirical research questions this matter. Also, it has been shown that security returns often fail to follow a normal distribution.
- There are no taxes, transaction costs, or other market imperfections. There are a large number of perfectly divisible assets, all of which are marketable. There are also numerous fully informed buyers and sellers, all of whom are price-takers. In reality, market imperfections are known to exist and they have been elaborated upon by researchers (see for example the after-tax CAPM).
- All investors have homogeneous expectations regarding the probability distribution of security returns. This is one of the most heavily criticised assumptions. Without it, the market portfolio is no longer, necessarily, the most efficient portfolio for all investors and therefore most of the CAPM's foundations fall apart.

---

12 It is clearly possible that there is a survivorship bias included in this premium and therefore the real risk-premium should be lower. This matter has lately been identified and addressed in e.g. Brown, Goetzman and Ross (1995) and Jorion and Goetzman (1999).

13 In an analysis of the Norwegian stock market (Oslo Børs), Gjesdal and Johnsen (1999) conclude that the market premium is likely to be approximately five percent, though it could be even lower than that.

- A risk-free asset exists, and all investors can borrow and lend unlimited amounts at a given, riskless, rate of interest. In reality, there is great doubt whether a risk-free security exists, and whether it is the same for all investors.

The CAPM generates expected returns, but tests of the model must be based on historical (realised) returns. When researchers want to test an *ex ante* model using *ex post* data, they must assume that investors will make unbiased estimates of expected returns, which over time and on average, will equal realised returns. This is called a *rational expectations assumption*. But a problem is that the relationship between realised and expected returns seem to have some systematic variance over time.

The elegance of the theoretical development known as CAPM is offset by the difficulties we have with applying it to the real-world. All empirical tests of the CAPM must be based on approximations of the true market portfolio, which is unobservable. The problems related to this fact were pointed out to the research community in an influential article by Roll (1977). He forcefully argued that the CAPM is untestable, i.e., that no empirical test can really determine whether the CAPM works or not. If this is true, researchers are left in a 'no-man's land' not knowing whether markets are efficient or whether their asset pricing models work. For all securities in a portfolio the securities' expected returns are linearly related to their beta-values (calculated in association with the portfolio). If the CAPM is wrong, the empirical test can support it, as a misspecified market proxy still can be mean-variance efficient. Another plausible outcome of the empirical test is that the theory is correct, but as the market proxy is not mean-variance efficient the theory is (wrongly) rejected. As it is difficult to define the true market portfolio, *Roll's critique* is indeed justified. His fellow colleagues have discussed whether there are ways around the problem, or whether it is possible to ignore it. They still do not agree.

6.2.4 Basic empirical tests

The CAPM is a robust theoretical construct that has empirical problems. Over the last thirty years researchers have tried to assess whether security return is determined by portfolio risk or not. In this section one of the techniques used to test the association is exemplified. The model we use, is one where expected returns are modelled using the equity premium in the basic CAPM equation. The expected risk premium of an individual security is then expressed as the expected return minus the risk-free rate (Expression

6.18). Similarly, the expected risk premium of the market portfolio is defined as the expected return minus the risk-free rate (Expression 6.19).

$$E(R_i') = E(R_i) - R_f \qquad (6.18)$$

$$E(R_m') = E(R_m) - R_f \qquad (6.19)$$

The expected risk premium of an individual security equals the market premium multiplied by the beta-value of the individual security. This can be expressed as:

$$E(R_i') = E(R_m') \cdot \beta_i \qquad (6.20)$$

Empirical tests are based on a *cross-sectional regression model*, such as that in Expression (6.21).[14] In other words, the mean excess return over a certain time interval for a set of securities is regressed on estimates of the systematic risk, β_i, of each of the securities.

$$R_i' = \gamma_0 + \gamma_1 \cdot \beta_1 + \varepsilon_i \qquad (6.21)$$

We can then easily specify the results that the CAPM predicts. *First*, the return on a security is linearly and positively related to the security's estimated systematic risk, β_i. From this follows that γ_1 should be positive and significantly different from zero. In fact, γ_1 should be equal to $(R_m - R_f)$. *Second*, the intercept, γ_0, should be significantly different from zero. If it is not, then the risk-free rate is incorrectly set or unstable. *Third*, realised returns should not be related to anything else except beta. When other explanatory variables are entered into the equation they should be insignificant. *Fourth*, the model should be inter-temporally stable, in other words, the beta-value should not change over time.

Research on the CAPM started at the beginning of the 1970s. The early studies offered general support for the CAPM, but there were already some problems then with the results. Black, Jensen and Scholes (1972) used the method described above and found that security returns are positively associated to beta. But they also found that high-beta securities had significantly negative intercepts whereas low-beta securities have significantly positive intercepts. Speaking in practical terms this means that our measure

14 A cross-sectional regression is a statistical analysis where each observation corresponds to a particular object, such as the return of Volvo and the beta-value of Volvo. A more thorough description of cross-sectional regression models can be found in e.g. Gujarati (1995).

of risk, beta, is priced too low and that there is not a perfect linear relationship. Other early studies were marginally positive to the functionality of the CAPM, despite low explanatory factors, or other disturbances.[15]

It is not the intention to go into details regarding all the various tests of the CAPM that have been done over the years. After the critique made by Roll (1977) and all the confusing results coming from tests in the 1980s, two additional contributions are worth mentioning. As it so happens both come from initial contributers to asset pricing theory. Roll (1988) showed that systematic factors account for less than 40 percent of the cross-sectional variation in stock returns. He furthermore shows that this is including a "hindsight bias", which means that the model cannot even explain what has happened (it is even worse when it shall explain what is about to happen). Roll's new critique applies not only to the CAPM, but also to the APT, which is about to be covered. Richard Roll is one of the "founders" of APT, and, if nothing else, this might make his critique extra truthful. The second contribution (source of empirically based critique) comes from Fama and French (1992).[16] Fama and French find that the relationship between return and beta is flat, in other words, beta has no significant explanatory power. What they do find is a negative association between security return and market capitalisation (value), and a positive association between security return and book-to-market value. In a series of articles Fama and French declare beta as more or less dead and they then propose other, empirically-oriented, models instead (e.g. Fama and French, 1992, 1993, 1995, 1996; Davis, Fama and French 2000). There are others who believe CAPM still works. A notable study here was conducted by Kothari, Shanken and Sloan (1995) who criticise the methodology and the data set used by Fama and French. CAPM has been seriously empirically wounded, but until somebody really provides a solid alternative theory it is unlikely that it will be fully abandoned.

15 See for example Fama and MacBeth (1973).

16 Yes, this is the same Eugene Fama who 25 years earlier embraced market efficiency and then acclaimed what he, at the time, thought was valid empirical support for the CAPM.

6.3 Alternative Asset Pricing Models

6.3.1 Arbitrage Pricing Theory (APT)

Parallel to an emerging critique of the CAPM during the 1970s an alternative model named the *Arbitrage Pricing Theory* (APT) made its appearance (Ross, 1976; Roll and Ross, 1980). For our purposes, we differentiate between the two models by concluding that the APT focuses on the interrelationship between security returns, and that these returns are generated by a number of industry- and economy-specific factors. A correlation between securities exists when they are affected by the same factors. In comparison, the CAPM allows correlation between securities, but it never specifies which factors are causing the correlation. The APT tries to do that, and to get the model to function one identifies the factors that systematically influence security returns.

The actual *arbitrage process* from which the theory has earned its name, comes from the fact that investors in a market, where any asset offered a too high or too low return, can earn a (risk-free) arbitrage return only by selling/buying some (correctly valued) assets and buying/selling the incorrectly valued asset. Ross (1976) shows that total value of the assets (the portfolio) an investor holds can have a total value of zero. There is thus no commitment of wealth.

A portfolio consists of securities of various kinds. The purpose of forming the portfolio is to avoid unnecessary variance. This unnecessary variance is due to unsystematic risk, i.e., effects caused by individual securities. Consider an investor who buys a share in an individual company. This investor runs a risk when the company puts a new product on the market. If the product is not well accepted the share price might drop. But if the investor instead invests the same amount of money in all companies within the same industry he/she is less affected by unique happenings such as an individual company's release of a new product. If consumers are dissatisfied with the product they will instead buy from another manufacturer. The investor's portfolio is only sensitive to factors affecting the whole industry, such as e.g. the industry growth rate. However, if the investor invests in all shares, he/she can become insensitive even to these issues. If e.g. new regulations or taxes change people's willingness to buy certain products, they will buy something else. By owning shares in all companies, the investor's portfolio is only affected by market factors which systematically affect all companies. This is the practical implication of portfolio theory and the search for systematic factors is of significant importance for APT.

A systematic risk is a risk that affects all assets to some extent. An example is the interest rate, or the economic growth within a certain area. An unsystematic risk is a risk that only affects a single asset or a limited group of assets. The unsystematic parts of different companies' risk are uncorrelated to each other. But the systematic parts are correlated to each other in various ways and as companies are affected by the same systematic risks, their returns will be related.

With the APT we search for factors that have an effect on security returns and we then estimate quantitatively the impact each factor has on the security return. The model we search for is called a *factor model*, and the systematic sources of risk, labelled F, are referred to as the factors. Expression (6.22) contains an n-factor model where each stock's return is generated by:

$$R_i = E(R_i) + \beta_{i1}F_1 + \beta_{i2}F_2 + \ldots + \beta_{in}F_n + \varepsilon \qquad (6.22)$$

where R_i = the random return on asset i
$E(R_i)$ = the expected return on asset i
F_n = the mean zero j^{th} factor common to all assets under consideration
β_{in} = the sensitivity of asset i's return to movements in the jth factor

We need to specify some assumptions for the APT to hold. *First*, we assume that capital markets are perfectly competitive and frictionless. *Second*, investors have homogeneous expectations about the process generating expected returns. *Third*, we can specify a linear relationship between the factors in the model mentioned above, and expected return of an individual security. *Fourth*, these specified factors are all that matters to security return and therefore the error terms of the individual securities are uncorrelated. A *fifth* assumption is that the number of systematic factors is much smaller than the number of assets.

If these assumptions are met, the model in Expression (6.22) can be converted into an *ex ante* model, where expected returns are expressed as a function of the individual securities' sensitivity to factors, and the risk-premium associated with each factor.

$$E(R_i) = \lambda_0 + \lambda_1 b_{i1} + \lambda_2 b_{i2} + \ldots + \lambda_n b_{in} \qquad (6.23)$$

where λ_n = expected return (risk-premium) on factor n
b_{in} = sensitivity to the return on the ith security to the nth factor

If we now assume that there is a risk-free asset, its return must be equal to λ_0. Why? A risk-free asset is an asset to which all investors will have the same sensitivity. In Expression (6.23) all the factors influencing the return are specified, and hence the return achieved without being influenced by these factors must be a risk-free return.

$$R_f = \lambda_0 \tag{6.24}$$

On the basis of this, we rewrite Expression (6.23) as:

$$E(R_i) - R_f = \lambda_1 b_{i1} + \lambda_2 b_{i2} + \ldots + \lambda_n b_{in} \tag{6.25}$$

So far we have said little about the risk-premium, λ_n. This premium is equal to the difference between (1) the expectation of a portfolio that has a one unit response to the kth factor and zero unit response to all other factors, and (2) the risk-free return, R_f. Here is an example. If one factor affecting stock return is identified as the change in inflation rate, then λ for this factor will be the expected change in stock return when inflation changes by one unit. To clarify the previous let's rewrite Expression (6.25):

$$E(R_i) - R_f = (\delta_1 - R_f)b_1 + (\delta_2 - R_f)b_2 + \ldots + (\delta_n - R_f)b_{in} \tag{6.26}$$

where δ_n = expected return on a portfolio with a one unit sensitivity to the kth factor and zero sensitivity to other factors

R_f = Risk-free return

It is easy to see how the CAPM can be a special case of APT.[17] If we find that there is only one systematic factor affecting share prices; the covariance between the individual share's return and the market return, then:

$$E(R_i) = R_f + (R_m - R_f)b_k \tag{6.27}$$

where b_k is the beta-value according to the Capital Asset Pricing Model. Whereas the CAPM assumes that all risk can be expressed using one measure, the APT identifies all systematic factors and then the importance of each factor is identified for each asset.

The Arbitrage Pricing Theory is much more theoretically robust than the Capital Asset Pricing Model. Therefore researchers often prefer the APT. The problem with the model is that while the CAPM lets investors (implicitly) identify the systematic factors, the APT needs us to empirically

17 This is however not at all always the case. See e.g. Copeland and Weston (1992) for further elaboration.

identify systematic factors affecting share prices. This has to be done empirically using a statistical technique called factor analysis. In so doing, several factors have been identified, but to find inter-temporally stable factors has been difficult. Most empirical studies of the APT are based on macroeconomic factors (see e.g. Chen, Roll and Ross, 1986; Burmeister and McElroy, 1988; Jagannathan and Wang, 1995). Some of the macroeconomic factors identified by researchers are: (1) changes in the level of industrial production in the economy, (2) changes in the shape of the yield curve, (3) changes in the default risk-premium, (4) changes in the inflation rate, (5) changes in the real interest rate, (6) the level of personal consumption, and (7) the level of money supply in the economy. Because of the instability, the theoretical and empirical critique provided by Roll (1977; 1988) is thus applicable also here.

6.3.2 *Other models of risk and return*

The CAPM and the APT are by no means the only two models used in practise to measure the expected return on risky assets. As we discussed before both of these models are risk-based, and they measure the risk of a security by its beta(s) on some systematic factor(s), and they both argue that the expected return must be proportional to the beta(s). There are similar approaches that can be used to price risky assets.

In the section on empirical tests we mentioned that a number of tests suggested that security returns were systematically affected by certain characteristics such as, for example, size, time-period, market-to-book value. Researchers have investigated whether security returns can be explained and forecasted using this information, rather than some theoretically derived systematic factors. One of these *empirically-based asset pricing models*, has been suggested by Fama and French (1996) as a response to their previous finding that CAPM did not work (Fama and French, 1992). In contemporary research it has been common to include company-specific factors in the modelling of security return. Both company size (market value) and market-to-book value have then been included in the asset pricing models in order to assist beta in explaining returns. It is not sure whether such models lacking solid theoretical foundations are going to stand up to tests over time and tests in various capital markets around the world.

6.4 Behavioural Finance

6.4.1 The causes of market inefficiency

Standard capital market theory makes a number of assumptions with regard to the behaviours of individual market actors, as well as the aggregated functioning of capital markets. Violations of these assumptions are possible causes of disruptions in the asset pricing models, and likewise in the efficiency of capital markets. In conjunction with the capital market efficiency debate in Chapter Five there were some indications that capital markets are not always efficient, but that it is possible to come up with investment strategies where security return is not determined by risk (as measured using the CAPM and a portfolio perspective).

In our following analysis we shall differentiate between market-specific and investor-specific factors. The market-specific factors are those which we can contribute to frictions in the financial market. As mentioned in Chapter Five a 'January-effect' has been identified, in which security prices seem to increase comparatively more in the month of January. This finding has been explained by tax-loss redemption before the end of the year. This seasonal effect is particularly strong for small companies. The size of the company is also a market-specific factor. Transaction and information costs are higher for companies with a low market capitalisation. Also, the liquidity of these companies is lower and therefore there might be a liquidity risk premium added to these companies. Although both size and seasonal effects are of considerable importance we shall spend less time on the market-specific factors in the following analysis.

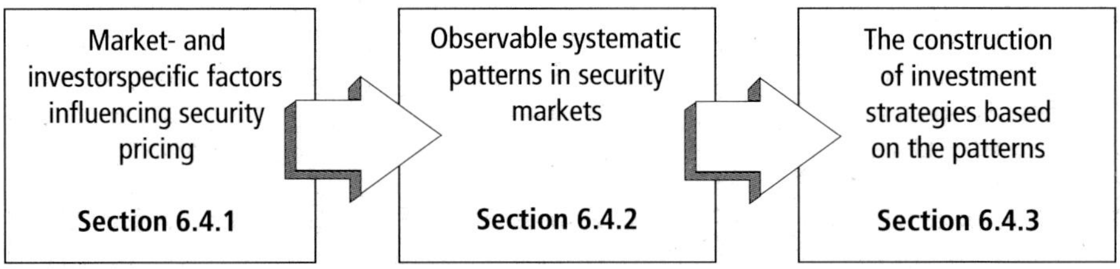

Figure 6.7 – Underlying reasoning in behavioural finance-based investment strategies.

Most of the analysis will focus on investor-specific (behavioural) factors. There is, arguably, no coherent theory of *behavioural finance* (or a behavioural theory of capital markets) as of today. What we have are scattered observations of security mispricing, and at the most, researchers have tried to couple these observations to underlying behavioural factors.[18] In this section we shall only briefly mention the underlying rationale of these factors, as it was discussed in Chapter Four. Capital market theory, as well as all other economic theories, cares little about the actual decision-making process. For a better understanding of the factors that can potentially cause a mispricing of securities it is vital to return to the model described in Chapter Four. Figure 6.8 is therefore similar to Figure 4.4, but shows nonetheless the decision-making process we refer to here.

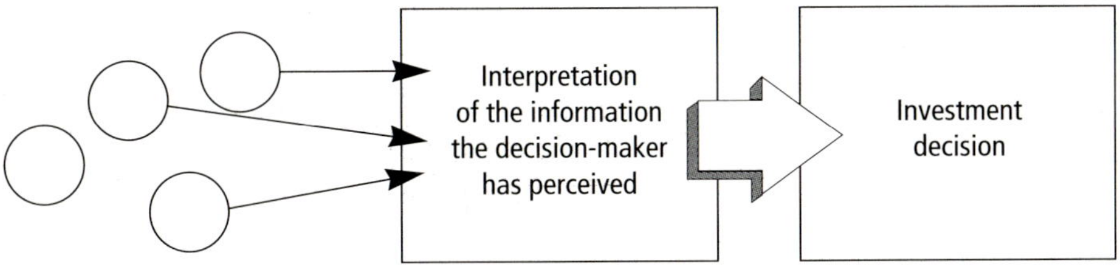

Figure 6.8 – A tentative model of decision-making.

In Chapter Four it was argued that individuals are biased both in their search for information and their evaluation of the information. Naturally this is true also for investors who use the same kind of heuristics when handling them. The *availability of information heuristic* has been given as the reason for the 'home bias' in equity portfolios, i.e., investors in Sweden have a much higher proportion of Swedish securities in their portfolios than they ought to have if they desired to be optimally diversified (Cooper and Kaplanis, 1995). The *imitating heuristic* is obvious as there is plenty of evidence that investor attention shifts from one industry (or company) to another in systematic ways. The *framing heuristic* is exemplified by how market actors desire to frame the policies of central banks. If investors frame an increase in the interest rate as something that increases the discount factor then the reaction is that share prices will go down. On the other hand, if they frame it as something that reduces future inflation and enhances economic stability then the reaction ought to be that share prices will go up. The *representativeness heuristic* is well documented. When judging companies, investors often argue that "... this can be a new Microsoft", or "...this is the same situation as in Framfab in March 2000...". It is likewise possible that investors think that a company performing well is a good company to invest in. They think so because it has been a good in-

18 Unfortunately, a great deal of the research still lacks even the most fundamental explanations as to why the patterns exist and the trading strategies work. All they do is document the potential market inefficiencies.

vestment in the past, but forget that increases in security value only come from *unexpected* future high performance. A surprisingly high performance in the past is not necessarily representative for the unexpected future performance (in fact it is more often unrepresentative). Finally, *overconfidence* among financial analysts is also well documented (Tversky, 1995). To be confident might, however, not just have the effect that investors overestimate their ability to make predictions. It might also mean that they filter out certain information in order to retain their previously made prediction. This particular behaviour has been referred to as *cognitive dissonance* (Daniel and Titman, 1999).

All of these biases in human decision-making can be used when explaining systematic, and thus biased, security price movements. Researchers often argue that combinations of them cause patterns. Now let us turn to some of these patterns that researchers have looked at.

6.4.2 Patterns in security prices

The next step in our analysis is to focus on some of the patterns identified in financial markets. Over the years there has been a great number of studies indicating that security returns are not just determined by portfolio risk.

Excess volatility

Traditional finance tells us that the share price reflects the intrinsic value of a company where all value-relevant information is incorporated. The share price should only change when new value-relevant information reaches the market. In an early study made by Shiller (1981) it was argued that share prices are much more volatile than they ought to be given the information they reflect. Shiller arrived at this conclusion by estimating an ideal dividend-discount share price. He found dividends too stable to explain share price volatility. Although this is a study that has spurred much of the research within the area of behavioural finance, it has substantial shortcomings. First of all, dividends can purposely be set stable (while earnings and cash flows vary), and secondly, Shiller assumed a stable discount rate over time (which is unrealistic). This issue of excess volatility is highly relevant given the large changes in share prices that occur on a daily basis.

Excess volume of trading

Recently it has been argued that financial markets have a higher trading volume than expected (Thaler, 1999). Heterogeneous expectations of the future must play a part here. Every investor can ask himself/herself before engaging in a trade why the other (anonymous) trader does the opposite. If you buy something for 100, the other trader must think it is worth less than 100. In an efficient market investors should only trade when rebalancing their portfolios (adjusting them in relation to risk and return) and for liquidity reasons.

Price under- and overreactions

There is a number of studies indicating that security prices do not follow random walks but that they are both persistent and mean reverting (not at the same time, however). It seems as if there are short term trends during which there is a positive autocorrelation in security returns. After this there is a correction, or a reversion back to the mean. Such patterns violate even the weak form of market efficiency.

Delays in market response to new information

Event studies, which were mentioned in Chapter Five, have frequently been used to investigate how quickly financial markets respond to new information. As mentioned already in Chapter Five, financial markets are reasonably good at incorporating new information into share prices as soon as it is released. But reasonably good is not the same as perfect. Over the last twenty years, many studies have documented various forms of delays in financial markets' response to new information.

6.4.3 Basing trading strategies on systematic market inefficiencies

Can investors base their trading strategies on systematic market efficiencies? In Chapter Five we learned that there are good reasons to believe that investors themselves make temporary inefficiencies disappear by trading on them. Nonetheless researchers have come up with numerous studies indicating that some forms of trading strategies have (in the past at least) been able to earn excessive returns for substantial periods of time. We shall here examine some of the strategies which heavily rely on the behaviours of market actors.[19]

19 As opposed to those dependent on market frictions (such as information costs and transaction costs).

Momentum strategies

Momentum strategies are based on the results of e.g. Lo and MacKinlay (1988) who found that security returns are positively correlated in the short run. This is then a violation of the weak form of market efficiency and a rationale for technical analysis. A momentum strategy capitalises on short term autocorrelations. Jegadeesh and Titman (1993) performed an initial study in the area and found that short periods of 3 to 12 months contained enough autocorrelation for investors to earn excessive returns. A second article by Chan, Jegadeesh and Lakonishok (1996) confirm the results and suggest that they partly relate to the so-called post-earnings announcement drift. International studies verify that excessive returns on momentum strategies are not limited to US stock exchanges (Rouwenhorst, 1998; Schiereck, DeBondt and Weber, 1999). Momentum strategies might be possible because of overconfident investors chasing past trends. Even though momentum strategies are shown to be profitable, trading costs do play an important role in their success. Chasing momentum can generate a much too high turnover. Phenomena such as day-trading are much more common in bull markets than in bear markets. It is likely that momentum strategies are also overly attractive in good times when transaction costs are more easily overlooked.

Contrarian investment strategies

An investor using a *contrarian investment strategy* is going to buy those shares whose price other investors are currently bidding down, while selling those that other investors are currently bidding up. The first of the studies that documented the merits of such a strategy was DeBondt and Thaler (1985). They found that securities that had performed badly in the past do better than average in the future. A trading strategy based on this study would therefore suggest that one identifies past losers, and then acquires and holds them for some period of time. Figure 6.9 shows that portfolios containing previous losers do consistently better than previous winners. It also shows that while this is true it takes up to 18 months until the winners lose value. It takes guts to suggest that one should abandon a previous high performer when it takes more than a year before this strategy, on average, pays off!

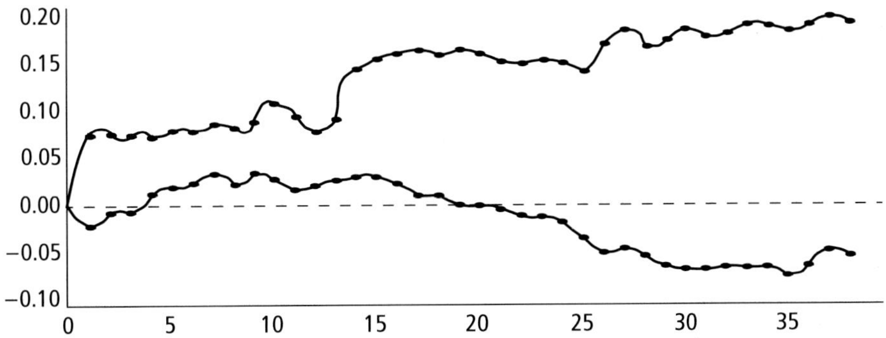

Source: DeBondt and Thaler (1985).

Figure 6.9 – Contrarian investment strategies.

It might seem as if the contrarian investment strategy opposes the momentum strategy. In fact they both capitalise on the same phenomena: Market overreactions and mean reversions. Whereas the momentum strategy relies on short term movements (away and back from the "true" share price), the contrarian investment strategy relies on the long term mean reversion. Market overreactions and mean reversions are two sides of the same coin.

The trading strategy suggested by Debondt and Thaler is a rather passive strategy; it only relies on the securities' past performance. A more active contrarian investment strategy can be achieved by identifying whether securities lately have under- or over-performed in relation to some measure of their fundamental value. One of the more interesting findings over recent years in finance is the seemingly systematic difference between value and glamour stocks. *Value stocks* are those stocks where the price of the company is low in relation to measures of company performance. *Glamour stocks* are those stocks where the price of the company is high in relation to the same measures of company performance. These measures can be e.g. a company's book value, its earnings, or its cash flows (Lakonishok, Shleifer and Vishny, 1994). Several studies have shown that it is possible to earn substantial excessive returns by investing in portfolios formed on the basis of such company-specific variables.

Evidence of the superiority of value stock investment strategies have been found in several national markets, such as Sweden, the US and Britain. Table 6.2 below contains information from the best known study within the area (Lakonishok, Shleifer, and Vishny, 1994). In this particular study American data was collected from between 1968 and 1989 and portfolios were constructed on the basis of companies' book-to-market ratio, cash flow-to-price ratio, earnings-to-price ratio, and historical growth in sales. The return of these portfolios was then estimated for the coming five years. Value portfolios contain the decile of companies having the highest fundamental value in relation to share price, and the glamour portfolio contains the deciles of companies having the lowest fundamental value in relation to share price.

Table 6.2 – Differences in return of value and glamour strategies.

	Stock return					
Single measures:	Glamour strategy		Value strategy		Difference	
	Avg.	Cum.	Avg.	Cum.	Avg.	Cum.
Book-to-market value (B/M)	9,3 %	56 %	19,8 %	146 %	+10,5 %	+90 %
Cash flow-to-price (C/P)	9,1 %	54 %	20,1 %	149 %	+11,0 %	+95 %
Earnings-to-price (E/P)	11,4 %	72 %	19,0 %	139 %	+7,6 %	+67 %
Growth in sales (GS)	12,7 %	82 %	19,5 %	143 %	+6,8 %	+71 %
Combination of measures:						
C/P and GS	11,4 %	71 %	22,1 %	171 %	+10,7 %	+100 %
E/P and GS	10,9 %	67 %	22,1 %	172 %	+11,2 %	+105 %
B/M and GS	13,0 %	84 %	21,2 %	162 %	+8,2 %	+78 %
B/M and E/P	10,0 %	61 %	19,9 %	148 %	+9,9 %	+87 %
B/M and C/P	10,3 %	63 %	20,3 %	152 %	+10,0 %	+89 %

Source: Lakonishok, Shleifer and Vishny, 1994.

The results are amazing! Single measures can be used to earn between 67 and 95 percent higher cumulated returns. A combination of measures seem to be even better, with up to 105 percent higher returns for value strategies as opposed to glamour strategies. Value portfolios are not just outperforming glamour portfolios but they also outperform the market index and their beta-values are lower than those of glamour portfolios. There have been several replications of this study and they all show basically the same thing.[20]

Perhaps you are still wondering what the fuss is all about? After all, it seems likely that some companies are better than other companies. Then you should remember from the section on market efficiency that there should be no other explanatory factor to return than risk, considering all the information which is being processed by market actors. It is clear that some companies perform better than other companies and that leads to higher profit margins and a higher profitability. But investors in the capital market see this and adjust the market value of a company to its prospects.

20 A replication of this study has been carried out on Swedish data with more or less the same kind of significant results (Hagnell, et al., 2000). Their contrarian investment strategy worked in 17 out of 20 years.

Being a value or a glamour company should not matter. It is systematic risk, measured as beta that explains security return. Company-specific factors should not matter. Systematic differences between value and glamour stocks thus cause problems for financial theorists. There are alternative ways of explaining the dilemma caused by these systematic findings. Believers in classical financial theory explain the results by arguing that either the results are evidence of market inefficiencies we are aware of (such as information costs, transaction costs, etc.), or that the results provide empirical support for models in which risk is captured using more complex models involving more than one factor (see Fama and French, 1996).

Size effects

Market capitalisation has an effect in almost all studies. Both in momentum and contrarian investment strategies the excessive returns are much higher in portfolios with small companies than in portfolios with large companies. Size in itself also has an effect on security return (Fama and French, 1992). An explanation is therefore that transaction costs and liquidity constraints help sustain the phenomena. An alternative explanation is that size itself approximates for risk. It could be, for example, a premium paid for dealing with a less liquid stock.

Information delay strategies

Some of the most interesting and influential recent studies employing the event study methodology are by Bernard and Thomas (1989; 1990). Based on a massive empirical database they show among other things that companies reporting high/low quarterly earnings have an abnormally high/low return for a substantial time after the announcement. It is still today not known why this is the case. The phenomenon is referred to as a *post-earnings announcement drift*. According to Bernard and Thomas' study it takes some time before investors incorporate all information into share prices. Figure 6.10 shows how there is a delayed positive reaction from investors when companies announce a good report, and a delayed negative reaction from investors when companies announce a bad report. The number of observations used in these studies is vast and the explanatory power of the models is rather low. Nonetheless it is argued that the drift (even when transaction costs are taken into account) is so large that investors can base successful trading strategies on it.

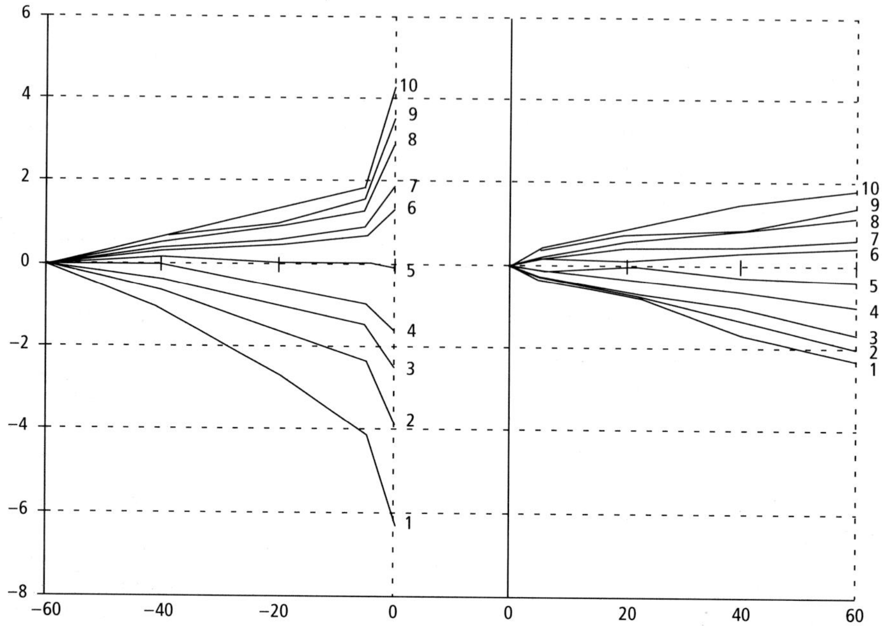

Source: Bernard and Thomas, 1989.

Figure 6.10 – Event study methodology applied to earnings announcements.

Note: The study includes 84,792 observations (quarterly earnings announcements from American companies). Ten portfolios are formed based on the difference between actual earnings and expected earnings. Portfolio Ten therefore contains those companies announcing the unexpectedly most positive earnings. Abnormal returns are measured as actual share return less average share return (adjusted for size). The left-hand side of the figure shows the cumulated abnormal returns (CAR) for the ten portfolios *before* the earnings announcements. The right-hand side shows the CARs for the ten portfolios *after* the earnings announcements.

6.4.4 Behavioural finance answers to the security price patterns

Overconfidence and extrapolation of previous performance (representativeness bias) cause a general excess volatility. This effect is probably reinforced by imitating behaviours. In the short run, investors can gain on riding the extrapolation wave, but sooner or later a contrarian behaviour is needed. There is a reversal to the mean. Note that overconfidence does not necessarily mean that investors do not listen to anyone else, or do not mimic the behaviours of others. It just means that he/she believes that a certain decision is correct and that he/she therefore is reluctant to change it once it has been made (cognitive dissonance). There is sluggishness in the incorporation of new information. This sluggishness is not substantial, but enough to be evident in studies. Once the new information is incorporated it is likely that it will be extrapolated too far.

In general, market overreactions can be explained by the extrapolation of past performance in the share market. Also, imagine what it is like making an investment in a company that nobody else wants to invest in and that investment then goes bad. Double loss! It is then better to make the same bad investments as everyone else. Everything else being equal, this leads to a situation where investors bid up the prices of growth stocks, while the prices of value stocks are kept low. Furthermore, there is a lot of media attention on companies whose shares have increased in value in the past. It is always easier to pick out past winners than future winners ...

Most of the behavioural finance ideas are based on the information constraints and the cognitive biases, and then the results coming from having investors using simplifying methods to solve the problems. Behavioural finance still has a way to go before mainstream financial theorists accept it (Thaler, 1999), but its emergence is evidence of the current standstill in traditional capital market research. Perhaps the solution to some of the problems financial researchers have encountered can be explained by human behaviours. Behavioural finance does however entail its own weaknesses, of which internal inconsistency is the most evident one. Fama (1998:291) criticised it, and stated that "... it is safe to predict that we will soon see a menu of behavioural models that can be mixed and matched to explain specific anomalies". In the midst of the debate stands the concept of market efficiency. Can the anonymous interactions in financial markets reduce the biases individual investors have in their decision-making? The truth is, we do not fully know. Excess volatility, momentum strategies, contrarian investment strategies and information delay strategies all thrive on biases in human decision-making.

6.5 Summary

This chapter reveals the current state of uncertainty that asset-pricing theory is in. Megginson (1997:130) has summarised the current state quite well. His words are hardly flattering, but indeed very true when it comes to research findings.

> *"First, it seems clear that the single-factor, constant-risk-premium CAPM is almost useless as a model either to explain observed returns or to generate expectations concerning future returns. Second, few other variants of the CAPM appear to offer much hope of emerging as the standard asset pricing model of the future. Third, a three- to five-factor APT appears to explain more of the cross-sectional differences in returns than any other single model, although the lack of observable variables in this model makes it a purely statistical construct that is maddeningly difficult to understand or explain economically. Fourth, the empirical evidence linking firm size to positive abnormal returns is unambiguous, but very strange, and must be explained before real progress can be made in asset pricing. Clearly size must be proxying for some other risk factor, but what? Fifth, it seems clear that the actual return generating process for stocks has multiple factors and the parameters of the process vary through time. Furthermore, at least part of this variation in risk premiums is predictable based on macroeconomic, business cycle-related data."*

So is this a hopeless case, are we back to the times when asset pricing was much more an art than a science? The answer must clearly be No. Researchers have undoubtedly a much better understanding of how investors ought to act when making investment decisions, and we have something of an understanding of why they act as they do when making decisions. We know that capital markets are reasonably efficient, and beating the market consistently using legitimate methods is almost impossible. This, as we have showed, lies in the nature of competitive markets. We also have an understanding of why and how investors benefit from using portfolio investment strategies rather than single asset investment strategies. From a theoretical point of view it is also hard to beat the two asset pricing models portrayed here, as they provide highly reasonable models of asset pricing. The CAPM is intuitively appealing and easily understood but seems to be too simple only allowing for one explanatory factor. The APT allows multiple factors but suffers currently from the inability to specify what these factors are and why they need to be used.

The emerging field of behavioural finance has so far contributed more questions than it has answered. It is doubtful that it will ever substitute the existing capital market theory. Investors can learn from any behavioural theory and then change their own behaviour to capitalise on it. If they do so the theory will ultimately change itself. To take an example; if sluggishness in the incorporation of new information into share prices can be capitalised upon, then some investors should earn these excessive returns and thereby move markets back to equilibrium. By being based on a mishmash of empirical observations, behavioural finance has rightfully been criticised for being too ad hoc. Theoretical support is created for whatever systematic pattern one can find when scanning security prices.

There are important corporate finance patterns that seem to be linked to market anomalies (see e.g. Daniel, Hirshleifer and Subrahmanyam, 1998). It has been documented that companies tend to issue relatively more new equity (rather than debt) in periods when they are highly valued (in relation to current earnings/cash flows or book value). The large number of Swedish IT-oriented companies who issued new equity and listed themselves on the SSE in 1999 and 2000 is a splendid example of this. There is evidence supporting this as newly quoted companies which have issued new equity perform considerably worse than other companies for many years (Loughran and Ritter, 1995). In the United States it has likewise been documented that share repurchases are particularly frequent in periods when the companies' share prices are relatively depressed. Although the area of mergers and acquisitions is complex to study, there is also evidence that acquisitions are more frequently paid for with new equity in periods when the acquiring company is relatively highly valued. If this is true, managers and insider owners can benefit greatly from understanding the psychology of the market. The effect is however that they gain on behalf of external shareholders.

Key Concepts

- > Security return
- > Security value
- > Realised return
- > Expected return
- > Standard deviation
- > Variance
- > Risk aversion
- > Risk neutrality
- > Risk taking behaviour
- > Mean-variance analysis
- > Covariance
- > Correlation coefficient
- > Portfolio return
- > Portfolio diversification
- > Nondiversifiable risk, systematic risk
- > Diversifiable risk, unsystematic risk
- > Minimum variance portfolio
- > Efficient frontier
- > Capital market line
- > Beta
- > Capital Asset Pricing Model
- > Market risk premium
- > Time-series regression model
- > Risk-free return
- > Reinvestment risk
- > Rational expectations assumption
- > Roll's critique
- > Cross-sectional regression model
- > Arbitrage Pricing Theory
- > Arbitrage process
- > Factor model
- > Empirically-based asset pricing model
- > Behavioural finance
- > Excess volatility
- > Excess volume of trading
- > Momentum strategies
- > Contrarian investment strategies
- > Value stocks
- > Growth stocks

Key Issues to Discuss

1 Explain why the realised returns of companies are not likely to be the same as their expected returns.

2 A mean-variance analysis of security return is based on a number of assumptions. Explain these assumptions as well as how the analysis works.

3 Explain the merits of moving from a risk-return analysis of individual securities, to a risk-return analysis of portfolios with risky securities. To answer the question you must discuss both the covariance between security returns and the definition of portfolio return and risk.

4 It is in the text stated that portfolio diversification is greatly affected by high correlations between securities. Explain why, and discuss whether the Stockholm Stock Exchange is affected by security pricing on other other stock exchanges.

5 By performing a mean-variance analysis we can identify a minimum variance portfolio. Why is this portfolio called "efficient"?

6 For every level of return it is possible to create a minimum variance portfolio, but on what grounds do investors choose between them?

7 Make a distinction between the correlation coefficient and the beta-value. In what ways are they similar?

8 Describe the risk-premium for an individual share in terms of its association with the market risk premium and the risk-free interest rate.

9 The expected market premium can either be calculated as the historical security return, or as the expected future return. Paradoxically a high security return in the past can mean both that the expected market risk premium becomes higher and lower. Explain how this can be possible. Hint: What happens with the relationship between security value and company performance when returns are high?

10 Explain the main differences and similarities between the Arbitrage Pricing Theory and the Capital Asset Pricing Model.

11 Provide an explanation as to how momentum strategies, contrarian investment strategies and information delay strategies can exist in a world characterised by information constraints and cognitive inconsistencies.

12 Why do managers need to know how investors put a price on securities? Give as many (conceptually different) practical examples as you can of situations where a manager can be disadvantaged by not knowing the expected return on its company's shares.

13 Discuss how managers can take advantage of security mispricing as described within the field of behavioural finance.

14 Is it beneficial to the company that management "fool" investors and arrange for cheap financing? Discuss the matter in terms of both current and future investors, and in terms of the short- and the long-run.

Further Readings:

Copeland, T. E., & Weston, J. F., 1992, *Financial Theory and Corporate Policy,* Reading, Massachusetts: Addison-Wesley. Chapters Six and Seven.

De Bondt, W. F. M., & Thaler, R. H., 1987, "Further Evidence on Investor Overreaction and Stock Market Seasonality", *Journal of Finance*, pp. 557–581.

Fama, E. F., & French, K., 1992, "The Cross-Section of Expected Stock Returns", *Journal of Finance*, pp. 427–466.

Fama, E. F., & French, K., 1996, "The CAPM is Wanted, Dead or Alive", *Journal of Finance*, pp. 1947–1958.

Roll, R., 1977, "A Critique of the Asset Pricing Theory's Tests – Part I: On Past and Potential Testability of the Theory", *Journal of Financial Economics*, pp. 129–176.

Thaler, R., 1999, "The End of Behavioral Finance", *Financial Analysts Journal*, pp. 12–17.

Chapter 7

Capital Structure Decisions

This chapter aims at:

- Describing different patterns in the capital structures of Swedish companies.
- Providing an understanding of how the value of a company is affected by management's choice of capital structure.
- Discussing how different factors influence management's choice of capital structure, and how the influence of the factors varies from situation to situation.

7.1 Introduction

7.1.1 Categorising liabilities

All capital structure decisions concern how different sources of capital should be mixed when financing projects. But often we take capital structure decisions to mean the long term (or permanent) financing of the company's overall operations, rather than just its individual projects. A capital structure is nothing one can touch or see in reality, but it is measured using accounting and financial information. It can hence be calculated for organisations sophisticated enough to portray their operations in the form of a balance sheet. From this it follows that the capital structure is socially constructed and thus not always an objective and uncontroversial measure. In most textbooks on capital structure decisions authors use the terminology of debt and equity when categorising companies' liabilities. *Debt* then refers to liabilities bearing a contractual cost, whereas *equity* refers to liabilities bearing a residual, or implicit, cost. We will also use this terminology (i.e., debt and equity) here, but our definitions will be slightly more precise. In accordance with the discussions in Chapters Two and Three debt can be split into interest bearing and non-interest bearing debt. Debt, as it is used here, refers to interest-bearing debt, and equity, as it is used here, refers to risk-bearing capital. The fundamental difference between debt and equity is that debt financing is based on a *contractual relationship* between the debtholder and the company as a legal entity. This provides the debtholder with certain legal rights. The contract often specifies the interest (return) given on the debt and the conditions under which capital has been provided to the company. This reduces the risk for the financier who regards debt as less risky and thus requires a lower return on a debt contract than an equity-holder does. From a company perspective debt might at first sight seem to be a relatively cheap source of capital. You will soon learn that it is not. The investors provide equity to the company and unlike debtholders, investors lack contractual rights giving them a certain return. We say that they hold a *residual relationship* to the company, meaning that they get the residual amount left after all contractual relationships with the other stakeholders (including debtholders) have been fulfilled. Because shareholders are not guaranteed anything they take a greater risk and hence we can expect them to ask for a higher return than debtholders.[1]

1 Companies can issue special classes of shares providing them with certain rights. These are called preference shares, and can for example return a higher dividend, or give its bearer priority in comparison to shareholders of common stock.

In essence, equity consists of capital invested by investors (typically common stock and preferred stock) and earnings after dividends from previous years (*retained earnings*). Debt consists of numerous different items, such as for example bank loans, issued corporate bonds, convertible securities, deferred tax liabilities, and supplier credits. Often the debt liability is subdivided into short term and long term debt. In Chapter Two we defined some of the most common measures of capital structure as:

Solvency: $$\text{Solv}_t = \frac{\text{RBC}_t}{\text{CE}_t}, \text{ alternatively } \frac{\text{EQ}_t}{\text{A}_t} \quad (2.16)$$

Debt ratio: $$\text{d}_t = \frac{\text{IBD}_t}{\text{RBC}_t}, \text{ alternatively } \frac{\text{D}_t}{\text{EQ}_t} \quad (2.17, 2.18)$$

The cost for possessing interest bearing debt was estimated as:

Interest rate: $$\text{i}_t = \frac{\text{nbc}_t}{(\text{IBD}_{t-1} + \text{IBD}_t - \text{po}_{t-1} - \text{po}_t)/2} \quad (2.19)$$

Alternatively: $$\text{i}_t = \frac{\text{fe}_t}{(\text{IBD}_{t-1} + \text{IBD}_t)/2} \quad (2.20)$$

The balance sheet presented in the annual report contains the book values of assets and liabilities. These can differ from the market values. This is particularly true for equity, where the market value often is much higher than the book value. The reason for this is, as discussed in Chapter Two, the conservatism of accounting. The market value stems from trading in financial markets where investors estimate future cash flows from the company's current and expected future projects. Existing assets might be worth more than their historical acquisition cost, and they can be expected to generate substantial future cash flows. The market value of debt can differ from book value, but usually to a much lesser extent.

The analysis in this chapter will focus on the capital structure of larger companies. Moreover, almost all prominent contributions to capital structure theory have been based on American public companies. This is somewhat unfortunate for us studying and managing companies in other environments. In this chapter we therefore spend time and effort distinguishing the problems of Swedish companies, in comparison to those of American companies. It is in particular the corporate governance system that causes differences.

7.1.2 Patterns of capital structure

In the analysis of capital structure decisions we will start by examining a case where capital markets are frictionless and where rational decision-makers try to maximise the value of their company. However, before this analysis takes place, it is relevant to acknowledge some patterns (or lack of patterns) in the capital structures of real-world companies. For a long period of time practitioners (and lately also theoreticians) have seen that there are systematic differences in capital structure between companies in different industries, time-periods and situations. Four of the most interesting findings are that:

1. Different companies have considerably different capital structures.
On average companies within an industry seem to have quite similar capital structures. The reason is usually said to be the similarity in business operations and hence in operating risk. In Chapter Two we defined operating risk as the *ex post* variance in ROCE, or alternatively as the *ex ante* probability that future ROCE will deviate from expected ROCE. Companies which face a great operating risk are less likely to also accept a great financial risk. Financial risk is mainly caused by the extent to which operating risk is magnified through *financial leverage* (the debt ratio). Between financial risk and operating risk there is usually said to be a negative association (Mandelker and Rhee, 1984). It has been identified in several international studies and Hamberg (2000) verifies that there is a negative association between operating risk and financial leverage also among Swedish companies.

But it is not true that companies within the same industry always have the same capital structure. Some information concerning the Swedish clothing industry is used to illustrate this. There are five companies with a primary focus on this sector listed on the Stockholm Stock Exchange. Hennes & Mauritz has a solvency of 76 %, JC has a solvency of 66 %, Fjällräven has a solvency of 55 %, Lindex has a solvency of 44 %, and Wedins has a solvency of 28 %.[2] These five companies are fairly similar and exposed to the same factors. Still it does not seem as if only industry grouping always determines the choice of capital structure.

2 According to statistics gathered from Affärsvärlden in May 2001.

2. The capital structure is different for companies within different industries.
Although there are differences between different companies, the differences are much smaller for companies within an industry category than for companies in different industries. For example, real estate companies have on average a higher debt ratio than manufacturing companies, while research-oriented companies tend to have a lower debt ratio.

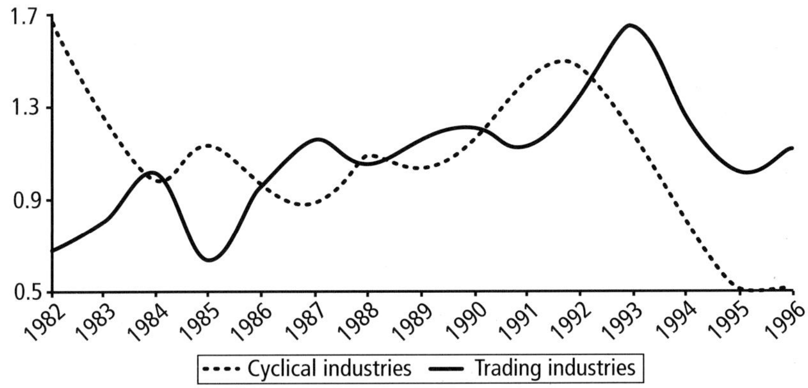

Note: Differences over time between trading industries and cyclical industries.

Figure 7.1 – Differences in capital structure between industries.

Figure 7.1 shows the debt ratios for Swedish public companies belonging to cyclical industries (primarily forestry companies and raw material oriented companies) and trading companies (such as for example the clothing companies just mentioned). Over a 15-year period it seems as if there is basically no correlation between the two industries, for either the level of debt financing or the changes in debt financing.

3. The capital structure is negatively associated with profitability.
Within virtually all industries, and countries, it is evident that more profitable companies have a lower debt ratio than less profitable companies. This is odd as researchers assume that capital structures are either unimportant, or chosen based on exposures to future business risk. If the observed capital structure is related to past profitability this indicates that it is an artefact of past performance rather than a deliberate policy decision.

Table 7.1 – Differences in profitability depending on capital structure.

Deciles				Quintiles			
	n	Debt ratio	Profitability		n	Debt ratio	Profitability
1	24	3.3	14.7 %	1	48	2.6	15.3 %
2	24	1.9	16.0 %	2	50	1.4	15.2 %
3	25	1.5	14.1 %	3	50	1.1	17.4 %
4	25	1.3	16.4 %	4	50	0.8	17.9 %
5	25	1.1	19.4 %	5	49	0.4	23.6 %
6	25	1.0	15.4 %				
7	25	0.9	17.7 %				
8	25	0.7	18.1 %				
9	25	0.5	24.0 %				
10	24	0.3	23.1 %				

Take a look at Table 7.1, which contains information from the annual reports of 123 Swedish industrial companies between 1982 and 1996.[3] It contains information regarding the debt ratio, measured as IBD/RBC, and the profitability, measured as RRBC. The table shows that in particular profitable companies have less debt than unprofitable companies. The 50 observations containing the highest debt ratio had a profitability of only 15.3 percent, whereas the 48 observations with the lowest debt ratio had a profitability of 23.6 percent. A remarkable difference. The correlation between debt ratio and profitability is –0.20, and statistically significant.

4. Observed capital structures seem not to vary greatly between countries. While there are substantial differences in the capital structures of companies in different industries, there is a much smaller difference in capital structure between companies in the same industries but operating in different countries (Rajan and Zingales, 1995; 1998). First of all, there are institutional factors affecting the choice of capital structure. Governments have the ability and willingness to sometimes influence the choice of capital structure. This can be done by selecting an appropriate tax rate, or differentiating taxes between different sources of capital. Secondly, comparing

3 To avoid biases from individual companies and individual years, the observations have been aggregated. For each company the average debt ratio and profitability during a five-year period (1982–96, 1987–91, or 1992–96) has been calculated. This gives us 247 five-year observations. These are grouped into ten and five categories based on capital structure. The first decile thus contain 120 one-year observations. No adjustments for business cycles or industries have been made. Debt ratio is measured as IBD/RBC and profitability as RRBC.

capital structures of companies in different countries can be difficult. Not only do tax systems differ, but also accounting standards.

With these patterns in mind we embark on a journey with the purpose of understanding what drives management's choice of capital structure. As we move along throughout this chapter we will pretty much follow the path research has taken over the last forty years. Along the journey we will encounter new capital structure patterns and find tentative explanations as to why some companies have higher debt ratios than other companies.

7.2 The Capital Structure Irrelevance Theorem

Although companies have been able to borrow capital for hundreds of years and although there have been reasonably active markets for debt and equity instruments for a long time, researchers have until lately wondered little about why managers choose a certain mix of debt and equity financing instead of another. Almost all modern theoretical analyses of capital structure decisions start from the path-breaking work set out by Miller and Modigliani in 1958. Their work has its origin in the principle of value-maximisation, i.e., that managers make decisions that maximise the company value. Meanwhile, the financial environment the company acts in functions without any frictions. As you should know by now, this is the obvious starting point for economic theory. To be specific we have listed the explicit and implicit assumptions of the Miller and Modigliani model of capital structure (also known as the *capital structure irrelevance theorem*).

Assumptions of the capital structure irrelevance theorem

1. Companies own all physical assets.
2. Capital markets are not influenced by income taxes or bankruptcy costs, and securities can be bought and sold costlessly and instantaneously.
3. Only two forms of securities can be issued: risky equity and risk-free debt.
4. Both investors and companies can borrow/lend at the risk-free interest rate.
5. Investors have homogeneous expectations about companies' future cash flows.
6. As there is no growth, all cash flow streams are perpetuities.

7 The company can be classified into an "equivalent return class", and the returns of all companies in one such class have proportional and perfectly correlated returns.

Despite the obvious lack of reality in some of these assumptions they form an excellent starting point for an economic analysis. After all, we know that the real-world does not function fully according to the assumptions, but on the other hand, to know how it does function if all the assumptions are correct is a great advantage. We can thereafter slowly adjust this original model to test which factors are the most important ones, and how violations of each factor affects companies' needs for a certain capital structure.

We will start with an idea that is elaborated in more detail later on in the book, namely what constitutes the value of a company. With the help of investment theory we can write the value of a company (or project) as the present value of all future cash flows into perpetuity. This can be written as in Expression (7.1), where V_t equals the present value of the asset generating cash flows, r_e equals the required rate of return, and cf_t equals the cash flow at time t.[4]

$$V_t = \sum_{i=1}^{\infty} \frac{cf_t}{(1+r)^t} \tag{7.1}$$

To make things as uncomplicated as possible, we then assume that future cash flows do not change over time, and thereby it is possible to simplify Expression (7.1), so that it becomes Expression (7.2). The value is then given by dividing the cash flow with the discount rate.

$$V_t = \frac{cf}{r} \Rightarrow r = \frac{cf}{V_t} \tag{7.2}$$

To show that this is correct a graphical proof in given in Figure 7.2, where three projects each providing steady cash flows of SEK 100 into infinity are shown. The discount rates for the three projects are 5, 10 and 20 percent respectively. A high discount rate means that the time-value of money is relatively higher. The project with a lower required return reaches a higher

4 If you have had no previous introduction to basic investment models, you might find it beneficial to first look at parts of Chapter Nine. Please note that Expression 7.2 is a simplified way of estimating the value of a company/project, which is based on steady growth in perpetuity. Chapter Ten provides much more extensive and realistic models of company valuation.

market value but it takes relatively longer to get there. Eventually all three projects displayed in Table 7.2 and Figure 7.2 reach their market value (2000, 1000, and 500 respectively). As shown in Expression (7.2) the required return equals the steady stream of cash flows divided by the value of the company.

Table 7.2 – Cash flow profiles of three investment projects.

	r	cf_1	cf_2	cf_3	cf_4	cf_5	cf_6	cf_7	cf_8	cf_9	Total
Project A	5 %	100	95,2	90,7	86,4	82,3	78,4	74,6	71,1	67,7	2000
Project B	10 %	100	90,9	82,6	75,1	68,3	62,1	56,4	51,3	46,7	1000
Project C	20 %	100	83,3	69,4	57,9	48,2	40,2	33,5	27,9	23,3	500

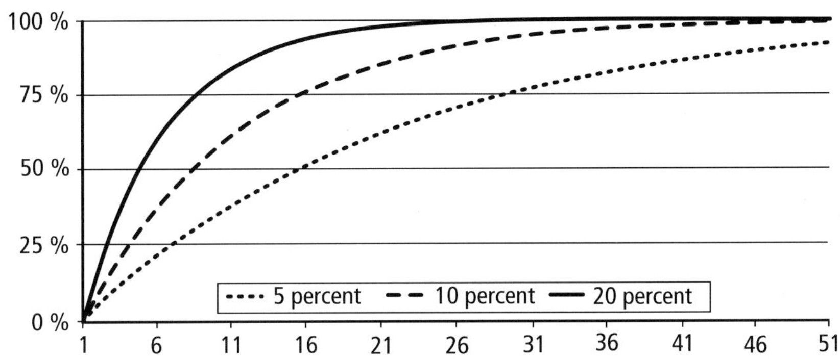

Figure 7.2 – Accumulated value of a no-growth investment with steady business risk.

The investors' expected return is the same as the company's cost of capital (for a 100 % equity-financed company). In the example below we shall use a company with an expected return of 20 percent (given the business risk of the company) and future perpetual cash flows of 400. Using the valuation model in Expression (7.2) we find that the value of equity is 2000 (400/0,20).

Now the question is if its value changes when the capital structure is altered? When the debt ratio is increased (solvency goes down), the market value of equity decreases proportionately to the increase in debt. If the company acquires debt (borrows capital from the bank or issues bonds) for 1000, it only needs to issue equity with a value of 1000 and the total value of the company is thus still 2000. This is obvious as the value of the company comes from future operating cash flows and they have not changed. The company only acquires capital, which it can invest profitably in assets giving a fair return. In this case it is just the value proportion between debt- and equity-holders that has changed.

Let's be more specific. Cash flows from operations were 400, but now the company has to pay the fixed costs that come with the debt contract. If one assumes that debt-holders require a 10 percent return on their investment (given the operating risk of the company and the terms of the contract) an additional fixed cost of 100 (1000 × 10 %) is introduced to the company. The periodic cash flow to the investors changes to 300 (400 – 100). In perpetuity investors will receive cash flows of 300, while the market value is 1000. Their required return has therefore changed. Previously it was 20 percent (400/2000), but now it is 30 percent (300/1000). We will soon learn the reason why investors increased their expectations. We can write the relationship that this reasoning is based on, as in Expression (7.3).

$$V^{Firm} = V^{D} + V^{EQ} \Leftrightarrow \frac{OCF}{r_t} = \frac{CFD}{r_d} + \frac{CFE}{r_{eq}} \tag{7.3}$$

where

V^{Firm} = Value of the whole company
V^{D} = Value of outstanding debt
V^{EQ} = Value of equity
OCF = Operating cash flows
CFD = Cash flows to debt holders
CFE = Cash flows to equity holders
r_t = expected return on total capital
r_d = expected return on debt
r_{eq} = expected return on equity

Prior to the contribution made by Miller and Modigliani (1958) people frequently thought that investors were willing to pay a premium price for the shares of levered companies. This is exactly the same as arguing that investors would accept a "too low" expected return on their investment, i.e., that their valuation is not based on the fundamental operating cash flows of the company. One of Miller and Modigliani's main contributions is that they show that such a valuation is impossible in an efficient market. It would create an *arbitrage* opportunity, where investors can buy underpriced securities ("too high expected return"), while selling overpriced securities ("too low expected return"). Very soon the price of a security will return to its correct price, given its intrinsic risk.

What has been described above is referred to as the first proposition of Miller and Modigliani. It is utterly basic, but immensely important, as it implies that the total value of a company is not affected by its financing policies.

The second proposition made by Miller and Modigliani follows tautologically on from the first proposition. It specifies what the expected return on levered equity must be for the market equilibrium to hold. To calculate this expected return we need to introduce a formula that is further discussed in Chapters Nine and Ten: the *Weighted Average Cost of Capital*

(WACC) formula. It is very straightforward and intuitive in nature, as it simply says that a company's cost of capital is a weighted average of its cost of debt and its cost of equity. The weight applied to the debt is the proportion of debt in the capital structure and the weight applied to the equity is the proportion of equity in the capital structure. The WACC formula is shown in Expression (7.4).

$$r_{WACC} = \left(\frac{D}{D+EQ}\right) \cdot r_d + \left(\frac{EQ}{D+EQ}\right) \cdot r_{eq} \tag{7.4}$$

The unlevered company (ULC) described above will have the following weighted average cost of capital:

$$r_{WACC}^{ULC} = \left(\frac{0}{0+2000}\right) \cdot 10\ \% + \left(\frac{2000}{0+2000}\right) \cdot 20\ \% = 20\ \% \tag{7.5}$$

The levered company (LC) described above will have the following weighted average cost of capital:

$$r_{WACC}^{LC} = \left(\frac{1000}{1000+1000}\right) \cdot 10\ \% + \left(\frac{1000}{1000+1000}\right) \cdot 30\ \% = 20\ \% \tag{7.6}$$

If Expression (7.4) is rearranged it can be written as:[5]

$$r_{eq}^{LC} = r_{WACC} + (r_{WACC} - r_d) \cdot \frac{D}{EQ} \tag{7.7}$$

This is referred to as Miller and Modigliani's second proposition. Here the impact of debt financing on the expected return on levered equity is emphasised. To illustrate the congruence between this model and the WACC we use information from the previous example. The shareholders of the levered company require a return of 30 percent.

$$r_{eq}^{LC} = 20\ \% + (20\ \% - 10\ \%) \cdot \frac{1000}{1000} = 30\ \% \tag{7.8}$$

The second proposition specifically points out that the required return on leveraged equity increases as the amount of contractual interest-bearing debt increases. The reason is simple. The company is still exposed to the same amount of business risk, but as more and more contractual debt is

5 Alternatively we can write this as in Chapter Two: RRBC = ROCE + d × (ROCE – i), which is the same formula but with slightly different notations.

introduced, the investors, who hold a residual relationship to the company, have to bear more and more of the operating risk themselves. An increased proportion of debt leverages the operating risk for investors holding equity shares in the company. An increased operating risk must mean increased expectations on the investors' return on investment.

The consequences of Miller and Modigliani's propositions are vast. *First*, given the assumptions they made, the value of a company is not affected by its capital structure. Market actors see through the financial policies management choose and make objective evaluations of operating risk and how that is distributed among the financiers. *Second*, the cost of capital is not affected by the capital structure management chooses. With efficient markets management has no opportunity to e.g. issue "cheap debt" and thereby lower their WACC. *Third*, the propositions open up for a separation of the investment and the financing decision. Regardless of which capital structure management chooses, a bad project will always be a bad project. Also, almost no matter what capital structure you choose, an investment appraisal will render the same end result (accept or reject the project).

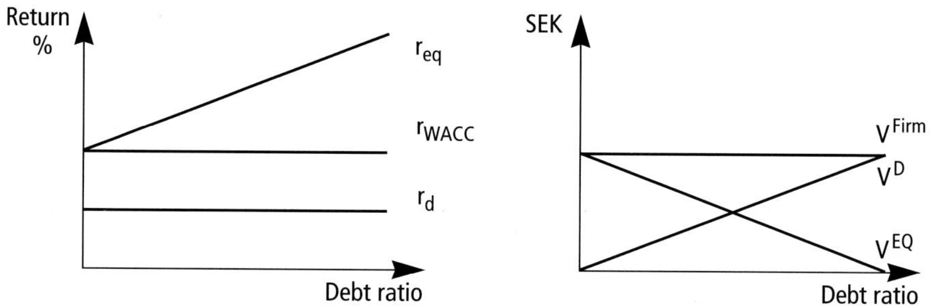

Figure 7.3 – Capital costs and company value under the conditions of M-M (1958).

Figure 7.3 illustrates graphically what happens when the debt ratio is increased. The first graph shows that as more and more debt is used to finance operations, the cost of equity rises and therefore the average required return (WACC) is constant. The second graph considers the value of the company. As more debt is employed, the value of total outstanding debt increases, but the value of outstanding equity diminishes at the same rate. Because of this, the total value of the company remains constant and hence the choice of capital structure is irrelevant.

7.3 Determinants of Capital Structure Policy

The message that Miller and Modigliani sent out to the world is clear: In a perfect world the choice of capital structure made by management is irrelevant for the value of the company. But as we have already pointed out capital structures do differ, and they seem to do so systematically. Researchers have since 1958 used the Miller and Modigliani framework to deepen the analysis of corporate capital structures.

The question that these researchers have tried to answer is when financing decisions might be value-relevant. It has to be said already here, however, that financing decisions are not as important as investment decisions. Financing decisions can contribute to company value only when there are any violations of the assumptions of the capital structure irrelevance theorem. These violations can roughly be divided into two kinds: Market inefficiencies and asymmetrically distributed information. In the rest of this chapter we will study four factors (based on these violations) that might be affecting the choice of capital structure made by management. The factors are:

1. The tax system
One of the most fundamental assumptions made by Miller and Modigliani is that capital markets work without frictions. There are several reasons as to why real-world financial markets contain frictions. One of them is that there might be institutional factors, which systematically make some means of financing more beneficial than others. The current tax system is unarguably one such factor, as it makes one financial source preferable to the other.

2. Bankruptcy costs
Debt financing involves fixed financial costs that have to be paid regardless of the underlying operating cash flows. Fixed financial costs create a higher probability of bankruptcy if the company exists in an environment where operating cash flows are uncertain. When there is a higher likelihood of bankruptcy, additional costs (such as legal costs, auditing costs and restructuring costs) decrease the value of the company.

3. Managerial welfare maximisation
Managers are likely to have other goals than both investors and debtholders, and asymmetrically distributed information about the firm's activities enables them to pursue financial strategies that are more in their own

interests. Both the providers of debt and of equity can react to this, which has an effect on the capital structure.

4. Investment activities

Most industries are characterised by economic growth and restructuring. Investment policies of different companies and industries thus vary. Some companies have to make large investments in tangible assets, whereas others have to make investments in intangible assets. Companies with good operating cash flows today, are likely to retain a great proportion of themselves, if they know the cash is needed in the future and that there are transaction costs related to the issuance of new equity.

Also, agency costs interact with investment activities. Companies where past investments currently generate high operating cash flows, usually retain a big proportion of them, as they provide greater freedom and flexibility. Internal financing becomes important and the capital structure relies on both the returns from past investments, and needs/desires to make new investments.

7.4 Capital Structure Under the Influence of Corporate Taxes

For obvious reasons, the capital structure irrelevance theorem (Miller and Modigliani, 1958) quickly came under attack. One of the most common arguments was that corporate taxes influence capital structure decisions. Neither companies nor investors act in a frictionless environment and the existing tax system creates a bias towards debt financing. The Swedish tax system, just like most other tax systems, bases corporate taxes on earnings after financial costs (and a number of other accounting items) have been deducted. More debt financing means lower taxes. More equity financing means no reduction in tax payments. The costs of using debt create a *tax shield* which adds some additional value to the company for every additional krona used to debt-finance operations.

In 1963 Miller and Modigliani came out with a corrected capital structure model in which they incorporated the effect of having corporate income taxes. To illustrate the effect of corporate income taxes, we shall take a second look at the example used in Section 7.2. Let us therefore assume we have a company with perpetual cash flows of 400, which is initially financed entirely with equity. The investors' required rate of return, given the business risk, is still 20 percent. But now the company exists in an environment where corporate taxes of 30 percent apply. The periodic return to investors is 280(400 · (1–30 %)). The market value of this equity-financed company is therefore 1400(280/0,20).

From the previous example we learned that in a no-tax environment the value of the company did not change when management substituted debt for equity. But let us again consider a case where management borrows 1000 to finance operations. The interest rate on debt is 10 percent. Operating cash flows are 400, which are reduced by contractual financial costs of 100(1000 · 10 %). The company is being taxed on the remaining part, 300, and therefore the investors are left with 210(300 · (1–30 %)). Figure 7.4 illustrates how the perpetual cash flows are distributed among different stakeholders. In Pie Chart A 100 percent of the cash flow goes to investors holding a residual relationship to the company. In Pie Chart B corporate taxes of 30 percent are introduced, and in Pie Chart C debt financing is used which reduces the negative effect of corporate taxes. While Pie Chart B displays that 30 percent of the generated value of the company is paid in taxes, Pie Chart C shows that this is reduced to 15 percent with debt financing.

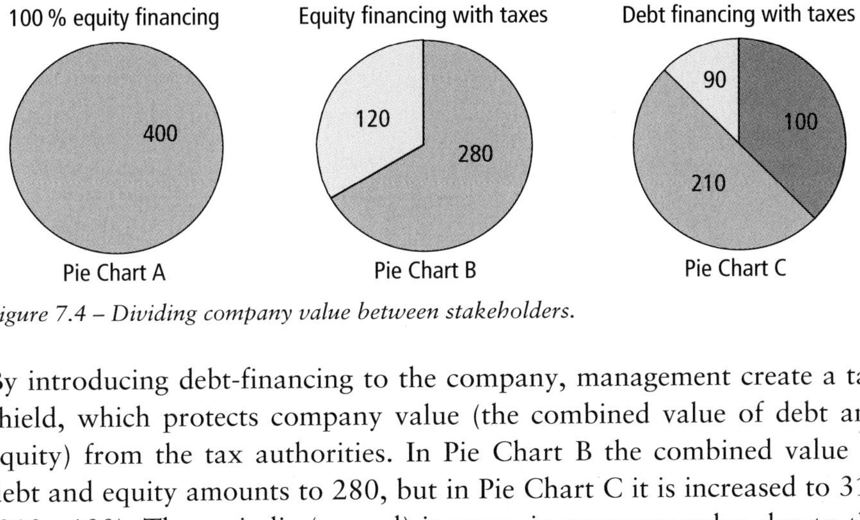

Figure 7.4 – Dividing company value between stakeholders.

By introducing debt-financing to the company, management create a tax shield, which protects company value (the combined value of debt and equity) from the tax authorities. In Pie Chart B the combined value of debt and equity amounts to 280, but in Pie Chart C it is increased to 310 (210 + 100). The periodic (annual) increase in company value due to the tax shield is 30, which means that with perpetual cash flows of 400, the total value of the company increases by 300(30 % · 1000).

Also in this second article Miller and Modigliani (1963) stated two propositions. The first proposition had odd consequences, and was even more controversial than the capital structure irrelevance theorem. Miller and Modigliani proposed that the total value of a leveraged company is equal to the value of an unleveraged company plus the value of the tax shield. Considering the existence of corporate income taxes all companies should be financed entirely by debt, something we know is not true.

$$V_{LC} = V_{ULC} + t \cdot D \tag{7.9}$$

The total value of the leveraged company is now increasing proportionally to the introduction of debt financing. The total value of the unleveraged company was 1400 and the value of the tax shield is in the example above 300, and so the total company value with debt financing is 1700. Moving on to the second proposition of Miller and Modigliani, this one concerns the investors' required rate of return for a leveraged company. Here Miller and Modigliani modify the previous second proposition (Expression 7.7) to fit a tax environment.

$$r_{eq} = r_{WACC} + (r_{WACC} - r_d) \cdot \frac{D}{EQ} \cdot (1 - t) \tag{7.10}$$

How does this work for the company we have discussed above? We import the information given above into Expression (7.10) and see that investors' required return should not have changed, although the market value of equity is lower than before.

$$r_{eq} = 20\,\% + (20\,\% - 10\,\%) \cdot \frac{1000}{700} \cdot (1 - 30\,\%) = 30\,\% \tag{7.11}$$

Finally we can again show the changes graphically. As more debt is introduced to the capital structure, the value of a leveraged company in a tax world increases. As you can see in Figure 7.5, it increases from the value of an unlevered company (in a tax world) towards the value of a company in

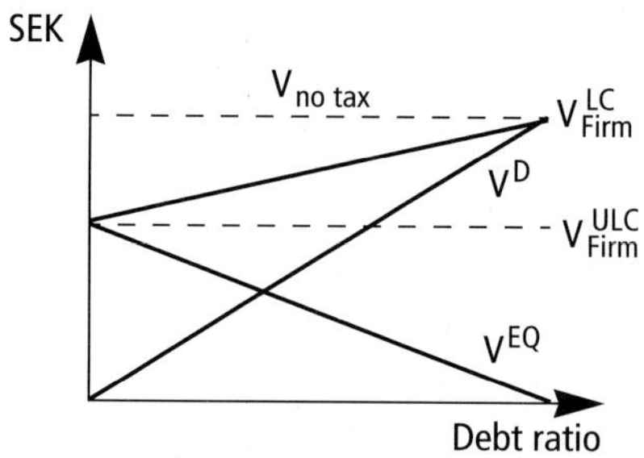

Figure 7.5 – Value of debt financed company in a tax world.

a no-tax world. The reason for this is that the value increase in debt (nominal outstanding debt plus tax shield) is higher than the value decrease of outstanding equity.

7.5 Introducing Bankruptcy and Agency Costs

The tax advantage occurring when debt is substituted for equity should in theory have the consequence that all companies finance their operations with contractual debt. But we all know that is not the case. Researchers therefore continued to systematically search for and incorporate factors into the original Miller and Modigliani model. The two most important factors with a negative effect on debt ratio are bankruptcy costs and agency costs. Whereas the tax system has one relatively clear effect on the choice of capital structure, these other factors are more complex. It is thus less common to formalise them in models as was done in the previous sections.

7.5.1 Bankruptcy costs

First of all, think of what will happen to a company that chooses to finance all of its operations with debt. The debt-holders are given a contractual return on their investment, which creates a fixed cost for the company. A highly leveraged company with revenues that vary over time might find itself in a situation where it suddenly cannot afford to pay its fixed financial costs. Such a company would then be in *financial distress*, which ultimately might lead to bankruptcy. Even if it does not, a financial reconstruction of the company might be costly and take time. The financial impact of bankruptcy is determined by:

$$\alpha_B \cdot C_B \tag{7.12}$$

Bankruptcy costs will only be of interest if there is a probability that the company will go bankrupt (α_B), and hence one has to consider both the *probability of bankruptcy* and the actual costs affecting the investors in the case of bankruptcy (C_B). The probability of bankruptcy is zero if (1) sales price, sales volume and production costs are constant or (2) all production costs vary in accordance with sales volume and price and there are no fixed contracts regarding future sales prices or input goods. The higher the fixed costs of a company are and the more volatile the sales are, the greater is the probability of running into financial distress. Debt financing will magnify the risk of financial distress that any normal company faces.

To understand the impact a bankruptcy might have on the choice of capital structure one has to understand the asset structure of the company together with the characteristics of the industry. A real estate company with long term lease agreements can afford to have a high debt ratio simply because revenues will be relatively easy to predict. The same goes for a company with no fixed costs but very unstable revenues, as long as it can alter input costs in relation to sales price and volume. For most companies, doing business involves large fixed costs, long term contracts and an uncertain (and volatile) market for finished goods. They face the probability of bankruptcy.

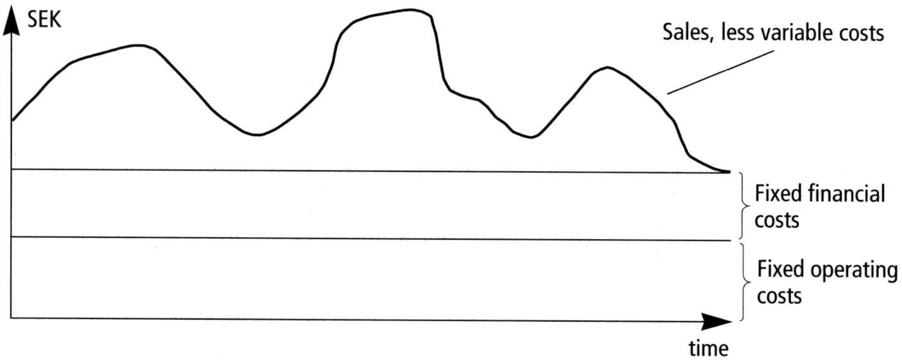

Figure 7.6 – The probability of bankruptcy.

Bankruptcy is however primarily the result of corporate failure and not the cause of it. All the company's valuable physical assets will still be employable by the company itself, or by somebody else. The issue is really the extent to which a situation of financial distress influences future cash flows. Bankruptcy is best described as a legal process involving a reorganisation of financial claims and the transfer of corporate ownership. Two kinds of costs exist; (1) *direct bankruptcy* costs like for example legal fees, auditing fees and reorganisation fees,[6] and (2) *indirect bankruptcy* costs such as lost supplier, employee and customer confidence causing a worsened competitive situation.[7] In today's business environment one can only imagine what

6 Warner (1977) provides evidence that the direct bankruptcy costs are limited for larger companies.

7 Altman (1984), Opler and Titman (1993), and Philips (1995) provide evidence that indirect bankruptcy costs are of significant importance for capital structure decisions.

will happen to the value of a company if rumour has it that it is close to filing for bankruptcy. As of this writing, E-commerce companies are having a hard time convincing their stakeholders that they can sustain their operations. Lost faith in the companies leads to lost customers, lost employees, and particularly a loss of capital. Even though E-commerce companies are not highly leveraged their current misfortune provides evidence of how important stakeholder confidence is for business.

The size of the bankruptcy costs is obviously hard to estimate, especially since the indirect bankruptcy costs constitute the most important part. There is one argument which goes against the importance of bankruptcy costs. Investors should not be particularly sensitive to the indirect costs of bankruptcy if they have well-diversified portfolios. Lost customers, suppliers and employees will end up somewhere else and as long as there are "industry lock-up" effects little harm is caused. If competition in the car industry forces one manufacturer (such as, e.g., Saab or Volvo) into bankruptcy that will not change total cash flows from the car industry to investors (because it would have a beneficial effect on the revenues and profit margins of other car manufacturers). There is however good reason to believe that management fear bankruptcy more than investors as they have invested all their "human capital" in one particular company. If this is the case, the relative importance of bankruptcy costs for *actual managerial decisions* is higher than what financial theory stipulates (c.f. Donaldson, 1961).

From an investor perspective, it seems reasonable that companies with unique complex products, where the after-market is relatively important, suffer more from indirect bankruptcy costs than companies selling commodity-like products do. Another, related, issue to consider is the *asset characteristics* of the company. Owners of companies with mostly tangible assets having a well-established secondary market, fear bankruptcy less, than owners of companies with intangible assets or specialised machines. This is one of the reasons why companies with mainly intangible assets have low debt ratios. Bank managers are reluctant to provide credits to someone who cannot raise a mortgage against assets with reasonable security.

So far the actual choice of capital structure has been explained using two factors, which have opposite effects on management's capital structure decision. The choice of capital structure can be illustrated by expanding Figure 7.3 so that it encompasses a trade-off between corporate taxes and bankruptcy costs. Figure 7.7 shows that the increase in company value caused by the tax shield (of increased debt) is countermined by the negative effects of bankruptcy costs. Somewhere there should be a point where the marginal utility of an increased debt ratio is equal to zero. Given only these two variables this is the company's optimal debt ratio.

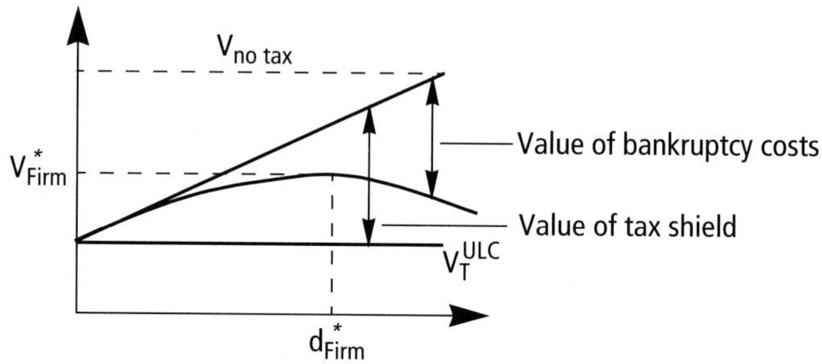

d^*_{Firm} = Optimal Capital structure. V^*_{Firm} = Optimal value of the company.

Figure 7.7 – The trade-off model between corporate taxes and bankruptcy costs.

7.5.2 Agency costs of debt

Agency costs were discussed in Chapter Three. Researchers tend to believe that there are two forms of agency costs affecting a company's capital structure, but that they do so in completely different ways. In this section the *agency costs of debt* are discussed. As you probably remember all agency costs stem from a goal incongruence leveraged by asymmetrically distributed information.

When debt is introduced to a company's capital structure a conflict of interest arises between shareholders and debtholders. Shareholders are assumed to be well informed, whereas debtholders are assumed to be poorly informed about the business activities. As the proportion of debt increases, so does the probability that shareholders pursue selfish strategies. We will consider three such selfish strategies illustrated in the short story below.

The case of the selfish owner and asymmetric information

Imagine that you attend the management meeting of a company that has performed badly for some time. Losses have been mounting up, and over the last month the latest project, which management had invested a considerable amount of time and money in, has turned out to be a fiasco. The company has increased its financial leverage and the fixed financial costs are getting harder to bear. On the daily agenda three, rather selfish, strategies are to be discussed. Stunned you listen to the three proposals.

#1 – The high risk strategy

The first proposal is about two mutually exclusive projects. One is a low risk/low return project and the other is a high risk/high return project. The low risk/low return project is however more profitable (higher NPV considering the risk). During an extended discussion representatives for the main shareholder suggest that if they should go for one of the projects it definitely has to be the high risk/high return project, as the magnitude of a possible loss is rather unimportant. It will just affect debtholders. If something goes wrong, shareholders will lose everything anyway. Finally the meeting decides to drop the issue and move on to the next proposal.

#2 – The underinvestment strategy

The next proposal is about a single project. The project itself is profitable and will bring an almost certain profit that can save the company from bankruptcy. But the investment requires additional capital, which has to externally funded. Asymmetric information prevents debtholders from evaluating the project properly and the management team knows that additional debt is out of the question. Current shareholders have to make the full investment, but they have to share the benefits with debtholders. After a long discussion management decide not to accept the profitable investment although they fully understand this means almost certain bankruptcy. The final word from the main owner is that if the company had been a fully equity-financed company it would have made the investment.

#3 – The "milking the cow" strategy

Finally a consultant stands up at the back of the room. He says he has gone through the company's records carefully and that he is of the same opinion as the others; the company is indeed very close to bankruptcy. His suggestion is to make no new investments at all, but to use what he refers to as "accounting strategies" that will raise disclosed earnings momentarily. Thereby a higher dividend payout ratio can therefore be supported. The others first listen stunned, then argue that it is immoral. The consultant replies that although it will quicken the bankruptcy it will certainly be the best option for current owners. No official decision is taken at the meeting, but as you leave the room you see how the consultant hands over documents to the representatives of the main shareholder...

The case clearly shows why debtholders are afraid of a too high financial leverage. In this case debtholders should add a risk-premium to their required return and the combined value of debt and equity then becomes lower as the debt ratio increases. The agency costs of debt are primarily driven by two factors; (1) shareholders' ability to be better informed than debtholders and influence decision-making, and (2) the asset characteristics of the company. If shareholders are weak they cannot act as forcefully in their own interests, and if fixed assets have an realisable market value they can be resold and debtholders are less likely to lose their stake. Also, if the company is financially healthy (positive cash flows) and far from bankruptcy, the agency cost of debt is minimal and likely to have little or no impact on company value.

7.5.3 Agency costs of equity

Shareholders can be pressured by agency costs and therefore increase their required rate of return, which leads to a reduced company value. While the agency costs of debt hypothesis assume a strong owner with great influence over business operations, the *agency cost of equity* hypothesis assumes a weak owner with little insight into management's activities and little control over management's activities. The result of such a situation was discussed in Chapter Three, but should be mentioned again. If shareholders believe management will not act in their best interest they will automatically bid down the value of the company (which is the same as saying that they require a higher return on their investment). As argued by Jensen and Meckling (1976), there are two ways for this company to go. Either shareholders take more control over the company (for example by going private), or else management introduce debt. Increased debt forces management to pay fixed financial costs rather than waste the money on non-profitable projects (see Jensen, 1986). Equity-financing is likely to be more expensive than it has to be (given the operating risk) because of agency costs. Similarly, company value is lower.

7.5.4 The static capital structure model

As you have seen, the original trade-off model has now been extended to include four factors. We have moved further and further away from the original model where the value of the company was split only between shareholders and debtholders. Figure 7.8 displays a tentative model of how company value is distributed. The category organisation represents both the managers' and other employees' parts. It forms part of the total agency costs, but this proportion of the generated cash flows is consumed by the organisation ("self-fulfilment" in various ways). The residual proportion of agency costs (labelled "agency costs" in the figure) are overlooked prof-

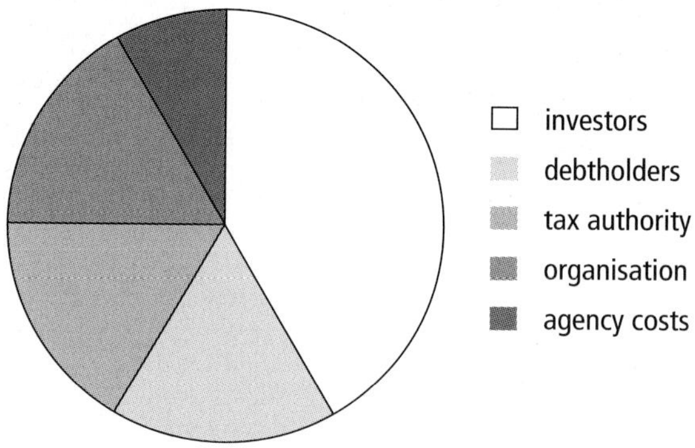

Figure 7.8 – Dividing company value between stakeholders.

itable investment opportunities. The model we have ended up with here is something of a stakeholder model where a number of parties are involved in the capital structure decision, and where they all derive some benefits from the activities of the company.

So far in this chapter we have introduced the pillars of a *static capital structure model*. According to this model the capital structure is optimised on a period-by-period basis, in which costs of having too much debt (bankruptcy and agency costs) are weighted against tax benefits. Management's role is then to choose an optimal capital structure maximising company value. According to Expression (7.1) company value can be described as:

$$V_t^{OA} = \sum_{i=1}^{\infty} \frac{cf_t}{(1+r)^t} \qquad (7.1)$$

and since this value is determined by the operating activities it should not be influenced by the choice between different sources of capital. By introducing agency costs, bankruptcy costs and corporate taxes the value of a company can be expressed as:

$$V_t = V^{OA} - (V^T + V^{TS}) - V^{BC} - V^{ACD} - V^{ACE} \qquad (7.13)$$

where

V^{OA} = Value of operating activities
V^T = Value of corporate taxes
V^{TS} = Value of tax shield
V^{BC} = Value of bankruptcy costs
V^{ACD} = Value of agency costs of debt holders
V^{ACE} = Value of agency costs of equity holders

The relationships between these factors are not linear and very much different for different companies. Based on these four factors an optimal capital structure might be designed. The optimal capital structure is one in which the value of the company can be increased through financial policymaking. One of the basic premises of the static capital structure model is, however, that management *want* to choose a capital structure that maximises company value. Against this static idea stands the more dynamic, and management-oriented, pecking order model to which we turn in the next section.

7.6 Other Capital Structure Models

7.6.1 The pecking order hypothesis

At the beginning of the chapter some patterns of capital structure were stated. One of the most interesting patterns found by researchers is related to the level of profitability that companies experience. When making comparisons between different companies, those having a higher return on invested capital also have a higher solvency (see e.g. Bertmar and Molin, 1977; Baskin, 1989; Hamberg and Store, 1994). But also when comparing companies over time the same pattern exists. Once companies start to make money they tend to retain it rather than pay it out as dividends. This implies that investment and financing decisions are not fully separated.

Table 7.1 – Differences in profitability depending on capital structure.

Deciles				Quintiles			
	n	Debt ratio	Profitability		n	Debt ratio	Profitability
1	24	3.3	14.7 %	1	48	2.6	15.3 %
2	24	1.9	16.0 %	2	50	1.4	15.2 %
3	25	1.5	14.1 %	3	50	1.1	17.4 %
4	25	1.3	16.4 %	4	50	0.8	17.9 %
5	25	1.1	19.4 %	5	49	0.4	23.6 %
6	25	1.0	15.4 %				
7	25	0.9	17.7 %				
8	25	0.7	18.1 %				
9	25	0.5	24.0 %				
10	24	0.3	23.1 %				

While the static trade-off model discussed in the previous two sections can explain some of the phenomena we relate to capital structure decisions, it can hardly explain all of them. In fact, sometimes that model predicts an opposite behaviour. According to the static capital structure model a profitable company should increase the debt-to-equity ratio because the probability of bankruptcy is lower and management can therefore take advantage of the tax shield. But instead management of most profitable companies seem to decrease the debt-to-equity ratio.

A tentative answer as to why this paradoxical behaviour exists has been proposed using the so-called *pecking order hypothesis* of capital structure. It has its foundation in the notion that managers and investors have different goals and that management might not always want to maximise the value of the company. As financial economists hardly see a foundation of "irrational, value-decreasing managerial behaviours" as solid enough for their analyses, it was not until the 1980s that it was seriously discussed (Myers, 1984).[8] In recent research, where the two models' explanatory power have been compared, it does seem as if the pecking order hypothesis does a better job explaining corporate capital structure (see e.g. Shyam-Sunder and Myers, 1999; Fama and French, 2000).

The pecking order hypothesis provides us with a simple answer to the recently mentioned patterns. Managers want control over cash flows and as outside stakeholders are both suspicious of management and less well informed, management desire financial slack. Financial slack is capital resources at management's disposal whenever needed.

The pecking order hypothesis is based on three observations/assumptions.

1. management prefer internal financing to external financing.
2. since management prefer internal financing to external financing, the dividend policy changes so that cash flows from past investments match the expected future investment needs.
3. when forced to use external financing management choose the safest and least demanding source first, and as they are forced to obtain more external financing, they will do so by working their way down the pecking order.

The *first* observation has as a consequence that cash flows from current projects determine to some extent whether new projects are started or not. The investment and financing policies of a company are integrated because of management's desire to have control over cash flows (c.f. Donaldson, 1984). The *second* observation was identified empirically already in the 1950s (Lintner, 1956) and has since then been a frequently found pattern in many studies. In essence, it means that management change their transfer of cash to shareholders so it matches the internal flow of capital. It also means that management will try to satisfy shareholders' needs for dividends, rather than maximise their dividends. Chapter Eight will discuss this matter in much greater detail. The *third* observation implies that if management have to approach external stakeholders to receive financial funds they will rather approach a stakeholder that they know well from previous commitments rather than an unknown stakeholder. More man-

8 Donaldson (1961) was however the first one to outline the pecking order of financial choices.

agerial control is better than less control. From this follows a pecking order that for a typical company could be:

1 Internally generated funds	High preference
2 Already approved bank credits	
3 Bank loan from current main lender	
4 Issue of bonds	
5 Issue of convertible securities	
6 Issue of preferred stock	
7 Issue of common stock to main owner	
8 Issue of common stock to new investors	Low preference

According to the pecking order hypothesis management are likely to accumulate financial slack so that they are not forced to move too far down on their priority list. The pecking order hypothesis of capital structure provides a more dynamic solution to the capital structure puzzle than the trade-off model previously discussed. Whereas the static model looks at the aggregated proportions between debt and equity, the dynamic pecking order model instead views the set of opportunities management have to finance their current investment projects.

Although the pecking order model is management-oriented, claims have been made to make it feasible also in the light of economic theory (Myers and Majluf, 1984). First assume that managers know much better than investors about the company's investment opportunities and outside investors are likely not to believe them (after all, management have an incentive to announce unjustifiably profitable projects in order to gain further control). Then asymmetric information will undeniably force investors to assign a lower value to the stocks of a company and new equity issues will only be bought at prices underneath the "true" value (the agency cost of equity). Management understand this and will therefore in certain cases even refuse to accept profitable projects because of asymmetric information when issuing new equity. If they issued new equity, new shareholders would benefit on behalf of current shareholders. This problem cannot be solved through lowering transaction costs or additional bonding activities. The solution given by Myers and Majluf (1984) is financial slack, which enables management to finance profitable projects internally.

If management choose the capital structure according to a pecking order, then it is beneficial for investors to take responsibility in corporate decisions. The governance structure should thus emphasise collaboration between investors and management. Otherwise, the pecking order-based choice of capital structure is likely to give rise to sub-optimal value-decreasing decisions from an investor perspective. This is particularly true if management decide not to make profitable investments because they do not have enough internal funds. The pecking order hypothesis is relatively simple and relies heavily on the fact that information is asymmetrically distributed. It does suffer from an inability to explain how taxes, bankruptcy costs and other market frictions affect the choice of capital structure, but on the other hand, it explains many managerial behaviours and choices related to the issuance of securities. Arguably, it works better on the marginal than the static trade-off model does.

7.6.2 The signalling hypothesis

Another idea sometimes used to explain the decision of capital structure, is based on a *signalling hypothesis* (Ross, 1979, Blazenko, 1987).[9] We will, however, spend less time on explaining this hypothesis, as it sheds relatively little light on the matter, particularly for Swedish companies. The origin of the theory is somewhat the same as for the pecking order hypothesis, namely asymmetric information problems between well-informed managers and poorly informed shareholders. A solution to the problem is that management signal to shareholders that they are in a favourable situation with good investment opportunities. Given the asymmetric information, shareholders are not satisfied with cheap talk but they want to see action. In the light of asymmetric information, a signal is credible if engaging in signalling is prohibitively costly for weaker firms, and therefore the poorly informed shareholders can rely on the signal.

When management signal to shareholders using the capital structure they will accept more debt, with its adjoining fixed capital costs, than poorly performing companies can afford to risk. The dead-weight costs of bankruptcy will thus on the marginal inhibit some companies from certain capital structures. While this model is intuitively attractive, it lacks empirical support, and is probably also of less relevance for Swedish companies. It was previously recognised that one of the most prominent patterns of corporate capital structures is that more profitable companies have lower debt ratios than less profitable companies. Clearly these companies would not be signalling to shareholders that they are better than average – quite the contrary. Another pattern is that high growth companies are equity

9 See Harris and Raviv (1991) for a good coverage of this, and other, theories of capital structure.

financed to a greater extent than asset-rich low growth companies. At the same time the signalling hypothesis predicts that industries rich in growth opportunities should employ more debt as they have more severe problems with information asymmetry and thus greater needs of signalling. Finally, it is worth mentioning that the differentiated voting rights we have in Sweden shorten the distance between the main owners and management. Obviously many of the main owners of Swedish companies have a better insight into their companies' operations than their American counterparts. Signalling makes less sense in such environment.

So is the signalling hypothesis worthless? Probably not entirely as researchers believe it can be used to explain individual issues of capital (in the US, bonds or new equity). Debt issues signal good news (management are confident about the future), whereas equity issues signal bad news (management have a bad feeling about future earnings). Recent research suggests that an issuance of debt signals that management believe the company is valued below its intrinsic value, whereas an issuance of equity often signals that management think that the company is valued at par, or above, its intrinsic value (e.g. Daniel, Hirshleifer and Subrahmanyam, 1998). Maybe these models will be refined in the future and then provide better explanations to empirical observations. While it makes intuitive sense, the pecking order hypothesis has a much stronger empirical support.

7.7 Summary

We started out with a very simple model of capital structure policy and worked our way towards much more realistic models, and while doing so the models also became more complex. Identifying determinants of capital structure is not easy and it would be misleading to argue that there is *one* correct capital structure for any given company, or *one* way of describing managerial behaviour.

The two main descriptions of how capital structures are chosen is the static trade-off model, and the pecking order model (Myers, 1984). According to the static trade-off model management set a target debt-to-equity ratio and try to maintain this over a period of time. The target ratio represents the optimal, value-maximising, capital structure given the tax shield, agency costs, and bankruptcy costs of the company. The pecking order model of capital structure is of a different nature. It is dynamic and less normative. According to it, management have no optimal capital structure to aim for, but instead the capital structure is changed depending on the investment opportunities and the financial sources management dare to rely on at the moment.

Several studies have compared these two models, or combined their major strengths (Shyam-Sunder and Myers, 1999; Fama and French, 2000). Pinegar and Wilbricht (1989) did something quite unusual for American financial researchers; they actually asked managers on what grounds they chose between debt and equity. Their study indicated that American managers were more likely to follow a financial hierarchy, such as the pecking order model, than to maintain a target debt-to-equity ratio, such as in the static trade-off model. Kjellman and Hansén (1995) made a very similar study on Finnish companies. They found that most Finnish companies set a target capital structure, and that corporate control is the main reason for this. The information is considerably less asymmetrically distributed in Finnish companies and thus the pecking order is less important. This could also be the case in Sweden.

It is time to summarise those factors which researchers are sure have a substantial effect on management's capital structure decision. Some potentially useful measures when explaining the actual mix of debt and equity are listed below.

Taxation and other government-oriented interventions in financial policy

Taxation plays a role as debt financing has a tax advantage provided by government. Companies operating in countries or industries where debt financing is particularly favoured will choose a higher debt-to-equity ratio. Companies operating in high-tax environments will also choose a higher debt-to-equity ratio.

Low corporate taxes	Lower debt-to-equity ratio
Great opportunities to make earnings dispositions	Lower debt-to-equity ratio

Bankruptcy risk and its consequences

The risk of bankruptcy influences the capital structure, as bankruptcies are costly for all claimants to the company's operating cash flows. There are primarily two factors causing bankruptcy risk; probability of bankruptcy and the cost of bankruptcy. The probability is determined by the operating risk of the company. Companies with high fixed operating costs and uncertain future cash flows will choose a lower debt/equity ratio. The cost of bankruptcy is primarily determined by the asset composition and the aftermarket for the company's assets.

High uncertainty regarding future sales volume and price	Lower debt-to-equity ratio
High proportion of fixed costs	Lower debt-to-equity ratio
High proportion of intangible assets	Lower debt-to-equity ratio
High asset specificity	Lower debt-to-equity ratio
Considerable amount of R&D	Lower debt-to-equity ratio
Many claimants to company assets in case of bankruptcy	Lower debt-to-equity ratio

Co-operation and trust between shareholders and management

The relationship between those controlling corporate resources and those owning them plays a role in the choice of capital structure. Little trust means that management will have difficulties issuing new equity when needed. This forces them to rely on internally generated equity (i.e., financial slack) in bad times. Trust can be established both if ownership is dispersed or not. A strong owner can act forcefully and ensure that management behaves as they should. Weak owners can establish incentive programs making management value-oriented. If shareholders trust management, there is less asymmetric information and the capital structure has then little signalling value.

Investment opportunities and internal cash flows

Although investment and financing activities should be separated, there is, according to the pecking order model of capital structure, good reason to believe that managers (a) consider cash-flows from past investments when deciding on new investments, and (b) consider investments in the near future when choosing between financial sources (and thus influencing the capital structure). Investments in intangible assets are less likely to be made using external debt. Instead, it is more likely that investments in research and development will be financed with internal cash flows, at least in profitable companies. After the start-up phase investments in physical assets are more easily funded with external debt, as debtholders then have assets to claim in the case of bankruptcy and therefore are more willing to provide cheaper debt. Sentiments in financial markets can also make it more favourable to issue equity in certain situations. In the spring of 2000 many Internet-oriented companies listed themselves on the Stockholm Stock Exchange. The main reason for this is said to be the favourable valuation of companies in the "new economy" at that period of time. In the fall, many investors became sceptical of Internet companies and as the valuations of them became lower, fewer companies were interested in listing themselves. When management (or the main current owner) behave in this way, they are likely to gain on the expense of future shareholders.

Value can potentially be created through financing decisions. The avoidance of taxes is the best example of this. Surprisingly, many companies do not pick a capital structure that optimises their value in respect to income taxes. These companies instead increase solvency in good times when they need the tax shield the most. As you know by now, this behaviour is hardly surprising, but indeed disappointing for some. Besides tax avoidance, value can (theoretically speaking) be enhanced through the creation of new financial instruments which cater better to the needs of specific investor groups. As competition in financial markets is so fierce, it is unlikely that such inventions can really provide major long term value increases. Managers might not always make decisions maximising shareholders' utility. As shown here, that does not make them irrational but on the contrary rather rational in their behaviour.

Key Concepts

- Debt
- Equity
- Contractual relationship
- Residual relationship
- Retained earnings
- Financial leverage
- Weighted Average Cost of Capital
- Capital structure irrelevance theorem
- Arbitrage
- Tax shield
- Financial distress
- Probability of bankruptcy
- Direct cost of bankruptcy
- Indirect cost of bankruptcy
- Actual managerial decisions
- Asset characteristics
- Agency cost of equity
- Agency cost of debt
- Pecking order hypothesis
- Signalling hypothesis
- Static capital structure model
- Dynamic capital structure model

Key Issues to Discuss

1. Discuss why is it so important for us to understand the value-relevance of corporate capital structures in the case of *perfect markets.*
2. The consequences of the Miller and Modigliani propositions are relatively easy to understand. Company value is unaffected by financial policies. But what is it then that affects company value in imperfect markets? How does the capital structure irrelevance theorem regard the level of competition in product markets as compared to the level in financial markets?

3 When corrected for taxes, the Miller and Modigliani propositions have some dramatic consequences. What are these consequences and how do they evolve?

4 The probability of bankruptcy can be forecasted by looking at the association between a company's fixed and variable costs. Give examples of companies who are likely to have considerably different probabilities of bankruptcy.

5 Is the probability of bankruptcy affected by management's choice between fixed and variable interest rates? Discuss the issue and while doing so you might benefit from some of the discussions in Chapter Two.

6 Why is it likely that managers care more about bankruptcy than investors? Does it matter if the company is owned by professional investors (such as e.g. mutual funds) or by private persons?

7 What are the differences between the agency costs of equity (ACE) and the agency costs of debt (ACD)? In what kind of companies are the ACE higher than the ACD?

8 Explain graphically how the capital structure of a company will develop over time as investment opportunities and the returns on past investments vary. Use the pecking order hypothesis as your starting point.

9 Discuss the differences between your answer to Question Eight and the predictions that the static capital structure model provides.

10 Obviously there can never be a single and uncontroversial model of corporate capital structure. But can the static and dynamic models be combined? In which situations do they function the best?

Further Readings:

Harris, M., & Raviv, A., 1991, "The Theory of Capital Structure", *Journal of Finance*, pp. 297–355.

Myers, S. C., 1984, "The Capital Structure Puzzle", *Journal of Finance*, pp. 575–592.

Pinegar, M. J., & Wilbricht, L., 1989, "What Managers Think of Capital Structure Theory: A Survey", *Financial Management*, pp. 82–91.

Shyam-Sunder, L., & Myers, S. C., 1999, "Testing Static Tradeoff Against Pecking Order Models of Capital Structure", *Journal of Financial Economics*, pp. 219–244.

Chapter 8

Dividend Policy Decisions

This chapter aims at:

- Describing different patterns of dividend policies among Swedish companies.
- Providing an understanding of how the value of a company is affected by management's choice of dividend policy.
- Discussing how different factors influence management's choice of dividend policy, and how their influence vary from situation to situation.
- Showing the differences between different forms of capital transactions between shareholders and the company.

8.1 Introduction

8.1.1 Cash transactions between shareholders and the company

Any company's main activity is to make and manage investments, which will earn back their invested capital. This chapter deals with the cash transactions between shareholders and the company. These cash transactions can take several forms: They can be cash flows from shareholders to the company, in terms of issues of shares in the company or other financial instruments that can be converted to shares. They can also be cash flows from the company to shareholders, in terms of dividend payments or the repurchase of previously issued shares. The primary focus lies in this chapter on the dividend policy that is one of the major financial decisions management engage in and also one of the more complicated issues to understand.

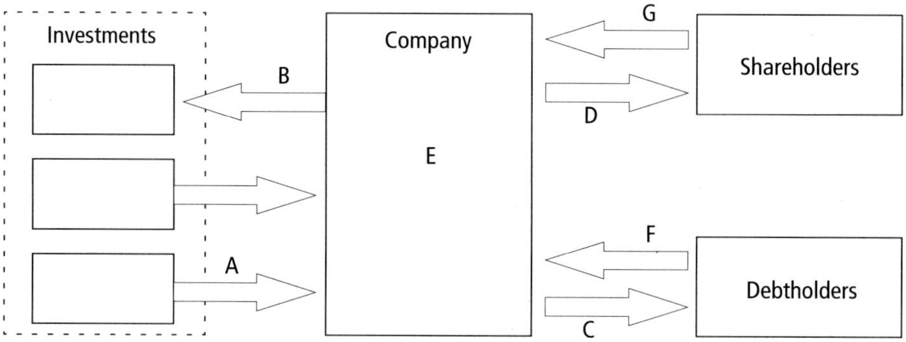

Figure 8.1 – Cash transactions between shareholders and the company.

Figure 8.1 illustrates the flow of capital between the company and its investment projects and financiers. Needless to say the picture is simplified but it does tell us what options management have. Existing investments bring an inflow of cash to the company (A) and there are several alternatives available for which management can make use of this capital. One of them is to make new investments in desirable projects (B). Another one is to reduce the amount of debt (C) and/or equity (D). A third alternative is to do nothing and just retain the cash (E). If management decide to make a new investment that requires more capital than what is at management's immediate disposal, they also have to increase the amount of debt (F) and/ or equity (G). The cash flows we are interested in in this chapter are (D) and (G), but in order for them to be relevant cash flows (A) and (B) usually need to be in place as well.

In Chapter Seven Miller and Modigliani taught us that the choice of capital structure would not have any effect on the value of a company when capital markets are efficient (the separation of investment and financing decisions). The same idea holds for the cash transactions between shareholders and management. As long as management make profitable investments and the shareholders can understand what it is management are investing in, the dividend policy and the issuance of new shares will have no impact on company value. Management will of course only retain the capital they can place in investments earning the required rate-of-return. When financial theorists speak with practitioners, dividend policy is a sensitive issue and one that often causes confusion. As early as 1956 Lintner identified that companies have different dividend policies and that these varied somewhat systematically. The question is, of course, why they do so and this issue has puzzled researchers ever since.

In this chapter we start to look at some patterns of companies' dividend policies, and thereafter we cover the theoretical reasons as to why the dividend policy should not matter in the case of efficient markets. Then it is time to challenge the basic assumptions of such a dividend irrelevance model. This basically leads us to the same kind of factors that were important for the capital structure decision discussed in Chapter Seven. After studying this chapter you will have an understanding of which factors it is management, consciously or unconsciously, take into consideration when making their dividend policy decisions. Although the dividend policy decision mainly concerns the setting of a dividend payout ratio it often concerns several sub-decisions, such as if the dividend should be in cash or new stocks, or if there are incentives for the company to buy back its own stock rather than pay dividends. We integrate these issues in the final discussion, and try to do so using a Swedish perspective.

To discuss the theoretical reasons for choosing a certain dividend policy we need to be able to measure it practically. A company's dividend policy is usually determined by calculating the relationship between, on the one hand, dividends and, on the other hand, earnings/cash flows necessary to pay the dividends. Alternatively, the relationship between dividends and the stock of capital employed in the company (such as market or book value of equity) is calculated. Throughout this chapter we will mostly relate dividends to the company's ability to generate earnings.[1] From a shareholder perspective it is usually discussed what portion of earnings is re-

1 We can define dividends as: $EQ_{t-1} - EQ_t + NP_t$. It is thus the periodic change in equity plus the net profit.

turned to shareholders, whereas managers often care about how much is retained within the organisation after shareholders have been compensated satisfactorily.

Dividend payout ratio: $$dp_t = \frac{Div_t}{NP_t} \quad (8.1)$$

Retention rate: $$r_t = 1 - \frac{Div_t}{NP_t} \quad (8.2)$$

To illustrate how one calculates these ratios please take a look at Table 8.1. Atlas Copco is a large Swedish company with an industrial orientation. Below you will find information from its annual reports in 1998, 1999 and 2000. Dividends are announced as dividends-per-share (DPS). This makes it easier for shareholders to keep track of changes over time. The DPS from previous years is recalculated to enable calculations of dividend growth. In the annual report of 1999 the DPS for 1998 is stated as 4.32.

Table 8.1 – The dividend policy of Atlas Copco.

	2000	1999	1998
Net earnings	2,924,000,000	2,247,000,000	2,283,000,000
Number of shares	209,602,184	195,309,247	183,515,920
Earnings per share (EPS)	13.95	11.50	12.44
Dividends	1,100,411,466	995,610,374	825,821,640
Dividends per share	5.25	4.75	4.50
Retained earnings	1,823,588,534	1,251,389,626	1,457,178,360
Dividend payout ratio	37.6 %	41.3 %	36.2 %
Retention ratio	62.4 %	58.7 %	63.8 %

The dividend payout ratio and the retention rate can vary even though the DPS is relatively stable. Three things affect the two ratios; besides the actual DPS, the net income and the amount of outstanding shares have an effect. During these three years Atlas Copco explicitly state that 30–40 percent of the earnings shall be redistributed to shareholders through dividends. A question we shall soon ask ourselves is why they want to have this particular dividend payout ratio, instead of any other.

8.1.2 Patterns of corporate dividend policies

Before examining the theory behind dividend policy irrelevance, it is interesting to note the extent to which dividend policy actually varies. Table 8.2

shows figures of the expected dividend payout ratios for the fiscal year 2000 for all companies listed on the Stockholm Stock Exchange. Some interesting patterns are evident. Dividend payout ratios vary between 0 percent and 100 percent. The far right column shows that the variance within each industry category is substantial. In fact, in many industries the standard deviation is higher than the average payout. For some companies the dividend payout ratio is exceptionally high, that is the case of, for example, the shipping, pharmaceutical, and investment companies. Other companies show very low dividend payout ratios and companies in some industries, such as research and prospecting companies, offer no dividends at all. When we study the reports of individual companies, we find that 116 out of 259 companies are expected not to pay any dividends at all next year (not shown in Table 8.2). At the same time 59 companies are expected to pay more than 50 percent of next year's net earnings in dividends. Obviously dividend policies are very diverse.

Table 8.2 – Differences in dividend policies.

Industry	**Dividend payout ratio**			
	n	**mean**	**median**	**Stand.dev.**
Heavy manufacturing	55	30 %	29 %	20 %
Paper and Pulp	9	31 %	34 %	19 %
Trade	21	37 %	38 %	29 %
Real estate and construction	23	52 %	58 %	26 %
Shipping	7	76 %	71 %	76 %
IT consulting	27	12 %	0 %	24 %
Computer software	17	8 %	0 %	14 %
IT-dealers	4	−3 %	0 %	41 %
Construction oriented	2	43 %	43 %	18 %
Research	9	0 %	0 %	0 %
Chemicals	5	35 %	39 %	22 %
Conglomerates	6	45 %	46 %	18 %
Consumer oriented	8	43 %	42 %	13 %
Electric utility	2	53 %	53 %	11 %
Pharmaceutics	2	58 %	58 %	17 %
Media	6	17 %	0 %	26 %
Medicine technology	7	15 %	0 %	19 %
Prospecting	3	0 %	0 %	0 %
Technical consulting	6	52 %	54 %	20 %
Services	15	18 %	19 %	20 %
Transportation	2	46 %	46 %	65 %
Office and printing	7	37 %	39 %	7 %
Investments	4	103 %	88 %	33 %
Banking and finance	12	37 %	37 %	23 %
Mean	259	34 %	32 %	23 %
Variance (between industries)		25 %	36 %	18 %

Source: Affärsvärlden (2000/08/10). Industry classification according to Affärsvärlden.

Although it is difficult to judge whether the observed patterns are systematic or not, we can clearly see that there is a substantial variance both within individual industries and between different industries. We end this short look at dividend policies by comparing companies in different countries. Figure 8.2 show some data the Economist published a few years ago. The figure speaks for itself: British and American companies have higher dividend payout ratios than Japanese and German companies. Differences in dividend payout ratios seem to be systematic, as they have existed for more than twenty years in a row. Swedish companies are not included, but their dividend payout is somewhere between that of German and American companies.

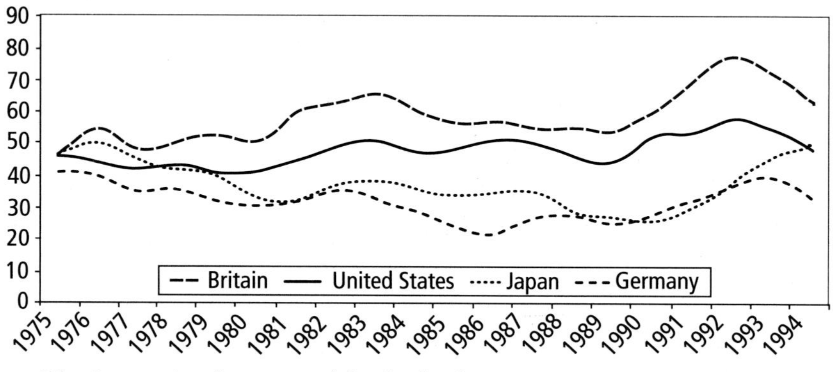

Figure 8.2 – International patterns of dividend policies.

In short, these empirical studies indicate that there are substantial differences within industries, between industries, and between companies in different countries. The figures shown in Table 8.2 and Figure 8.2 are merely illustrations of findings from the many research studies conducted over the years. These differences have existed over an extended period of time and the same kind of company and industry differences have been observed in various countries. In the classic empirical study of dividend policies carried out by Lintner (1956), there was a mentioning of a number of dividend related issues managers had to consider. These issues are pretty much the same today, as managers still wonder whether they should maintain dividend payments or change them? They still wonder how investors judge changes in dividends, and if they prefer a stable nominal DPS or accept that it will vary along with corporate earnings? Managers still wonder if investors prefer high payout ratios or if marginal tax rates make them favour longer investment horizons and low payout ratios? Dividend policies are still puzzling, but this chapter does attempt to provide answers to some of the questions. It will do so using the massive amount of research conducted over the last forty years.

8.2 The Dividend Irrelevance Theorem

Together with capital structure decisions, dividend policy decisions were one of the first areas in corporate finance to be analysed by researchers using rigorous theoretical models. From an economic standpoint the ultimate question to ask is whether dividend policy has an effect on the value of a company. Given the similarities between capital structure decisions and dividend policy decisions it is no coincidence that Miller and Modigliani (1961) were the first to provide an analytical framework under which companies' dividend policies can be analysed.

Similarly to their analysis of capital structure decisions, this analysis is based on a number of simplifications. The purpose is again to state dividend policy in an idealised world so that we can examine what happens when one variable at a time is changed to resemble reality. We can sum up their assumptions as follows:

Assumptions of the dividend irrelevance theorem

1. Investors are utility maximising (and thus prefer more wealth to less).
2. Investors are indifferent to the source of wealth (dividends or capital gains).
3. All companies issue a single class of security (common stock).
4. Buyers and sellers are price takers (they are not large enough to influence market prices).
5. Investors have information regarding the company's investment program and future profits of all companies.
6. All traders have equal and costless access to the same set of information.
7. There are no transaction costs (when issuing new equity and paying dividends).
8. There are no tax differentials between dividends and capital gains (or between distributed and undistributed profits).

The return investors require was formalised in Chapter Six and is restated in Expression (8.3). Standing at the beginning of period one, investors' return is equal to dividends during the period plus the change in company value, divided by the current value of the company.

$$r_t = \frac{(Div_t + V_{t+1} - V_t)}{V_t} \tag{8.3}$$

where

r_t	= The asset's return	V_{t+1}	= Market value (end-of-period)
Div_t	= Cash dividends for the period	V_t	= Market value (beginning-of-period)

Expression (8.3) can be turned around to express the value of the company (8.4a), and it can also be transformed into a formula stating the value of an individual share (p), where dps equals the dividend-per-share (8.4b).

$$V_t = \frac{Div_t + V_{t+1}}{1 + r_t} \tag{8.4a}$$

$$p_t = \frac{dps_t + p_{t+1}}{1 + r_t} \tag{8.4b}$$

In other words, the current value of the company equals what is paid out in dividends plus the value of the company's future cash flows at the end of the next period. If a company chose to pay larger dividends (i.e., to have less capital invested in the company) the value of future cash flows would be lower. At the same time, a company not paying any dividends, but reinvesting it all into operations, is increasing its future cash flows that can be used to pay future dividends. It is necessary to consider three issues here. *First*, the value of a company is, for a shareholder, only determined by the stream of dividends. But it is not necessary to know when those dividends occur as long as it is properly adjusted for (using the discount rate). *Second*, as management is assumed to invest only in profitable projects the choice of dividend payout ratio reflects the number of profitable projects management has. *Third*, management does not have to retain profits today just because new investment opportunities might show up in the future. If new investments require capital which management does not have, it simply issues new equity (and/or debt). Investors have access to the same information management have about future projects and their profitability. Because of the dividend policy the number of shares outstanding, and the price of these shares might vary. But the total value of the company will always mirror the business opportunities and risk the company confronts. Dividend policy must be irrelevant under such circumstances.

To show how simple but elegant this trade-off model is; take a look at the following example concerning two companies competing head-to-head in the same industry and thus having the same business opportunities. The companies are of equal size and both have 500,000 shares outstanding, each worth SEK 20. This gives them both a market value of SEK 10,000,000. Both companies earn a steady-state return of 10 percent, equal to annual operating profits of SEK 1,000,000. As they earn a steady-state return of 10 percent investors' required return is 10 percent.

Now both companies have the opportunity to make a profitable investment which will give them SEK 1,000,000 during period t. The two companies will (as you have probably guessed) be using different dividend policies. The first company, Company A, will have a retention rate of 100 percent, whereas the second company, Company B, will have a retention rate of zero percent. Instead of using internal financing, management of Company B will issue new shares. The questions are, of course, whether these two dividend policies work and if they both maximise company value?

First consider Company A. The shareholders of this company will not receive any dividends as the retention rate is 100 percent. All operating cash flows during period t are retained and used to internally finance the SEK 1,000,000 investment. At the end of period t this company is worth SEK 11,000,000 (10,000,000 + 1,000,000). The value of Company A's shares is SEK 22 (11,000,000 ÷ 500,000). If we insert these figures into Expression 8.3 it looks like this:

$$r = \frac{(Div_1^A + V_1^A - V_0^A)}{V_0^A} \Leftrightarrow 10\ \% = \frac{(0 + 11{,}000{,}000 - 10{,}000{,}000)}{10{,}000{,}000} \qquad (8.5)$$

Similarly, we can use Expressions (8.4) to calculate the market value of the company. Each of the 500,000 shares is worth SEK 22 at the end of the period. Dividends (of no value) plus this end-of-period value total SEK 11,000,000, which is equivalent to SEK 10,000,000 in today's value.

$$V_0^A = \frac{Div_1^A + V_1^A}{1 + r} \Leftrightarrow 10{,}000{,}000 = \frac{0 + (500{,}000 \times 22)}{1 + 10\ \%} \qquad (8.6)$$

What happens then to Company B that chose a zero percent retention rate? Lets examine the situation by looking at Company B on a per-share basis. This company pays dividends of SEK 2 on its 500,000 shares. From an investor perspective the company is worth SEK 2 (dividends) plus SEK 20 (future cash flows) at the end of the period, which is equal to a return of 10 percent.

$$r = \frac{(Div_1^B + V_1^B - V_0^B)}{V_0^B} \Leftrightarrow 10\ \% = \frac{(2 + 20 - 20)}{20} \tag{8.7}$$

But the management of Company B have an investment opportunity that they do not have sufficient internal cash to finance. They therefore raise capital to finance the investment by selling new shares. The investment requires SEK 1,000,000 and as the beginning of period t share price is SEK 20, the company has to issue 50,000 shares (1,000,000 ÷ 20). This yields a value of the company at the end of the period equalling 550,000 · SEK 20 = 1,100,000. This is similar to Company A.

$$V_0^A = \frac{Div_1^A + V_1^A}{1 + r} \Leftrightarrow 10{,}000{,}000 = \frac{(2 \times 500{,}000) + (500{,}000 \times 20)}{1 + 10\ \%} \tag{8.8}$$

You might think that it is almost too easy to make these calculations. In fact, all we do is play around with the numbers assuming that value is created somewhere else other than in the financial policies. But if investors can understand and evaluate all investments the company is making, managers do their best in maximising the value of the company and capital can flow freely between investors and the company, this is the right thing to do. It is important to remember that the investment policy must be kept fixed. A dividend paying company only has an equal value to a non-dividend paying company if it finances future investments with the issuance of new shares. Keep in mind that we assume that companies always invest when they have profitable projects.

8.3 Determinants of Dividend Policy

In the first section of the chapter it was shown that dividend policies vary between companies. At the same time the previous section implied that the dividend policy should have no value-relevance. In the rest of this chapter we will look at factors that explain the choice of dividend policy. These factors are going to be more or less the same as those discussed for capital structure relevance. They can be classified as either being factors inhibiting market efficiency, or factors relating to corporate control.[2]

2 We will violate each of the last four assumptions of the dividend irrelevance theorem, as they were specified in Section 8.2.

The most obvious factor affecting dividend policies is *taxation*. Structural differences in the taxation of income from different capital sources can make one corporate finance policy favourable to another. The same goes for *transaction costs*. If management cannot alter the amount of equity capital, or investors cannot alter the disposition of their wealth without incurring costs, then both management and investors will shy away from certain behaviours and policies.

A third violation of the assumptions Miller and Modigliani set up is that management do not have the same goals as investors, *goal incongruence*, and investors know less about the company's current activities and future prospects. In reality there is *asymmetric information* between investors and management. Under such conditions dividends can be used as a signal.

Although this was not fully accounted for in the assumptions of Miller and Modigliani, it seems reasonable that the *corporate governance system* influences managerial behaviour and the need for management to send signals to shareholders (in the form of dividends). This relates to the discussion in the previous chapter on the need for and use of financial slack by company management. In the rest of this section we shall consider these factors and see when, and in which ways, they affect dividend policy.

8.3.1 Taxes

In Sweden, as in many other countries, shareholders pay taxes on dividends. If management of a company decide to payout dividends in such an environment shareholders would no longer be indifferent between full payouts and full retention of earnings. We illustrate the effect of taxation by returning to the example of Companies A and B. In a no-tax world the dividend payout of SEK 1,000,000 for Company B was compensated by the rise in value (the investment's future dividends) of SEK 1,000,000 for Company A. But with taxes on dividends the value of a dividend paying company has to be written as in Expressions (8.9).

$$V_t = \frac{Div_t \times (1 - t_t) + V_{1+t}}{1 + r_t} \tag{8.9a}$$

$$p_t = \frac{Div_t \times (1 - t_t) + (s_{nt} \times p_{t+1})}{1 + r_t} \tag{8.9b}$$

where s_n equals the amount of outstanding shares, and p equals the price of an individual share. In the example this causes an imperfection, which clearly makes a dividend paying policy unprofitable. Now lets investigate the value implications corporate taxation has. Let us assume that dividends are to be taxed with a 30 percent tax rate (t = 0.30). Company A, having chosen a 100 percent retention rate then still has a value of SEK 10,000,000.

$$V_0^A = \frac{Div_1^A \times (1 - t) + (s_n^A \times p_1^A)}{1 + r} \Leftrightarrow 10{,}000{,}000 = = \frac{0 \times (1 - 30\,\%) + (500{,}000 \times 22)}{1 + 10\,\%} \tag{8.10}$$

But Company B is suffering because of taxation on dividends. The value of Company B has now decreased to SEK 9,727,000. The difference in value between these two companies can be expressed as (Div · t) ÷ (1 + r).

$$V_0^B = \frac{Div_1^B \times (1 - t) + (s_n^B \times p_1^B)}{1 + r} \Leftrightarrow 9{,}727{,}000 = = \frac{1{,}000{,}000 \times (1 - 30\,\%) + (500{,}000 \times 20)}{1 + 10\,\%} \tag{8.11}$$

But some of you are probably thinking that even though this simple calculation is correct this is not what the world looks like. After all, in most countries shareholders pay taxes on capital gains (increases in share price) as well. This is true, but there can be a difference between the tax rate on dividends and capital gains. Moreover, also in countries such as Sweden, where the is no difference between taxation of capital gains and dividends, taxation still plays a most important role as capital gains are taxed upon realisation. A delayed tax payment causes less damage and as long as there is a tiny tax advantage with internal financing then companies should choose to payout low or no dividends.

Existing tax regulations thus give companies the incentive to retain a greater portion of earnings. In real-life, this tax-related bias is probably the greatest for companies with large controlling owners (insiders) who have no need for cash. Such owners are likely to find it better to have their wealth being accumulated in one company rather than have it paid out to the tax authorities.

8.3.2 Transaction costs

Transaction costs should be taken to mean dead-weight costs, which are associated with transferring capital from one market actor to another. The transaction cost usually occurs because of the necessity to use an intermediary whose services are not for free. A transaction cost can affect dividend policies in two different ways. First of all, if it is more costly to use an intermediary when buying and selling shares than it is when paying dividends, then having dividends paid out to him/her on a periodic basis helps the investor. Such a payout would reduce that investor's loss of cash. This is, of course, not true for an investor who wants to keep all of his/her fortune in shares. Such a person would be given additional costs because of dividend payouts. From this respect the transaction cost will affect the dividend payout ratio on the basis of whether investors want cash dividends or not.

The other effect of transaction costs have is more of interest from a management perspective. For the dividend irrelevance theorem to hold, Miller and Modigliani assume that the company can issue new equity without cost whenever it has a need. But, if the issuance of new equity entails large costs, such as brokerage fees and prospectus, then companies have an incentive to choose a higher retention rate. One can assume that the effect transaction costs have on a company's dividend policy, is determined by the balance between the individual company's future cash flows and investment needs. High growth companies with capital-intensive operations should be less willing to pay dividends than low growth companies with less capital-intensive operations. Why would you pay out dividends if you as a manager know that you will need that capital within the nearest investment period? The transaction cost thus forces managers to consider financial decisions in conjunction with investment decisions. This is an issue we return to in Chapter Eleven when considering an internal financial system.

Both taxes and transaction costs have a negative effect on dividends. They are likely to play some role in the dividend policy puzzle, but as both of these factors promote a high retention rate there must be some other factor that promotes a lower retention rate. Such a factor has to have a substantial effect, and be independent of these two factors. Obviously companies pay dividends and some do so even the same year that they issue new equity.[3]

3 It is also quite common that companies pay dividends the same year they issue new equity, which makes very little economical sense. Atlas Copco constitutes one good example. It issued new equity worth SEK 4.1 Billion in 1999 when they also paid dividends of almost SEK 1 Billion.

8.3.3 Asymmetric information

Nobody should have the ability to understand a company's true financial performance better than its management. Management sit on lots of information that outside shareholders never gain access to. We have discussed these information asymmetries in several of the previous chapters and return to them again here. Dividends represent one of the best transmitters of information that management have available.

When it comes to the dividend puzzle the signalling role dividends can have, has received much attention over the last years. Its foundation is exactly the same as for the signalling model within capital structure theory – the difference is only that here it makes more sense. Management and shareholders do not have access to the same set of information (information asymmetry) and therefore management have an incentive to signal to shareholders the company's future prospects. As before, investors consider talk to be cheap – anyone can make statements that they will be the market leaders within three years, or that they have the ability to enforce an abnormally high profit margin. But will any management team pay out costly dividends if they are not absolutely sure they are performing well?

Investors need to overcome the information asymmetry and they do so by relying on costly, but for some companies affordable, signals of company performance. Dividends fit this definition of a signal very well. *First*, companies can only pay out (long term) dividends if their projects generate positive cash flows. Few managers would consider paying (short term) dividends unless they are currently earning money. *Second*, to pay dividends means to give up capital that could have been used for future investments. This then signals that management is expecting high future cash flows from operations. Cash flows that are sufficient to finance future profit-making activities. *Third*, to pay dividends is to give up financial slack. As financial slack is deemed as an insufficiently profitable investment, this is a positive signal in the eyes of investors. Higher dividends mean fewer opportunities to retain slack. Investors feel they have greater control over a company with little slack.

The combination of goal incongruence and asymmetric information means that shareholders view dividends positively. Empirical studies have also shown that when companies announce dividend increases, the value of the company increases; which obviously is contradictory to the dividend-irrelevance models in Expression (8.4) (see e.g. Aharony and Swary, 1980). The effect is particularly large when companies who did not previously pay dividends make an announcement (Michaely, Thaler and Womack, 1995). One has to be cautious when interpreting such findings however. If managers know of and take advantage of such interpretations of dividend changes then they might disappear. It is all about how investors interpret the reasons behind the change in dividend policy. Dividends can signal both changes in cash flows from previous investments and the level of future investments. If investors interpret the reason for dividend changes to be unexpected value-relevant changes in these underlying matters this can drive share prices in either direction. It is clearly possible that a manager who wants to create a short term increase in the share price can then make conscious cut-backs on investments and make believe increased cash flows come from operations whereby it is likely investors view this signal as positive. A short term valuation above the company's true economic value could be beneficial to management when they e.g. want to issue new equity, or for an insider owner who is selling her stake in the company to an outsider. Likewise, a temporary short term cash flow and dividend "boost" might possibly force management to reduce corporate wealth and/or forego profitable investments.

This discussion gives rise to the *dividend-signalling model.* Some want to see the dividend-signalling model as a more dynamic model explaining changes in dividend policy over time. Just as in Chapter Seven, where the pecking-order theory was said to explain changes in capital structure over time, the signalling model connects investment policy with financing policy. Figure 8.3 shows a typical long term dividend policy of a company acting according to the signalling model. The earnings-per-share has a much greater variance than dividends-per-share has. Management sets its dividend policy so that it usually shows a slowly upward trend. It is only in the case of a severe downturn that dividends are cut, and as soon as earnings recover, dividends are raised to the previous level. Such a behaviour signals

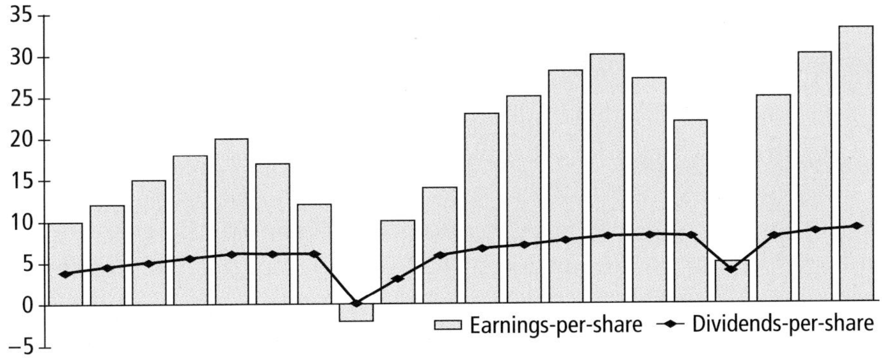

Figure 8.3 – Dividend policy according to the signalling model.

to shareholders (as well as other stakeholders) that the company is doing well and that management has everything under control.

Whether dividends really have this comforting effect on anxious and uninformed shareholders we cannot be fully sure, even though evidence cited above does indicate so. It is important to note that if management use their dividend-per-share to send comforting signals to their stakeholders, then the dividend payout ratio will vary greatly over a business cycle. When observing dividend patterns over a business cycle one might find signalling patterns, but such patterns always revolve about a more stable long term dividend payout ratio. In Figure 8.3 it is approximately 30 percent, which also seems to be the current norm for many Swedish industrial companies.

8.3.4 Governance structure

So far we have been able to establish a number of factors affecting dividend policies. That dividends have a signalling value that reflects information asymmetries might be true, but that does not fully explain why dividend policies are so different in e.g. different countries. As shown in Figure 8.2 at the beginning of the chapter, American and British companies do on average pay out more in dividends than Japanese companies. Some differences in dividend policy might be explainable by looking at the growth rates of the economies wherein companies function. It would be reasonable to assume higher retention rates in Southeast Asia than in Europe, as macro-economic factors signal a higher overall growth rate there. But it does not explain the systematic differences between Germany and Britain; two geographically close countries with similar economic wealth and who are both members of the European Community.

The reason for these international differences is probably due to differences in the agency problems within the different corporate governance systems. German companies more often tend to have strong inside-owners whereas American companies are characterised by a more dispersed ownership. Dispersed ownership and weak main owners cause greater information asymmetries than concentrated ownership and strong owners. Not even the largest owner of a company might want to take an active role in the governing of the company, particularly if he/she only holds a fraction of his/her wealth in this particular company. This gives the main owner very little real insight into operations (the situation for the other owners is of course even worse). Dividends then become more important (Rozeff, 1982). The signalling effect of dividends makes less sense in a company where the owner has direct control over his/her investment. In such companies it makes more sense to retain earnings (because of transaction costs and taxes).

The importance of information asymmetry related to the governance structure has also been proven important when previously government-owned companies go public. It has been found that companies doing so, increase their dividend payout ratio quite substantially (Megginson, Nash, and van Randenborgh, 1994). There is also a difference between, on the one hand, private and newly introduced companies and, on the other hand, large public companies. The latter do in general pay much larger dividends (Walker and Petty, 1978). The essence is that there is a much wider separation of ownership and control in large public companies than there is in small private or government-owned companies.

The problem escalates in mature companies, as these tend to have greater free cash flows and fewer opportunities to make profitable investments. Management in these companies have greater opportunities to increase financial slack. As investors realise this they should demand higher dividends. Strong owners of a mature company can enforce a certain dividend policy, whereas weak owners have a harder time doing so. The effect coming from the governance structure (agency problem) is thus interfered with company-specific production-oriented factors such as free cash flows and investment opportunities.

8.4 Share Repurchases

8.4.1 The nature of share repurchases

Dividends represent just one of the capital transactions between shareholders and the company. An alternative to a dividend payout is the repurchase of shares. This activity reduces the number of outstanding shares and if the purchase is paid with excessive cash and not interfering with long term investments the value of the remaining shares should increase. From year 2000 and onwards, Swedish companies are allowed to repurchase their own shares. This no longer makes their situation different from that of most other European companies. The share repurchase programs of European companies have increased immensely over the last three to four years. Only in Europe shares worth more than SEK 672 Billion were repurchased in 1998. Whereas share repurchase is a relatively new European phenomenon, American companies have been able to do so for a long time and hence most of the empirical studies of these transactions have been carried out there.

We shall focus the analysis on the advantages of share repurchases, and the reasons why companies choose to reduce the number of outstanding shares instead of simply paying additional dividends. While so doing, we shall adopt a managerial perspective and see whether there are reasons for management to choose one policy instead of another.

First of all, share repurchasing means that the company uses liquid assets to purchase its own shares on the stock exchange. There are differences between different countries regarding for example who makes the decision of repurchasing shares, how many shares companies are allowed to repurchase, and from whom they can be purchased. In Sweden a general meeting of shareholders has to approve a repurchasing scheme. According to Swedish law a company can own a maximum of ten percent of its own shares, and those shares can be purchased either through a tender offer to all shareholders, or anonymously through the open market. Several restrictions apply, of which we will not go into details of here. In the past, companies have been allowed to redeem shares, so the reduction in the number of outstanding shares that share repurchases enable is not something totally new. But share repurchases are easier to make and add flexibility to management. With a share repurchase the company can own its own shares for some time and then sell them at a later stage, for example, in combination with an acquisition of another company.

Both dividends and share repurchases are used to remove an overcapitalisation in companies with high free cash flows or an excessively high stock of capital, which is not appropriately used. In a world with no market frictions and no asymmetric information the choice between cash dividends and share repurchases would have no value-relevance. In order to choose correctly between the two alternatives we must therefore, again, look at violations of the dividend irrelevance theorem. In contrast to a dividend payout, share repurchases increase the value of existing shares and thus current investors do not have to pay instant taxes on their gain. The world with taxes that we live in thus provides an advantage for share repurchases over cash dividends. Transaction costs can also, possibly, be reduced if the company buys it own shares, and then uses them when acquiring another company.

From society's point of view, there is one major drawback with a share repurchase scheme; the risk of share price manipulation. For many companies ten percent of outstanding shares represent a significant portion of the free float. Severe price manipulation can potentially be the end result, particularly since Swedish companies often have very close ties between owners and management. In the case of a takeover current owners could use their own company's shares to increase the value of the company, i.e., increase their wealth on behalf of future owners' wealth. There are restrictions as to when the company can buy shares and to what extent it can do so, but such restrictions only reduce some of the negative effects. One must not forget that share repurchases in themselves are value-relevant and drive value. It is impossible to say that no share repurchasing may occur in connection with the announcement of value-driving information.[4]

8.4.2 Example of a share repurchase

At the special general meeting of Volvo in year 2000, which was held because of the company's sale of the car division to Ford Motor Corporation, it was announced that the company wanted to repurchase ten percent of the outstanding shares for approximately SEK 10 Billion. With the sale of the car division the company has liquid assets of more than SEK 60 Billion and so without current restrictions the company could have repurchased much more of its outstanding shares. The estimated operating earnings from the remaining business units amounted to SEK 5 Billion this year. It is assumed that the money used for share repurchase, SEK 10 Billion, could have been used for little else than safe investments in the financial market, yielding 3.5 percent in return. We therefore get the figures shown in Table 8.3.

Table 8.3 – The share repurchase program of Volvo.

(MSEK)	With share repurchase program	Without share repurchase program
Operating earnings	5,000	5,000
Financial income	0	+350*
Earnings after fin.income	5,000	5,350
Corporate taxes (28 %)	–1,400	–1,498
Net earnings	3,600	3,852
Earnings per share	9.06	8.72
Number of shares outstanding ('000)	397,350	441,500

* = 10,000,000,000 × 3.5 %

After the repurchase program the earnings-per-share increases and since Volvo's business operations are the same, shareholders should experience

4 There seems to be two ways of framing information regarding a share repurchase program. Either it is seen as good news to investors because the program raises earnings per share, or it is seen as bad news to investors because it signals a lack of profitable investment opportunities.

an unchanged risk. The share repurchase program therefore increases the value of Volvo. Please note the tax shield removal, which reduces the benefits of share repurchase by (1 – t).

8.4.3 Managerial strategies

In a world with taxes the repurchase of shares is a more efficient way of transferring capital from the company to the shareholders. Still most companies pay dividends. This behaviour cannot be explained by saying that share repurchases involve high transaction costs as most companies repurchasing shares still pay dividends. American studies have however showed that the share price response to large repurchases through tender offers is substantial (e.g. Dann, 1981). In fact, it is larger than equivalent dividend payouts. There have not been many Swedish studies in this area so far. Smaller repurchases made anonymously through the open market are not likely to have any major different effect than a dividend payout.

The reason for retaining dividends when making share repurchases is probably that a reduced dividend sends out more bad information, than a share repurchase sends out good information. Particularly if the market interprets the dividend cut as permanent and the share repurchase as a one-off event. The same argument is probably true when it comes to the retention of dividends when issuing new equity. The cash that shareholders receive from the dividend is possibly also conceived as more definite and secure than a paper-gain in the share price.

8.5 Summary

8.5.1 The agency cost – contracting model

In short, the agency cost – contracting model explains dividend policy as value maximising attempts by managers acting in an environment where the separation of ownership and control causes agency conflicts, and thus additional deadweight costs, to arise. As agents, management should maximise the value of the company but instead they are thought to pursue their own personal goals, which usually involves an establishment of financial slack and an investment in unprofitable projects. We have so far identified a number of factors determining the "trade-off" within this model. Taxes and transaction costs reduce the amount of dividends paid out, whereas agency costs (goal incongruence and asymmetric information) increases the amount of dividends paid out. To understand the level of dividends any certain company should pay out one must look at company-, governance- and context-specific factors, and see how they interact with the four issues mentioned previously in the text.

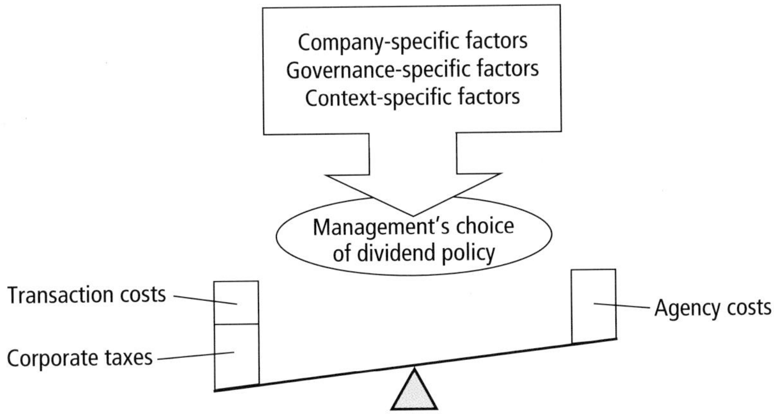

Figure 8.4 – The Agency Cost – Contracting Model.

The dividend policy is determined by company-specific production-oriented factors such as for example the amount of free cash flows, investment opportunities, capital intensity of business operations, company size in comparison to competitors, etc. High free cash flows make agency costs relatively more important for the dividend policy. A large amount of investment opportunities make transaction costs relatively more important, and so on. At the same time there are governance related factors such as for example the existence of active equity markets, monitoring ability of shareholders, the number of shareholders, etc. A relatively low ability to monitor managerial activities will make agency costs important, and so on. Below we summarise all the market imperfections we have covered throughout the chapter, and their effects on the choice of company dividend policy. The actual dividend policy is unique for the company in question, and determined by the relative importance of each of the factors in Table 8.4.

Table 8.4 – Summary of factors included in the Agency Cost – Contracting Model.

Context-specific factors	
High personal taxes on dividend income	Lower dividend payout ratio
High personal taxes on capital gains income	Higher dividend payout ratio
High transaction costs in financial markets	Lower dividend payout ratio
Governance-specific factors	
Weak owners	Higher dividend payout ratio
Many owners	Higher dividend payout ratio
Extensive bonding arrangements (e.g. options)	Lower dividend payout ratio
Extensive use of monitoring devices	Lower dividend payout ratio
Company-specific factors	
Little other information about company performance	Higher dividend payout ratio
High company growth rate	Lower dividend payout ratio
Many profitable investment opportunities	Lower dividend payout ratio
High capital intensity in production	Lower dividend payout ratio
High level of free cash flow	Higher dividend payout ratio

Key Issues to Discuss

1. Explain the dividend policy irrelevance theorem, and while doing so point out the similarities between it and the capital structure irrelevance theorem.
2. Discuss the impact that market frictions (or various kind) have on the choice of dividend policy.
3. Discuss the impact that goal incongruence between management and investors have on the choice of dividend policy.
4. Discuss whether (and if so, how) management can take advantage of the signalling aspects of dividends. What are the motives for managers to do so? Can such a behaviour have negative long term effects on managers?
5. Is it likely that dividend pay-out ratios are higher, lower or about the same in Swedish companies as compared to their American counterparts? Why?
6. Share repurchases are often suggested to be a better way to transfer cash from the company to the shareholders. Why is this so?
7. Is it likely that management would benefit from cutting down dividends while making increased share repurchases? Discuss the signalling effect such behaviour would have.

Chapter 9

Investment Decisions

This chapter aims at:

- Describing how capital costs are determined and used when evaluating investments.
- Providing a brief coverage of how the most common techniques of investment appraisal work.
- Discussing how and to what extent management uses investment appraisal models when deciding to make investments.

9.1 Introduction

One of the fundamental ideas of financial theory is that management should focus on making investments in product markets rather than focus on how to finance investments. Financial markets are far more efficient than product markets, and it is relatively speaking easier to earn abnormal returns in product markets. To put it differently: There are hardly any business success stories in which the manager seriously considered the capital structure before knowing which investment she needed to finance. This is not to say that the financing function is unimportant, just that it is dependent on good investment ideas. In this chapter we learn how to examine whether an investment is profitable or not.

Investment and financing decisions are usually treated separately in the theoretical literature. The reason for this goes back to the basic principles of investment and consumption that were established by economist Irving Fisher (1930). To make an investment is to forego consumption. Although Fisher was not interested in share markets per se, he demonstrated that capital markets provide a single interest rate that both borrowers and lenders can use in consumption and investment decisions. This is known as *Fisher's separation theorem.*[1] The practical aspect of this theorem is that management does not have to rely on specific individual investors and their investment preferences. They simply present information concerning the investment opportunities they have to the market, where it is evaluated and priced. On the other hand, those individuals having surplus wealth (investors) do not have to worry about making the actual physical investments themselves. They evaluate the existing information and price investment projects in accordance to their risk. Of course this requires efficient capital markets where information about investment projects is abundant. Both transaction costs and information asymmetries cause disturbances. In small companies requiring capital for investments this can cause a substantial problem. For them the separation of financing and investment is more difficult to make, as transaction costs are greater and, sometimes, information is more asymmetrically distributed.

1 Irving Fischer never applied his ideas to capital markets, but discussed them only in general. The application of the Fischer Separation Theorem to capital markets was made by e.g. Williams (1938), Durand (1952), and Rubinstein (1973).

Although financing and investment decisions are separated, financiers (shareholders) and investors (managers) need to understand each other.[2] The link between them is the *required rate of return* (as it is called from a financier perspective) or the *discount rate* (as it is called from an investor perspective). We can also refer to it as the *cost of capital.* With perfect capital markets, the cost of capital is unaffected by capital structure (remember Chapter Seven) and dividend policy (remember Chapter Eight). It is only the operating risk that matters. When transaction costs and asymmetrically distributed information exist the cost of capital will rise in proportion.

There is a continuous trade-off between the return coming from investments and the costs of capital used to finance the investments. The ultimate objective for a profit-maximising company is to approve all investments that have an expected return on investment higher than their cost of capital. This idea is illustrated in Figure 9.1. If a company finances its operations with capital coming from a frictionless capital market and all its investment opportunities bear the same risk, one can illustrate the cost of capital as being independent of the amount of investments made. Management does not have to be concerned about how operations are financed, it just makes the profitable investments and when additional capital is required this is asked for and collected from the capital market.

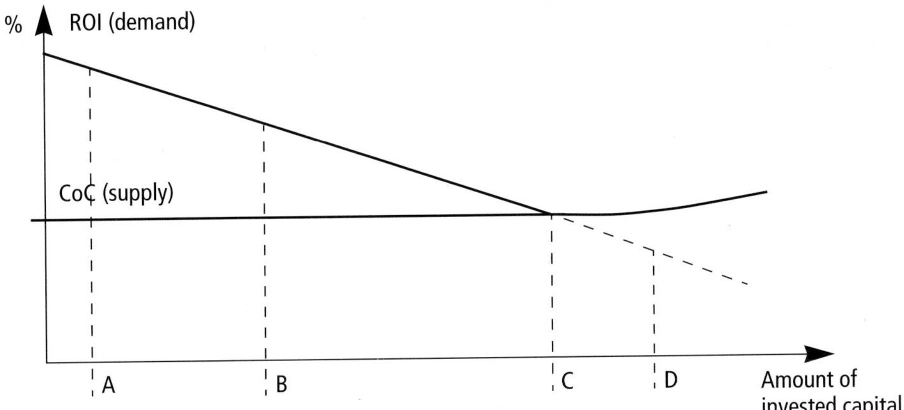

ROI = Return on investment, CoC = Cost of capital.

Figure 9.1 – The demand and supply for capital in a corporation.

2 The terminology here can be confusing. Since we are talking about *product markets* managers are referred to as investors, i.e., they are the ones making physical investments. Shareholders are, from a management perspective, financiers although they are investors in the capital market.

Consider the situation illustrated in Figure 9.1. This company has many different investment alternatives, which are illustrated using the ROI solid line. Among these investments four particular ones have been shown in the figure; Projects A, B, C, and D. The company's cost of capital (CoC) is assumed to be independent of the amount of invested capital. The most profitable investment is Project A, which is clearly expected to earn a return higher than the cost of capital, and it will undoubtedly be made. Also Project B will be made. Project C has an expected return on investment equal to the cost of capital, whereas Project D is expected to earn less than the cost of capital. It can be expected that the company will invest in Project C but not in Project D. The supply and demand for capital in this company is therefore in equilibrium at the point where ROI intersects CoC, in this case being Project C.

The typology of different investments

The most typical investment is probably that of a machine used to produce a certain product. But to enable a meaningful discussion of investment decisions we need to distinguish between different investments. In reality these distinctions are not always easy to make. The first distinction to be made is between *financial investments* (made in monetary assets, such as bonds, certificates and shares in other companies), and *operating investments* (made in physical assets, such as production plants, buildings, machines and suchlike). Acquiring shares in other companies is to some extent dealt with in the next chapter (including mergers), but, apart from that this text deals with operating investments. Most often investments in financial assets are assumed to create no additional value – financial markets are too efficient. They are therefore simply valued at their current market value. More of this in Chapter Ten.

The second distinction is between new investments and reinvestments. The new investment aims at providing the company with the ability to produce products and/or services it has yet not been able to produce or alternatively to increase the amount of products currently being produced. The reinvestment is made because existing machinery has worn out and thus needs to be replaced. The *reinvestment* has no additional effect on company cash flows. Reinvestments are relatively certain and rarely need careful evaluation. They are also often so in line with existing strategies they cannot be avoided. New investments increase the size of company operations and create what is referred to as *organic growth*, i.e., growth based on an expansion of the company's own operations.[3] In comparison to reinvestments, the new investments are usually more uncertain and they involve more parameters management have little knowledge of.

But in between these two types of investments there are various others. Some investments are made in order to enhance the *quality* of existing products and services. Some investments are made to improve *cost efficiency*. Others are forced upon the company because of changing *legislation*. In reality most investments are made because of several of these reasons in combination. A forest company which decides to make an investment in a new paper mill probably expects to increase capacity, improve quality, improve cost efficiency and possibly also better conform to new environmental standards.

Theoretically speaking there is little difference between the above-mentioned reasons for making investments; the real problem lies in detecting their cash-flow effects. Investments that are made to improve product quality might just sustain a company's position in the market and not improve it – which means no explicit cash flow effects. But withholding the investment would lead to lost market shares and thus lost cash flows. Although there is, theoretically speaking, little problem dealing with this, it is rarely dealt with in the investment theory literature. We return to this later on in the chapter. Table 9.1 summarises major differences between investments.

Table 9.1 – Generic cash flow effect coming from investments.

Reason for investment	Cash flow effect	Comment
Produce more products	Higher cash inflows.	
Produce more different products	Higher cash inflows.	
Improve quality	Perhaps higher cash inflows.	Strategic consequences? Profitability depends on competitors' reactions.
Decrease production costs	Lower cash outflows.	
Conform to standards	No effect.	Often made although unprofitable. No choice.

In this chapter the most fundamental issues of evaluating individual investment projects are covered. In the next chapter we move on to evaluating whole businesses. The discussion in Chapter Ten is based on the same ideas of discounting future cash flows as this chapter but it contains some refine-

3 As opposed to acquired growth, which is achieved by acquiring the operations of another company.

ments of the models. At the end of that chapter there is furthermore a discussion of mergers and acquisitions. These are investments in assets that management make, but instead of setting up the investments themselves (organic growth) they acquire them as stand-alone units (acquired growth).

In comparison to previous chapters of this book, this one contains slightly more techniques and less theory. Wherever it is appropriate, references to current research have been added to support ideas brought forward in the text. For a much more thorough coverage of investment decisions the reader is directed towards more specialized texts within the area.[4]

9.2 Determining the Discount Rate

9.2.1 The risk-free interest rate

When you put money in the bank, you usually require an interest on that money. Perhaps you have not reflected on why it is that you "want" that interest (or why you deserve to get the interest). The basis for our decision criteria used when evaluating projects is that time is money. All creditors require an interest and hence all borrowers are forced to pay for using someone else's money. But let's get back to the issue of putting money in the bank. Why do you require interest? It is possible to distinguish between a couple of reasons. The first one is that when you place your savings in the bank you forego consumption. That is, capital is a financial means used to satisfy your needs and wants. The mere possession of money is not enough to make you happy, but it is having the ability to satisfy your current and future desires that counts. When one's capital is placed in the bank account one has fewer opportunities. The interest is therefore a compensation for the opportunities that are lost; an *opportunity cost*. The second reason is that there is a tendency of price rises (inflation) within society. Continuous price increases will lead to a situation where the money placed in the bank is worth less when you get it back than when you placed it there. Those who postpone their consumption need compensation for this as well.

4 A book with the same kind of critical perspective on investment decisions that is given here, is Åkerblom (2001), which obviously is highly recommended.

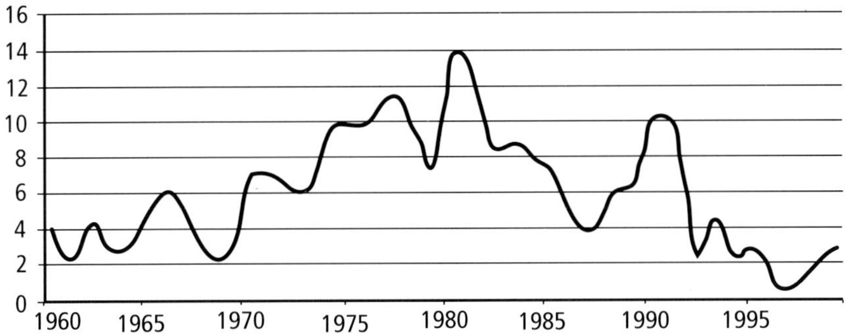

Figure 9.2 – Swedish inflation 1960–99.

Figure 9.2 shows that on average inflation in consumer prices has been approximately six percent over the last fifty years. Since 1993 the Swedish inflation rate has been kept below four percent, which is lower than any other time-period of substantial length. As discussed in Chapter Six, the risk-free interest rate is often approximated using the 10-year government bond. Because of low inflation (and low inflation expectations) the interest on this bond is currently at about six percent, lower than it has been in the past. Over the last twenty years, the ten-year government bond has consistently been a bit above the expected inflation rate, as shown in Figure 9.3.

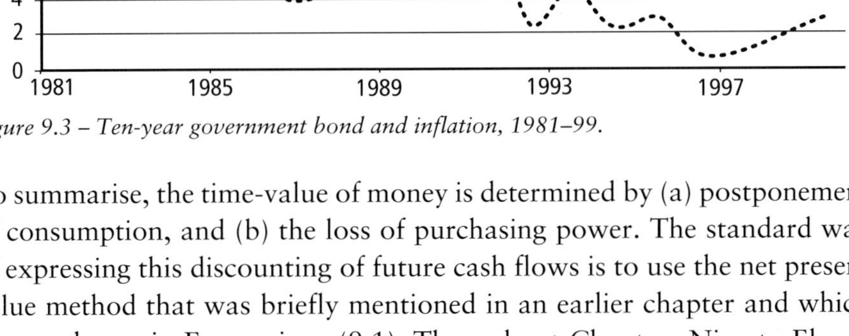

Figure 9.3 – Ten-year government bond and inflation, 1981–99.

To summarise, the time-value of money is determined by (a) postponement of consumption, and (b) the loss of purchasing power. The standard way of expressing this discounting of future cash flows is to use the net present value method that was briefly mentioned in an earlier chapter and which is now shown in Expressions (9.1). Throughout Chapters Nine to Eleven it will be used frequently.

$$V_t = \sum_{t=1}^{\infty} \frac{cf_t}{(1+r)^t} \qquad (9.1a)$$

$$V_t = \frac{cf_1}{(1+r)^1} + \frac{cf_2}{(1+r)^2} + \ldots + \frac{cf_n}{(1+r)^n} \qquad (9.1b)$$

If the time-value of money is 10 percent, the value of an investment with annual cash flows of 100, 100, and 100 is not 300, but instead Expression (9.1b) gives us:

$$V_t = \frac{cf_1}{(1+r)^1} + \frac{cf_2}{(1+r)^2} + \frac{cf_3}{(1+r)^3} =$$

$$= \frac{100}{(1+10\,\%)^1} + \frac{100}{(1+10\,\%)^2} + \frac{100}{(1+10\,\%)^3} =$$

$$= V_t = 90.9 + 82.7 + 75.1 = 248.7 \qquad (9.2)$$

Even under certainty, future cash flows are worth less in today's value the further into the future it is received, and the higher the cost of capital is. By asking for an annual interest of 10 percent the investor is compensated for the postponement of consumption and the loss of purchasing power.

9.2.2 Including risk in the discount factor

In the modern financial world large companies have hundreds, if not thousands, of different ways of sourcing capital. Similar to the discussion in Chapter Seven the following discussion is limited to two forms of capital: the interest-bearing debt and the risk-bearing capital (mainly equity). These are two conceptually different forms of financing, where the first relies on a fixed legal contract, which guarantees the holder of the debt-contract certain rights, whereas the second provides the holder the right to all residual claims to the company. The reason why different financiers are treated separately is that their contracts with the company are different and therefore their risk differs. With the help of *the weighted average cost of capital formula* (WACC) the cost of capital for a company is identified. This cost is, primarily, determined by the risk of the portfolio of projects management have invested in. In Expression (9.3), r_n represents the cost of capital source n, and w_n represents the weight of capital source n.

$$r_{WACC} = w_1 \cdot r_1 + w_2 \cdot r_2 + w_3 \cdot r_3 + \ldots + w_n \cdot r_n \quad (9.3)$$

where $w_1 + w_2 + w_3 + \ldots + w_n = 1$

In Expression (9.3) an unlimited number of financial sources can be included. But if we limit ourselves to only debt (D) and equity (EQ) financing, Expression (9.3) can be re-written as in Expression (9.4). As you can see, a risk-premium is added to the risk-free interest rate (Expressions 9.5 and 9.6).

$$r_{WACC} = \left(\frac{EQ}{D + EQ}\right) \cdot r_{eq} + \left(\frac{D}{D + EQ}\right) \cdot r_d \quad (9.4)$$

$$r_d = r_f + rp_d \quad (9.5)$$

$$r_{eq} = r_f + rp_{eq} \quad (9.6)$$

where

r_d = the cost of debt

r_f = risk-free interest rate

rp_d = risk premium for debt

r_{eq} = the cost of equity

rp_{eq} = risk premium for equity

In previous chapters it has been discussed more in detail how to estimate the cost of debt and the cost of equity. This discussion is not repeated here. By far the most common way to adjust for risk when making investment decisions is to include the risk-premium in the discount factor. Further on in this chapter an alternative approach is discussed, in which the expected values of future cash flows are reduced with a factor representing the uncertainty (risk) involved. This risk-adjusted amount is thereafter discounted using the risk-free interest rate. We return to this approach further on, but will for now stick with the standard method.

9.2.3 *Different discount rates for different projects*

Most companies are running a number of projects at the same time. Although many of them might be in the same area, they are not likely to bear the exact same risk.[5] This can cause problems when evaluating individual investment projects. Let's take an example. Assi-Domän is a Swedish com-

5 Risk refers to deviations from expected future cash flows. Differences in risk therefore refer to differences in the predictability of future cash flows.

pany listed on the Stockholm Stock Exchange. It operates mainly in two business areas: one that is industrially oriented (aimed at producing paper materials such as corrugated board, containerboard and cartonboard), and another that is forestry oriented (Assi-Domän is currently Europe's largest listed forest owner.).[6] The risk of doing business within these two sectors is considerably different. Whereas the industrial part is in a relatively turbulent competitive situation, the forestry part is facing a much more stable situation. The low risk environment of the forestry part should earn investors low/moderate returns, while the industrial part should earn them higher returns.

The cost of capital for the entire company is reasonably easy to estimate, one simply has to observe the capital structure, calculate the cost of debt and the cost of equity (using e.g. the CAPM). But since Assi-Domän's business operations are so diverse, this WACC is hardly representative for any individual investments within each of the two business sectors.

Two ways of handling this are possible. Both aim at determining the actual risk of the project. Unfortunately, both suffer from the same limitation. The first suggestion is to identify the industry that the individual project is operating in, and then find a company that has its entire operations within the same industry. The beta-value of this company can be used directly, or after a transformation to that of Assi-Domän with adjustments for differences in capital structure.

In order to adjust for differences in capital structure, use of the so-called "unleveraged" beta-value (Myers, 1974) is often suggested.[7] With efficient markets the transformation is straightforward.[8]

$$\beta_{EQ} = (1 + D/EQ) \cdot \beta_A \tag{9.7}$$

But as debt is tax-deductible this formulation is often altered to incorporate the "tax-shield" effect caused by debt financing. The model that is most commonly used is one developed by Hamada (1972).[9] This beta-value (β_A) can be plugged into the standard capital asset pricing model generating the cost of equity for an unleveraged company.

6 As of this writing at the beginning of 2001, there is a discussion of whether these two parts of Assi-Domän should be placed into two separate companies.

7 This method is only briefly covered here, but can be found in several textbooks on investment decisions.

8 When using Expression (9.7) one has to assume risk-free debt.

9 See e.g. Grinblatt and Titman (1998) for a pedagogical coverage of these techniques.

$$\beta_A = \frac{\beta_{EQ}^{competitor}}{[1 + D/EQ \cdot (1 - t)]} \tag{9.8}$$

The other alternative is to carefully compare the cash flows of the particular area in which the investment is made, with those of the entire company. It can thereby, at least in theory, be possible to estimate beta-values for each individual project the company is involved in. Business areas in which projects are earning stable cash flows will have a lower beta-value and additional investments in these areas should be evaluated using a lower discount rate, and vice versa.

The problem with these two methods is identical. In order to estimate the risk of the project one has to be able to forecast the patterns of future cash flows. But can we be sure that the cash flow pattern of an investment will be similar to that of a competitor? Can we be sure that it will resemble that of the operations we currently have, or have had? There is something paradoxical with investment appraisal models and forecasting cash flows. If one knows the future well, there is usually little need to use precise evaluation models, the decision is obvious anyway. If one does not know the future well, little additional help will come from refined models.

9.3 Models Used to Appraise Investments

9.3.1 Introduction

Several alternative models are used to appraise investments, and three of these are described in this section. It is important to note that all models that take the value of time into account will, under the same assumptions, provide the same answer. The choice of evaluation method is therefore very much determined by individual preferences and the decision-making environment. The first of the methods described here is a simple payback method, in which time is not taken into consideration. The other two models are more sophisticated as they do not only take the size of the cash flows into consideration but also when in time they occur. These models are the net present value (NPV) model and the internal rate of return (IRR) model.

When making investment decisions, cash flows are all that matter. Cash flows are for real, they cannot easily be manipulated, and have a value that can be agreed upon by all. Accounting earnings have only a limited effect on investment decisions. An effect we will not discuss further until the next section.

9.3.2 The pay-back method

The *payback method* is the easiest model to understand and apply. It measures the time it takes to recover the initial outlays in a project. If the future cash flows are annuities, i.e., the same throughout the whole investment period, simply dividing the initial outlay with the value of the annuity will identify the payback time. If the investment generates a varied stream of future cash flows the periodical cash flows will have to be summarised and compared with the initial outlay. The investment is made if the initial investment is regained within a reasonable time. Obviously it should never be made if it is never regained.

Table 9.2 shows capital expenditure data for four projects in the company Mercumin AB. When evaluating Project A that has annual cash inflows of SEK 26,000 the payback period is found simply by dividing the initial investment with the annuity (100,000/26,000). This gives a payback period of 3 years and 10 months.[10] Project B has irregular cash flows over the project's economic life, which have to be considered. After one year 50 percent of the initial investment has been paid back, after two years 85 percent has been paid back, and after three years 110 percent has been paid back. If cash flows are equally distributed throughout the year the payback period is 2 years and 7 months.

Table 9.2 – Capital expenditure for three projects in Mercumin AB.

(SEK)	Project A	Project B	Project C	Project D
Initial investment (year 0)	–100,000	–100,000	–100,000	–100,000
Cash flows (year 1)	26,000	50,000	45,000	0
Cash flows (year 2)	26,000	35,000	35,000	10,000
Cash flows (year 3)	26,000	25,000	20,000	30,000
Cash flows (year 4)	26,000	10,000	–20,000	50,000
Cash flows (year 5)	26,000	10,000	50,000	65,000
Total cash flows	**30,000**	**30,000**	**30,000**	**55,000**
Payback time (year:month)	**3:10**	**2:7**	**3:0, 4:5**	**4:4**

The payback method is usually viewed as a rather unsophisticated capital budgeting technique. It ignores the previously discussed point that time is

10 After three years the investment had paid back 78,000 of the initial investment of 100,000. During the fourth year cash inflows of 26,000 are expected. (100,000– –78,000)/26,000 gives us 0.85 years, equal to 10.2 months.

money. The payback method only recognises the liquidity (cash) consequences of the investment decision. Already from the beginning of this book it has been emphasised that investors care little about liquidity, but focus on profitability. The payback method is thus not in line with the shareholder wealth maximisation idea. A second weakness is the method's failure to take the whole investment period into account. To illustrate this, look at Project C in Table 9.2. The initial investment is paid back in the first three years. But Project C requires an additional investment during year four. This additional investment is compensated by a higher cash flow (in comparison to the other investment alternatives) in year five. Because of the negative cash flow in year four Project C has two "payback periods": One after three years and one after four years and five months. Project D earns back the highest total amount of cash, but it takes two years to generate the first positive cash flows and its payback time is four years and four months. If management had to choose between these four projects it is likely that they would choose Project B first.

Despite the critique against the payback method it has been known to be one of the most commonly used method by practitioners. Such results have been found in several countries such as e.g. the United States (Gitman and Maxwell, 1987), Japan (Hodder (1986), and Sweden (Segelod, 1986).

9.3.3 The net present value method

The *net present value* (NPV) method is the most frequently discussed capital budgeting technique in investment literature. It is also a method that is well-aligned with financial theory and the idea of shareholder wealth maximisation. The NPV method assigns an explicit value to time and does not give consideration to liquidity aspects of the investment decision. To be precise, the net present value of an investment is the sum of all future cash flows brought back to today while considering when in time they occur. The value given to time is dependent on the opportunity cost of the investor, who could have made an equivalent investment (same risk) elsewhere in the financial markets.

$$NPV = \sum_{t=1}^{\infty} \frac{cf_t}{(1+r)^t} = -I_0 + \frac{cf_1}{(1+r)^1} + \frac{cf_2}{(1+r)^2} + \ldots + \frac{cf_t}{(1+r)^t} \tag{9.9}$$

The investment should be made if the NPV is greater than zero, but rejected if it is less. When the NPV is greater than zero the cash inflows, valued at today's present value, are greater than the capital costs. If such an investment is made the market value of the company is increased, and shareholder wealth is maximised.

9.3.4 *The internal rate of return method*

The *internal rate of return* (IRR) method is conceptually the most difficult of the three capital budgeting techniques. It has nonetheless been found to be quite common in practise (Gitman and Maxwell, 1987). The IRR is the return that is generated by a project's cash flows. To compare with the NPV method one can say that the IRR represents the discount rate for which the NPV of a project is equal to zero. This is the same as when the NPV of all future cash flows are the same as the initial investment. Mathematically the IRR can be found by solving either of the two equations:

$$NPV = 0 = \sum_{t=1}^{t} \frac{cf_t}{(1 + IRR)^t} - I_0 \quad (9.10a)$$

$$I_0 = \sum_{t=1}^{n} \frac{cf_t}{(1 + IRR)^t} \quad (9.10b)$$

Unless the cash inflows are annuities, there is a substantial difficulty calculating the internal rate of return of an investment. Fortunately there are both calculators and software programs that do this for us. The alternative is to estimate the IRR using a trial-and-error process. This latter method is exemplified in the next section where the NPV and IRR methods are compared. An investment should be made if the IRR is greater than the cost of capital, but rejected if it is less. When the IRR is greater than the cost of capital, the present value of future cash inflows is greater than the initial outlay. When such an investment is made the market value of the company is increased, and shareholder wealth is maximised.

9.3.5 *Comparing the NPV and IRR methods*

Both the net present value and the internal rate of return method are based on the same principles and will therefore generate the same results as long as the underlying assumptions are the same. Differences in the accept-reject decision only occur when the rule of equal underlying assumptions is violated.

Now we shall compare the two approaches using the data from Table 9.2. Mercumin had four investment alternatives. Let's look at Projects B and D and assume that the cost of capital for Mercumin is 12 percent.[11] Table 9.3 shows the NPV of the two projects.

Table 9.3 – Using the net present value method to evaluate projects.

Project B							
Year (t)	0	1	2	3	4	5	**Summary**
Cash flows	–100,000	60,000	25,000	25,000	10,000	10,000	**30,000**
Discount factor, 12 %	1.000	0.893	0.797	0.712	0.636	0.567	
Present value	–100,000	53,571	19,930	17,795	6,355	5,674	**3,325**

Project D							
Year (t)	0	1	2	3	4	5	**Summary**
Cash flows	–100,000	0	10,000	30,000	50,000	65,000	**55,000**
Discount factor, 12 %	1.000	0.893	0.797	0.712	0.636	0.567	
Present value	–100,000	0	7,972	21,353	31,776	36,883	**–2,016**

The NPV is positive for Project B, which should be undertaken, whereas it is negative for Project D. Intuitively we can make a guess that the internal rate of return for Project B is higher than 12 percent (WACC), whereas the internal rate of return for Project D is lower than 12 percent. To find the IRR of each project we can use a trial-and-error approach as illustrated in Table 9.4. The cash flows of Project B are discounted using various discount rates. First, when eight percent is used, the NPV is clearly positive. Thereafter we try with a discount rate of 12 percent. Also here the NPV is positive. The third time the discount rate is set at 15 percent and then the NPV is negative. The IRR must lie between 12 and 15 percent. The discount rate that generates a zero NPV is 13.92 percent. This is Project B's internal rate of return (IRR). In an identical way (not shown) we can find that the IRR for Project D is 11.43 percent.

11 In Table 9.4 a discount factor is multiplied to future cash flows. The discount factor is estimated as $1/(1 + r)^t$.

Table 9.4 – Finding the IRR of Project B.

Period	CF	8 %		12 %		15 %		13,92 %	
		df	dcf	df	dcf	df	dcf	df	dcf
0	−100,000	1.000	−100,000	1.000	−100,000	1.000	−100,000	1.000	−100,000
1	60,000	0.926	55,556	0.893	53,571	0.870	52,174	0.878	52,671
2	25,000	0.857	21,433	0.797	19,930	0.756	18,904	0.771	19,265
3	25,000	0.794	19,846	0.712	17,795	0.658	16,438	0.676	16,912
4	10,000	0.735	7,350	0.636	6,355	0.572	5,718	0.594	5,938
5	10,000	0.681	6,806	0.567	5,674	0.497	4,972	0.521	5,213
NPV			**10,991**		**3,325**		**−1,795**		**0**

Note: df equals the discount factor and dcf equals the cash flow when multiplied with the discount factor.

But to compare the NPV and IRR methods more closely we shall look at their so-called net present value profiles, which are described graphically in Figure 9.4. To obtain the coordinates necessary for the graph one needs to find the NPV given certain discount rates. The NPV using a discount rate of twelve percent was calculated to be 3,325, and −2,016, respectively, in the text above. Adding all positive cash flows and subtracting the initial investment gives us the NPV at a zero percent discount rate. For Projects B and D the following calculations are used:

$$NPV^{B}_{0\,\%} = -100{,}000 + 50{,}000 + 35{,}000 + 25{,}000 + 10{,}000 + 10{,}000 =$$
$$= 30{,}000$$

$$NPV^{D}_{0\,\%} = -100{,}000 + 0 + 10{,}000 + 30{,}000 + 50{,}000 + 65{,}000 =$$
$$= 55{,}000$$

Figure 9.4 shows that for any discount rate above 9.1 percent Project D will be preferred to Project B. Below this breaking point however, Project

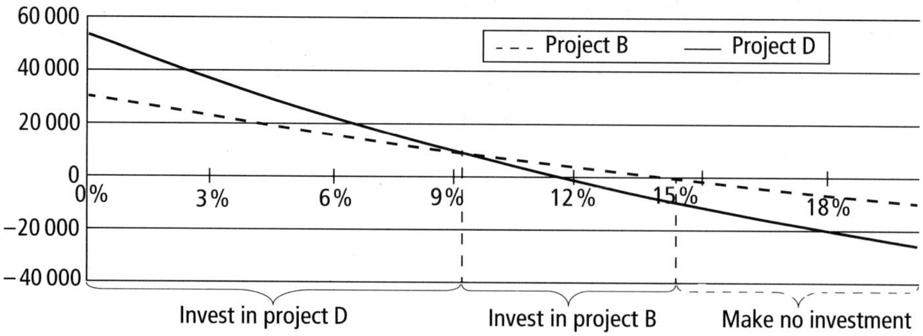

Figure 9.4 – Net present value profiles for Mercumin's Projects B and D.

B is preferred to Project D. When comparing these two models it is important to understand that as long as the NPV profiles for Projects B and D cross at a positive NPV the IRRs for the two projects will cause conflicting rankings *below* the breaking point (here: 9.1 percent).

It was mentioned before that the IRR method is slightly more common among practitioners. On a purely theoretical basis, the NPV method is a better investment appraisal method. This is for several reasons. The internal inconsistency achieved among the investment alternatives shown in Figure 9.4 is due to assumptions regarding reinvested cash inflows from the projects. When using the IRR method cash inflows are assumed to be reinvested at the IRR, which is usually quite high. The NPV method on the other hand assumes that intermediate cash inflows are reinvested at the cost of capital, which is more realistic. If the company lacks investment opportunities earning this rate of return, such cash flows can be redistributed to investors by having a more generous dividend policy.

A second reason is that investments having irregular cash flows (both net cash inflows and net cash outflows) will show multiple IRRs (Lorie and Savage, 1955; Hirshleifer, 1958).[12] This problem is similar to the problem the payback method suffered from. On the other hand, the NPV method is much more straightforward. Being the theoretically most correct method does not however mean it is the most desired method. Managers often prefer the IRR method to the NPV method. The IRR is seen as a measure of profitability and is therefore easier to communicate throughout the organisation.

9.4 Handling Future Cash Flows

9.4.1 Introduction

This chapter does not aim at giving a complete guide as to how all investment situations should be handled. It is suggested that the reader uses other more specialised texts on the subject. In this section however, some of the most common technical problems are illustrated and dealt with. They are also returned to in the final discussion of management's usage of capital budgeting techniques.

12 The reason for this is based on the mathematical propensities of the model. Please see e.g. Gitman (1992) for a thorough discussion of the subject.

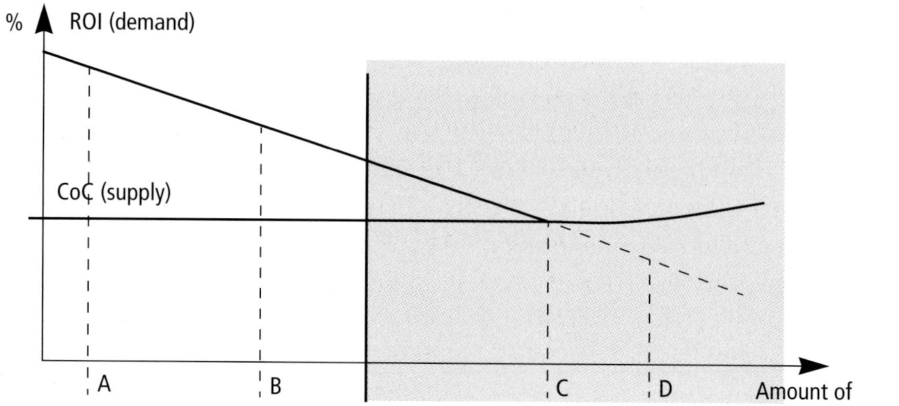

ROI = Return on investment, CoC = Cost of capital.

Figure 9.5 – Capital rationing and unlimited funds.

So far we have only been concerned about technical differences between the three different models. The only thing that has been said about the actual investments is that it is cash inflows and cash outflows that are discounted. First of all it must be recognised that investment appraisals are made in various different environments. One of the factors here is in regard to the availability of funds. Companies which have access to efficient capital markets should not be overly concerned about capital rationing, yet they are. *Capital rationing* means that the amount of capital that can be allocated to investment projects is limited. The opposite case is obviously to have unlimited funds. With unlimited funds all investments earning a return above the cost of capital are made, and with capital rationing investments earning the highest possible combined NPV are made. One then has to consider both the profitability of individual projects and liquidity constraints (initially and throughout the investment period). Compare management's decision concerning the situation portrayed in Figure 9.5. With unlimited funds management would invest until they have no more profitable investments. Projects A, B, and C would therefore be conducted. With capital rationing only Projects A and B would be undertaken.

A second factor to consider is whether it is merely to reject or accept a project or whether two or more projects have to be *internally ranked*. The reject-accept situation is usually the case when the company has unlimited funds, although it can be used as a screening process when capital is rationalised. In this case only profitable projects are given further consideration. The ranking approach is based on some evaluation criteria, such as NPV or IRR. The project with the highest NPV/IRR is ranked first, and the project with the lowest NPV/IRR is ranked last.

A third and final factor to consider is whether the investment projects are independent or mutually exclusive to each other. For a company with unlimited funds there might be many different investment alternatives that need to be investigated independently. In some cases investment alternatives are *mutually exclusive*. That is the situation for a company choosing between acquiring a small contractor, increasing computer skills among the personnel, and implementing a new quality control system. As long as one of these alternatives is profitable it should be implemented. But the same company might be faced with limited production capacity. To solve the problem management has three alternatives. One is to set up a new production facility abroad, another to acquire a competitor, and a third to expand the current production capacity at the main plant. Even though management has access to unlimited funds and all projects are profitable, the acceptance of one of the alternatives eliminates the need for either of the others. The situation here is thus similar to the one above when comparing situations characterised by either accept-reject or ranking of alternatives.

In the following discussion the NPV method will be used rather than the IRR method.

9.4.2 Initial investments and operating cash flows

The initial investment in a project and the operating cash flows coming from running the project form the core of the analysis. The initial investment consists of all the negative cash flows coming from the decision to go ahead with the investment and which occur until production has been set up properly. This involves e.g. acquisition of land, hiring of architects/consultants, erecting buildings, setting up production plants, acquiring production machines, et cetera. It is of course the total outlays for setting up a building that are considered including personnel, planning and other overheads.

The operating cash flows are those coming from the initiated investment project. It is the initiated project that needs to be evaluated and therefore all its effects on the company's cash balance needs to be identified. These include the inflow of cash coming from sales of produced goods and services and the outflow of cash coming from the production, administration and marketing (PAM) of goods and services. In most investment projects it is the cash inflows that are the most difficult to estimate and cash outflows generally come in relation to the cash inflows from sales. The degree to which PAM outlays follow cash inflows depends on the proportion of variable and fixed expenses, which one needs to keep track of.

9.4.3 Sunk costs

A *sunk cost* is a capital expenditure, related to an investment currently under consideration, which has already been made or to which there is a commitment. A company in the oil and gas business, such as e.g. Statoil, regularly make test drillings at various sites. The planning and implementation of these tests are costly but will of course not affect the actual decision to set up regular operations. In many real-life decisions the treatment of sunk costs are less obvious. This is particularly true when considering new investments where the alternative is to keep old production facilities.

Although most students and managers have no problem identifying and understanding how to treat sunk costs in theoretical examples given in textbooks, such as this one, they have much greater problems remembering what they have learnt when making real-life investment decisions. Sunk costs are in real-life just as much a psychological problem as a technical one. If you have made prior commitments to a certain business area and invested a lot of funds there, it is hard to give it up. The recognition of a sunk cost is in many situations just as much a recognition of a previous mistake.

9.4.4 Working capital requirements

Most investments in fixed assets have to be accompanied by investments in working capital. Working capital is used when raw materials are purchased, it is used when employees are paid a salary, and it is used to finance the inventories the company stocks before delivering to the customers. Working capital is usually connected to the size of company operations, i.e., when sales grow so do customer receivables and inventories. If an investment project has a finite lifetime (for reasons of simplicity) we often assume that in capital budgeting exercises, although it is seldom the case in reality) the working capital is regained when terminating the project. Investments in working capital have no impact on company profit, but since time is money it creates an interest cost to the company. The project needs to earn back the cost of tying up capital. Finally it should be noted that often increased working capital requirements is not a liquidity problem for the company itself. An increased need for working capital comes from increased sales from which additional cash inflows are generated.

9.4.5 Corporate taxation

Investment decisions are made on the basis of cash flows. Accrual accounting concepts have no cash flow effect, they are there in order to keep assets' reported values in line with their economic values. When taxation is taken into consideration one moves from just considering cash inflows and outflows, to considering income and costs (which are accounting concepts). Corporate taxes therefore does not have a straightforward effect on investment cash flows and deserve some special attention. Taxation affects investment decisions in three ways.

Effect One:
First of all the company has to pay taxes on its income. Although operating income is not exactly the same as operating cash flows, the company has to pay taxes on operating cash flows as long as it is generating a positive net income (making a profit). Obviously it pays no taxes if taxable income is negative. Under the condition that the company is earning money, it pays taxes on sales revenue (≈ cash inflows).

Effect Two:
Investments in many assets of a substantial nature where economic benefits are likely to occur beyond the period when the investment is made are capitalised. This means that they are written-off over the expected economic life. This is particularly so for physical assets, such as plants and machines, but also R&D or immaterial rights are sometimes capitalised. The periodical "cost" of the investment is then referred to as depreciation. The depreciation has no cash-flow effects – only accounting effects – but if the company is showing a profit before taxes, the depreciation gives rise to a *tax shield.* Under the condition that the company is profitable, the tax shield value of depreciation can be described as:

$$I_0 \cdot \frac{1}{el} \cdot t \tag{9.11}$$

where el equals the *economic life* of the investment and t equals the prevailing tax rate. In reality, the economic life is a subjective estimate made by management of how many accounting periods into the future the investment will be in use and generate cash flows.

Besides those cash flows that are with the accounting terminology classified as income and cost, there are investment-related cash flows. One example is changes in working capital, which often occurs throughout the length of the investment. Another is for example additional investments in production facilities. These cash flows are not affected by corporate taxation.

Effect Three:
Corporate taxation has a third major impact on investment decisions – although it is not a cash flow effect. Just as depreciation has a tax shield effect, so does debt financing. This is one of the practical implications of the issues that were discussed in Chapter Seven. Because of the tax benefits given to debt financing one has to adjust the weighted average cost of capital formula.[13] The discount factor is reduced when more debt is employed in the capital structure. The new discount factor, where t is the effective tax rate, can be written as:

$$r_{WACC} = w_e \cdot r_e + w_d \cdot r_d \cdot (1 - t) \quad (9.12)$$

9.4.6 *Opportunity costs*

An *opportunity cost* is the same as the monetary benefits that would have occurred if the proposed investment had not been made. If a new machine is invested in while the old one is scrapped, one cannot ignore the cash flow effects that the old machine would have had on the company if it had not been scrapped. Perhaps the old machine could have been used for another year or two and could have generated the same cash flows as the new machine. Why then change? The opportunity cost is dealt with similarly to the treatment of individual investments when ranking different alternatives. It is then the monetary differences between the alternatives that have to be analysed, and not only the cash flows of one of the alternatives.

9.4.7 *Terminal value and contingent claims*

Usually when investments are appraised one determines a lifetime during which the project's cash flows are mapped and investigated. At the end of this time-period the value of the initial investment is determined. This we refer to as the *terminal value.* A terminal value can only exist if the economic lifetime of the appraised investment is longer than the investigated

13 Actually it is not debt financing that is advantageous, but equity financing that is disadvantageous. Companies (borrowers) pay no tax on interest costs, but the interest income that the bank (lender) receives is taxed. Equity financing on the other hand is fully taxed in the company (using the corporate income tax) and then taxed again when dividends are paid to investors. A Swedish company thus pays taxes once on debt financing, and twice on equity financing (so-called double taxation).

time-period. In many simple capital budgeting examples one sets a terminal value and say this is the value of the initially acquired machine when sold to another party. Another way is to say that the initial investment is kept in the company but one cannot determine its cash flows after a certain point in time. This method is used substantially when determining the value of companies (which is discussed in Chapter Ten), where more stereotyped techniques are used to determine the terminal value as compared to that of the current.

Over the last decade or so, the standard capital budgeting literature has usually contained some discussion of *contingent claims*. This is in essence an application of option pricing theory to investments in physical assets. The idea is intuitively very appealing, even though it will here be argued that the idea is more intellectually appealing than it is practically implementable. The problem in the past has been that standard finance looks at investments as if one can plot all future cash flows and then takes their uncertainty/risk into consideration and out comes a quantitative measure of the investment's profitability. Investment projects are stand-alone happenings that can be separately evaluated. Three different forms of contingent claims are usually mentioned. These are:

1 the option to make additional investments
2 the option to accelerate or slow the pace of an investment's development
3 the option to incorporate changes in the existing investment as it proceeds

In reality companies make continuous investments and they learn from making the investments. A new car model from Volvo is never a totally new project, but it evolves from past experiences. The current product portfolio of Ericsson stems from past products and past research. The digital technology that modern switchboards are based on, have been developed from knowledge established by those working with analogue technologies. Ericsson cannot evaluate a new investment solely on what cash flows it will generate, but also on what cash flows the investment might create coming from other future investments. This opens up a new dimension to investment appraisal. Investments that seem to be unprofitable are merely steps towards future profitable investments. Although this is intuitively appealing (after all, this is probably the way management makes decisions) it is hard to estimate the value of future investments. The pioneering work within the area was carried out by Brennan and Schwartz (1985), who showed how option-pricing theory could be applied to a mining operation. By using a few assumptions regarding variable and fixed operating costs, and output prices they could calculate the opening, closing and mothballing of a project.

Also the timing option (to accelerate or slow down the investment's development) is conceptually a very appealing extension to the classical investment appraisal. The classic NPV (or IRR) analysis assumes that management has the choice of either making the investment now, or abandoning it forever. This analysis thus ignores the option of postponing the decision in order to avoid uncertainty such as e.g. new legislation, changes in interest rates, and competitive pressures. Another type of timing option is the choice of temporarily closing down a production facility if its profitability is too low. Again this idea is most easily described for investments in natural resources. An oil drilling company working in the North Sea will only earn money when the oil price is above a certain level. Let's assume that the economically feasible level is $20 per barrel. In the past the oil price has been lower than $20 at numerous occasions, and for extensive periods of time. If the past is the best predictor of the future one might expect that oil prices will drop and operations will become uneconomic. Hence no drilling should commence. But one then ignores the option of closing down operations while oil prices are low. As long as liquidity is no problem (remember our focus on profitability) the company can use its option to only pump oil when it is profitable. Management can change its mind depending on how exogenously determined factors develop.

The contingent claims idea generally requires an exogenously set output/input price, which is often the case in natural resource projects. It seems far more applicable to investments in natural resources than in complex production processes involving considerable R&D, high value added and where output products are unique. Still it is in such projects that the need to account for flexibility is the greatest. While the benefits of integrating contingent claims into investment decision literature are indubitable, the practical problems are worse. It is probably enough if we acknowledge this way of thinking without being pressured to quantify the monetary effects. If one does this one also has an economically feasible reason to accept investments on "strategic" grounds. Arguably, managers have already understood and appreciated the contingent claims idea in investment decision-making in the past, interpreting it as 'strategic fit'.

9.4.8 Summary

In this section a number of issues have been described that need to be dealt with when appraising investments. The description here has focused on their technical side, i.e., their effect on cash flows. To learn the techniques of capital budgeting requires practise, and then again more practise. As already said, it is recommended to look for more specialised literature on the subject to get this practise.[14]

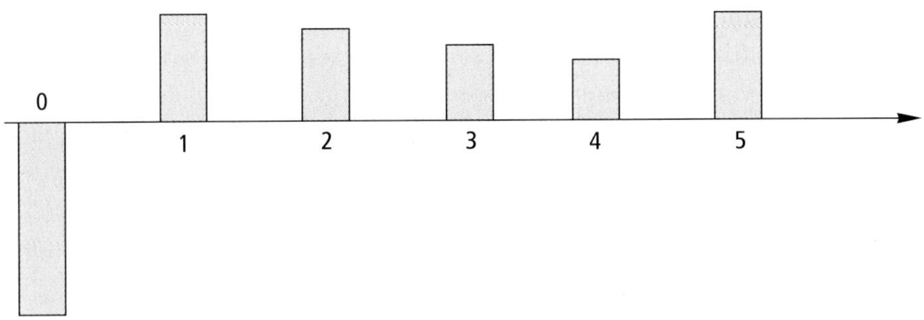

Figure 9.6 – Illustration of a time-line.

As a summary I now provide an example of an investment proposal, which contains all of the factors described above, together with a few other problems. To illustrate the time and size of the investment's cash flow consequences a *time-line*, as shown in Figure 9.6, is used.

Example 9.1 – Mercumin revisited

Mercumin is, as previously described, a company with substantial manufacturing operations. One of its divisions is currently considering making a new investment, which will enable it to expand its current operations. Mercumin Electronics produces equipment used for the production of microchips. This market is turbulent and rapidly undergoing changes. The manager of the Electronics division has seen the possibility to expand the division's customer group by also focusing on companies in the telecommunication industry. She has done an extensive amount of research herself and has also hired an external consultant to get an objective picture of the project. The cost of hiring the consultant is 200,000. The Mercumin manager estimates that she and her subordinates have set off time to work on the project worth approximately 300,000. Below are all the activities they have considered together with their monetary consequences.

The plan involves setting up a new production unit at an existing production plant. The manager of the Electronics division reckons that this does not require any additional acquisition of land, but it does require the

14 Åkerblom (2001) contains a number of different capital budgeting problems to practise on.

expansion of current buildings and the purchase of new production equipment. A moderate estimate she has been given by the consultant is ten million for setting up the new operations. It is estimated that it will take four to six months before the production is running from when it is initialised. Although the machinery is likely to be usable for a longer period of time, Mercumin never evaluates projects beyond a six year time-horizon. In this case a terminal value has been set at two million. The initial investment is written off using a straight-line depreciation plan.

Initially the investment will require four million in working capital. This is after the first year reduced to ten percent of outstanding sales.

The following information has been estimated by the division controller:

Sales volume:	120,000 units
Sales growth (units):	35 percent the first three years, thereafter 10 percent.
Contribution margin:	40 percent
Fixed production costs:	4.2 million
Semi-fixed product. costs:	4 million per 100,000 produced units
Fixed administrative costs:	0.5 million
Fixed S&M costs:	0.3 million

The Sales and Marketing manager at the Electronics division has estimated that this expanding market offers great opportunities. The total market volume is believed to be more than five million units next year. Mercumin is aiming at an increased market share over the first three years. The 120,000 units Mercumin believes it can sell will be in the more expensive segment of the market. Mercumin will work closely with its customers and produce integrated chips. Although competition for such contracts is fierce the reputation that the name Mercumin carries has already given it some positive acknowledgement. The sales price, based on selling 100,000 units is 20 million. Any additional first-year sales are likely to generate approximately the same price-per-unit. Due to competitive reasons, Mercumin estimates that the unit sales price will be reduced by 5 percent per year.

All units within Mercumin operate with substantial independence. They are, officially at least, free to acquire funds from external sources although the actual transfer of funds go through the internal financial centre. The floating rate is at the moment five percent, whereas the five-year fixed interest rate is approximately six percent. When going to the bank, Mercumin got an interest rate of seven percent. Mercumin is listed at the stock exchange and has a beta-value of 0.80. The market risk premium is believed to be four percent. The Electronics division is believed to be in a slightly more risky industry than Mercumin in general. The long term objective for the debt ratio is 0.67 (debt-to-equity). The current debt ratio is 1.0. The current corporate tax rate is 30 percent, not likely to change over the planning period.

Solution

There are many issues that needs to be considered in this case. Here follows some of them. First of all there are some sunk costs to be identified. These are the cost of the external consultant (200,000) and the opportunity cost coming from having people planning and evaluating the project (300,000). These costs have to be covered regardless of whether the project is carried out or not, and they are therefore not affecting the investment decision.

Then let's consider the operating costs. Volume and price effects are considered separately in the table. The contribution margin is assumed to be kept at 40 percent, regardless of changes in the unit sales price. This gives us the following figures:

Table 9.5 – Example: Mercumin revisited. Cash flows.

Operating cash flows	**year 1**	**year 2**	**year 3**	**year 4**	**year 5**	**year 6**
Sales volume (units)	120	162	218.7	295.25	324.77	357.25
Unit sales price	200.0	190.0	181.0	171.5	162.9	154.8
Sales revenue	24,000	30,780	39,585	50,635	52,905	55,302
Variable production costs	14,400	18,468	23,750.8	30,380.7	31,743	33,181
Semi-fixed production costs	4,000	4,000	8,000	8,000	12,000	12,000
Fixed production costs	5,000	5,000	5,000	5,000	5,000	5,000
Total operating cash flows	600	3,312	2,833.88	7,253.8	4,162	5,120

Other investment-related cash flows						
Taxes, operating cash flows	−180	−993.6	−850.1	−2,176.1	−1,248.6	−1,536.2
Change in WC	1,600	−678	−880.5	−1,105	−227	−5,290.5
Tax shield (depreciation)	300	300	300	300	300	300
Terminal value						2,000
Total other cash flows	1,720	−1,371.6	−1,430.6	−2,981.1	−1,175.7	6,054.3

Cost of capital is estimated using the tax-adjusted weighted average cost of capital model, in which the Capital Asset Pricing Model is used to determine the cost of equity, and the bank interest rate is used to determine the cost of debt. This gives us the following estimate:

Table 9.6 – Example: Mercumin revisited. Discount rate.

Estimate	Value	Formula	Calculation	Comment
w_d	0.4			
r_d	7 %			assumed stable
w_e	0.6	1 – (debt-ratio/2)	1 – (0.67/2)	
r_e	9.6 %	$r_f + \beta \cdot (r_m - r_f)$	$6\,\% + 0.9 \cdot (10\,\% - 6\,\%)$	5-year interest rate used as r_f
r_{WACC}	8 %	$w_e \cdot r_e + w_d \cdot r_d \cdot (1-t)$	$0.6 \cdot 10\,\% + 0.4 \cdot 7\,\% \cdot (1-30\,\%)$	7.68 percent

There is one matter that complicates the analysis slightly. The cash flows from operations come at various occasions throughout the year. This needs to be considered. In this example it takes six months until the investment will be ready. Operating cash flows are assumed to be evenly distributed within each annual period and hence discounted after six months ($t+0.5$, $t+1.5$, etc.). The initial investment was made at $t-0.5$.[15] When these cash flows are summarised using a time-line, the cash flow profile looks like this:

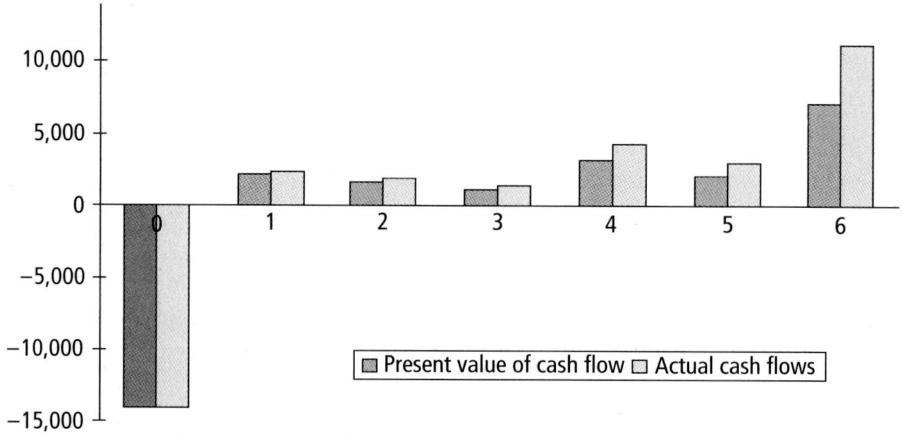

Figure 9.7 – Example: Mercumin revisited. Cash flow profile.

Initially, investments worth 14,000 have to be made (10,000 plus 4,000). In the end of the investment period 2,000 of the investment in the production unit is recaptured and all of the capital invested in the working capital (5,530.2).

15 The only cash flow which differs from this pattern is the tax shield, but this amount is so small it can be neglected here.

Table 9.7 – Example: Mercumin revisited. Final calculations.

	year 0	year 1	year 2	year 3	year 4	year 5	year 6
Total cash flows	–14,000	2,320	1,940.4	1,403.2	4,272.7	2,986.3	11,174
Discount factor	1.000	0.926	0.857	0.794	0.735	0.681	0.630
Present value of future cash flows	–14,000	2,148.1	1,663.6	1,113.9	3,140.6	2,032.5	7,042.1
Net Present Value	**3,140.8**						

According to the information that has been used the investment project is profitable and should be considered. There are many issues that can affect the decision however. In the Section *Key Issues to Discuss* there are several questions related to this example. Please answer them to make sure you understand the basic techniques.

9.5 Handling Uncertainty

9.5.1 Two alternative techniques

Investments would be easy to decide on if it was not for the uncertainty of future cash flows. In this section the issues of risk and uncertainty, which were discussed in Chapter Four, are returned to, but here they are discussed in a more practical, and perhaps more appropriate, setting. As all practitioners know, the real problem in investment appraisal is not to choose the appropriate valuation model, but to forecast future cash flows with a reasonable precision. This tendency by academicians to focus on the "wrong" problem has also been recognised in a number of research studies (e.g. Donaldson, 1984; Pruitt and Gitman, 1987; Pohlman, Santiago, and Markel, 1988; Butler and Schacter, 1989). The uncertainty in forecasting cash flows has a direct effect on the estimated value of the investment, and hence also on the actual accept-reject decision.

In the first section of this chapter the cost of capital was discussed, and then primarily as the link between finance and investment decisions. In this section the handling of uncertainty is dealt with explicitly. Indeed, there are two alternative ways of adjusting for uncertainty: one which has an effect on future cash flows, and one which has an effect on the discount rate. The method where uncertainty/risk is adjusted for in the discount rate has already been covered and here the focus is on risk-adjusting the cash flows. In addition, some light is shed on the usage of sensitivity analyses.

If one were to make an investment under certainty, the net present value method would merely be an illustration of the obvious. Under certainty one knows all cash flows and hence the net present value is a simple calculation. To illustrate this let's again turn to the investment plans of Mercumin, which were shown in Table 9.2. But now let's assume that we stand at time (t + 5) – at the end of the project – and that management decided to invest in Project A for which the given figures also turned out to be the actual ones. When we, *ex post*, evaluate the project we do have to take postponement of consumption and price changes into consideration, but risk is of no interest. Let's assume that the risk-free interest rate during the investment period is constant at five percent. This gives us the following estimate of Project A's NPV:

$$\text{NPV} = \sum_{t=1}^{\infty} \frac{cf_t}{(1+r_f)^t} =$$

$$= I_0 + \frac{cf_1}{(1+r_f)^1} + \frac{cf_2}{(1+r_f)^2} + \frac{cf_3}{(1+r_f)^3} + \frac{cf_4}{(1+r_f)^4} + \frac{cf_5}{(1+r_f)^5} =$$

$$= -100{,}000 + \frac{26{,}000}{(1+0.05)^1} + \frac{26{,}000}{(1+0.05)^2} + \frac{26{,}000}{(1+0.05)^3} + \frac{26{,}000}{(1+0.05)^4} + \frac{26{,}000}{(1+0.05)^5} =$$

$$= -100{,}000 + 24{,}762 + 23{,}583 + 22{,}460 + 21{,}390 + 20{,}372 = 12{,}567$$

If we then move from a situation characterised by certainty to one characterised by uncertainty there are two alternative ways of handling it. Either we add a risk premium to the discount rate, or we reduce the forecasted future cash flows. The two alternative models are expressed below.

$$\text{NPV} = \sum_{t=1}^{\infty} \frac{cf_t}{(1+r_f + \text{riskpremium})^t} \qquad \text{NPV} = \sum_{t=1}^{\infty} \frac{cf_t \cdot (1 - \text{risk}_t)}{(1+r_f)^t}$$

The standard way of handling uncertainty is to include a compensation for it in the denominator. This method was covered in Section 9.2 of this chapter. The discount rate is determined by (i) postponement of consumption, (ii) price changes (usually increases), and (iii) compensation for risk. To use risk-adjusted discount rates is a practical approach to handling uncertain cash flows. Its practicality is however counteracted by practical flaws. Not all cash flows have the same uncertainty as they can vary both over time, and between different sources of cash flow.

9.5.2 Making adjustments in the discounted cash flows

When confronted with uncertainty one usually tries to come up with the best possible guess. When analysts forecast the earnings of companies for the coming year, they usually estimate a most likely value, but they also often state an interval within which this estimate lies. The span of the interval is a measure of how uncertain the analyst is when making his/her decision. If it is an estimate of the return on a one-year government bond that is determined the span is close to nil, but if it is the earnings of an Internet company the span is quite substantial. The determination of a span is similar to the variance used in the probability analysis described in Chapter Four (see Figure 4.2). The greater the variance is, the lower the probability of getting the expected value is (assuming a normal distribution).

Making adjustments in the discounted cash flows requires the decision-maker to estimate the most likely value of each cash flow together with its probability. In the case of high uncertainty the probability is lower and hence the cash flow to be discounted is lower. Two important rules apply: (i) each expected value is multiplied by its probability ($cf_t \cdot \alpha_t$) which gives us a *certainty equivalent*, and (ii) certainty equivalents are discounted using the risk-free interest rate. Sick (1986) contains a good discussion of the use of certainty equivalents in capital budgeting, although similar ideas had been presented before that (see e.g. Bogue and Roll, 1974).

Table 9.8 – Capital expenditure in Mercumin using certainty equivalents.

Project A							
Year (t)	**0**	**1**	**2**	**3**	**4**	**5**	**Summary**
Cash flows	–100,000	26,000	26,000	26,000	26,000	26,000	**30,000**
Probability	1.0	0.95	0.9	0.9	0.9	0.8	
Certainty equivalent	–100,000	24,700	23,400	23,400	23,400	20,800	**15,700**
Discount factor, 12 %	1	0.893	0.797	0.712	0.636	0.567	
Discount factor, 5 %	1	0.952	0.907	0.864	0.823	0.784	
Present value, 12 %[A]	–100,000	23,218	20,722	18,512	16,536	14,742	**–6,270**
Present value, 5 %[B]	–100,000	23,514	21,224	20,218	19,258	16,307	**521**

[A] Discounted using the average cost of capital in Mercumin.
[B] Discounted using the certainty equivalent.

Project B

Year (t)	0	1	2	3	4	5	Summary
Cash flows	–100,000	60,000	25,000	25,000	10,000	10,000	**30,000**
Probability	1	0.9	0.85	0.8	0.8	0.65	
Certainty equivalent	–100,000	54,000	21,250	20,000	8,000	6,500	**9,750**
Discount factor, 12 %	1	0.893	0.797	0.712	0.636	0.567	
Discount factor, 5 %	1	0.952	0.907	0.864	0.823	0.784	
Present value, 12 %	–100,000	53,580	19,925	17,800	6,360	5,670	**3,335**
Present value, 5 %	–100,000	51,408	19,274	17,280	6,584	5,096	**–358**

In most cases the probability of receiving a certain cash flow is higher at the beginning of the investment period, and for cash outflows. Table 9.8 shows the two Projects A and B of Mercumin that were evaluated earlier on. In the previous estimates we found that Project B should be preferred to Project A when discounting using the average cost of capital of Mercumin (twelve percent). Project A actually had a negative NPV. In this example the risk-free interest rate is assumed to be five percent, and the probability of each cash flow is shown in the table. Please note that for the sake of simplicity the certainty equivalent has been estimated on an annual basis rather than a cash flow basis. There is thus only one aggregated cash flow per year and only one aggregated probability per year (instead of one for each event causing a cash flow during each year).

From the previous comparison of these two projects we have seen that with a discount rate of twelve percent Project A is unprofitable whereas Project B is profitable. In Table 9.4 the same basic information is provided. However, when individual cash flows are individually risk-adjusted and then discounted a totally different pattern emerges. As it turns out, the cash flows of Project A have on average higher probabilities than those of Project B and therefore the certainty equivalents are relatively higher. When certainty equivalents are used it is Project A that generates a positive NPV, whereas Project B has a negative NPV.

Theoretically speaking this approach is appealing. It recognises that the uncertainty of cash flows can be heterogeneously distributed over time and between events. Early cash outflows are very certain, whereas future cash inflows are less certain. The problem is of course that one has to look at individual cash flows and determine their likelihood. This requires both more time and effort than before. As always certainty equivalents are based on subjective estimates.

9.5.3 Sensitivity analysis

A recommended way of handling uncertainty and understanding how the investment decision is affected by changes in some of the input variables is to perform a *sensitivity analysis*. Here the expected values that were used in the actual calculation can be accompanied by probability distributions for each relevant input variable. The first step is therefore to identify those variables having a key impact on the analysis. In most cases those variables are related to cash inflows. Initial investment outlays, working capital expenditures, and cash flows related to production are relatively easy to determine. Often they are, at least partly, dependent on the much more uncertain cash inflows.

The next step is to estimate the probability of each relevant input variable. This step can be divided into several substeps, of which the first is to estimate by how much actual outcomes can differ from expectations, and the second is to estimate the probability distribution. The decision-maker within modern corporations is supported by numerous computer packages, which can ease the technical part of this estimation. By far the most important task is however left to the individual: To estimate the input values. When the probability distribution and the spread for each input variable has been chosen, the computer software can estimate the NPV/IRR of the project.

The impact of changes in these critical input variables is estimated for the whole investment decision. As this can be difficult it might be easier to utilise a few different scenarios instead. A *scenario analysis* is in this context something inbetween a fully-fledged probability analysis (where all cash flows are given a probability distribution and a spread) and the standard investment appraisal (where only the expected value is used). The decision-maker has to imagine a couple of relatively likely situations, often a "worst case" scenario, a "most likely" scenario, and a "favourable" scenario. Table 9.9 describes how a summary of such a scenario analysis can be made.

Table 9.9 – Scenario analysis.

Worst case scenario

Competitive barriers are small and competing products enter the market place which drives profit margins down. Product demand is therefore considerably lower than expected. At the same time the economy hits a recession, which causes medium-term growth to be sluggish.

Effect

Operating profit margins:	8 percent
Cash flow growth:	12 percent
Sales and marketing costs:	15 percent higher than expected

Most likely scenario

Competition can be reasonably reduced for a limited period of time. Profit margins will be slightly higher than normal. Market demand is as before and thus the company's market share will grow slightly.

Effect

Operating profit margins:	12 percent
Cash flow growth:	15 percent
Sales and marketing costs:	As expected

Favourable scenario

Market growth is stronger than expected. Overall production shortages in the industry creates a favourable situation and profit margins can be increased. Although market growth is strong the new products are favourably viewed by customers and the company can raise its market share.

Effect

Operating profit margins:	13 percent
Cash flow growth:	20 percent
Sales and marketing costs:	As expected

It is critical that the decision-maker has an understanding of which variables are most important for the outcome of the analysis, and how the outcome will change when, or if, these variables are changed. There can, however, never be too much emphasis on the fact that this "risk analysis" is nothing but an "uncertainty analysis" based on highly subjective judgements. It is not an objective measure providing definite answers. Its main purpose is therefore to provide decision-makers with a structure that enables them to think systematically about the monetary consequences of their decisions, under the influence of time and an uncertain future.

9.6 Managerial Implications

9.6.1 The rational investment appraisal process

How is an investment decision taken? Most people would hope that they behave relatively rationally and thus make consequent decisions. In this section we address managerial behaviours in investment decisions. In most investment literature it is however common that one rather finds more normative descriptions of how management ought to behave. We start out in this section reviewing five steps commonly found in such a rational decision-making process. At the end of the section we spend some time discussing how managers might behave, why they would do so, and what overall implications this would have.

1. *Proposal generation.* Proposals are generated in various ways, as some are desperately needed to solve an existing problem, some are derived from an excess of capital, and others spring out of normal business activities. The urgency and access to resources, particularly financial, will determine the quality of the proposal generation process. Large and more uncertain outlays are also likely to be more carefully scrutinised.
2. *Analysis.* The analysis of investment proposals should determine their strategic fit and economic viability. In accordance with the techniques covered previously in this chapter and elsewhere, the cash flows and their respective probability should be estimated whereupon an appropriate discounted cash flow technique is used to determine the value of the investment. No investment analysis is complete however without a qualitative judgement of its overall feasibility, strategic fit and uncertainty. This judgement is usually put forward in a summary report.

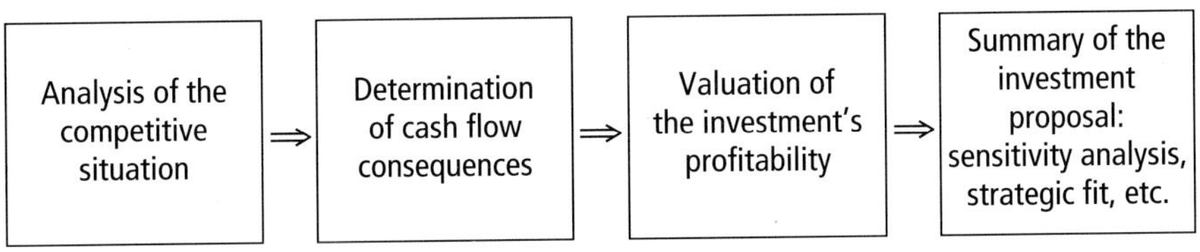

Figure 9.8 – Steps in the analysis of investment proposals.

3. *Decision-making.* The person responsible for the invested capital should take the decision of whether or not the investment will be made. For large investments this is usually the CEO or the board of directors. It is common that companies delegate capital-expenditure authority downwards in the organisation. Such delegation is usually based on dollar limits. Depending on the urgency and capital access the decision-making

process differs. In the case of, for example, investments to solve production stops, decision-making is quicker and more decentralised than in the case of unlimited funds and the ranking of mutually exclusive projects.

4 *Implementation.* Most of the actual work on major investments occurs after the decision has been taken. Responsibility for physical and capital resources has to be delegated and regular follow-ups must occur.
5 *Reviewing.* Continuous review of project development in terms of performance, time and cost is carried out and, whether performance is too negative, initial investments might be viewed as a sunk cost and the whole project is terminated. Other alternatives might be to cut costs, improve benefits or delegate more resources to the project.

9.6.2 Some final thoughts on the actual use of investment models

Within economic theory it is unarguably so that managers are assumed to invest in projects that have a positive net present value. In cases of mutually exclusive projects the one with the highest NPV should be chosen. In reality, one can ask if profitability is always the norm and if it is not, what other criteria could management have when choosing among investments?

With the separation of investment and financial decisions comes the notion that managers should focus on what they do best: make (profitable) investments. From finance literature we have learnt that risk-averse investors get a return in relation to the risk they dare to take. One of their main tasks is to diversify their portfolios and hold assets that are unrelated to each other (as close to a "free lunch" that you can ever get in finance). Because financial markets are more efficient it makes sense that investors do the diversification themselves. But what about managers? They are also averse to risk, and prefer less risk to more risk. From a managerial perspective it is little comfort knowing that the company's owners are diversified and will not suffer when or if the company runs into problems. Managers will suffer substantially as they have their whole investment in just one asset: the company they are managing.

From a managerial perspective it makes sense to hold a group of investments that have unrelated cash flows. When one of them performs below expectations, there is a chance that another one, which performs better, balances it out. All business areas should not be in the same phase at the same time. What if all business units were growing at a substantial rate? Such a situation would cause the company to have substantial negative cash flows and it is not sure creditors and investors would accept that. The same if all business units were in mature industries having substantial positive cash flows. Such a situation might at first sight seem less problematic, but in the long run pressure from stakeholders could be unbearable. Investors require new investments earning adequate returns.

A major problem with the funding of investments is that managers have much more information about the investments than shareholders do. Several researchers have also developed signalling models of corporate investments (e.g. Miller and Rock, 1985; Ambarish, John and Williams, 1987). The idea is that making investments is a good signal that the company is likely to prosper in the future, meaning both high cash flows and high profitability. The empirical results from such studies have been mixed. Managers who currently have a lot of cash (abundant cash inflows) also make more investments. This supports the ideas of Donaldson (1984) and Findlay and Whitmore (1974) reported in Chapter Three, that growth is important. Contrary to the findings of Donaldson, other researchers have argued that the shareholders are not very hostile towards new investments. Several studies have documented that new investments have a positive effect on share prices (e.g. McConell and Muscarella, 1985; Chan, Martin, and Kensinger, 1990)[16], although this trend declined in the 1980s. Researchers have also documented differences between companies in different industries. Investors are much more positive towards investments made in companies in high growth industries, than in mature industries (Pilotte, 1992), which does make a lot of sense. In mature industries managers are driven by slack incentives, whereas in growth industries managers are driven by true cash flow growth opportunities.

Finally, management might choose not to make an investment if that would leave them with too little financial slack. It is likewise possible they select projects with a quick payback time but a low net present value simply because such a strategy would more corporate wealth and/or better short term cash flows demanded by the investors.

If managers are not totally devoted to the shareholder wealth maximisation idea they will see access to capital as restricted and therefore rationed. Because of this, some investment projects might be overlooked and sometimes profitable projects are foregone. To management corporate wealth and control are of fundamental importance and they influence in-

16 Please note that this discussion solely deals with investments in physical assets. When it comes to making corporate acquisitions it is a totally different story, which is returned to in Chapter Eleven.

vestment decisions. Also management does pay attention to the interaction between different projects and the overall liquidity effects that individual projects have; the self-sufficiency motive does influence investment decisions. Economic theory tells us one thing, but without strong incentives making managers more focused on shareholder wealth there is a good chance they will diversify the company's operations, create slack and create a situation where their desires are more aptly covered. Because of asymmetric information it is more rational, also from an investor point of view, to take liquidity into consideration.

Moreover, when managers identify an investment opportunity they make biased forecasts of the information they have in hand. They can never estimate cash flows perfectly as these are uncertain by nature. The idea of risk is based on objective probability distributions, not subjective ones. Yet in investment decisions it is nothing more than subjective views of an unclear future that are the foundation for the analysis. In fact, if the probabilities of future cash flows could be objectively determined it is likely that no formal investment appraisals would be made. This is also evident in empirical studies: It is only for complex and highly uncertain projects where a substantial amount of money is at stake that managers actually perform such a structured analysis that is discussed in investment literature. This can be referred to as the *paradox of capital budgeting*. In real-life we most often use the capital budgeting techniques for those situations where they are difficult to apply.

Finally, we should not be overly pessimistic about the models described throughout the chapter. On the contrary, they help us a lot. But it is important that one has an understanding of how they ought to be used, what problems they bring with them, and the deficiencies human beings are suffering from when they use rational decision-making models in real-life decision-making. Many times managers have more gut feelings they are correct, than they are mathematically sure. Issues such as product quality, competitive pressures, and additional investment opportunities play important roles. Knowing that without an investment the company is not at the technological forefront but is outdistanced by its competitors can make any manager scared and feel without control. Such feelings are bound to be influential on rational managers.

Key Concepts

- > Fisher's separation theorem
- > Discount rate
- > Financial investments
- > Operating investments
- > Reinvestment
- > Organic growth
- > The weighted average cost of capital
- > Payback method
- > Net present value method
- > Internal rate of return method
- > Capital rationing
- > Internal ranking of projects
- > Mutually exclusive projects
- > Sunk cost
- > Tax shield
- > Economic life
- > Opportunity cost
- > Terminal value
- > Contingent claim
- > Time-line
- > Certainty equivalent
- > Sensitivity analysis
- > Scenario analysis
- > Paradox of capital budgeting

Key Issues to Discuss

1. Explain the roles of management and investors according to the Fisher separation theorem.
2. When management evaluates new investment projects they need to use a discount rate. Discuss how they determine it. Your answer should include explanations of the following terms; WACC, CAPM and cost of debt.
3. Can the ownership structure influence the discount rate management uses? Discuss the matter while referring to different forms of risk and asymmetric information.
4. The discount rate shall reflect the risk of the evaluated project. There are obvious problems with determining the discount rate, as different projects have different risks. Discuss management's ability to determine the discount rate of future projects and ways to handle the uncertainty. Also discuss whether the discount factor ought to be constant over time or not.
5. Estimate the net present value of Projects A and C (Table 9.2). Are these investments profitable?
6. First, estimate the internal rate of return of Project A (Table 9.2) using the trial-and-error approach shown in the text. Then estimate the internal rate of return of Project C (Table 9.2) using the same technique. Project C generates two IRRs. Can you find them? How can management overcome this problem?
7. Discuss the advantages and disadvantages with the certainty equivalent method, as compared to the discounting method.
8. In relation to the capital budgeting example made in the text (Mercumin revisited); answer and discuss the following questions.
   a) At which discount rate is the project (as described here) unprofitable?
   b) To what extent can the fixed production costs increase before the project is unprofitable?
   c) Do you think management can be reluctant to this investment given that they are relatively more concerned about liquidity and the timing of cash flows? Motivate your answer!
   d) Discuss if there are any strategic matters related to the project that need to be considered. Could such affect the decision? How?
   e) Contingent claims could perhaps be a matter here. In what ways could they have an effect on the calculations?

f) Make a sensitivity analysis and while doing so, you should pay particular attention to the cost of equity.

9 From a strictly managerial perspective, is it likely that the WACC is always used as the discount rate? Discuss managerially oriented factors that might influence the evaluation.

10 If a profitable investment is made, the company value increases. State your opinion concerning the relationship between the company value and the investment policy. Why are investors sometimes negative to investments? Try to support your opinions with examples from real-life.

Further readings:

Åkerblom, M., 2001, *Evaluating and Financing Company Projects*, Uppsala: Företagsekonomiska institutionen.

Chapter 10

Company Valuation

This chapter aims at:

- Providing coverage of the most common company valuation models, with a particular focus on discounted cash flow models.
- Identifying the main steps in the valuation process, and discussing their importance for the overall valuation.
- Discussing how value is created and sustained within businesses and how analysts can make estimates of these value drivers.
- Examining the extent of mergers and acquisition activities and discussing briefly the main drivers of acquisition behaviour.

10.1 Introduction

To estimate the value of a company is to bring together knowledge from several areas of corporate finance. There is thus good reason to have this chapter at the end of the book as it draws on ideas presented in several previous chapters. In essence company valuation is nothing more than investment appraisal, although a few extensions of those models covered in Chapter Nine are made. In general, modern financial theory does not deal as much with the techniques of how to estimate the value of a company as it deals with the consequences of a correct valuation. In our previous coverage of capital market theory, capital structure theory, and dividend policy theory (Chapters Five to Eight) we have frequently assumed efficient markets. Well, in order to have efficient markets, investors will have to engage in the technique of putting a value to assets. As we will soon see this is about determining the amount and probabilities of future income streams of corporate entities.

The activity on stock exchanges around the world has increased dramatically over recent decades. This pushes for more sophisticated valuation techniques. Also during the last decades there has been a remarkable increase in structural changes within most industries. The consolidation of industries has been driven by changes in both product and capital markets. Increases in the proportion of fixed costs in companies' value chain (not just production, but also in e.g. marketing, and computer services), a focus on the core business, and global competitive forces are some product-market related factors. Another reason is that investors (often anonymous institutional ones) have been successful when crying out for ever higher returns and managers have tried to respond to this. The whole financial industry has been pushing for more structural changes in product markets. To determine the value of companies, or parts of companies, has in this context been increasingly important. In response to this development practitioners and academicians have sought more sophisticated tools.

In the finance literature several different valuation models exist. An important characteristic of the models covered here is that they are based on the idea of viewing companies as *going concerns*. This means an assumption that the company remains in operation indefinitely under normal circumstances. There is thus no termination value for the portfolio of projects that the company constitutes. The basic model applied throughout this chapter is the Discounted Cash Flow model outlined in Chapter Nine. The value of a company is therein determined by three factors; the company's ability to generate cash flows, the time perspective during which the cash flows are generated, and the degree of (un)certainty surrounding the occurrence of cash flows.

It is important to note that there are other valuation models than those explained here, such as e.g. the residual income model and its offspring; the economic value added (EVA) model. The EVA model is to some extent described, as a corporate control device, in Chapter Eleven. The reader interested in a considerably more in-depth coverage of residual income models is recommended to read e.g. Penman (2001). In general, we can say that as long as one makes the same assumptions when using the different models the end-result will be the same (for evidence see Lundholm and O'Keefe, 2001). Levin (1998) provides an analysis of differences between these valuation models and under which conditions they are congruent. Such comparisons can also partly be found in other texts on company valuation (e.g. Lundholm and O'Keefe, 2001; Copeland, Koller, and Murrin, 2000).

The difficulty with company valuation is not to choose a valuation model, but to estimate the future cash flows that the company will generate. Regardless of which model one finally chooses the value of a company can alter substantially just by a slight change of the discount rate or the growth expectations of future cash flows. This is particularly true for companies characterised by a lot of uncertainty.

At the end of this chapter it is recognised that many company valuations are not made simply in order to value a company on a stand-alone basis, but also to value it in combination with another unit. In relation to acquisitions of related businesses or mergers *synergy effects* are frequently discussed. In the last section of the chapter we try to estimate the amount of synergy an acquisition can generate, and which factors it is that makes some mergers and acquisitions more successful than others. When doing so we again find that the managerial welfare maximisation idea is an important part of explaining merger and acquisition activities.

10.2 Models Based on Discounted Income Streams

10.2.1 The dividend and free cash flow discount models

In Chapter Nine we studied some models to be used for discounting future cash flows. Explicitly or implicitly, the investor applies them when he/she buys shares in a company. For the investor owning shares in a company but having little interest in the control of the company, cash flows come in the form of dividends. The value of a company can therefore be described using Expression (10.1).

$$V_0^{EQ} = \sum_{t=1}^{\infty} \frac{Div_t}{(1 + r_{eq})^t} =$$

$$= \frac{Div_1}{(1 + r_{eq})^1} + \frac{Div_2}{(1 + r_{eq})^2} + \frac{Div_3}{(1 + r_{eq})^3} + \ldots + \frac{Div_t}{(1 + r_{eq})^t} \qquad (10.1)$$

This is known as the *dividend discount model* (DDM), which states that the NPV of a company is found by discounting all future dividends to present time. This is the "classical way" of determining the value of a company (Williams, 1938). Please note that the discount factor is the investors' required rate of return (r_{eq}). We are thus in this case only interested in the value of the investors' part of the company. Dividends form the ultimate transaction between a company and its owners (shareholders).

In Chapter Eight we learnt from Miller and Modigliani that in an efficient market dividend policy is irrelevant for company value. Shareholders are indifferent between getting a return in the form of a cash dividend or an increase in share price (as long as management invests in profitable investments). The actual return (r) an investor receives during time-period t can be written as:

$$r_t = \frac{[Div_t + (V_{t+1}^{EQ} - V_t^{EQ})]}{V_t^{EQ}} \qquad (10.2)$$

The increase in value comes from reinvestments of capital which otherwise would have been returned to shareholders. Since this reinvestment is supposed to be made in projects earning the same return as already existing investments, the increases in share price the investor benefits from are due to changes in the expectations of future dividends caused by the reinvestment of cash.

The DDM requires the analyst to estimate company dividends. But, of course, in order to estimate dividends one also has to estimate cash flows from operations. Over the last decade NPV models based on different forms of *Free Cash Flow* (FCF) have been developed and extensively used. Whereas the DDM is used to value the investor's part of a company, FCF models have a greater application. Free cash flow is referred to as the capital that is at disposal after all necessary investments have been made. As we move along throughout this chapter it is the basic Free Cash Flow model shown in Expression (10.3) that is elaborated and expanded.

$$V_0 = \sum_{t=1}^{\infty} \frac{FCF_t}{(1+r)^t} = \frac{FCF_1}{(1+r)^1} + \frac{FCF_2}{(1+r)^2} + \frac{FCF_3}{(1+r)^3} + \ldots + \frac{FCF_t}{(1+r)^t} \quad (10.3)$$

While the upcoming FCF models might seem more sophisticated than the DDM they involve no more components, but perhaps a slightly better structure for understanding what drives company value. In order to get all of these models right one has to understand the impact that factors such as cash flow growth, capital structure, and discount factors have on the estimation.

10.2.2 Determining the value of a company

The most common way of estimating the value of a company's equity is to first place a value on the company's total operations and then subtract the value of debt and other claims superior to common stock. This section has been split into two sections. First we learn to estimate the value of the whole company, and then we use this in order to generate the value of the shareholders' part of the company. The value of a company's operations, regardless of its capital structure, can be estimated as:

$$V_0^{Firm} = \sum_{t=1}^{\infty} \frac{FCFF_t}{(1+r_{WACC})^t} =$$

$$= \frac{FCFF_1}{(1+r_{WACC})^1} + \frac{FCFF_2}{(1+r_{WACC})^2} + \ldots + \frac{FCFF_t}{(1+r_{WACC})^t} \quad (10.4)$$

When using this valuation model one is interested in the total cash flows a company generates beyond its investment needs, the so-called *free cash flows to the firm* (FCFF). The FCFF can be split into two parts: gross cash flows and gross investments. Roughly speaking, gross cash flows are returns from previously invested capital, whereas a gross investment is newly invested capital that will earn a return in the future. Because it is changes in cash from operations (before any financial costs have been subtracted) this value is independent of how the operations have been financed.

$$FCFF = \text{Gross cash flows} - \text{Gross investments} \quad (10.5)$$

The gross cash flows (GCF) are usually defined as *NOPAT* + *depr*, and the gross investments (GI) are defined as *NetInvest* + *depr*. *NOPAT* stands for Net Operating Profit After Taxes. It will be discussed more thoroughly shortly. *Depr* stands for depreciation, and represents the value of past investments that are written off during the period. *NetInvest* refer to all investments made during the period, both in fixed assets (such as production plants and machines) and in working capital (e.g. raw materials, and inventory of finished goods). FCFF is defined as GCF – GI, which obviously can be re-written as *NOPAT* – *NetInvest*. The, at first sight, seemingly unnecessary treatment of the depreciation is conducted for pedagogical reasons. As discussed in Chapter Two depreciation is just an accounting concept, a subjectively set portion of previous investments. By moving it to gross investments it is treated in conjunction with new investments (to some extent made to replace these old investments). The Net Operating Profit After Taxes is the most important of all the variables in the FCFF model. This is the value that investments have generated. It is calculated using the formula in Table 10.1. Note the consistency with the discussion in Chapter Two on financial statement analysis.

Table 10.1 – Calculating Net Operating Profit After Taxes.

+	Sales from core business
–	Cost of goods sold
–	Selling, general and administrative expenses
∑	**Gross profit**
–	Depreciation
∑	**Operating profit**
–	Actual taxes on core business
–	Deferred taxes
∑	**NOPAT**

One should not just look at the income statement when judging a company's NOPAT, but it is important to be aware of the process in which NOPAT is generated. That process can be described as:

$$\text{NOPAT} = \text{NOA} \cdot \text{RNOA}^{\text{aT}} \tag{10.6}$$

This shows the important link between NOPAT, which is a measure of the value that has been created, and the capital that has previously been invested in the company. NOPAT is equal to the *net operating assets* (NOA) multiplied by the return on net operating assets after taxes (RNOA^{aT}). NOA is the current value of all past net investments including their depreciation in economic value. This value is reasonably well described in the company's balance sheet.[1] When NOA is estimated it is very important that one identifies those assets which generate NOPAT. The following definition of NOA is congruent with the previous definition of NOPAT, and thus follows the matching principle of ratio analysis outlined in Chapter Two.

Table 10.2 – Calculating Net Operating Assets and Capital Employed.

+	Operating current assets
–	Short term NIBD
∑	**Operating working capital**
+	Operating fixed assets
–	Long term NIBD
∑	**Net Operating Assets**
+	Goodwill
∑	**Net Operating Assets incl. goodwill**
+	Non-operating current assets
+	Non-operating fixed assets
∑	**Capital Employed**

In Table 10.2 all of the non-interest bearing debt (NIBD) has been deducted. For pedagogical reasons the NIBD has been split into two parts (short term and long term). The previously invested capital (NOA) is estimated both with and without goodwill. There are different opinions regarding the treatment of goodwill in these valuation situations. The most appropriate treatment is likely to be an inclusion of it, but with a shorter write-off period. Regardless of how goodwill is viewed and treated it is important that this is done consistently.

Please note that the relationships specified in Chapter Two hold here also. Three forms of capital are used to finance the company's operations: risk-bearing capital, interest bearing debt, and non-interest bearing debt. In the regrouping of balance sheet items above, the capital employed equals risk-bearing capital plus interest bearing debt. The difference between capital employed and net operating assets is non-operating assets, such as short term investments in financial markets, and long term non-strategic holdings in other companies.

1 It says, "reasonably well described" because of the conservative accounting regime discussed in Chapter Two. No more detailed discussion of these accounting problems is carried out here.

So far we have covered the numerator in the FCFF valuation model. For the denominator the matching principle is of importance. When expected free cash flows to the firm are discounted, the weighted average capital cost for the firm has to be used. To the actual discount rates to be used in the valuation models' denominator we will return later.

10.2.3 Determining the value of share capital

In Chapter Seven the assumptions of Miller and Modigliani (1958) in regard to capital structure irrelevance were outlined. The market value of a company is determined by the risk and return of its investments. According to Miller and Modigliani company value is not altered by different combinations of equity and debt financing. When more cheap debt is acquired this only causes equity capital to become more expensive. Total company value is determined by the investment policy, and not the financing policy. With an efficient capital market there is no combination of debt and equity that adds value to the company.[2]

$$V^{Firm} = V^{EQ} + V^{D} \Rightarrow V^{EQ} = V^{Firm} - V^{D} \tag{10.7}$$

The indirect approach to finding the value of equity is therefore to first estimate the NPV of all future FCFF and then subtract the value of debt. This idea is formulated in Expression (10.8).

$$V_0^{EQ} = \sum_{t=1}^{\infty} \frac{FCFF_t}{(1 + r_{WACC})^t} - \sum_{t=1}^{\infty} \frac{FCFD_t}{(1 + r_d)^t} \tag{10.8}$$

The value of a company's debt is equal to the free cash flow to debt-holders (FCFD) discounted with an appropriate adjustment for the risk they face.[3] In an efficient debt market debt-holders will ask for a risk-premium corresponding to the risk they take on. Therefore one can assume that future borrowings have a zero NPV. Thus it is just the market value of outstanding debt at the valuation date (t = 0) that matters. The same reasoning is used for the non-operating assets the company possesses. These assets are merely investments in capital markets and, given that these markets are reasonably efficient; they will earn no additional value beyond their cur-

2 Even though we rejected the "capital structure irrelevance theorem" in Chapter Seven this has no impact here. Tax effects are taken care of in the discount factor. Potential agency and bankruptcy costs have no effect here.

3 Free Cash Flow to Debt-holders is defined as financial expenses – new loans + amortisations on past loans.

rent market value. We can hence rewrite Expression (10.8) in the following way to get the final *indirect valuation model of shareholder capital*:

$$V_0^{EQ} = \sum_{t=1}^{\infty} \frac{FCFE_t}{(1 + r_{WACC})^t} - (D_t + FA_t) \tag{10.9}$$

But why do we use an indirect approach to value equity, instead of finding the free cash flow to equity straight away and then discount it with an appropriate adjustment for the risk of equity-holders? This method would generate exactly the same results if all conditions were the same. The *direct valuation model of shareholder capital* is shown in Expression (10.10) where the *free cash flow to equity* (FCFE) is measured as FCFF – fe –/+ –/+ ΔIBD.

$$V_0^{EQ} = \sum_{t=1}^{\infty} \frac{FCFE_t}{(1 + r_{eq})^t} =$$

$$= \frac{FCFE_1}{(1 + r_{eq})^1} + \frac{FCFE_2}{(1 + r_{eq})^2} + \frac{FCFE_3}{(1 + r_{eq})^3} + \ldots + \frac{FCFE_t}{(1 + r_{eq})^t} \tag{10.10}$$

The main reason why the indirect method is more commonly used is that the direct method makes it difficult to understand what drives future free cash flows from operations. It is investments in the company's core operating area that will be its strategic base for the future and the return from this base makes up virtually all of its value-creation. But FCFE prevents a closer study of this strategic base as changes in capital structure (debt financing) impacts the FCFE. Speaking in terms of the models, they are nevertheless the same. As you see, our choice of valuation model is affected by its ability to get us focused on the most important value-drivers. We now move into the area of forecasting future free cash flows. Before that we shall however say a few things about the discount factor and then try to simplify the models slightly.

10.3 Estimating the Discount Factor

Not much can be said about the discount factor that has not been said previously. The approach is the same as the one in Chapter Nine. The discount factor is determined by the cost of the different sources of capital used to finance the project generating the cash flows that are to be discounted. If we, for example, evaluate the dividends paid to investors, we have to use the investors' required return. If we discount the cash flows from a subsidiary within a large group, we need to have the weighted costs of those capital sources used to finance the subsidiary. The costs for all sources of capital are determined by three factors; postponement of consumption, compensation for inflation, and compensation for risk. Since the first two components are more or less the same in spite of the financial source chosen, it is the last part that really causes differences. We have described the choice between capital sources in Chapter Seven and will not repeat these issues here. We will however point out the mathematical formula, which expresses the cost of capital for a company:

$$r_{WACC} = \left(\frac{EQ}{D + EQ}\right) \cdot r_{eq} + \left(\frac{D}{D + EQ}\right) \cdot r_d \qquad (10.11)$$

The tax shield has to be considered here as well. Whenever debt is used the weighted average cost of capital is changed. The correct discount factor is thus Expression (10.12), where t equals the expected tax rate.

$$r_{WACC} = \left(\frac{EQ}{D + EQ}\right) \cdot r_{eq} + \left(\frac{D}{D + EQ}\right) \cdot r_d \cdot (1 - t) \qquad (10.12)$$

One of the most questionable issues in the DCF model is the commonly used assumption of constant capital structure. In Chapter Seven we noted that capital structures vary over time. Still the capital cost in the discount factor is based on one optimal combination of debt and equity. It is important that one does find a sustainable capital structure, or else modify the valuation model.[4]

Finally, it should be mentioned that analysts often do change the discount factor when modelling cash flows into perpetuity. More of this later on.

10.4 Time Horizons and Estimates of Continuing Value

10.4.1 Certainty regarding future income streams

So far when we have used the discounted cash flow (DCF) models we have not been concerned about the possibility of actually making forecasts of

4 Levin (1998) discusses this matter and provides suggestions on how to handle the issue.

what future cash flows are going to be. The only thing we have done is to set up an appropriate model. To estimate the value of a company our models have valued income streams from now until perpetuity, but can we ever really know what the company's income streams will be tomorrow, next year, and in thirty years time? In this section we shall make some assumptions and thereby simplify the job of forecasting cash flows into eternity.

But in order to create more complex models we first need to introduce a couple of simpler models. Regardless of which DCF model we use, it can be simplified by assuming constant income streams. If dividend payouts are constant the DDM can be rewritten as:

$$V_t^{EQ} = \sum_{t=1}^{\infty} \frac{Div_t}{(1 + r_{eq})^t} \Rightarrow \frac{Div}{r_{eq}} \qquad (10.13)$$

Expression (10.13) is referred to as the *constant cash flow formula*. There is nothing extraordinary about this transformation, but it does help us value assets with constant income streams.[5] However, hardly any assets we are concerned with here will have a constant income stream, with the exception perhaps of bonds. But what about constant increases in the income stream? A growing company will experience growth in both cash flows and dividends. The simplified DCF model shown in Expression (10.13) can then, provided that the dividend growth rate is constant, be transformed into:

$$V_t^{EQ} = \frac{Div_t \cdot (1 + g)}{r_{eq} - g} \text{ or } \frac{Div_{t+1}}{r_{eq} - g} \qquad (10.14)$$

This model is known as the *constant-growth formula* (Gordon, 1962). To illustrate it, let's take an example. Mercumin AB has a dividend policy of paying out 40 percent of its earnings over a business cycle. It is expected that earnings, and dividends, will rise by 5 percent per year into infinity. Currently Mercumin AB pays dividends of SEK 10, and its business risk corresponds to a cost of equity of 12 percent. What is the value of the company using the DDM under the assumption of constant growth in dividends? The answer is that one Mercumin share is worth SEK 150 [(10 · · 1.05) ÷ (0.12 – 0.05)].

5 The formula was, as you might remember, introduced already in Chapter Seven.

10.4.2 Uncertainty regarding future income streams

In the two previous models the future income streams were known. In reality this is of course never the case. Both the assumption that future cash flows will be constant and the assumption that they will have a constant growth is unrealistic. By just looking at historic cash flows we know that they do fluctuate substantially over time. More important is that there one shifts in trends meaning that extrapolation of the past does not necessarily work when forecasting the future.

Obviously it will be more and more difficult to forecast cash flows the further away from the present that we get. When turning to financial analysts they seldom provide detailed forecasts for more than the next two or three years. They know there is too much uncertainty when they look further into the future. In contrast to this uncertainty stands the fact that most of the value attributed to a company will arise beyond the observable near future; in the unobservable and unknown future.

Table 10.3 illustrates the portion of a company's value that is generated during a five-year time-period. Please note that it functions only as an illustration of the relationship between market value and profits, and that it therefore contains some simplifications.[6] The far right column states the proportion of each company's 1997 market value that was retrieved between 1997 and 2001. The portion of company value arising beyond the observable time period varies. Some companies who operate in uncertain low-growth industries, such as paper and pulp, are often valued at an exceptionally low level (in this case illustrated by Rottneros and SCA). For a traditional manufacturing company the future is relatively stable and certain and the overall growth in its (mature) industry is often low. For these companies the earnings of the next five years might add up to 30 to 50 percent of total value.[7] But for some companies in high growth industries the earnings over the next five years are perhaps no more than 10 percent of the company value. Netcom is one such company and although its profits

6 In the left-hand column one finds the market value of each company in the beginning of 1997. The following five columns give the actual net earnings for each company in the years 1997 to 2001. The figures for year 2001 are based on estimates from Affärsvärlden in May 2001. Net earnings act as proxies for FCFF even though investment needs are considerably different for the various companies. Observe that no discounting has been made. The figures for SCA include some major non-recurring items.

7 Manufacturing companies are today often being given a low value because of the low growth expectations in the companies' future cash flows. However, sometimes some segments of mature industries, or whole industries start to expand. The telecommunication industry is one such example. In the 1970s Ericsson's future certainly did not look brighter than that of Electrolux. Well, as time goes by things do change ...

accounted for 25 percent of the market value in 1997, its investments made cash flows considerably lower. On average, when discounting the cash flows of the coming five years, it is fair to say that they constitute no more than 40 percent of the value. The rest lies beyond the observable future.

Table 10.3 – The foreseeable future's importance for the valuation of Swedish companies.

Company	MV, -97	Profit -97	Profit -98	Profit -99	Profit -00	Profit -01	Profits/MV
Ericsson	201,844	11,941	13,041	12,130	21,018	12,717	35.1 %
Netcom	9,712	49	67	3,769	−381	−1,057	25.2 %
H&M	39,018	1,691	2,287	3,705	2,553	3,443	35.1 %
SCA	27,241	2,759	3,379	3,602	7,148	6,107	84.4 %
Finnveden	1,295	140	141	280	116	179	66.1 %
Rottneros	1,884	-5	121	91	642	485	70.8 %

10.4.3 The foreseeable and unforeseeable future

When discounting future cash flows it is more or less the norm to separate the future into one time period for which explicit forecasts are made, and another for which a more general forecast is made. This is a natural consequence stemming from our view of the company as a going concern. Deciding on how far into the future explicit forecasts are to be made is something that has to be done early on. The objective should always be to make explicit forecasts as far into the future as possible. But at some stage it will make no sense spending time estimating NOPAT, gross investments and suchlike. There is too much uncertainty. Figure 10.1 shows how the forecast period is split in two.

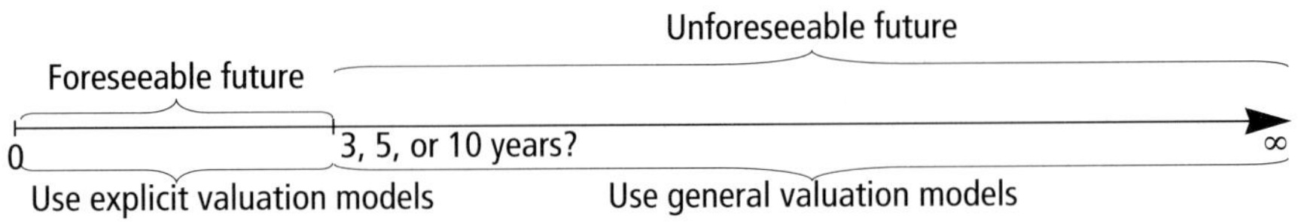

Figure 10.1 – Splitting the future into two parts.

Theoretically speaking, one should try to get the length of the explicit forecast period to coincide with any abnormal growth in the company's cash flows. Thus enabling the time period thereafter to be more "normal". In reality most analysts are probably choosing a time period as long as possible given the possibility to foresee what will happen. The best suggestion to give in regard to deciding the length of the time horizon is to make it as long as possible, and make it at least long enough to incorporate the time-period which is believed to contain the company's abnormal growth in cash flows.

Another matter is that we must recognise that some companies will have a *lower* growth than their competitors and their market. In fact some companies might even be shrinking instead of growing. For forecasts of the nearby explicit time period, the analyst will make use of detailed strategic and financial analyses while trying to understand the company's prospects and its *explicit value*. For forecasts of the distant unforeseeable time-period, for which company value often is referred to as *continuing value*, he/she will instead rely on standardised valuation models, such as e.g. the constant-growth formula. The rest of this section is devoted to modelling the unforeseeable forecasting period, whereas the next section gives some basic insight into the prognosis of the foreseeable forecasting period.

10.4.4 Perpetual abnormal growth in cash flows is impossible

A reasonable assumption is to say that we have few clues concerning most companies' structure and earning capability in ten years. Indeed we can forecast earnings with reasonable accuracy for the next quarter, the next year and perhaps even the year thereafter. But just as we humans often extrapolate what has happened in the past too far into the future, we also extrapolate what we think will happen in the near future too far into the distant future. This in undoubtedly one of the most common causes of inaccurate valuation models. Perpetual abnormal cash flows are in reality impossible. During the 1980s Nokia could hardly be described as a high performer. It was a conglomerate with an average level of profitability. After the financial crisis at the very beginning of the 1990s it decided to focus on one of its smaller business segments; telecommunications. Not many people in 1992 could imagine that a company with a long and stable history suddenly could be transformed into one of Europe's greatest corporate success stories ever. Ten years later Nokia's market value had increased about 700 times. But just like investors could misjudge Nokia's future in 1992, they can do so today. Will Nokia continue to expand? Will they continue to hold a market share of 35 percent in a market growing by more than 50 percent a year? Will they continue to have operating profit margins higher than 20 percent?

Perhaps. This text is not a critical analysis of Nokia in particular. But in most cases things do change. Some industries and companies suddenly excel, while others weaken. The only thing we know for sure is that no tree grows to the sky. If these last years have brought an extraordinary growth in cash flows for a company such as Nokia, this will not necessarily happen again in the next decade. We can assume that in the next ten years most of the short term barriers currently protecting the extraordinary cash flows of Nokia will be removed. Nokia should not be able to earn a return much higher than industry average. In fact, the telecommunication industry should not earn a higher return than other industries because of the breakdown of protective barriers. In the long run no company can earn a higher return than industry average and no industry can earn a higher return than the market average (possibly with an adjustment for risk).

There are two reasons for this. The first reason should be obvious to us as it was discussed extensively in Chapter Five. Reasonably competitive markets will in time ensure that new products enter a profitable market so that companies earning short term "monopoly rents" do so no more. Competitors will mimic the behaviour of high-performers, design similar products and enter their markets or market segments. Remember the consequences from Figure 10.2 that were discussed also in Chapter Five.

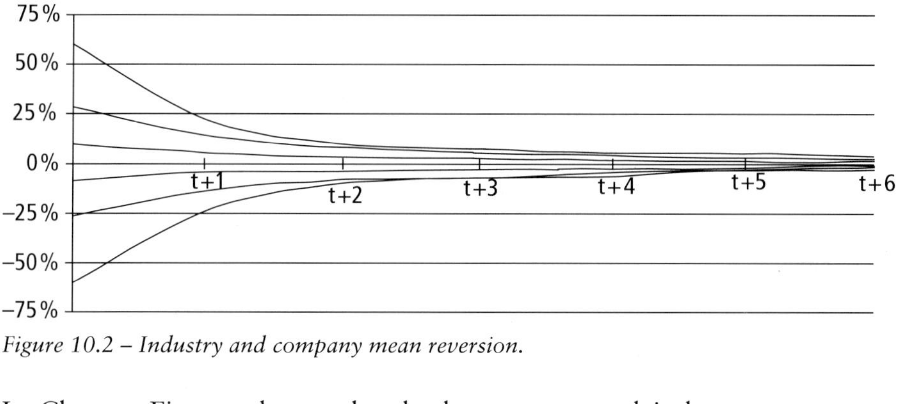

Figure 10.2 – Industry and company mean reversion.

In Chapter Five we learnt that both company and industry returns are mean reverting. It is only logical to incorporate this knowledge into the valuation model. Thus we determine an explicit forecast based on historical information and identify the growth in free cash flows during that time-period. At the same time the overall industry and market growth rate in free cash flows is estimated. During the transformation period the company-specific free cash flows are allowed to revert to the mean. Companies earning returns above industry average during the explicit forecast period will hence gradually get a lower return. Companies earning returns below the industry average during the explicit forecast period will at same time gradually get a higher return.

The second reason for not believing in excessive growth rates in cash flows is that if a company constantly grows quicker than its competitors (i.e., the market) then it will eventually become the market. As it gets bigger it will be more and more difficult to maintain the relatively higher pace. Let's take Nokia as the example again. In the beginning perhaps the higher growth rate in cash flows is due to improved profit margins but sooner or later it will have to be because of a higher growth rate in sales than the competitors. Nokia is thus increasing its market share. But as its market share increases so will the growth rate of the telecommunications industry and sooner or later Nokia will dominate the whole industry. If Nokia then continues with its exceptional growth rate, which is higher than the overall market growth, then the telecommunications industry will make up a greater and greater portion of all production in society. Growth is likely to stagnate at some point in time, probably sooner rather than later. Competition authorities also play a role here inhibiting too dominating market positions for individual companies.

10.4.5 Modelling cash flow growth in a single period

As you probably understand, we need to modify Expression (10.3) so that it encompasses both a foreseeable forecast period and an unforeseeable forecast period. This is easy to do as shown in Expression (10.15).

$$V_t^{Firm} = \sum_{t=1}^{T} \frac{FCFF_t}{(1 + r_{WACC})^t} + \frac{\left(\sum_{t=T+1}^{\infty} \frac{FCFF_t}{(1 + r_{WACC})^t}\right)}{(1 + r_{WACC})^{T+1}} \qquad (10.15)$$

In Expression (10.15) there are two explicit forecast periods based on the same technique of discounting separate cash flows. For the sake of order let's rewrite Expression (10.15) so that the second period can be generalised. For the foreseeable forecast period we can use explicit forecasts of the FCFF for each year, whereas we can use a general valuation model for the unforeseeable forecast period.

$$V_t^{Firm} = \sum_{t=1}^{T} \frac{FCFF_t}{(1 + r)^t} + CV_T \qquad (10.16)$$

where CV stands for continuing value. The most common way of estimating continuing value is to use the *constant cash flow formula*, or the *constant-growth formula*. In the valuation literature, as well as among practitioners, it seems to be more common to use the constant-growth model. We shall soon provide some criticism of this technique but first let's look at the constant-growth model of continuing value. Expressions (10.17) contain three ways of measuring the continuing value, each generating the same result.

$$CV_0 = \frac{[(FCFF_T^{normal} \cdot (1+g))/(r_{WACC}^{market} - g)]}{(1 + r_{WACC}^{firm})^{T+1}} \tag{10.17a}$$

$$CV_0 = \frac{[(FCFF_{T+1}^{normal})/(r_{WACC}^{market} - g)]}{(1 + r_{WACC}^{firm})^{T+1}} \tag{10.17b}$$

$$CV_0 = \frac{FCFF_{T+1}^{normal}}{(r_{WACC}^{market} - g)} \cdot df \text{ where df equals } \frac{1}{(1 + r_{WACC}^{firm})^{T+1}} \tag{10.17c}$$

All models are essentially equal and consist of the same four components. The first is the free cash flow to the firm at the end of the foreseeable forecast period. This measure needs to be "normalised" as described in the next section (10.5). The second component is the growth rate during the unforeseeable forecast period. The last two components are the WACC for both the company itself, during the foreseeable forecast period, and the expected WACC for an average company with the same capital structure in the unforeseeable forecast period. We shall briefly discuss the last three components here.

In most valuation situations the growth rate is lower in the unforeseeable forecast period than in the foreseeable. This can lead to biases if one is not careful. Lower growth rates mean that less NOPAT needs to be reinvested and hence FCFF will be higher. Therefore successful companies might maintain a high growth in FCFF for some time after the profitability has decreased. There is however no reason to believe that excessive growth can hold forever and ever. To say that a company will grow at a pace higher than its cost of capital stipulates can be dangerous. In fact it should, according to economic theory, be impossible if we continue to have reasonably efficient markets. Financiers should place a value on companies based on their investments, and nothing else. The weighted average cost of capital that is in the denominator of Expression (10.17) includes a compensation for the postponement of consumption and price increases, as well as risk. If these actors have judged the company's future correctly (and why should we not expect this?) expected growth is already incorporated into the model.

Another thing to think about when estimating the continuing value is the discount factor in the unforeseeable future. Free cash flows for individual companies were not, in the long term, expected to grow faster than average. As they revert to the mean it is likely that also discount factors (or more correctly; compensation for risk) revert to the mean. This is why it is suggested that one does not use company-specific capital costs, but the market-specific.

Remember that the continuing value you receive here is the value at the beginning of the unforeseeable forecast period and this needs to be discounted back to the beginning of the foreseeable forecast period. Since the value is transferred from the end of the explicit forecast period to its beginning, one uses the appropriate company-specific discount rate.

10.4.6 Modelling cash flow growth in multiple periods

Is it likely that cash flow growth in the unforeseeable period can be modelled in a single period, or would the analysis benefit from extending it into multiple periods? The answer would be no if the unforeseeable period was truly unforeseeable, but as uncertainty comes gradually there is reason to look further into the problem. Figure 10.3 shows three different patterns in cash flow growth.

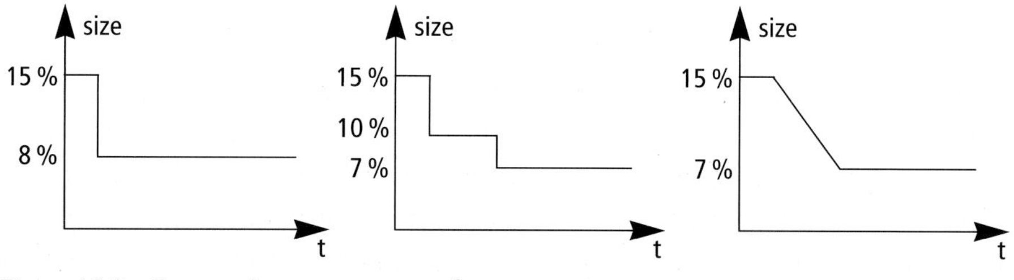

Figure 10.3 – Patterns in company growth.

Scenario A: Growth in foreseeable period 15 %. Constant growth rate in unforeseeable period of 8 %.
Scenario B: Growth in foreseeable period 15 %, then growth of 10 % in constant transition period, and thereafter growth of 7 %.
Scenario C: Growth in foreseeable period 15 %, then a continuously decreasing growth rate in transition period, and thereafter growth of 7 %.

Scenario A contains a first period in which there is first a company-specific period of cash flow growth, and then a reversion to the mean industry growth in the unforeseeable forecast period. This is according to the previous estimation of continuing value. Scenario B contains the same company-specific period of cash flow growth, but thereafter there is first a period of slightly higher growth in cash flows than the market, and some time later that growth finally reverses fully to long term market growth. In Scenario C there is a continuous and gradual reverse from company-specific growth in cash flows to long term market average. Intuitively this makes a lot of sense, but the obvious problem is to determine when each period starts and ends.

In Chapter Five it was discussed how the mean reversion process of abnormal company returns could be divided into a company-specific and an industry-specific component. We learnt that the company-specific component should disappear faster than the industry-specific component. A workable angle of incidence is to say that the foreseeable forecast period should comprise the time when we believe that the company itself earns excessive returns. The transition period is when company-specific growth rate have transformed to the industry, and in which industry-specific growth rates are reverting towards the long term market averages.

10.5 Estimating Future Cash Flows From Operations

10.5.1 Fundamental analysis

Most people get so involved with trying to understand the technical aspects of the valuation models that they forget the by far most important part of making a company valuation; the estimation of future cash flows. It is the most important part both because it is the most difficult part and because it has the greatest impact. By just making slight changes in the expected growth in free cash flow the value of the company can change substantially. The effect is greater the further away the majority of expected cash flows come and the higher the discount rate (the uncertainty being greater). To find estimates of future FCFF the analyst perform a fundamental analysis.

The *fundamental analysis* is about discovering the strengths and weaknesses of the company's core operations and relate this to company value. It is about understanding where the company is today, and where it is likely to be heading in the future. To perform it properly one has to mix a strategic analysis with a financial analysis. The *strategic analysis* aims at creating an understanding of how the company will interact with stakeholders and industry competitors in the future. It is just as much an analysis of the competitive environment as it is an analysis of actual company performance. To perform the strategic analysis a number of different "tools" or "guidelines" can be used. Textbooks in corporate strategy often recommend models such as SWOT-analysis, BCG-matrix, or Porter's industry-structure model. Questions to find answers to are e.g. how is the company's market going to develop in the short- and long term? What is the competitive situation going to be? How will customers' needs be satisfied? What production means are needed to satisfy them? These questions will link to the financial analysis, where sales growth, profit margins, investment plans, and production structure can be determined.

The *financial analysis* is also about discovering the strengths and weaknesses of the company's core operations. A financial analysis is primarily based on historical figures of earlier company performance. The job is to extend these historical figures into the future, and thereby determine expected free cash flows. A good financial analysis can never be done without a strategic analysis. Historical cash flows have to be understood in the light of the historical competitive environment, and future changes in that environment is what will cause changes in future free cash flows. After the analyst has done her financial analysis properly she knows what the key success factors are and she can measure them and potential changes in them via the financial analysis. No deep coverage of financial analyses is provided here.[8] But to give an idea of one we might use the Dupont-formula (also shown in Expression 2.30) to distinguish between the profit margin and the capital turnover.

$$\text{RNOA} = \frac{\text{OPc}_t}{\text{S}_t} \cdot \frac{\text{S}_t}{(\text{NOA}_{t-1} + \text{NOA}_t)/2} \tag{10.18}$$

The profit margin component might be decomposed further to highlight any particular key success factor. Some of these factors are described in Expression (10.19).

$$\frac{\text{OPc}_t}{\text{S}_t} = \text{S}_t - \frac{\text{SellExp}_t}{\text{S}_t} - \frac{\text{R\&D}_t}{\text{S}_t} - \frac{\text{ProdExp}_t}{\text{S}_t} - \frac{\text{Other}_t}{\text{S}_t} \tag{10.19}$$

8 See Penman (2001) for an excellent coverage of this topic.

The operating profit margin can also be separated to incorporate differences in variable and fixed costs, or to separate between different product areas/geographical markets. Which categories one chooses to use is dependent on the strategic analysis where key success factors must be determined.

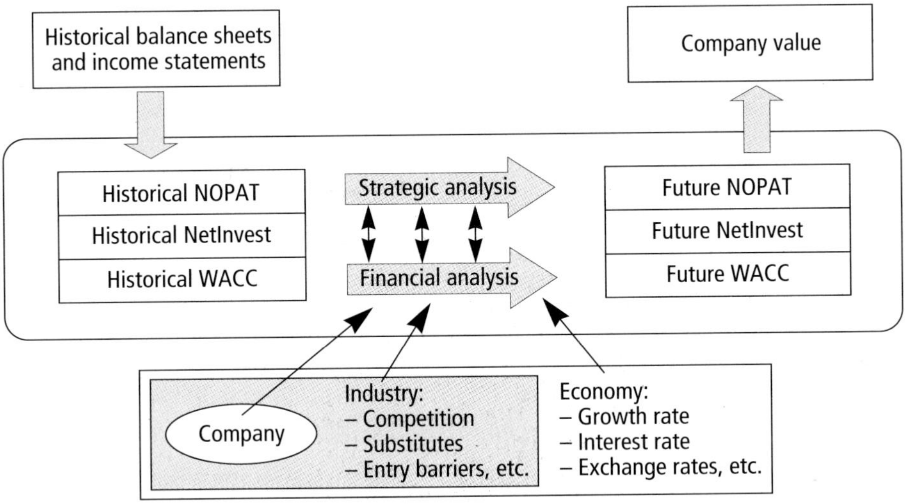

Figure 10.4 – The combined strategic and financial analysis.

To summarise the process of estimating future cash flows from operations we use Figure 10.4. The primary input data is historical accounting information in the form of income statements and balance sheets covering at least the last business cycle (or five to ten years). This information can be used to estimate historical NOPAT, NetInvest and the discount factor. Based on a strategic and financial analysis these figures are extrapolated into the future. Again the estimates should reach as far into the future as possible. Accounting information is primarily used for the specific company to be analysed (although comparisons with some of close competitors are recommended), whereas the strategic analysis takes in both competition at the industry level and macro-economy factors (such as economic growth, inflation, and exchange rates).

10.5.2 Normalised free cash flows and operating earnings

What is normal when it comes to business operations? To answer such a question the analyst will have to look at the current organisational structure of a company and judge, on the basis of past operations, how much money has been earned in the past. When the continuing value needs to be estimated it is very important to identify a "normalised" FCFF at the end of the foreseeable forecast period. A personal opinion is that future free *cash flows* are easier to determine when based on historical *earnings*. This personal empirical experience also receives support from research, partly covered in Chapter Two. Because of this we talk of operating earnings (NOPAT) instead of cash flows (FCFF) here.[9]

Normalised operating earnings must be based on the average over a full business cycle. As one usually expects most organisations to grow, organically or through acquisitions, the trend component is important. Often it helps to understand the growth in operating earnings by comparing it to a size-related measure. That could be e.g. sales (operating profit margin), or capital employed (return on capital employed).

Just as the historical free cash flows can be a bad indicator of future free cash flows so can historical earnings be a bad indicator. When studying the normalised operating earnings it is important to evaluate the figures in the income statement further. The pharmaceutical company AstraZeneca disclosed substantially lower operating earnings in 1998 than in the past but that was only due to merger costs. As the merger between Astra and Zeneca was an extraordinary event not likely to happen every year in the future it cannot be considered to be part of normal business. The same goes for Volvo who sold off its car division in 1999. The extraordinary gains coming from that divestment is not part of normal business activity. Having said this, it should be remembered that most costs (it usually is costs) that companies call extraordinary are indeed quite ordinary. Restructuring costs do seem to be quite normal, smaller divestments and investments seem to be part of normal business for most companies. Analysts need to discover the sustainable level of growth.

10.5.3 Modelling fluctuations in operating earnings

Is it possible to identify patterns in company earnings? Most financial analysts will clearly say that in the short-run there are both company-specific and industry-specific patterns, and these move with the business cycle. As for all forecasting the real challenge is not to extrapolate a trend, but to

9 Gross investments can be normalised by looking at past investment and separating between reinvestments and new investments, operating and financial investments, and organic and acquired growth.

identify when a trend is broken. Clearly there are many historical patterns that are observable when it comes to fluctuations in company earnings. Below we look at four common patterns in company performance; these are (1) organic growth, (2) acquired growth, (3) cyclical growth, and (4) stable growth.

The organic growth company

This company has products and services for which there is an above-average demand and therefore growth is above market-average. Companies within this category are companies where many things, usually positive, are happening. New products and services are launched, new sales offices are opened and investments are being made. Often these companies have low cash flows (although earnings can be higher) because of new investments. When judging this kind of company it is most important to judge whether current expansions are likely to transform into future cash flows. A growing company has a high market value in comparison to fundamentals, such as current earnings, cash flows, and book values. This reflects the current growth prospects, but there is usually also a greater amount of uncertainty. These companies are, above all, extremely sensitive to changes in expected future growth rates. For these companies the mean reversion process will be an extremely influential part of the valuation.

The acquired growth company

This company produces accounting statements that portray an expanding organisation. It is usually not a company in a growing industry, but a growing company in a mature and stable industry. These companies are also surrounded by many events but as mergers and acquisitions often tend to be stressful for the organisation as a whole it is important to judge how the units fit together. The acquired growth company is often found in mature industries and the reason for consolidating the industry is often cost-cutting. Cost cutting is usually a "defensive" strategy, which has short- and medium-term effects. It is important to judge whether the long term effects of the acquired growth company is growth in operating earnings/cash flows. Usually there are much greater opportunities for the organic growth company to sustain a continuous earnings growth than it is for the acquired growth company. When identifying the normalised earnings of this kind of company it is important that one determines first the underlying growth rate of existing operations, and then judge whether the structural changes are likely to remain and to what level they will be kept.

The cyclical company

The cyclical company has operating earnings that vary substantially over time. This is either due to severe fluctuations in the demand for the offered product/service or because of smaller fluctuations in the demand, which are levered by high fixed operating costs. In the case of a large degree of fixed operating costs it is common that a company in a cyclical industry also acquires growth. A typical cyclical company is a forest company, which is influenced both by severe fluctuations in demand (and with changing prices) and a high portion of fixed production costs. When identifying the normalised earnings of this company it is important to consider the whole business cycle. It is often in the economic downturns that these companies really distinguish themselves from the others.

The stable company

If all companies formed part of this category life as an analyst would be much easier. The stable company usually performs in a mature market where it has a dominant role. Its growth rate is both at market-average and relatively predictable. For various reasons there is little consolidation in the industry, one of these reasons can be that fixed costs are not an important factor in determining industry performance. Another reason can be that the industry is so consolidated that further mergers are unlikely. A third reason can be an owner who is running the business with other intentions than expansion and value-maximisation. This kind of company is usually the easiest to determine the normalised earnings for.

It is important to note that according to financial theory none of these categories is "better" than the others. As of this writing, there is a great belief in growing companies and particularly in companies having an organic growth. But the value of a company quoted in an efficient market should always reflect all future cash flows discounted to today's value, despite the company's cash flow pattern. Table 10.4 contains a categorisation of companies for which past performance places them in one of the earnings pattern categories.

Table 10.4 – Examples of companies within each category.

Organic growth	Acquired growth	Cyclical growth	Stable growth
Hennes&Mauritz	Assa-Abloy	Trelleborg	Svedbergs
HL Display	Pharmacia	StoraEnso	AGA
WM-Data	Electrolux	SAPA	Sandvik
Nokia		Holmen	

Assumptions regarding normalised FCFF will have the greatest impact on companies with high expected organic growth. Unexpected changes in their "true" normal FCFF just as dramatic consequences for their valuation as unexpected changes in the growth rate and the cost of equity.

10.6 Summarising the Valuation Model

Step by step we have worked our way towards a final equity valuation model based on the free cash flows to the firm. This model is now expressed in Expression (10.20).

$$V_t^{EQ} = \sum_{t=1}^{T} \frac{FCFF_t}{(1 + r_{WACC})^t} + \frac{(NOPLAT_{T+1}/r_{WACC}^{norm})}{(1 + r_{WACC})^{H+1}} - D_t + FA_t \qquad (10.20)$$

For reasons of simplicity, this model has no transformation period for the calculation of continuing value. Also, in accordance with the critical view expressed in the previous section, the unforeseeable forecasting period is estimated without assuming a constant abnormal growth in cash flows. The steps to be gone through when making the evaluation are reviewed below.

1. Determine the forecast horizon.

The forecast horizon has to stretch as far into the future as possible. If there is a lot of uncertainty it is probably wise to do more explicit forecasts as they force the analyst to consider all the problems there are with forecasting. Companies with stable growth rates, or predictable cash flow patterns, are easier to use general valuation models for.

2. Understand the company's past.

The second step is to review the company's past, both in terms of historical accounting statements, and in terms of industry analyses. The analyst has to make a combined strategic and financial analysis to enable an extrapolation of the figures into the future. It is wise to use accounting information covering at least the last business cycle if meaningful extrapolations are to be made. Understanding a company's performance is just as much about understanding its competitors and its competitive environment. If these factors are changing, extrapolations of historical accounting information can be largely irrelevant.

3. Extrapolate the past into the future.
When judging a company's future cash flows it is important to consider both past cash flows from historical investments and its new investment needs. Because of irregular past investments historical cash flows are difficult to use for forecasts of future cash flows. It is often recommendable to use average historical investments (perhaps in a ratio to sales or capital) and then deduct them from forecasted cash earnings.

4. Estimate the discount rate.
Discount rates are often discussed less than they deserve. But as shown elsewhere in this book, it is indeed difficult to determine the cost of equity. Market premiums have varied between three and eight percent in different studies. For equity-financed companies such variations have huge effects on company value. An alternative is to discount certainty equivalents, although management must set them subjectively. Remember that risk is likely to reverse to market averages in the distant future, or at least that is our best guess of what the future will look like.

5. Determine "normal" FCFF at the end of the foreseeable forecast period.
If the explicit forecast period is supposed to end when the economy is expected to be in a particularly bad or good shape the cash flow of this last period is a terribly biased starting value for estimates of the continuing value. Both NOPAT and net investments have to be normalised, based on the cash flow pattern seen during the explicit forecast period.

6. Determine the value of outstanding debt and financial assets.
This is a straightforward process where non-operating assets are valued according to their current market value. If shares in private companies are held, their values can be estimated using comparisons to public companies in the same industry. Future debt used to finance future investments is usually assumed to have a zero net present value. Tax effects are taken care of in the discount factor as long as the capital structure is maintained constant.

7. Sensitivity analysis.
The final step in the analysis is to perform various kinds of sensitivity analyses. These are in general performed in similar manners as to those described in Chapter Nine. In other words, the most influential and uncertain events, and their monetary consequences, have to be understood. In this

analysis the use of different scenarios is appropriate. Some factors that are of importance are future profit margins, industry growth rates, company market share, risk, and risk-free interest rates. What happens if the risk premium is changed? What happens if one uses a growth rate above market rate? What happens if the persistent profit margins shrink because of increased competition?

10.7 Mergers and Acquisitions

10.7.1 Introduction

For the creation of wealth in society, it is important to have an employment of resources in product markets that is as efficient as possible. The combination of production units within an industry has to be such that the long-run production costs are as low as possible relative to their utility. If the current combination of production units within an industry is less efficient than it could be, there are incentives to find ways of changing the organisation of the industry and take advantage of the benefits from such a restructuring. One of the prime motives for having active efficient capital markets is to enable such structural changes in companies/industries. In some cases a restructuring calls for a *combination* of previously separate business units, and sometimes it calls for a *separation* of previously combined business units.

During recent years the amount and size of structural changes within industries have undoubtedly increased. In this section we shall look at the combination of production units. The restructuring of industries has a tendency to cause larger and larger production units rather than smaller ones. A *merger* is an event in which two companies are combined into one new company. It is distinguished from an *acquisition*, which is an event in which one company acquires another company. The main distinction, although often hard to see, is that a merger is a friendly amalgamation between partners, whereas an acquisition is a friendly or unfriendly combination where one party dominates the other. Because of the fuzzy line between the two events they are often used interchangeably.

Since the latter half of the 1990s many of these mergers and acquisitions have been on a global scale. British Petroleum (BP) have merged with Amoco, Daimler-Benz have merged with Chrysler, and Ford has acquired Volvo, just to take a few examples. In the global economy the allocation and reallocation of resources works quickly and mergers and acquisitions (hereafter referred to as M&As) are an important part of it[10]. In fact, many companies have acquisitions and divestitures as their prime strategy. Their competitive advantage is that they are better than other companies at restructuring industries. Obviously these companies want to earn excessive returns and when they restructure an industry this is not necessarily beneficial for society in general. Whether merger and acquisition activities in general benefit society is an often-discussed matter. Such discussion is mostly refrained from here and instead the focus lies at the corporate level, and particularly the shareholder and management aspects of M&As.

Almost all industries have seen companies pushing for more and more acquisitions. It seems as if big is undoubtedly beautiful. From a managerial perspective there are of course good theoretically grounded reasons for this. Donaldson (1984) stated that growth is the ultimate objective, as management want to handle the pressure from stakeholders. According to Donaldson survival, independence, self-sufficiency and self-fulfilment were the motives for management's desire to grow. Managers have great incentives for making use of excessive growth strategies.

From an investor perspective the size of a company's operations is of no real interest. It is only when a larger size is transformed into growth in cash flow per share, i.e., in value-creation that shareholders are benefited. For shareholders the prime consideration is whether an acquisition or a merger creates value to shareholders.

We can distinguish between three forms of acquisitions: (1) strategic investments, (2) financial investments, and (3) conglomerate investments. Of these, strategic investments are the most important to cover here. *Financial investments* are mainly conducted because the company has excess cash, which is needed in the near future. Most financial investments are made in unrelated business areas. A special case of financial investment is when a company acquires a smaller part in a competitor, supplier or any other related party. This can be done as a short term financial investment (no con-

---

10 Technical aspects of how mergers and acquisitions actually are conducted are not discussed in this book. An acquisition usually involves a cash payment for the shares of another company, or an exchange of shares. A merger usually involves the exchange of shares in one company with those of another. Control over resources is extremely important, and perhaps the most important distinction between a merger and an acquisition is that with a merger the control over the combined resources is split (in "fair" proportions) between the merging entities. In an acquisition, on the other hand, the acquiring company takes control over the other company's resources. Hardly surprising, many acquisitions are officially announced as "mergers", simply because that causes fewer official conflicts. In reality most, if not all, "mergers" consist of one stronger party taking control of a majority of the resources.

trol over the other party is exercised), but it paves the way for future strategic investments. In 1998 the Irish forest company Jefferson Smurfit acquired a smaller part in Munksjö, a competing, although smaller, Swedish forest company. No attempt has been made to increase the ownership, but the financial investment is likely to be followed up by a future bid for the whole company. *Conglomerate investments* are nowadays often seen as unnecessary and perhaps even value destroying. They involve a long term active engagement in a unit not operating in the acquiring company's strategic areas. The economic motives for making them are that they stabilise total cash flows, reduce excessive cash positions, and increase scale economies in corporate overheads and in the financing of investments. Conglomerate investments make particular sense in environments where there are substantial bankruptcy or transaction costs. The main explanation as to why companies make conglomerate investments is the agency cost hypothesis based on a survival motive (Denis, Denis and Sarin, 1997).

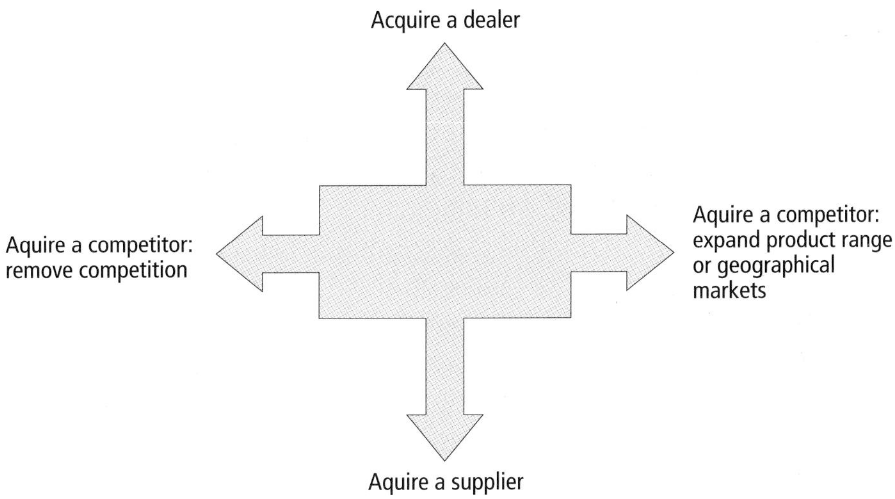

Figure 10.5 – Forms of strategic investment activities.

Strategic investments are engagements in activities that affect the core business of a company. They are the prime objective in the rest of this discussion. Figure 10.5 shows its two dimensions: vertical and horizontal integration. *Vertical integration* is to acquire or merge with units before or behind the company in the value chain. *Forward integration* is to acquire a dealer, which previously has bought products or services from the company. A *backward integration* is to acquire a supplier, which previously has delivered products or services to the company. A vertical integration can be motivated by the reduction of transaction costs, the ability to increase coordination in production and to assure the supply of input goods and/or demand for output goods. *Horizontal integration* is to either acquire a direct competitor, which sells similar products in the same markets as the company. This primarily reduces direct competition and might reduce overhead costs. Or it is to acquire a competitor, which sells different products or sells the same kind of products in different markets. Whereas the first case of horizontal integration is a defensive move, reducing production costs, the latter is usually an offensive move, increasing market penetration.

In the following discussion the emphasis is on quoted companies purchasing or merging with other quoted companies. The reason is simply that in those cases value-creation is easy to measure and evaluate, as market values (and changes in them) are readily available. The same ideas are however applicable to private companies as well. One of the underlying assumptions of studies of the value created by M&As is that capital markets are efficient, i.e. before the announcement of a merger or an acquisition the companies affected by the deal are valued correctly in regard to their cash flows generated on a stand-alone basis. After the deal they are valued correctly in regard to their cash flows generated as a combined unit.

10.7.2 The creation of synergies

Mergers and acquisitions create value for shareholders if, *ceteris paribus*, the combined value of the two units after the merger is higher than the stand-alone values of the two companies before the merger. This increase in combined value comes when investors believe that *synergies* between the two companies will cause future cash flows to be higher when the two units work together instead of separately.

$$V_t^{A+B} = \sum_{t=1}^{\infty} \frac{FCF_t^A}{(1+r^A)^t} + \sum_{t=1}^{\infty} \frac{FCF_t^B}{(1+r^B)^t} + \sum_{t=1}^{\infty} \frac{FCF_t^{synergy}}{(1+r)^t} \tag{10.21}$$

From a shareholder perspective, no acquisition or merger is needed unless synergies can be expected.[11] Naturally researchers have frequently studied the synergies stemming from mergers and acquisitions. Questions they have asked are for example (1) if mergers and acquisitions create synergies, (2) how often do they do so, and (3) what the size of the synergy effect is.

11 Without synergies shareholders are not benefited by M&As. Instead they just hold a portfolio consisting of all companies within the industry.

Researchers still do not agree fully on the answers to these questions. Synergies will have to be found in the combined companies' operations. The size of the companies increases but is that effect being transformed into the operating profit margin, the capital turnover and finally into the companies' return on capital? The consolidation of industries is often said to be an effect of the "fixed-cost" game of business. A larger company can reduce the fixed cost per unit. Fixed costs occur everywhere; in the production process, in service functions (such as information systems), in sales and marketing, and even in finance. It is likely that some fixed costs can be reduced when units are joined together. It is also likely that some competition is lost which gives the combined unit better control over prices.

A number of empirical studies have looked at the *ex post* economic performance of merged companies. Most of these studies have perhaps surprising results. Herman and Lowenstein (1988) have reported that profitability actually declined after hostile takeovers. Mueller (1985) found declines in market shares for as long as eleven years after manufacturing companies had merged. A McKinsey study reported in Copeland, Koller and Murrin (2000) stated that 61 percent of all studied merger programs were failures as they were unable to earn back their cost of capital. The results are perhaps supportive of the often claimed notion that companies, which are performing well, are so busy running their own business that they have no time to get involved in acquisition programs. Most studies in the area are American and they come to the conclusion that managers have higher expectations of mergers than economic consequences motivate. It is not likely that similar Swedish studies would come to any other conclusions. Synergies do arise, but only infrequently and in smaller sizes than expected.

In a large American study, Sirower (1997) estimated the maximum synergy gains to be only three to four percent. Why is the synergy effect not larger when there are substantial "fixed-cost gains" in many industries? The answer is that the reduction of fixed costs is not the only cash flow effect M&As has. In relation to a merger and/or acquisition two or more units will have to be integrated, and such a process is both lengthy and costly. Production facilities will have to be run jointly, some employees might have to be laid off whereas others might have to be hired, computer systems will have to integrated, sales offices will have to be integrated, etc. Perhaps the most costly, and most difficult, tasks to evaluate *a priori* are the cultural differences and the conflicts that can arise when merging two organisations. Although researchers have identified these problems they still know rather little about their actual effects and it can only be studied on a case-by-case basis. The evaluation of synergies arising from M&As is also complicated by the fact that we do not know what would have happened if the merger had not occurred. Perhaps the two companies would have been worse off without merging and the low synergy effects were due to the fact that the environment had changed? Perhaps competitors responded to the merger by also merging and thus created a *status quo* within the industry?

10.7.3 Mergers, acquisitions and shareholder value

Even if synergy effects are low, mergers and acquisitions are still beneficial to society. But an important question for us to answer is whether they do add any significant value to shareholders. When answering this question, researchers start out by assuming that capital markets are efficient, which implies that companies are always correctly valued. From a shareholder perspective the success of an individual acquisition (merger) is not only based on the synergies that are created but also on the price of the acquisition. Usually the acquiring company pays a *takeover premium* on top of the existing market value. From the perspective of the acquiring company the success of the acquisition is calculated as:

$$NPV_0 = -\text{Premium}_0 + \sum_{t=1}^{\infty} \frac{\text{synergy}_t}{(1+r)^t} \qquad (10.22)$$

Let's take an example. In year 2000 the Swedish industrial company Finnveden acquired another subcontractor in the industrial sector; Bulten. The market value of Bulten was prior to the acquisition bid SEK 560 million. Finnveden made a cash offer of SEK 45 per share, equal to SEK 840 million for the whole company. Finnveden thus paid an acquisition premium of a little more than 50 percent. If we first assume that the market is efficient, and hence Bulten was correctly priced as a stand-alone unit, then the total NPV of synergies stemming from the integrating of the two companies should be worth more than 280 million.

We can hereby identify three scenarios as illustrated in Figure 10.5. The *first* is that the synergy effects are higher than the premium paid. In such cases the acquisition is a success. The *second* scenario is that there are positive synergy effects, but that the acquisition premium is higher than the synergy effects. In such cases the acquisition is economically logical, but it is mismanaged by the acquiring company and therefore it reduces shareholder value for the acquiring company. The *third* scenario is that there are negative synergy effects exist. In such cases it makes absolutely no sense to go ahead with the acquisition (merger). If management pays a premium on top of it all, then even more valued is destroyed for the shareholders of the acquiring company.

Table 10.5 – Decision rule in mergers and acquisitions.

Synergy ≥ Bid premium	Make the acquisition. Economic benefits are greater than the price paid.
Bid premium ≥ Synergy ≥ 0	Economic benefits exist, but managers pay too much for the acquisition target. According to Sirower (1997) the most common situation.
0 ≥ Synergy	Why make the investment at all? No economic benefits whatsoever.

The results from almost all research studies show that on average mergers and acquisitions destroy value for shareholders of the acquiring company. This is beyond most doubt and investors usually know it and the value of an acquiring company frequently decreases after the announcement of an acquisition. Quite often the value of two combined companies becomes lower than the value of the companies on a stand-alone basis. The short term decrease in value for the combined unit is an indication of the long term decrease in value (see e.g. Jensen and Ruback, 1983; Magenheim and Mueller, 1988; Sirower, 1997). A Swedish study (Jonsson, 1995) indicates that while shareholders of the acquired company do gain on acquisitions, there is no consistent evidence of gains for shareholders of acquiring companies.

These results are likely to be more pronounced for mature companies who are merely getting rid of excess cash and want to increase size rather than return cash to shareholders. In some industries it might make more sense to acquire other companies. Two such areas could be banking and the forestry industry (where fixed costs are substantial), or high growth industries such as telecommunications (where access to new technology is of critical importance). Acquisitions in unrelated industries are also likely to be less successful than acquisitions in related industries (e.g. Caves, 1989).

10.7.4 The conflict between managers and shareholders

Who gains from acquisition bids? If the shareholders of the acquiring company loses in the "acquisition game", there must be some winners, or at least somebody who believes he/she will gain from the acquisition. The tentative winners and losers are portrayed in Figure 10.6. When the acquisition premium is higher than the synergy effect shareholders of the acquired company must be among the winners. They now get more for their shares than they would have received if no acquisition had been made or if they had received shares in the new company. However, their gains come from passive participation in the merger, i.e., they are not directly responsible for the bid. The other winner is management of the acquiring company. Obviously they will obtain the benefits outlined by Donaldson (1984). It has been documented that managers within the acquiring companies gain substantial power in the combined organisation. It is hardly surprising that they are the active winners in the acquisition game. At the same time the losers are management within the acquired company. It has been documented that they generally lose power in the combined organisation. Often the top management have to go or they choose to leave the new organisation voluntarily. Besides these parties shareholders of the acquiring company are often losers, subject to overly optimistic managers who eagerly desire growth.

	Aquiring company	Aquired company
Shareholders	Loser	Winner
Management	Winner	Loser

Figure 10.6 – Winners and losers in the acquisition game.

In an important contribution to the area Jensen (1986) outlined the importance of acquisitions as a re-distributor of free cash flow to investors. In his eyes management often use excess free cash flow to pay for the acquisition premium resulting in a return of financial slack to investors. The fact that the slack is returned to other shareholders than those owning the company is not a problem if investors are diversified and hold a proportional amount of their wealth in all companies. The, at first sight, presumably uneconomic behaviour of management is thus not harmful as long as shareholders behave rationally (i.e., diversify themselves).

10.7.5 Strategies for successful mergers and acquisitions

Managers have good reasons for pursuing excessive growth strategies, which often includes buying other companies at prices set too high. At the same time it is difficult to really judge whether a bid premium is motivated or not, as synergies are so hard to measure. The question that remains is then, of course, how do we know when the acquiring company pays too much? The study made by Sirower (1997) gives us considerable insight into the phenomenon. According to Sirower the best measure of *post-acquisition performance* is the acquisition premium expressed in terms of percentage. The higher premium you pay the greater is the probability that you pay too much.

Sirower also find that multiple bidders usually destroy value, as prices tend to be too high. Although it is not uncommon in Sweden with multiple bidders it is far less so than in the US. The corporate governance system and the traditions in Sweden cause many deals to take place directly between a seller and a potential buyer. It is more common in the US to announce public offers for the shares of a company, and without a contact between the buyer and seller it is more likely that additional buyers show up.

Companies used to making acquisitions are usually betters buyers of other companies. Some companies specialise in acquiring smaller companies and integrating them into an existing corporate structure. Common sense tells us that negotiating business deals requires skills, and those practising often are likely to be more skilful. Some Swedish companies, such as e.g. Electrolux, Securitas and Bergman & Beving, are known to continuously acquire and integrate smaller companies into their organisation. In particular Securitas have a good reputation for doing this well.

Sirower also finds that the size of the acquired company is of importance. If a company acquires another company of equal or larger size the deal is less likely to be successful. Smaller deals are usually much more successful.[12] The reason behind this is easy to understand. In a company created by two equals there will be many more power struggles. Smaller units will probably cause less harm and they will more easily see benefits arising from being part of a larger organisation and therefore fewer conflicts will arise.

Besides paying too much, there are other reasons for failing in merger and acquisition activities. The *first* one is the overestimation of synergies. Because of reasons previously mentioned, fixed costs related to all activities in the value chain cannot be reduced as heavily as anticipated. The *second* reason for failing is an overly optimistic view of the combined market potential. Clearly management think that the synergies will spill over onto

12 Also confirmed by the Mckinsey study reported in Copeland, Koller and Murrin (2000).

market activities, so that for example product assortment can be extended to both companies' sales agents. But one has to have a realistic view of market penetration rates and agents' willingness to promote new products. In many situations (of which banks form a prime example) the combined market power of two entities is lower than they are separately. Customers dislike the dominating position the new company achieves and therefore move their business elsewhere. In situations where this is likely the merging companies will have to weigh positive cost-cutting effects against negative market penetration effects. A *third* reason is because of high integration costs that arise both because of power struggles and cultural differences.

To describe a reasonably rational way of behaving when acquiring another company is not easy. It is bound to be subjective, normative and simplistic. As with the description of how investment appraisals are conducted, described in Chapter Ten, there is a great variation from case-to-case. Alas, managers are far from being as rational as is suggested here.

1. Thorough analysis of current situation

The first step is to know yourself before you decide what to do. One needs to identify the company's mission, its objectives and strategies in relation to the industry structure and industry's likely future development. A thorough strategic analysis will help management understand whether it needs to go through any structural changes at all.

2. Identify potential candidates

Once the company's position within its industry is well known and strategies for the future have been identified, it is possible to screen and identify potential acquisition targets. For most businesses the screening of candidates is an on-going process. Management knows fairly well who their competitors are (targets for horizontal integration) and who their suppliers and customers are (targets for vertical integration). Investment banks and corporate finance departments, which have suggestions regarding suitable targets, approach companies relatively often. One has to bear in mind however that such propositions are often given to more than one potential buyer, and that prices can be higher. Instead, being an active and knowledgeable player in the market helps management acquire the right companies at the right prices.

3. Assess potential candidates

When management knows the potential acquisition targets in relation to the company's objective it is ready to assess potential candidates. Often the identification and assessment of potential candidates take place simultaneously; all acquisitions are of interest only if the price is right. In general it should be the *strategic fit* that determines whether an acquisition is made or not. The assessment of the acquisition candidate has to be made on both a stand-alone and an integrated basis. The assessment follows pretty much that outlined previously in this chapter and it is not necessary to go through that further here.

If the acquisition target is a public company the stand-alone value can be determined with the help of for example the current market value and, perhaps, estimates from security analysts. As argued before, synergies form the sole reason for making the acquisition. These must be categorised and analysed whenever and wherever discovered. The time perspective of capturing synergy effects also has to be paid attention to, as well as the reactions of competitors.[13]

Although synergies are likely to be complex to identify and analyse they generally fall into three broad categories. If synergies can arise between two particular companies, and no others, it is less likely there will be more than one bidder. These kinds of company-specific synergies are the "cheapest" to acquire, as the acquisition price will not be affected by other buyers. An example of this can be a company acquiring a supplier that has no other, existing or potential, customers. If synergies can arise between companies in an industry it is likely that the price rises. Now there is competition for the synergy effects. Most of the acquisitions fall within this category. It might spread fixed costs over more produced units, or it might be getting control over a greater portion of the distribution chain. Finally, if synergies are available to more or less any logical acquirer the company is open for many bids. It can be due to general economies-of-scale in corporate overheads, such as management costs, rents, and transportation. It can also be that mismanagement has caused the company to currently perform worse, and with any new management team it is likely to do better. It is necessary that these synergies are determined for each and every acqui-

13 The reactions of competitors play an important role in the determination of whether to make the acquisition or not. Synergy effects are probably overemphasised just because of competitive reactions. To take an example; Scandinavian banks are perhaps in the short term gaining from being bigger. But size can only be determined when comparing a company to its peers, and as all companies in the industry go about the same acquisition streak, competition will increase and profit margins decrease again. On the other hand, if one company does not grow bigger in an environment where everyone else is, it will lose. Thus one can argue there is an opportunity cost involved with not acting in such an environment.

sition target so that the monetary consequences can be balanced against a possible bid premium.

4. Contact and negotiate the deal

The contact with the acquisition target(s) is often handled through an investment bank or corporate finance department. In the case of privately held companies negotiations are in general handled directly with the main owner. In the case of publicly held companies an acquisition can be made in stages, in which control is gradually achieved. This gives the acquirer the opportunity to get a more thorough understanding of the acquisition target and its performance. In such a situation the acquirer might also get a seat on the board of directors, which gives it considerable insight into the performance of the company. The information (sometimes non-public) one can receive through the board of directors can enhance the ability to make the offer on the whole company as timely as possible. In the case of Finnveden/Bulten mentioned previously, the acquisition came in several steps. This seems to be the case of the Jefferson Smurfit/Munksjö relationship as well.

It is rare that acquisitions in Swedish companies are made through hostile takeovers. This is of course because of differentiated voting rights, a relatively small dispersed ownership, and a small business community where most market actors know each other. In general, hostile takeovers bear the risks of both upsetting the management of the acquisition target (which might decrease synergies and increase integration costs), and make competitors aware of the structural changes within the industry. An awareness that might lead them to make quick countermoves, and possibly cause a bidding contest.

5. Integrate the unit within the new organisation

Most acquisitions are followed by a so called *due diligence process* where the buyer has come to an initial agreement with the seller but now gets the opportunity to carefully examine all internal and external information about the acquired company. The deal will thus go through given that previous information can be verified as being reasonably accurate. The information advantage the seller has will thus disappear. Obviously sensitive internal information cannot be handed out to potential buyers before a pre-agreement has been established. Most of the due diligence consists of a coverage and verification of documents. Naturally the outcome of a due diligence process can be that the buyer does not go through with the offer.

What remains now is nothing but the actual integration of the units – undoubtedly the most difficult part. To describe such a complex and situation-specific area is rather hopeless. One of the main issues in the integration process does not usually arise until now, and that is the issue of cultural differences and conflicts. The winners in most acquisitions were earlier said to be management of the acquiring company whereas the losers were management of the acquired company. Well, losers hardly fall easily and without a fight. Consider that two large companies with overlapping sales organisations are merged. This means that while there might be large economies-of-scale to be gained in each sales district, there will also be integration costs and potentially large conflicts in each and every sales unit. How to handle such issues will however have to be covered in other textbooks.

Key Concepts

> Going concern
> Synergy effect
> Dividend discount model
> Free cash flow
> Free cash flow to the firm
> Net operating assets
> Indirect valuation model of shareholder capital
> Direct valuation model of shareholder capital
> Free cash flow to debt-holders
> Free cash flow to equity-holders
> Constant cash flow formula
> Constant growth formula
> Explicit value
> Continuing value
> Fundamental analysis
> Strategic analysis
> Financial analysis
> Normalised operating earnings
> Merger
> Acquisition
> Financial investment
> Conglomerate investment
> Strategic investment
> Vertical integration
> Forward integration
> Backward integration
> Horizontal integration
> Takeover premium
> Post-acquisition performance
> Due diligence process

Key Issues to Discuss

1 Make sure you understand the association between the dividend discount model and the indirect valuation model of shareholder capital. Under which circumstances do they generate the same results?

2 To evaluate the return from past investments the free cash flow model uses the term NOPAT, which is equal to the return on the company's net operating assets. Discuss why it is the return on net operating assets that is used, rather than e.g. capital employed or total assets. To answer the question you might be helped by reviewing some of Chapter Two.

3 How shall goodwill be treated in the analysis? Discuss *both* the treatment upon acquisition and afterwards.

4 Make sure you understand the two models of valuing shareholder capital. Then explain why the direct valuation model in most cases makes more sense than the indirect valuation model. It might be beneficial if you make up your own numerical example while answering the question.

5 Explain why it is appropriate to "normalise" the discount rate the further into the future one discounts cash flows.

6 Use the constant-growth formula (Expression 10.14) and initially assume that the information concerning Mercumin is correct, i.e., that its shares are worth SEK 150. Then make the following corrections:
a) the risk premium is 8 %, rather than 6 %.
b) the expected growth rate is too high and is adjusted downwards to 2 %
c) the valuation was made at a time when dividends were higher than the sustainable rate. It should be decreased to 30 % of earnings.
d) All of the three corrections mentioned above are necessary.
How does this affect the share price of Mercumin?

7 Discuss the results provided in Table 10.3. What are the shortcomings of the method used there? What does the table tell us in regard to investors' ability to forecast company value?

8 In some of the previous chapters (such as e.g. Chapters Four and Six) we have discussed the cognitive biases humans have. In relation to the heuristics that were mentioned there, you should discuss investors' problems with determining company values.

9 Explain how mean reversion processes affect the valuation of companies. Can we expect companies to have a long term growth rate above the cost of capital? Discuss and outline the consequences on the valuation model that your conclusions have.

10 Discuss different techniques whereupon a *normalised* level of operating earnings can be established. Then use this technique to identify the current "normal" level of NOPAT for some real-life companies.

11 Why are financial investments valued assumed to earn no additional value to the company? Is this assumption always valid? Discuss the matter while referring to the discussions in Chapters Five and Six.

12 Why is it common that an acquiring company pays a takeover premium when acquiring another company? Your answer should not just be based on the creation of synergies, but also include other possible explanations.

13 Explain why acquisition activities often destroy value for shareholders of the acquiring company. Also explain how well-diversified investors can get around the problem.

14 What is the role of financial intermediaries in the restructuring of industries? Could they be one of the reasons why there is an (excessively high) level of M&As? Discuss the matter and, if necessary, do your own research.

Further Readings:

Copeland, T., Koller, T., & Murrin, J., 2000, *Valuation – Measuring and Managing the Value of Companies*, 3rd Ed., New York: John Wiley & Sons.

Levin, J., 1998, *Essays in Company Valuation*, Doctoral thesis, Stockholm School of Economics, EFI, Stockholm: Elanders Gotab.

Penman, 2001, *Financial Statement Analysis and Security Valuation*, New York: McGraw-Hill.

Chapter 11

Corporate Objectives, Growth Strategies and Value

This chapter aims at:

- Exemplifying how the theoretical ideas proposed in Chapter Three can be applied to a practical setting.
- Outlining the components of a corporate strategic plan and discussing it in relation to finance and investment decisions.
- Describing how investment policies, capital structure policies and dividend policies are connected to each other and how management has to consider them in an internal financial system.
- Explaining how shareholders can convert managers into focusing on shareholder wealth rather than managerial welfare.

11.1 Corporate Objectives and Strategic Planning

11.1.1 Reintroducing the conflict between management and shareholders

In this chapter some of the overall strategic financial policies management of large companies implement and live by are addressed. The discussion is very much a continuation of that held in Chapter Three. In this chapter, just as in that previous chapter, the conflicts between the Managerial Welfare Maximisation (MWM) perspective and the Shareholder Wealth Maximisation (SWM) perspective permeate the discussion. Corporate strategies aiming at both of these two conflicting perspectives are described. This first section of the chapter introduces the main parts of a corporate strategic plan and it links some previous discussions of product market competition to strategic financial decision-making. The second section of the chapter contains a discussion of how management can create a balance between the supply and demand of financial resources under the restriction that funds are limited and financial slack is desirable. The third section of the chapter contains a discussion of how shareholders can implement control systems to change the behaviours of management and get it to focus on profitability and value-creation rather than growth and survival.

The MWM view, presented particularly in the second section, is one rarely found in the textbooks on financial management and is one that does not receive full support from the normative financial theory. The discussion is not here to provide norms which management ought to live by under the conditions specified in economic theory, but rather to provide a description of the norms management often seem to follow. The aim is to bridge the gap between the financial theories and managerial practises, and to stimulate a further discussion of what consequences a separation of ownership and control of corporate resources bring.

11.1.2 The strategic planning process

Any business entity is foremost created in order to earn a return above its cost of capital. The cost of capital is determined by the intrinsic risk of the business venture. In Chapter Five we learnt that competition often normalises the profitability of companies, and when competition is really fierce abnormal returns will disappear fully. Those running the business entity must determine how they can earn a return above the cost of capital in the best possible way. The result of this determination then has to be communicated throughout the organisation so that its members know what they are expected to accomplish and how management think they can reach these expectations. The company's *strategic planning process* is a disciplined and well-defined organisational effort aimed at specifying ways of achieving returns above their cost of capital (Hax and Majluf, 1984). It contains both an analytical part and a communication part.

Corporate strategy is a subject on its own, and it usually renders its own university courses and textbooks. Most often strategy is taught within the management department, as it is seen as a broader field dealing with all aspects of doing business. This book is focused on strategic management's relationship to corporate finance. Obviously the question of how to finance and evaluate investments needed in order to earn a return is crucial for strategic planning.

Strategic analysis is the first part of the strategic planning process. It is performed to find a way in which competition can be reduced. A good strategic analysis identifies ways that enable a company to earn an abnormally high return. Strategists often talk about *competitive advantage*, which is really the key to these returns. Competitive advantages rely on a dynamic process. They depend on the relative skills and resources the company possesses (Grant, 1991): relative in terms of what the company has in relationship to near competitors within its industry, and distant competitors in other industries. It is a dynamic process as both the possession and desire for different skills and resources change over time. While the strategic planning process and the concept of competitive advantage are not so easy to get a grip of, they are relatively easy to link to investment and financing decisions. A company that is able to continuously make profitable investments is also one, which explores its competitive advantages and creates excessive returns.

In Chapter Nine we learnt how to evaluate individual investments. The techniques used in capital budgeting are developed to help management understand the monetary consequences of investment decisions. With the help of risk and return management can decide whether or not to make a decision. In reasonably competitive product markets we have seen that excessive returns disappear relatively easy. It therefore makes sense to coordinate the company's investment activities so that investments not only build on the competitive advantages the company possess today, but they sustain and enhance them for the future.

To do so, management has to relate its individual investments to the creation, use and maintenance of competitive advantages. Investments have to be evaluated in relation to their *strategic fit*; their contribution and closeness to the overall creation of excessive returns. If investments do not fit with the strategic plan management has set up, then it is likely management will soon find itself sitting with a number of projects not pulling together and not taking advantage of each other. Donaldson (1984) actually found that many managers see long term strategic importance of a project as more important than the short term cash flows. In this section we shall focus on how management can set up a viable financial plan that can be linked to financial decisions.

To say that the strategic planning process aims at exploiting competitive advantages and thereby create excessive returns is not opposing the view that management might recognise the pressures from more stakeholders than just the investors, nor the issue of goal incongruence between investors and management. An exploitation of competitive advantages enables management to expand the organisation and create corporate wealth. Instead a managerial perspective on the strategic planning process might primarily differ because of a different view on the distribution of wealth coming from the competitive advantages.

11.1.3 Components of the strategic plan

While the strategic planning process is far more than just a document outlining the strategic plan a company has, we focus here on its documentation. Other, specialised, textbooks within strategic analysis can give a much more appropriate view of the full strategic planning process. The analysis part is also considerably more situation-specific than the strategic plan, which primarily outlines the contents of the analysis. A *strategic plan* is really nothing but a communication device. Its main purpose is to get the organisation to pull uniformly in the direction management has identified. As a communication device the strategic plan should be formulated in a clear and straightforward manner so that its message is easy to understand. It usually contains three (or four) main elements; the corporate mission statement, corporate objectives and corporate strategies. Sometimes it also includes tactics – which is a means of implementing strategies further down the organisation.[1]

The corporate *mission statement* defines the nature and the scope of a business. Thereby it provides important guidelines for managing the cor-

1 An alternative way of expressing this is to say that corporate strategies are developed at the corporate, divisional and functional levels.

poration. It is usually short and concise, without details. With it, management communicates the real reason for the company's existence and its responsibilities to shareholders as well as other important stakeholders. The mission statement usually mentions who the customers are, which main markets the company targets, and which resources it utilises to do so. From a shareholder perspective the mission statement declares, in qualitative terms, within which area investments earning returns above the capital cost are to be made.

Table 11.1 shows the Volvo group's mission statement as it was expressed in the annual report of 1999. Volvo has divided its mission statement into three parts and included long term objectives. While the document is short and concise, Volvo's management has included its own comments in it, in order to make the text more easily understood.

Table 11.1 – The Volvo Group's Mission Statement in 1999.

Mission statement	Our mission statement expresses our business concept: our purpose, our offerings, and our identity.
By creating value for our customers we create value for our shareholders.	
We use our expertise to create transport-related hard and soft products of superior quality, safety and environmental care for demanding customers in selected segments.	*... hard and soft products...* Combined, our products and services constitute total solutions for our customers.
We work with energy, passion and respect for the individual.	*... selected segments...* We focus on customer segments that appreciate superior quality, safety and care for the environment.
Vision	The vision represents the objectives that we all share and work to achieve.
To be valued as the world's leading provider of commercial transport solutions.	*... to be valued...* To be valued by our customers, shareholders and employees.
Position in year 2005	Volvo's position is expressed in three long-term objectives. When we have fulfilled them we will be on the right track to achieving our ultimate objective: the realisation of our vision.
In each of its businesses Volvo shall be: Number one in image and customer satisfaction Sustainable profitability above average Number one or two in size or superior growth rate	*Sustainable...* Over economic cycles.

The second part of a strategic plan is made up of the *corporate objectives*. They specify the measures on which corporate success is based. Corporate objectives are implicitly linked to the mission statement and management's willingness to create shareholder wealth. A useful corporate objective needs to fulfil five criteria; it shall be specific, measurable, achievable, reasonable as well as timely. It has to be *specific* so one knows clearly what is to be measured. A growth rate above industry average is not very specific. It does not say which industry one is comparing with, whether acquired growth is acceptable or not, and it does not say if it is growth in assets, sales, or the number of employees that is important. The corporate objective also needs to be *measurable*. To say that the value of human capital shall grow by 20 percent annually is therefore not a good objective, as human capital *per se* is difficult to quantify. Hence, one can never know whether the goal is achieved or not. A corporate objective needs to be *achievable* given the structure of the industry and the context that the organisation works in. It would be unwise for a forest company to set an objective of annual organic growth exceeding 15 percent. Such growth is unlikely given the situation within the industry. The fourth criterion is that the objective needs to be *reasonable* within the organisation itself. Perhaps it would be beneficial to reduce capital tied up in production by 20 percent annually, but can it be done given the employees, managers and other resources the organisation currently employs? The fifth and final criterion is that there needs to be a *timeframe*. A statement saying that the company shall be the largest company within a certain well-defined segment, does not tell us when this will happen. With a timeframe it is much easier to judge whether the objective has been reached in time, or not.

Besides these specific criteria on individual corporate objectives it is necessary to put some restraints on the total set of objectives. It does not make sense to have *too many objectives*, at least not on the same organizational level. Objectives are used to direct management's attention to the most important issues, and not to confuse it by stating that everything is important. Three to five objectives are usually enough. It is also important that the *objectives are not mistakenly linked* to each other. In Section 11.2 we shall see in detail how financial objectives are linked to each other, but already in Chapter Two we learnt that financial ratios could be decomposed and combined. Using the so-called Dupont-formula, we learned that e.g. the return on capital employed could be decomposed into the capital turnover and the operating profit margin.

$$ROCE_t = \frac{OPc_t}{S_t} \cdot \frac{S_t}{CE_t} \tag{11.1}$$

If management then says it wants to maintain an operating profit margin of eight percent, but increase its return on capital employed from 16 to 20 percent over the next business cycle, we quickly realise that this can only be done by improving the capital turnover (from 2 to 2.5). It has been shown in the past that most industrial production is becoming more and more capital-intensive. To increase ROCE might therefore be impossible without increasing the operating profit margin objective. Based on the discussion held above, an example of a plausible set of corporate objectives is given in Table 11.2.

Table 11.2 – Setting corporate objectives.

The corporate objectives of Mercumin state that we shall:

- Have an annual organic growth in sales revenue of seven percent.
- Have an operating profit margin, excluding extraordinary items, which is at least six percent over a business cycle.
- Have a solvency of at least 30 percent at all times, and we shall never experience an interest cover margin of less than six times.
- Spend at least 15 percent of sales revenue on R&D, further training of employees, or other knowledge-related investments, as defined in the corporate handbook.
- Continuously maintain a number one or number two position within each of the targeted market segments in terms of sales revenue.

All of these five corporate objectives will lead towards the creation of shareholder value. The ultimate objective is to maximise company value given the operating risk of our investment portfolio. Our company will therefore always be valued at least in par with its industry competitors using measures such as the P/E-ratio and B/M-ratio.

The third part of the financial plan is the outlining of corporate strategies. Of course this part of the financial plan must also be closely connected to the other parts. A *corporate strategy* will broadly express how management believes it can practically reach the objectives it has set out. Some like to express close links between a particular strategy and individual objectives whereas others like to state general strategies. Again, this depends on what messages are communicated and to whom they are addressed.

In cooperation with the board of directors, top management establish guidelines for long term strategies. It should never be the intention that a corporate strategy changes each and every year (but of course management ought to adapt them to changing environments). If a company has two or more independent business units corporate strategies are often created in two steps. As top management develop their strategies together with shareholders (i.e., the board of directors), it is wise that business unit managers develop theirs together with top management. Corporate objectives should however be developed so that they are applicable to all business units.

The allocation of resources within an organisation is difficult to have clear thoughts about, as it is so dependent on individual contingencies. In economic theory (or at least according to shareholder ideas) top management decides not only which business areas the company will be engaged in, but also which resources each area/unit will be allocated. In practise the process is considerably more dynamic and complex. Resources are not just allocated, but created within business units and top management does not have complete control over and information about all of the operations of each business unit. A top-down approach, as suggested here, can also inhibit top management from realising which competitive advantages there are within the different business units. After all, the main reason with the strategic plan is not to merely have one, but to communicate a message of where to go, which is based on competitive advantages that will generate excessive returns. The competitive advantages are usually found in the operating units and hardly ever in corporate headquarters.

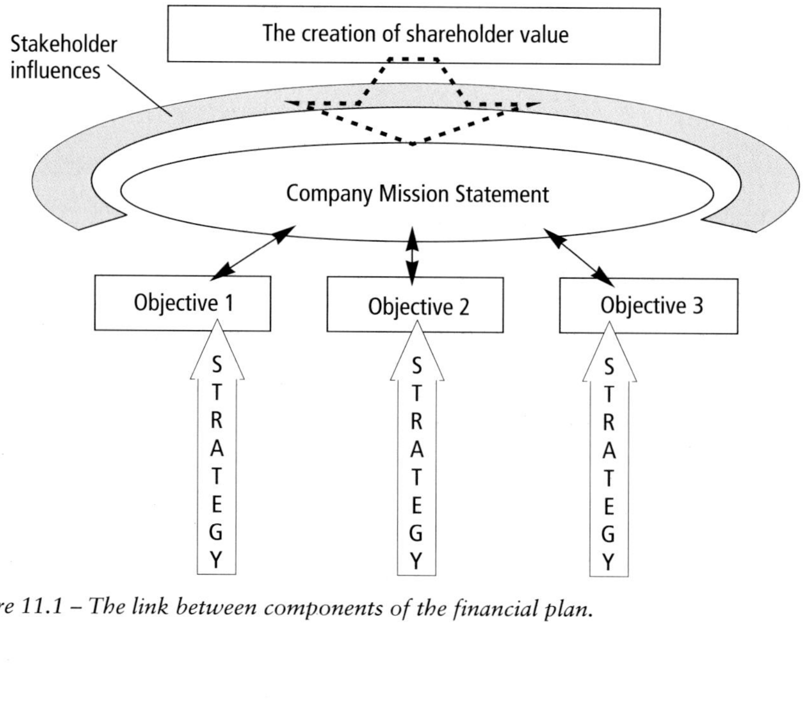

Figure 11.1 – The link between components of the financial plan.

11.1.4 The link between the strategic plan and financial decisions

As the strategic plan is the overall planning tool in the corporation it will have consequences on all decisions of major importance within the company. It will affect liquidity planning, risk management, and the allocation of resources within the corporation, to name but a few of the most common decisions. Of all these effects, the most influential one is on investment decisions.

The most important decision top management makes concerns the allocation of corporate resources to different business units and investment projects. The strategic plan will have a particular influence on management's choice of which investments it will make, and which ones it will maintain or get rid of. In Chapter Nine we discussed how management sometimes decide to make an investment even though it cannot show explicitly in the valuation that it will be profitable in a foreseeable future. But if the strategic fit of the investment is right, or if competitors are doing exactly the same thing, management might decide that the investment is justified anyway. Please note that this does not mean management is making an unprofitable investment, it simply means that it cannot measure its final impact completely. Sometimes these kinds of investments can turn out to be big failures, but if management has a gut feeling that it is vital (if the company wants to e.g. maintain a top position within the industry) then it is often made. Obviously it would be easier if all investments could be estimated using precise formulae. If a strategic plan is in place management can determine that even if an investment is not profitable within a foreseeable future its strategic fit makes it likely that it will contribute to long term prosperity.

Diversification is in general not looked upon positively by shareholders. But this still does not mean management should totally give up on profitable investments just because they are found in a non-core business area. It should seize the opportunity if it has the time and effort to manage the investment, and if there is a possibility to exit the investment whenever needed. Because of a lack of strategic fit, it can be argued that the discount rate ought to be set higher. There is a smaller chance that non-core business investments will generate beneficial spin-offs. With two projects earning exactly the same cash flows, management should choose the one that has the best strategic fit, as it is the likeliest to contribute to new future investments.

What kind of investments should management look for when desiring positive net present values? To a great extent, this depends on the structure of the industry the company operates in. In industries where *price competition* is fierce, management might want to make investments that reduce production costs. Often these investments include reinvestments in the same markets, and/or the same technologies that have been used in the past.

If management has identified a strategy based on *product differentiation*, then new investments might aim at introducing new products that meet customer requirements better, or to introduce variations on existing products that expands the product line. In the spirit of Michael Porter and the 'five-forces' model, discussed in Chapter Five, investments that are likely to earn excessive returns (investments reducing competition), can be achieved if management is able to set up entry barriers and avoid near substitutes. Innovative technology that is continuously updated, patents and copyrights are ways of achieving this.

In this section we have emphasised the financial consequences of the strategic plan. As a financial theorist it is easy to argue that all corporate decisions have monetary consequences and hence we need to understand, monitor and control them. In the following section we shall take an overall view of financial objectives and see how they fit together. Furthermore, we link strategic planning to not only investment decisions, but also to our alternatives when it comes to the financing of investments.

11.2 Managing an Internal Financial System

11.2.1 Supply- and demand-related goals

The prime objective of financial markets is to allocate financial resources from those who have more capital than profitable investments, to those who have profitable investments but not enough capital. Within financial markets there is thus a demand and a supply of financial resources and these two functions determine the amount of capital to be invested.

Actors in the share markets judge the prospects of investments in legal entities – the business enterprises – and in a similar way we can see management judging the prospects of its investments in business units and/or individual projects. From a management point of view there is a demand for financial resources and a supply of them. The demand stems from opportunities to invest in new projects earning positive net present values, or to maintain those old investments still generating a sufficient return. The supply of financial resources comes both in the form of debt and equity. The only real difference between the investment situation of actors in the share market and that of managers is that managers might be forced to consider liquidity constraints as well as control constraints. The internal financial system is not closed and management can and do interact with external financial markets – although they are thought to be reluctant to this.

Management will have to act in relation to both the supply and demand for financial resources within the company and set financial goals appropriately. As you have probably guessed after reading Chapter Three it is often likely that demand-related goals dominate, as management want to maximise company growth. But with the introduction of supply-related restrictions on the will to grow the growth-maximisation desire that Findlay and Whitmore (1974) laid out, is turned into a growth-optimisation desire. The optimal growth is hence as much growth as possible given restrictions forced upon management by the company's stakeholders, and particularly by investors and lenders.

Management's role is to manage the company's relations with external stakeholders. It seeks to balance their interests and thus the optimal level of growth is one in which the interests of the stakeholders are balanced. At the same time, company growth can never be perfectly balanced. Management therefore needs funds, which can be used to handle imbalances; to counter the pressures from stakeholders. This is where corporate wealth, as described in Chapter Three, comes in. We will soon see how the pressures from stakeholders, financial goals and corporate wealth all fit together in an internal financial system. But first we need to specify some prerequisites for such a system.

11.2.2 The assumptions behind the internal financial system

The financial system presented in this section relies on a number of assumptions. Of these the most important one is that managers are reasonably rational individuals who seek to maximise their own utility rather than anyone else's utility. This leads *to goal incongruence*, particularly between management and shareholders. By being rational management seek, within their limitations, the most efficient way to maximise their own benefits.

The problem coming from separating those who control and those who own the corporate resources is magnified by the existence of *asymmetric information*. One of the prime ideas behind the financial system is that investors do not have as much information as management about what goes on in the company. Investors are aware of both the asymmetrically distributed information and the goal incongruence. The main consequence of this is that the cost of equity increases, making some investments costlier than they actually should be in the eyes of the manager. In many cases, managers therefore prefer equity generated internally (retained earnings) to issuances of new equity. Some researchers even argue that managers are hostile towards investors and the share market (Donaldson, 1961; 1984). This hostility has been documented and confirmed by others (Myers, 1984) and is an important part of the *pecking order hypothesis* as discussed in Chapters Seven and Eight.

A final prerequisite is that management set relatively *stable financial policies*. These policies are set in order to control the organisation and guide its development during a foreseeable time-period. The pressures from stakeholders ultimately determine the financial policies.

11.2.3 The internal financial system

Introducing the basic parameters and variables

The internal financial system as described here is primarily derived from a study carried out by Donaldson (1984).[2] The system is determined by three financial policy items; the capital structure, the dividend payout rate, and the interest rate. In reality management can affect the capital structure and dividend policy whereas the interest rate is more or less determined by actors in financial markets (after they have judged e.g. the risk related to the company's investment projects). The interest is partly determined by company-specific factors, and partly by macro-economic factors. All three financial items are assumed to be relatively stable over a reasonably foreseeable planning period and are therefore labelled *parameters*. They are key elements in the process by which management tries to balance the

2 Professor Gordon Donaldson performed an in-depth study of the strategic financial management of 12 large US industrial companies in the late 1970s and early 1980s. Based on interviews he identified the internal financial system as described here in this chapter. It is notable that this financial system was not created by him, but identified by him as a prime planning tool within several of the studied companies. Donaldson did however provide theoretical reasons as to why this internal financial system was used. All of the studied companies were in mature industries with highly dispersed ownership, which is quite typical for many US companies. One has to interpret his findings, and this model, within this framework. Thus the model can be of less relevance for newly started companies, high-growth companies or companies in which agency costs are very low.

supply and demand for capital. When management desire funds for new projects, it is these three parameters that determine what can be financed internally.

The consequence of the making of investments is a growth in sales. We refer to sales growth, g(s), as a demand-related goal. To internally supply investments with capital the company needs to have a positive flow of capital, we therefore refer to profitability, return on capital employed ROCE, as a supply-related goal. In the rest of the discussion growth and profitability are referred to as *variables*, as they are allowed to vary in the internal financial system over time. The internal financial system that is based on these parameters and variables is shown in Expression (11.2).[3]

$$g(S) = r[ROCE + d \cdot (ROCE - i)] \tag{11.2}$$

where

g(S) = sales growth (percentage)
r = 1 – (dividends paid/net income)
ROCE = return on capital employed after taxes
d = interest-bearing debt/risk-bearing capital
i = interest costs/interest-bearing debt, after taxes

The left-hand side of the equation shows the *demand-related goal* and the right-hand side specifies the ability to finance investments internally; the *supply-related goal.* This equation is actually very similar to the leverage formula introduced in Chapter Two and the one used by Miller and Modigliani when illustrating the capital structure's irrelevance for company value. That latter formula was expressed as:

$$ROE = ROCE + d \cdot (ROCE - i) \tag{11.3}$$

Two major differences exist between Expressions (11.2) and (11.3). The first is that our management perspective makes us interested in the capital generated *after* the shareholders have received their cash dividends. This is the reason for introducing the retention rate parameter [r]. The second difference is that growth in equity is substituted for growth in sales. As ROE is the one-period growth in equity (assuming no capital transactions with shareholders) it might at first sight seem more appropriate to say that growth in equity, g(E), should be used rather than g(S). The reason for the substitution is that the internal financial system has to be communicated throughout the organisation and it is easier to do so with a sales growth target than an equity growth target. Different units might have different

3 Actually, before Donaldson (1984) made this model well known, it had been suggested by others such as Zakon (1976) and Higgins (1977).

capital structures, or they might have limited abilities to affect their capital structure. Growth in sales on the other hand is a measure, which is much easier to communicate and understand. The sales figure is obvious for each and everyone and it is indirectly linked to the financial system. The substitution causes no problem as long as the capital turnover is constant (Sales/Capital Employed).

Displaying the Internal Financial System graphically

The internal financial system can now be plotted graphically. The parameters enable us to see whether the two variables growth and profitability are balanced. Too much of either one will cause an imbalance that can be a threat to long term prosperity. Whether a certain combination of growth and profitability is sustainable depends on the parameters. The parameters form a 'line' to which growth and profitability will be close. This line is referred to as a *balanced goals line* (BGL).

Let's illustrate how the financial system works. The following information regarding the Company Mercumin is found in its latest annual report. Interest-bearing debt equals 1,000 whereas risk-bearing capital (mainly equity) equals 1,500. Dividends have been averaging thirty percent of company net earnings over the last six years (approximately one business cycle). The interest Mercumin paid on its interest-bearing debt was 100 last year, equalling an interest rate of ten percent. This interest rate is supposed to be relatively stable over the coming years. Mercumin pays thirty percent in corporate taxes.

With the help of this information we can estimate the r, d, and i parameters to be used in Mercumin's internal financial system. It is important to note that we use the information given above to forecast the future capital structure, dividend policy and interest rate of Mercumin.[4] If historical figures are unrepresentative for the future one should obviously not use them. In this case r equals 0.7 (1 – 0.3), d equals 0.67 (1,000/1,500), and i equals 0.07 (10 % × 1 – 30 %). To plot the balanced goals line we set ROCE to 0 and 20. When ROCE is set to 0, g(S) equals – 3.3 percent. When ROCE is set to 20, g(S) equals 20.1 percent. This enables us to display the internal financial system graphically as in Figure 11.2.

4 When using the internal financial system *within* a company one uses its financial objectives directly rather than going through estimates based on historical real figures. Also when making an analysis of a company for which the financial goals are known, this information should be used rather than anything else.

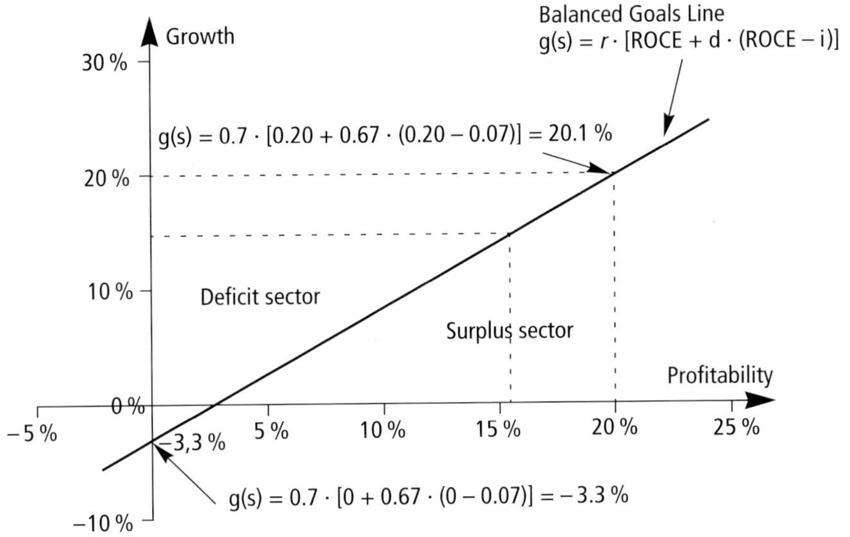

Figure 11.2 – The Internal Financial System expressed graphically.

The balanced goals line (BGL) is independent of which *actual* supply (profitability) and demand (growth in sales) of capital Mercumin achieves/desires. It is sloping upwards, which means that higher profitability enables higher growth (or higher growth requires higher profitability). If the combination of actual profitability and growth is above the BGL, the company is using more funds than its internal financial system can support. In the graph such a performance would mean that the company positions itself in the *deficit sector*. If the combination of actual profitability and growth is below the BGL, the company is generating more funds than it desires. We then say that the company is in the *surplus sector* as it generates a surplus of capital. Given the capital structure, dividend policy and interest rate of a company it is possible to calculate its optimal growth rate given any level of profitability. In the long run no company can deviate from a combination of demand- and supply-related goals that are in balance. When we look at the graph in Figure 11.2 it is thus unlikely that a target growth rate for the next five years can be 15 percent if the profitability is less than 10 percent. For Mercumin in the example above it turns out that a 15 percent growth rate requires an after-tax ROCE of at least 15.6 percent.

It is sometimes believed that it is better to be in the surplus sector than in the deficit sector. It is correct that in the short term, being in the surplus sector does not put any financial constraints on the organisation as management can finance the investments it wants to make. But external stakeholders are likely to be upset if financial slack increases and is invested in

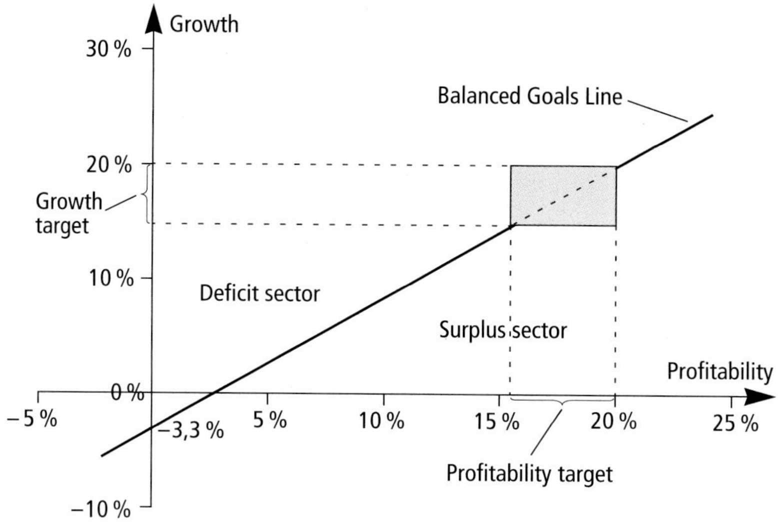

Figure 11.3 – Setting the growth and profitability targets.

insufficiently earning projects. In the long run it is equally bad to be in the surplus and deficit sectors.

The three parameters set the balanced goals line and determine the possibilities management has to balance the demand- and supply-related goals. Within this framework management also needs to have some targets for growth and profitability, and of course these have to be on, or close to, the balanced goals line. In Figure 11.3 the targets for corporate growth and after-tax profitability have been set, and together they form a "target box". An annual growth rate of fifteen to twenty percent is reasonable given that the company manages to earn a return of fifteen to nineteen percent. In reality it is difficult to stay within these limits in every period. It is instead only realistic as an average over a longer planning period. Figure 11.4 shows Mercumin's performance over time. As you can see it is only reaching its targets in one out of six years, but as it moves around its average is right in the target box, close to the balanced goals line. Mercumin starts out in the deficit sector in 1995, and while the next year takes it further into the deficit sector it thereafter moves back towards the balanced goals line, and in the last two years it is able to regain some of the corporate wealth by having investments returning more capital than what is needed for expansion.

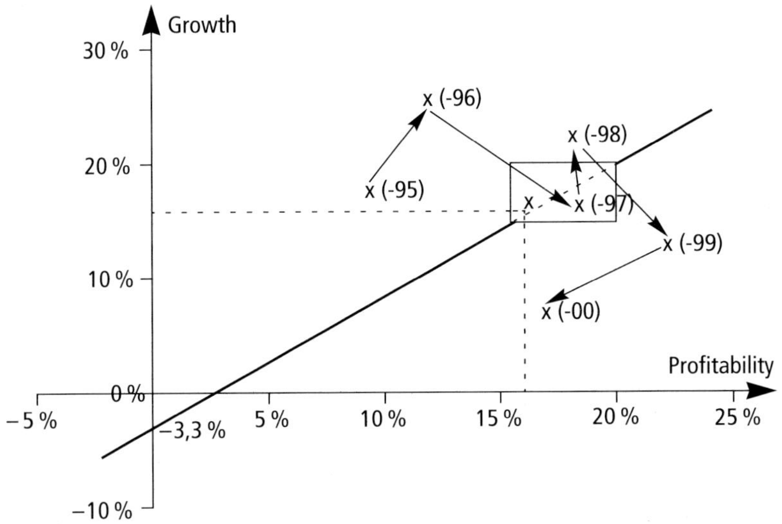

Figure 11.4 – Monitoring company performance within the internal financial system.

11.2.4 Management of the system

Making adjustments in corporate financial policies

The decision whether any certain combination of growth and profitability is sustainable is determined by the three parameters; r, d, and i. As you probably recall they are assumed to be fixed over a given planning period. It is however important to understand in what ways they affect the system. Thereby one can see whether changes in them can enable the company to adjust its supply of funds to its demand. The choice of any particular capital structure and dividend policy is thought to be dependent on the relationship management has with its financiers, and primarily the investors. To make changes in the parameters can have a significant signalling effect. Still, major strategic changes might be possible through conscious and careful changes in the parameters.

Changes in the capital structure have an effect on the leverage coming from the difference between profitability and interest rate (ROCE and i). As long as ROCE is higher than the interest rate (which must be the case in the long run for a surviving company – and is also usually the case in the short run) there is a positive leverage effect that is augmented by a higher debt ratio. Thus the BGL tilts more upwards as shown in Figure 11.5a. If the debt ratio is decreased (or if there is a short term negative relationship between ROCE and i when d is increased) the BGL is tilted downwards. The point on the BGL, around which this tilting movement centres, is determined by the point where ROCE equals i.

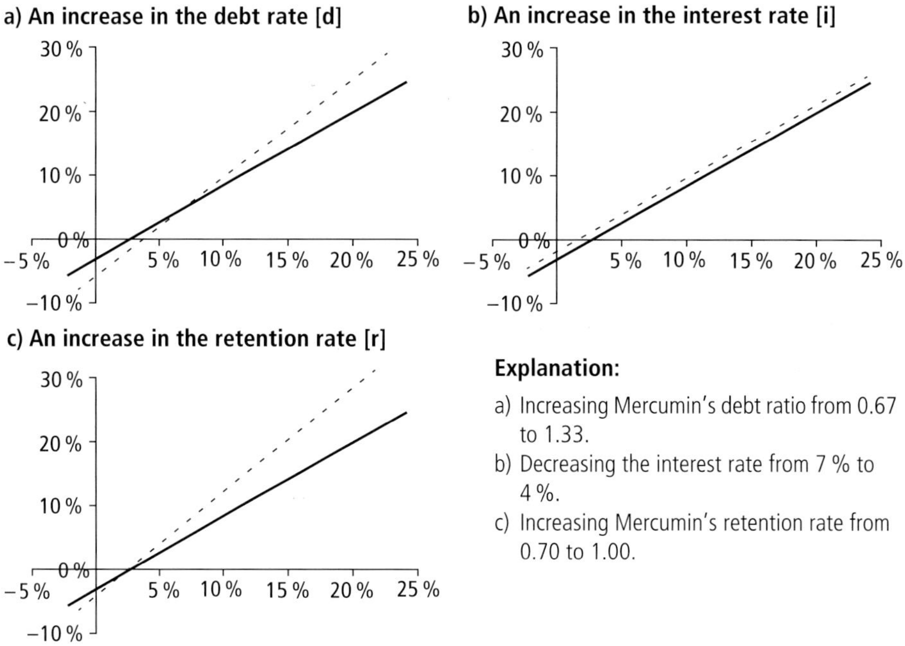

Figure 11.5 – Changes in the parameters.

If the interest rate changes the BGL moves upwards (interest rate goes down) or downwards (interest rate goes up). This movement is expressed in Figure 11.5b. An increased retention rate [r] means that more earnings are retained in the company, and can be reinvested in new projects. An increased retention rate allows a company to make more investments, and hence grow faster, *ceteris paribus*. The effects coming from an increase in the retention rate is shown in Figure 11.5c. An increase in the retention rate tilts the BGL upwards, whereas a decrease in the retention rate tilts it downwards. The point on the BGL, around which this tilting movement centres, is the zero growth point.

So far we have not been concerned about actual cash flows and their timing. The idea has simply been to hold the discussion at a strategic level. In reality there can be a substantial gap between the time when capital is invested and the time when it yields positive cash flows. Actually the internal financial system as described so far assumes that capital invested in one year generates sales growth that same year. This is clearly a simplification. The model does however function well as a general planning tool at the top level in large companies with a great deal of physical assets, particularly when a large degree of the company's investments are of a replacement character. But for many companies, e.g. those with many research and development activities, capital is invested which does not earn an adequate return nor generates any sales for many years.

For such companies there are only three viable solutions. *First*, if they have substantial operations in other areas that generate a sufficient amount of cash that is at management's disposal (i.e., corporate wealth), they can use this capital. *Second*, they might have a stock of corporate wealth hidden from previous investments. Or *third*, if management has close connections with its owners and if the owners are well informed and supportive of a long term strategy, then management can ask for a capital infusion. To pursue expansive growth strategies, for which it is hard to see the connection to profitability without having the internal funds for it, has many times proven to be impossible.

Movements within the internal financial system during a business cycle

It has been argued that no company in the long run can have an unbalanced growth. Being far above the BGL requires the company to either have an infinitely large corporate wealth from which it can finance its projects, or it will require the issuance of new capital (interest-bearing debt *and* risk-bearing capital).

To extend the discussion on balanced growth and the BGL, the relationship between a company's actual performance within the financial system and its targeted performance can be analysed further. We do this by categorising the actual performance into four categories as shown in Figure 11.6. In quadrant one (Q1) the company's performance is solely in the deficit sector. The company's operations are thus growing faster than its current internal financing is capable of coping with. This is only possible in the short run, and can then be sustainable for a few different reasons. The first is that management has corporate wealth with which they can finance the expansion.[5] A second reason as to why a company can be positioned in this quadrant is that continuous investments in the past are suddenly starting to pay off. This is almost like saying that value (corporate wealth?) has previously been created within the particular product/business area and it is now capitalised. It is common that start-up companies or companies in high growth market segments are found in this quadrant. It is also quite common that these companies are supported by their owners and hence are injected with external capital.

5 In Chapter Three there is an extensive discussion of what financial slack (or corporate wealth) is, using Åkerblom's definition.

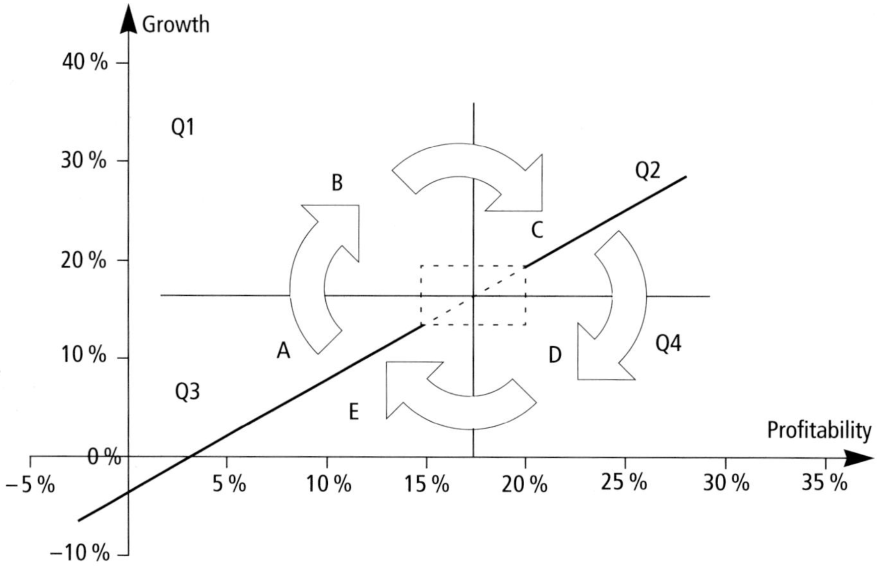

Figure 11.6 – The strategic cycle and financial performance.

In quadrant two (Q2) the distance between a balanced growth and actual growth is often not all that great. Companies within this sector can be either in the deficit or in the surplus sector. The important characteristic for these companies is that both their profitability and growth rate is higher than the target. Being above the targets but in the deficit sector sets financial constraints on management. They should however be of less importance, as capital infusions from investors are relatively easy to obtain. Investors tend to look positively at high growth, high profitability investments.

Companies performing in quadrant three (Q3) are solely in the surplus sector. These companies are thus generating substantial corporate wealth that can be used for future investments or as a buffer towards sudden capital needs. Although being in the surplus sector is convenient for management in the short term, it is likely to cause irritation among primarily investors who see that their investment is not yielding an adequate return. An example of this was seen among several Swedish companies who earned enormous returns in 1993 to 1996. Although they voluntarily paid off their interest-bearing loans (and hence changed one of the parameters in the financial system) they were still far into the third quadrant. Many of these firms were then "forced" to increase their dividend payout ratio. Performance affected financial policies, both in terms of capital structure policy and dividend payout policy.

Also in quadrant four (Q4) the distance between actual performance and target performance is not all that wide, but actual performance is inferior to the company's goals concerning both profitability and growth. This can only be sustainable in shorter periods of time. It can be in the start-up phase when capital needs to be heavily invested without a quick growth in sales. In this case management is probably tolerant for some time while making the investment. The other case is if the company has seen both profit margins and sales drop and the product, business area or company is in a weak position. This might be just before it is liquidated or heavily restructured. Companies positioned in the deficit sector of this quadrant can most probably only rely on financial slack when financing their operations. Investors are not likely to willingly infuse capital into investments earning an inadequate return.

It is only natural that a company, or business unit, move in a certain pattern within the internal financial system. In Figure 11.6 a *strategic cycle* is shown, which takes a newly started company (business unit) from A to E. Newly started projects often have a low profitability and no growth in sales. As the product and services enters the market more resources are invested into the project and profitability continues to be low. When the market slowly matures fewer resources have to be invested and a more stable position involving a sound profit margin is achieved. In a mature market sales growth will diminish and the performance will be centred to quadrant three. Eventually competition might increase, new technology might emerge, or customer demands might change so that the products and services offered are no longer needed. The company then ultimately falls back into quadrant four and, as stated above, has to be restructured or perhaps liquidated.

The divisionalised company's performance

One of the ideas with the internal financial system is that some units within a company can finance other units. It is in other words possible for a diversified company to have some units performing far above the BGL whereas other units perform below the BGL. For most companies this is the rule rather than the exception. Top management manages the whole system and while considering the needs of different units it must balance the overall financial need of the company. Clearly a diversified company has more relative freedom than a focused company. By being diversified management have more internal sources of capital to choose from when an investment alternative appears. Diversification also enables management to hide more corporate wealth in the organisation.

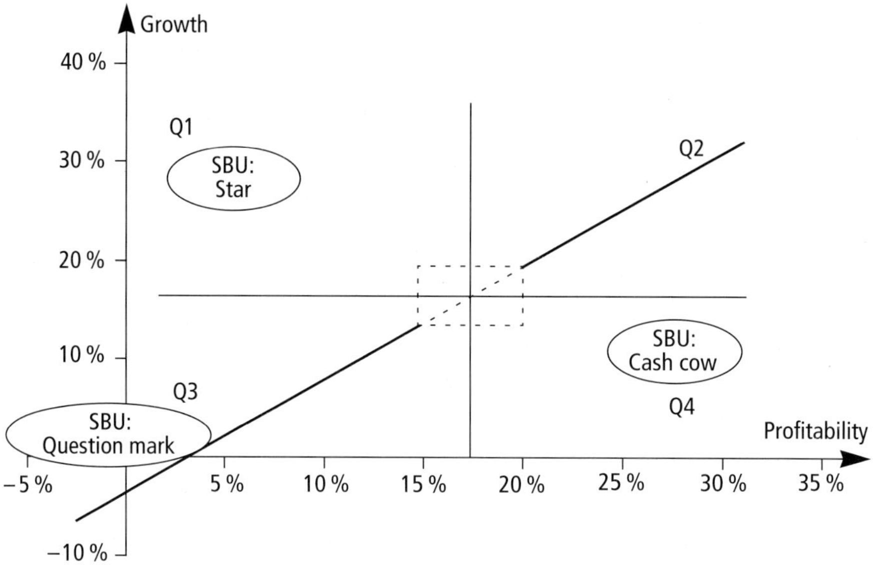

Figure 11.7 – Determining the financial performance of a multi-business company.

In Figure 11.7 the seemingly well-balanced performance of Mercumin is studied more carefully. It turns out that none of Mercumin's business units is close to the BGL. But overall management has a well-balanced investment portfolio. It uses the large and established main business unit, which is in a mature market, to finance its other investments. As you see in the figure, one might very well use the same terminology here that is used in the BCG matrix. Below the BGL one finds the "cash cow" of the company. Above the BGL one finds a business unit, which is growing rapidly, and which cannot sustain operations on its own. The rapid growth earns this business unit its reputation as a "star". In the future there is great hope that the star will follow the strategic cycle and turn into a cash cow. At the same time there is a unit we might label as a "question-mark". In this case it is a research and development company, not earning any money and as yet with no sales. It might turn into a star and then require substantial capital investments. If not it might be killed, or at least substantially restructured.

11.2.5 Some final comments

All companies governed within a reasonably stable environment are likely to show a medium and long term stability in their internal financial system. Imbalances mainly arise when there are structural changes. Acquisitions and mergers are good examples of this. They can, however, be adjusted for in the financial system. What happens is that growth becomes abnormally high during one observed period after which everything returns to normal – it does not disrupt the whole system. Also an issuance of new equity has an effect on company performance within the financial system. In theory, it should not have any greater effect as long as management maintains a stable capital structure. In reality it has often been shown that companies change their debt ratio when new equity is issued. Whenever the new capital is used for sales-increasing activities one has to adjust for them (or merely understand that they can occur because of the infusion of new equity).

As said before, this is not a precise system used for managing cash flows, but a general internal financial system used for strategic purposes in healthy companies operating in reasonably stable and mature industries. The internal financial system creates a strategic link between management's investment decisions and its financial policies. The reason why it is important to maintain a balance between supply- and demand-related goals should not be forgotten. Without it management runs the risk of upsetting its stakeholders. Among them, it is the shareholder group which has the ability, and the responsibility, to directly take away management's independence and replace them. Imbalances that temporarily occur in the system are most easily handled using corporate wealth, hidden within the organisation.

The obvious threat from being too far above the BGL is to run into financial distress. With no "cash cows" in the business portfolio, management will have to sell off parts of the company, or liquidate it. Bankruptcy is thus the main threat for companies above the BGL. But are there threats when the organisation is too far into the surplus sector as well? The answer is yes, as management's main priority is to survive and to remain the managers of this particular company. With too much financial slack current owners might either become so disappointed with management's performance that they replace them, or they might sell the company (voluntarily or involuntarily) to somebody else who is willing to take action. The risk of being taken over has been proven to be much greater for companies far away from the BGL, particularly if they are far below the BGL.

11.3 Value As a Managerial Objective

11.3.1 A system for managing the creation of company value

Given the theoretical reasons for managerial disinterest in shareholder value maximisation stated in Chapter Three, and the more practically oriented model suggested in the previous section of this chapter shareholders are likely to be distressed. One of their prime concerns over recent years has been to give managers incentives to act in shareholders' interests. Most companies today have incentive schemes implemented, which make the top decision-makers feel and behave more like shareholders. Their compensation is therefore to a great extent based on share performance and value creation. In this section we take a look at some forms of incentive programs and assess their capability to solve the agency problem between shareholders and managers. In particular we look at the measure Economic Value Added (EVA™), as it was this tool that initiated the wave of incentive systems that flooded the market in the 1990s.[6]

To start from the beginning: When somebody is employed to manage a business for somebody else, that person can be remunerated in numerous ways. Just like any other employee the person can be provided with a fixed salary and perhaps some fringe benefits, such as lunch coupons or a free car. This remuneration is not connected to the manager's actual behaviours in his/her work. Of course, if one severely misbehaves one can get fired, or if one performs exceptionally well one can get pay rises. But on the whole, the connection between performance and reward is rather weak. The threat of being fired and the opportunity of pay rises are rather slow and imprecise ways for shareholders to signal to the manager how his/her performance is evaluated. Somebody holding a purely contractual relationship to the company can never be expected to behave as somebody holding a residual relationship.

Within companies sales personnel are often rewarded based on their sales performance. Generating more sales is good for the company and so if they sell more they also get a bonus on top of their normal salary.[7] Those who have no sales responsibility on the other hand, such as back-up functions, cannot be given the same kind of rewards. The reason is that their performance is harder to measure. Getting back to managers the same idea can be implemented. Managers are responsible for the performance of the whole corporation. With the emphasis on the capital market that we have had so far, it is easy to say that management compensation would benefit

6 EVA is a trademark of Stern Stewart & Co.

7 But obviously the evaluation of sales personnel has to be based on the effect their customers' orders have on the net earnings. Misspecified incentive schemes might get sales personnel to focus on e.g. products with low profit margins, or products which have a high operating profit margin but high capital costs (due to capital intensive production or long production times).

from being tied to value-creation as measured in the company's share performance.

In the past it has been common to provide management with a bonus, on top of the basic salary, linked to some measure of company performance. Very often this measure has been accounting-based. It might have been the level or growth in sales and/or earnings. To tie management's bonus to sales performance seems to be not such a good idea, but of course sales growth does have positive implications also for shareholders. It has also been common to provide top management with shares in the company, or stock options. These options usually give management the right to buy shares in the company at some time in the future at a predetermined price. Obviously it is then in management's interest to maximise the price of the share. The higher the share price is when the options are exercised, the more money management will make. Stock options are important aspects of most modern remuneration schemes for top managers and they are returned to later on in this section. There are still many pitfalls one can fall into when designing these schemes and we need to address a few others before turning to stock options.

In Chapter Three it was said that agency costs exist because managers (the agents) do not maximise the interests of shareholders (the principals). Theoretically speaking two types of activities were suggested to handle the agency costs: monitoring activities and bonding activities. The agency problems come from asymmetrically distributed information; managers know more about the company's operations than shareholders do. The monitoring activity increases shareholders' understanding of company performance, whereas the bonding activity increases management's willingness to focus on issues shareholders find relevant. All sophisticated management compensation systems should comprise both these activities, as they complement each other.

Economic Value Added is a concept that was developed by the consulting company Stern Stewart & Co. in the late 1980s. Its success accelerated in the early 1990s in American companies, and came to Sweden in the mid-1990s. Although the EVA™ system in itself has not been a huge success here, most large companies have developed similar systems or taken ideas from the concept and implemented them.

Without giving too much credit to Stern Stewart it must be recognised that their idea is simple, but quite ingenious. Within a shareholder wealth maximisation framework they recognise agency costs and they come up with a system that in two integrated steps give management the right incentives to focus on the creation of shareholder wealth rather than the conservation of managerial welfare (Stern, Stewart and Chew, 1995). The two steps are of course the measuring of "true" company performance, and the aligning of interests. We will cover these two steps consecutively in the text below.

11.3.2 Finding measures of company value: RI, MVA and EVA

There are two main differences between the measures used in the EVA-system and an "old-fashioned" accounting measure of profitability (such as e.g. return on equity). *First*, the measures used in the EVA-system are based on the *residual income* concept, rather than the return-on-investment concept. This means that the measured outcome is not a ratio (i.e., earnings compared with invested capital), but an actual monetary sum, measured as the profit left after *all* costs have been deducted. *Second*, the "new" measures are related to the creation of value and they are adjusted for some of the flaws that accounting information has. We deal with these issues separately.

Developing a residual income model

Residual income (RI) is not a new concept at all, but has been used by economists for at least 100 years (see Marshall, 1890). Economists define residual income (also known as economic profit) as operating profit less a charge on all capital employed.[8] When the residual income is positive, operations have generated a surplus and when it is negative, operations have failed to earn back their costs. In an *efficient* market capital costs reflect the earnings capability and the risk of the operations and therefore long term residual income is expected to be zero. In reality some companies do over a limited period of time set competition temporarily out of place and generate residual incomes.[9]

The residual income (RI) model is mathematically connected to the net present value (NPV) model used in Chapter Nine. In fact, they are just the same. We shall start of with the NPV model and change it into a RI model. To begin with we have Expression (11.4), which shows us that the value of

8 Marshall defined Economic Profit as total net gains less the interest on invested capital at the current rate. The concept of residual income later appeared in accounting theory (e.g. Church, 1917) and was later heavily used in management accounting literature in the 1960s (e.g. Anthony, 1965; Solomons, 1965). Among practitioners, General Motors popularised the residual income concept in the 1950s.

9 As you probably remember, this was discussed in depth in Chapters Five and Ten.

a company is equal to future cash flows discounted to today's value using the appropriate cost of capital. When speaking about the value of equity, it is equal to all future dividends discounted using the cost of equity.

$$V = \sum_{t=1}^{\infty} \frac{cf_t}{(1+r)^t} \Rightarrow V^{EQ} = \sum_{t=1}^{\infty} \frac{Div_t}{(1+r_{eq})^t} \qquad (11.4)$$

From Chapter Eight we then borrow the following definition of dividends:

$$Div_t = EQ_{t-1} - EQ_t + NP_t \qquad (11.5)$$

The dividend concept is equal to the periodic change in equity plus the net profit. The next step is to define residual income. Residual income is, as its name indicates, the income that is left after all stakeholders have received their part from the company's operations. In relation to net profit, we can define residual income as:

$$RI_t = NP_t - EQ_{t-1} \cdot r_{eq} \Rightarrow NP_t = RI_t + EQ_{t-1} \cdot r_{eq} \qquad (11.6)$$

As you see Expression (11.6) can also be turned around so that net profit is defined in terms of residual income. This is important because we can then import this definition of net profit into Expression (11.5), which gives us Expression (11.7). Furthermore we can import Expression (11.7) into Expression (11.4), which gives us Expression (11.8).

$$Div_t = EQ_{t-1} - EQ_t + RI_t + EQ_{t-1} \cdot r_{eq} \qquad (11.7)$$

$$V^{EQ} = \sum_{t=1}^{\infty} \frac{EQ_{t-1} - EQ_t + RI_t + EQ_{t-1} \cdot r_{eq}}{(1+r_{eq})^t} \qquad (11.8)$$

Now we have a formula that expresses the value of equity in terms of residual income. But Expression (11.8) is more complicated than it needs to be. We shall simplify it using two steps. By separating out RI and writing out the rest of the formula we get Expression (11.9).

$$V^{EQ} = \sum_{t=1}^{\infty} \frac{RI_t}{(1+r_{eq})^t} + EQ_0 - \frac{EQ_1}{1+r_{eq}} + \frac{EQ_1}{1+r_{eq}} - \frac{EQ_2}{(1+r_{eq})^2} + \frac{EQ_2}{(1+r_{eq})^2} - \ldots + \ldots \qquad (11.9)$$

As the terms in the end alternate signs and cancel each other out, this expression can be simplified and all that is left are Expressions (11.10).

$$V^{EQ} = EQ_0 + \sum_{t=1}^{\infty} \frac{RI_t}{(1 + r_{eq})^t} \tag{11.10a}$$

$$V^{EQ} = EQ_0 + \sum_{t=1}^{\infty} \frac{NP_1 - r_{eq} \cdot EQ_{t-1}}{(1 + r_{eq})^t} \tag{11.10b}$$

The value of equity is now finally shown as the current value of equity plus the present value of all future residual income, discounted to today's value using the cost of equity. In most companies the market value is higher than the book value of equity, and in these cases management has been able to (or are expected to) create shareholder value.[10] The market value of a company therefore reflects both the value of capital that has already been invested in it, and the expectations of earning future returns above the capital cost of invested capital.

The difference between the market and book values of equity shows how much value has been added to the shareholders' cumulative investment since the inception of the company. It is also the share market's assessment of the company's net present value. Stewart (1994) refers to this difference as the *Market Value Added* (MVA). MVA is obviously then the sum of all the discounted future residual income, or the latter term in Expressions (11.10).

$$MVA = V^{EQ} - EQ_0 = \sum_{t=1}^{\infty} \frac{NP_t - r_{eq} \cdot EQ_{t-1}}{(1 + r_{eq})^t} \tag{11.11}$$

What drives a company's value is its ability to earn residual income in the future. Stern Stewart therefore argue that the periodic measure that drives future value is EVA; *Economic Value Added.* EVA is defined as in Expressions (11.12).

$$EVA_t^{EQ} = NP_t - r_{eq} \cdot EQ_{t-1} \tag{11.12a}$$

$$EVA_t^{EQ} = EQ_{t-1} \cdot (ROE_t - r_{eq}),$$
$$\text{where } ROE_t = NP_t / EQ_{t-1} \tag{11.12b}$$

10 Obviously those companies which have a market value of equity below the book value are expected to not generate, but destroy shareholder value in the future. These companies have a negative market value added.

Alternatively, we can express MVA and EVA in relation to all operating capital used to earn an operating return. Instead of just using equity we then use the net operating assets. We start with EVA and add net financial expenses to it. Expression (11.12b) is then redefined as:[11]

$$EVA_t^{NOA} = NOA_t \cdot (RNOA_t^{aT} - WACC_t) \qquad (11.13)$$

where NOA equals the net operating assets, $RNOA^{aT}$ equals the after-tax return on net operating assets, and WACC is the weighted average cost of capital. To be more precise, we can define $RNOA^{aT}$ as:

$$RNOA_t^{aT} = NOPAT_t / NOA_{t-1} \qquad (11.14)$$

Market value added is in a similar fashion defined as:

$$MVA = \sum_{t=1}^{\infty} NOA_t \cdot (RNOA_t - WACC_t) \qquad (11.15)$$

Expression (11.13) is the most common way to measure EVA.[12] Shareholders obviously desire a Market Value Added as high as possible. Economic Value Added (and Residual Income) is the periodic measure of wealth creation. If EVA is positive management has created value to shareholders and if it is negative they have destroyed value.

When EVA is used as performance measure there are only three generic ways of doing well. The *first* alternative strategy is to find a way of earning higher profits using the same amount of capital as today. This means increasing profit margins and often to also make 'offensive' changes in the organisation. The *second* alternative strategy is to reduce the amount of capital used to generate the same amount of profits as today. This means increasing the capital turnover and getting rid of unnecessary capital. If management can be convinced to do this, much of the financial slack will disappear as well. The *third* alternative strategy is to find new investments, which earn a return higher than the cost of capital. This means to pursue a growth strategy, but a growth strategy that is profitable. All three alternatives are congruent with the shareholder wealth maximisation idea.

---

11 Please note that EVA^{EQ} and EVA^{CE} are equal given that the company's activities in financial markets are made at their cost of capital. As discussed in e.g. Chapters Five and Ten this is a reasonable assumption.

12 Alternatively capital employed can be used instead of net operating assets, although this makes less sense since financial assets have nothing to do with the long term sustainability of operating cash flows.

Summary: ways of creating company value

1 Increase earnings coming from previously invested capital.
2 Reduce the capital used to generate current earnings.
3 Make additional profitable investments.

Making accounting adjustments

Proponents of the EVA-system, as well as other similar systems, point at two problems with the measures used in past reward systems. *First*, these measures are based directly on conservative accounting information, and do therefore not always describe the true value that has been created within the business. A company investing heavily in research and development might treat R&D investments as operating costs and they will thus not be recorded as assets generating future returns.[13] Problems like these were partly discussed in Chapter Two. The *second* problem is that accounting information can be manipulated. It is easy for management to adjust its reported earnings both in the short and the medium term. Hurrying or delaying the booking of contracts can create short term effects in reported earnings. Writing down the value of inventories can create temporary losses. Cutting down on critical and necessary investments can enable temporary increases in profitability (but eventually old investments will have to be replaced by new ones).

To handle these problems it is important to scrutinise the accounting information and adjust it to enable a more correct measure of the creation of economic value. In their guidebook of 1991, Stern Stewart speak of at least 164 changes that are of potential interest. They do however view these changes as business secrets and thus do not like to reveal them. It is likely that for most companies no more than a handful of them are used. To get an idea of what changes Stern Stewart suggest, see Table 11.3.

Table 11.3 – A few changes of accounting items when measuring value-creation.

Type of problem	Problem	What to do
Periodisation	Material assets	Long term investments are capitalised, even though materialisation is uncertain and far away in the future.
	Immaterial assets	R&D is not written off directly, but capitalised.
	Goodwill	No depreciation of goodwill.
Expenses		Write-downs are not allowed.
		Restructuring costs are not allowed.

13 The Swedish pharmaceutical company Astra (AstraZeneca) is one which has had a tradition of writing off R&D expenditures directly in the income statement. Since its investments (particularly in Losec) have been successful, the market value has been considerably higher than the reported book value.

11.3.3 Making management target the creation of company value

So now we have a measure of the value that has been created within the company over a certain time-period. But that only means we are halfway, now we need to link this measure of performance to the compensation plan. Management have got to have incentives to increase MVA further. There are numerous problems within this area, of which only a few are addressed here. We shall consider two of the features suggested by Stern Stewart: the bonus bank and the leveraged stock options. Before these two alignment mechanisms are dealt with, three issues related to holding management accountable for changes in EVA are to be commented on.

First, if EVA is zero during a certain time period, it means that management did what it was supposed to do. It earned an adequate return in correspondence with the actual business risk. When EVA is zero shareholders got full compensation for the risk they took. If EVA is positive, then management has performed above expectations and created shareholder value. Finally, if EVA is negative management has actually destroyed shareholder value (performed below expectations). The idea of EVA-based bonuses is that management is only compensated when shareholders have made gains. If the periodic EVA is split between shareholders and management both parties win (whenever EVA is positive). Figure 11.8 shows three alternative ways of dividing EVA between shareholders and managers. One (A) in which management always receive 40 percent of EVA (the actual percentage is of no interest here), one (B) in which management receive no EVA-related bonus, and finally one (C) in which management are not held

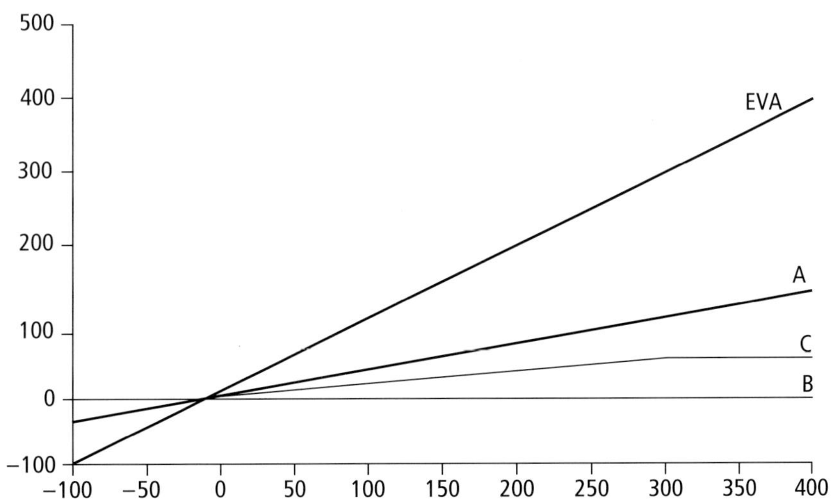

Figure 11.8 – A static approach to EVA compensation.

responsible for losses but do receive some compensation for gains up to a certain point. Obviously, if management are not accountable for negative EVA their risk is substantially lowered and the upside potential must similarly be adjusted downwards.

But a problem shows up if management are statically rewarded based on the actual level of EVA. Consider that you are asked to become the manager of a highly unprofitable company. Its EVA has been negative for several years and although you see a potential in its operations, you also see that it will take a couple of years before profits can be made. Would you take the job? Probably not if most of your remuneration is based on actual EVA. We need to understand that it takes time to bring a business around, and in the short term it is the change in EVA that is important.[14] It can thus be foolish to base compensation merely on the absolute level of EVA, but one needs to consider also the periodic change in EVA.

Although such a 'dynamic' management compensation scheme is fairer, it also gives management more incentives to make inappropriate accounting adjustments. Now managers can benefit not only from shifting long term EVA increasing activities to short term activities (such as avoiding strategic investments) they can also benefit from shifting operating earnings from one period to another. A small and steady increase in EVA might be most beneficial to management. Such performance would also have a positive signalling effect. Investments might be made with this in mind rather than with the idea of MVA maximisation.

A *second* issue that ought to be mentioned is the special case of negative EVA. Should management be held accountable for them? In theory it would be possible to implement such a system, but in reality it would probably be difficult to find managers willing to accept it. Shareholders bear a residual risk, but they do so in a diversified way. Managers on the other hand, would not be able to diversify away the unsystematic risk of their company and would therefore most likely ask for more in compensation. If management is held fully liable for negative EVA that would most certainly mean that investments, which are profitable in the eyes of shareholders, are not made because management applies a higher discount rate.

A *third* issue to be handled is management's ability to manipulate accounting figures. As management is the actual provider of the information

14 An opposite situation to the one described above is also easy to imagine. Think of a manager of a company that has spent considerable resources in the past to establish a competitive advantage. These investments are nowadays generating substantial EVA surpluses. But is SEK six Billion in EVA only good? Perhaps not if last year's EVA was ten billion. Then management has, relatively speaking, lost four billion in just one year.

they themselves are evaluated upon, there are some obvious problems concerning self-interest. This problem of asymmetric information can really only be solved by having somebody observing management more closely than what is possible through the existing accounting system. Stern Stewart suggest that consultants are the ones who should go through the company reports and adjust them appropriately.

Now we have two problems left to deal with in this section. The first is management's willingness, and ability, to change the timing of investments so that EVA turns out as beneficial as possible (for management, but not for shareholders). What happens if management decides to decrease current marketing expenses (and thus increase current NOPAT), which will not have a negative effect until next year? Such value-destructive behaviour cannot be fixed through the measurement system. It is a decision purposely taken by management to maximise its own interest on behalf of long term investors.

The Bonus bank

The solution that is suggested is a *bonus bank*. The bonus bank makes sure that management compensation is tied to medium-run EVA performance rather than the short-run EVA performance. By locking in most of the one-period earned EVA bonus in a "bank", management gets the incentive not to fool around with short term EVA.

Let's assume management's bonus is based on thirty percent of total EVA and that there is no downside risk in bonus payments. Negative EVA still has an effect on the account in the bonus bank. One third of the capital in the bonus bank is paid out to management each year. After a person has left his/her position one third of the next two year's EVA is paid out at the end of each year. Table 11.4 shows how EVA is distributed to management of the company Mercumin.

Table 11.4 – Bonus payments using a bonus bank.

Year	2000	2001	2002	2003	2004	2005	2006
EVA (MSEK)		100	300	−20	0	(100)	(100)
Compensation		30	90	−6	0	(30)	(30)
Bonus bank	0	30	110	67	45	(60)	(70)
Bonus payment		10	37	22	15	20	21

Management is hired at the end of year 2000 when there is nothing in the bonus bank. In year 2001 thirty percent of EVA (100 MSEK) is put in the bonus bank and of this management can collect one third (10 MSEK). The next year another thirty percent of EVA is put in the bonus bank and of the total amount (110 MSEK) management can collect another third (37 MSEK). In year 2004 management leave office. They get one third of the sum in the bonus bank that year and the next two years. As the bonus bank delays EVA payments, there is less incentive to maximise this year's EVA on behalf of next year's.

The leveraged stock option plan

Stewart (1991; 1994) suggests another tool that makes management focus even more on long term shareholder value. While the bonus bank focuses management's mind on EVA, periodic EVA has its shortcomings as discussed above. It is therefore suggested that the payment from the bonus bank is connected to the actual share price. By turning the bonus bank payment into share options not to be exercised within a certain time-frame, management will have a great incentive to combine the short term return they get in the bonus bank with long term strategic thinking. This is thus a way to handle the problem with managers taking advantage of short term EVA, while not maximising long term value.

11.3.4 Empirical evaluations of the merits of the system

Intuitively it is easy to understand that the agency problem is for real, and that it can be quite severe in some businesses. At the same time the EVA system clearly seems to be a solid incentive system that has been implemented in a large number of companies in different countries. But, although the problem is there and the method seems reasonable in theory, this does not mean these kinds of systems actually work. To shed some lights on their merits we will in this section ask whether:

1 Companies with EVA-based incentive systems perform better?
2 Shares of companies with EVA-based incentive systems perform better?

An evaluation has to be based on the company's performance both in the product and the capital market. The share price performance is of course based on expectations of improved profitability from product markets. As such one can expect investors to react more quickly to positive effects that EVA-systems might have. Changes in share prices do thus represent changes in expectations of future, unrealised, EVAs. But as shareholders react to expectations and not realised returns their reactions can later turn out not to be true.

Partly because EVA is a relatively new phenomenon there have not been very many studies of whether companies implementing EVA-systems perform better or not. Wallace (1997) studied forty companies which had adopted management compensation plans based on some kind of residual income model (such as for example the EVA-system). He then compared them to similar companies which had their management compensation plans tied to traditional accounting measures. He found that management actually did have a different attitude to important financial decisions when they were evaluated based on 'residual-income' performance measures. They did, for example, decrease the amount of investment, they increased their payouts to shareholders (particularly in the form of share repurchases), and they utilised their assets more intensely. It is important to note that we cannot be sure that these behaviours actually enhance long term value, only that current behaviours do change. Wallace's study also showed that the share price of the 'residual income companies' performed slightly better than the market average, which indicates that shareholders appreciate the changes.

Apart from Wallace's study, there are also studies from consulting companies wanting to sell EVA-based remuneration systems. There is a great problem taking such studies into serious consideration, as they are likely to be biased by the researchers' motives for conducting the studies in the first place. Several of the "success stories", which are used in the media, are also individual cases and it is not sure whether they represent the actual average performance of companies switching to EVA-systems. Nonetheless these consultants do report that companies implementing EVA-based control systems perform better both in the short and long term.

According to the EVA-model described earlier, the market value of a company is equal to the book value of equity plus the current value of all future EVA. This suggests that EVA is closely related to the market value of a company. A number of studies have looked at the association. All these studies do however have a serious problem to overcome: share prices are primarily based on expectations of future cash flows. Changes in the current share prices therefore reflect changes in future cash flows and in future EVA expectations. Because of this, current EVA can never explain current share prices very well. But based on the conviction that all other measures are equally flawed, researchers have explained share prices with models experiencing a relatively low explanatory power.

Stewart (1991), Uyemura, Kantor and Pettit (1996), and O'Byrne (1996) all come to the conclusion that EVA is a far better indicator of share prices and returns than other measures, but since all of these studies are conducted by people at Stern Stewart their trustworthiness is questionable. Most other studies are less positive. Milunovich and Tsuei (1996) do find that EVA has a higher correlation with MVA than earnings-per-share and return-on-equity, but the difference is not enormous. Two studies, by Dodd and Chen (1996) and Biddle, Bowen and Wallace (1997) present evidence that there is no higher correlation between EVA measures and stock returns. Currently there is an increasing number of studies within this area. From a theoretical perspective it would be surprising however if the majority of studies did not indicate that shareholders benefit from implementing the system.

11.3.5 Integrating 'value objectives' in the strategic financial planning system

Although many companies have implemented shareholder wealth oriented incentive systems it is not sure they have all been successful. Failure does not however have to be because the system was misspecified or mismanaged. One of the most important success factors is likely to be the cost of running the system versus the value-enhancement it generates.

If management is not going to behave much differently even though an expensive EVA system is implemented shareholders might simply find themselves stuck with additional operating costs. Expression (11.16) shows how the value of the company is affected both by changes in cash flows due to management's operating policies (lower agency costs: ResidAC), and changes in monitoring costs (higher MonitC) and bonding costs (higher BondC).

$$\Delta V_0^{EQ} = \Delta \sum_{t=1}^{\infty} \frac{\text{ResidAC}}{(1+r)^t} - \Delta \sum_{t=1}^{\infty} \frac{\text{MonitC}}{(1+r)^t} - \Delta \sum_{t=1}^{\infty} \frac{\text{BondC}}{(1+r)^t} \qquad (11.16)$$

The decision-rule is to implement the system if the total cash flow effect from reduced agency costs is greater than the costs of implementing the EVA-system. Having external observers examining all major decisions in a large multinational corporation will indeed be costly. If management at the same time is closely tied to the main shareholders there might be no incentive for setting up a full system. There is even a chance that if management is performing in the long term interest of the company, then the implementation of an EVA-system causes it to abandon the long term corporate success for its own personal short term benefits. There is no empirical evidence supporting this, but it is fully possible.

Another issue is to recognise who has control over corporate resources and how far one can delegate responsibility, and then measure performance and reward accordingly. The proponents of these shareholder wealth oriented incentive systems usually argue that the systems can be implemented throughout most of the organisation. Clearly there are problems with doing this and the main reason is that compensation has to be tied to measured performance. And then performance has to be controlled by those who are rewarded. Subsidiaries can be measured on the basis of EVA (where cost of equity is determined on the basis of subsidiary risk and the corporate cost of equity) but subsidiary management should only be rewarded from a bonus bank. The leverage stock option scheme would make little sense to make use of. Internal transfer pricing is another major issue causing severe problems. Both transfer pricing and asymmetric information within a corporation are issues that need to be handled so that the value creation process is transparent.

It is quite unlikely that shareholders would benefit from a system where individual employees, in for example the production units, are remunerated based on EVA. But if one finds ways of determining individual units' contribution to value creation at the corporate level one might find good indicators even of individuals' contributions. By implementing an EVA-system at the top of the organisation it is possible that all the company's activities will be focused on value creation. At least this is what its proponents hope and argue for.

The success of the EVA-system is likely to depend on several issues. One of them is whether, or to what extent, management can affect the output of the system. If measures can be superficially changed, the system will give the wrong signals. But if the system allows or even gives incentives for management to make uneconomic decisions, then it is even worse. Very often this has got to do with short term decisions versus long term decisions. Hardly any manager who gets most of his/her remuneration from short term bonuses will invest in major projects earning negative returns over the coming three to five years. It is easier to cut down on short term spending, earn major returns now and then retire before the backlash appears. Herein lies another of these agency conflicts. Just by introducing a shareholder wealth oriented incentive system does not mean the conflict goes away, it is merely its shape that changes.

The important thing is that any such system is so simple everyone understands how it works; both among those who are being evaluated and those who evaluate. Bearing this in mind, it is important to note that no system can ever be perfectly objective, but it is bound to be biased. There is a great tendency for managers to be keener on implementing EVA-systems in eras such as that of the 1990s where share prices increased enormously (see e.g. Yemack, 1995; Mayer, 1996). Managers are not likely to resist a system that is highly likely to provide them with some extra money. Herein lies perhaps one explanation as to why companies with EVA-based systems have performed better: they were more eager to implement the system in the first place because they knew they would benefit from it. Perhaps this is a reason why a large proportion of existing incentive systems work so that management is compensated solely on general increases in share prices?

As you see, the conflicts and controversies between shareholders and managers are just as great today as when Adam Smith commented on them 200 years ago. There is nothing today indicating that they will not be around in another 200 years, influencing strategic financial decisions taken within future companies.

Key Concepts

> Competitive advantage
> Strategic plan
> Mission statement
> Corporate objective
> Corporate strategy
> Demand-related goal
> Supply-related goal
> Balanced goals line
> Residual income
> Market value added
> Economic value added
> Invested capital
> Bonus bank
> Leveraged stock option plan

Key Issues to Discuss

1. Pick a company you have an interest in and analyse its strategic plan. What is its mission? Does it point out explicit corporate objectives and are these specific, measurable, achievable, reasonable and containing a timeframe? Does it have corporate strategies that makes sense to you? If you cannot find explicit information then perhaps you can "read between the lines".
2. Discuss the importance of investments' strategic fit. In what ways can we justify that an investment can be made even though it is less profitable than another investment (assume mutually exclusive projects)?
3. Is it reasonable that investments outside the company's core business are evaluated with a discount rate higher than investments within the company's core business area. Discuss the question and state your arguments.
4. Are the ideas behind the internal financial system totally inapplicable in a world where the Fisher separation theorem holds?
5. Discuss the relationship between the pecking order hypothesis (explained in Chapter Seven) and the internal financial system. Are they based on the same assumptions? Are there any assumptions that seem to be exceptionally different? Describe the pattern that

a company's performance would have in the internal financial system, given that management behaves according to the pecking order hypothesis.

6 Pick a company you have an interest in and analyse its performance in the internal financial system. Analyse both its actual performance during the last 3–5 years, and its forecasted performance for the coming 2–3 years. Is it performing in the deficit or the surplus sector? Is its overall performance balanced?

7 Given the information about Mercumin stated throughout the chapter; would you say that the following estimates of its performance can be supported within the company's internal financial system?

Year	Growth	Profitability
2001	4 %	18 %
2002	10 %	15 %
2003	20 %	11 %
2004	15 %	7 %

Explain your answer!

8 If you assume that Mercumin is earning an average ROCE of 15 % during the coming years, then how much faster can the company grow if it changes the debt ratio from 0.67 to 1.10, and the retention rate from 0.70 to 0.80? Also, discuss the potential problems with such changes and whether they are viable or not.

9 Make sure you understand the association between the discount model and the residual income model. Discuss potential empirical problems arising from the conservative accounting regime, i.e., is the value of equity always representing the value of past investments?

10 Discuss the association between market value added (MVA) and the book value of equity. What effect does the conservative accounting regime have on this association?

11 Explain the three generic ways of creating company value (increasing EVA and MVA). Which one is the easiest to carry out, and which one do you think will have the greatest long term effect?

12 How can management take advantage of asymmetrically distributed information when they are evaluated and compensated according to an EVA-system? There are many ways so you should be able to identify several.

13 Why is it so difficult in empirical capital market studies to explain changes in company value with the help of measures such as EVA (or earnings for that matter)?

14 A number of Swedish companies have over the last years implemented bonus programmes for their top executives. Based on the discussion in Chapter Eleven, what are some of the suggestions you have concerning the design of such programmes? Is it appropriate to just hand out shares or options to management?

Further Readings:

Donaldson, G., 1984, *Managing Corporate Wealth*, Westport: Praeger.

Stern, J. M., Stewart, G. B., III, & Chew, D. H., Jr, 1995, "The EVA®, Financial Management System", *Bank of American Journal of Applied Corporate Finance*, pp. 32–46.

Reference List

Aharony, J., & Swary, I., 1980, "Quarterly Dividend and Earnings Announcements and Stockholders' Returns. An Empirical Analysis", *Journal of Finance*, pp. 1–12.

Altman, E., 1984., "A Further Empirical Investigation of the Bankruptcy Cost Question", *Journal of Finance*, pp. 1067–1089.

Ambarish, R., Kose, J., & Williams, J., 1987, "Efficient Signalling With Dividends and Investments", *Journal of Finance*, pp. 321–343.

Anthony, R. N., 1965, *Management Control Systems*, Homewood, Illinois: Irwin.

Antonides, G., 1996, *Psychology in Economics and Business*, 2nd Ed., Dordrecht: Kluwer Academic Publishers.

Bachelier, L., 1900, *Theory of Speculation*, Paris: Gauthier-Villars, Translated by Boness, A. J., in Cootner (1966).

Bain, J. S., 1956, *Barriers to New Competition*, Cambridge, Massachusetts: Harvard Business Press.

Ball, R., & Brown, P., 1968, "An Empirical Evaluation of Accounting Income Numbers", *Journal of Accounting Research*, pp. 159–178.

Ball, R., 1995, "The Theory of Stock Market Efficiency: Accomplishments and Limitations", *Journal of Applied Corporate Finance*, pp. 4–17.

Baskin, J., 1989, "An Empirical Investigation of Pecking Order Hypothesis", *Financial Management*, pp. 26–35.

Bell, D. E., 1983, "Risk Premiums for Decision Regret", *Management Science*, pp. 1156–1166.

Berg, L., & Lyhagen, J., 1998, "Short and Long-Run Dependence in Swedish Stock Returns", *Applied Financial Economics*, pp. 435–444.

Berle, A. A., & Means, G. C., 1932, *The Modern Corporation and Private Property*, New York: MacMillan.

Bernard, V. L., & Thomas, J., 1989, "The Nature and Amount of Information in Cash Flows and Accruals", *The Accounting Review*, pp. 624–652.

Bernard, V. L., & Thomas, J., 1990, "Evidence That Stock Prices Do Not Fully Reflect the Implications of Current Earnings for Future Earnings", *Journal of Accounting and Economics*, pp. 305–340.

Bernstein, P. L., 1995, "Risk as a History of Ideas", *Financial Analysts Journal*, pp. 7–11.

Bernstein, P L., 1996, *Against the Gods*, New York: John Wiley & Sons.

Bertmar, L., & Molin, G., 1977, *Kapitaltillväxt, Kapitalstruktur och Räntabilitet*, Doctoral Thesis, Stockholm School of Economics, EFI, Stockholm: Gotab.

Biddle, G. C., Bowen, R. M., & Wallace, J. S., 1997, "Does EVA Beat Earnings? Evidence on Associations with Stock Returns and Firm Values", *Journal of Accounting and Economics*, pp. 301–336.

Black, F., 1972, "Capital Market Equilibrium with Restricted Borrowing", *Journal of Business*, pp. 444–455.

Black, F., Jensen, M. C., & Scholes M., 1972, "The Capital Asset Pricing Model: Some Empirical tests", in *Studies in the Theory of Capital Markets* (Jensen, M. C.) New York: Praeger.

Black, F., & Scholes, M., 1973, "The Pricing of Options and Corporate Liabilities", *Journal of Political Economy*, pp. 399–418.

Blazenko, G. W., 1987, "Managerial Preference, Asymmetric Information, and Financial Structure", *Journal of Finance*, pp. 839–862.
Bogue, M. C., & Roll, R., 1974, "Capital Budgeting of Risky Projects With 'Imperfect' Markets for Physical Capital", *Journal of Finance*, pp. 765–794.
Bowman, E. H., 1980, "A Risk/Return Paradox for Strategic Management", *Sloan Management Review*, pp. 17–31.
Brennan, M. J., & Schwartz, E. S., 1985, "Evaluating Natural Resource Investments", *Journal of Business*, pp. 135–157.
Brown, S., Goetzmann, W., & Ross, S. A., 1995, "Survival", *Journal of Finance*, pp. 853–874.
Brown, K. C., Harlow, W. V., & Tinic, S. M., 1988, "Risk Aversion, Uncertain Information, and Market Efficiency", *Journal of Financial Economics*, pp. 355–385.
Brozen, Y., 1970, "The Antitrust Task Force Deconcentration Recommendation", *The Journal of Law and Economics*, pp. 279–292.
Burmeister, E., & McElroy, M. J., 1988, "Joint Estimation of Factor Sensitivities and Risk Premia for Arbitrage Pricing Theory", *Journal of Finance*, pp. 721–733.
Butler, J. S., & Schacter, B., 1989, "The Investment Decision: Estimation Risk and Risk Adjusted Discount Rates", *Financial Management*, pp. 13–22.
Caves, R. E., 1989, "Mergers, Takeovers, and Economic Efficiency", *International Journal of Industrial Organization*, pp. 151–174.
Chamberlin, E. H., 1933, *The Theory of Monopolistic Competition*, Cambridge, Massachusetts: Harvard University Press.
Chan, L. K. C., Jegadeesh, N., & Lakonishok, J., 1996, "Momentum Strategies", *Journal of Finance*, pp. 1681–1713.
Chan, S. H., Martin, J. D., & Kensinger, J. W., 1990, "Corporate Research and Development Expenditures and Share Value", *Journal of Financial Economics*, pp. 255–276.
Chen, N-F., Roll, R., & Ross, S. A., 1986, "Economic Forces and the Stock Market", *Journal of Business*, pp. 383–403.
Claus, J., & Thomas, J., 2000, "Equity premia as low as three percent? Empirical evidence from analysts' earnings forecasts for domestic and international stock markets", working paper.
Coase, R. H., 1937, "The Nature of the Firm", *Econometrica*, pp. 396–405.
Cooper, I., and Kaplanis, E., 1995, "Home Bias in Equity Portfolios and the Cost of Capital for Multinational Firms", *Journal of Applied Corporate Finance*, pp. 95–102.
Copeland, T., Koller, T., & Murrin, J., 2000, *Valuation – Measuring and Managing the Value of Companies*, 3rd Ed., New York: John Wiley & Sons.
Copeland, T. E., & Weston, J. F., 1992, *Financial Theory and Corporate Policy*, Reading, Massachusetts: Addison-Wesley.
Cyert, R. M., & March, J. G., 1963, *A Behavioral Theory of the Firm*, Englewood Cliffs, New Jersey: Prentice-Hall.
Damodaran, A., 2000, "*Estimating Equity Risk Premiums*", from the website: www.stern.nyu.edu/~adamodar.
Daniel, K., Hirshleifer, D., & Subrahmanyam, A., 1998, "Investor Psychology and Security Market Under- and Overreaction", *Journal of Finance*, pp. 1839–1885.

Daniel, K., & Titman, S., 1999, "Market Efficiency in an Irrational World", *Financial Analysts Journal*, pp. 28–40.

Dann, L., 1981, "Common Stock Repurchases: An Analysis of Returns to Bondholders and Stockholders", *Journal of Financial Economics*, pp. 113–138.

Davis, J. L., Fama, F. E., French, K. R., 2000, "Characteristics, Covariance, and Average Returns: 1929 to 1997", *Journal of Finance*, pp. 389–406.

De Bondt, W. F. M., 1993, "Betting on Trends: Intuitive Forecasts of Financial Risk and Return", *International Journal of Forecasting*, pp. 355–371.

De Bondt, W. F. M., 1998, "A portrait of the individual investor", *European Economic Review*, pp. 831–844.

De Bondt, W. F. M., & Thaler, R. H., 1985, "Does the Stock Market Overreact?", *Journal of Finance*, pp. 793–805.

De Bondt, W. F. M., & Thaler, R. H., 1987, "Further Evidence on Investor Overreaction and Stock Market Seasonality", *Journal of Finance*, pp. 557–581.

Denis, D J., Denis, D. K., & Sarin, A., 1997, "Agency Problems, Equity Ownership, and Corporate Diversification", *Journal of Finance*, pp. 135–160.

Dodd, J. L., & Chen, S., 1996, "EVA: A New Panacea?", *Business and Economic Review*, pp. 26–28.

Donaldson, G., 1961, *Corporate Debt Capacity*, Boston, Massachusetts: Harvard Business Press.

Donaldson, G., 1969, *Strategy for Financial Mobility*, Cambridge, Massachusetts: Harvard Business Press.

Donaldson, G., 1984, *Managing Corporate Wealth*, Westport: Praeger.

Durand, D., 1952, "Cost of Debt and Equity Funds for Business: Trends and Problems of Measurement", in *Conference on Research in Business Finance* (New York: National Bureau of Economic research).

Elling, J. O., 1995, *Årsregnskabsteori*, Silkeborg, Danmark: FSRs Forlag.

Elling, J., Krogholt Hansen, C., & Sørensen, O., 1998, *Strategisk Regnskabsanalyse*, Silkeborg, Denmark: FSRs Forlag.

Fama, E. F., 1965, "Random Walks in Stock Market Prices", *Financial Analysts Journal*, pp. 55–59.

Fama, E. F., 1970, "Efficient Capital Markets: A Review of Theory and Empirical Work", *Journal of Finance*, pp. 383–417.

Fama, E. F., 1991, "Efficient Capital Markets: II", *Journal of Finance*, pp. 1575–1617.

Fama, E. F., 1998, "Market Efficiency, Long Term Returns and Behavioral Finance", *Journal of Financial Economics*, pp. 283–306.

Fama, E. F., & Blume, M. E., 1966, "Filter Rules and the Stock-Market Trading", *Journal of Business*, pp. 226–241.

Fama, E. F., Fischer, L., Jensen, M. C., & Roll, R., 1969, "The Adjustment of Stock Prices to New Information", *International Economic Review*, pp. 1–21.

Fama, E. F., & French, K., 1988, "Permanent and Temporary Components of Stock Prices", *Journal of Political Economy*, pp. 427–466.

Fama, E. F., & French, K., 1992, "The Cross-Section of Expected Stock Returns", *Journal of Finance*, pp. 427–466.

Fama, E. F., & French, K., 1993, "Common Risk Factors in the Returns on Stocks and Bonds", *Journal of Financial Economics*, pp. 3–56.

Fama, E. F., & French, K., 1995, "Size and Book-to-Market Factors in Earnings and Returns", *Journal of Finance*, pp. 135–155.

Fama, E. F., & French, K., 1996, "The CAPM is Wanted, Dead or Alive", *Journal of Finance*, pp. 1947–1958.

Fama, E. F., & French, K., 2000, "Testing Tradeoff and Pecking Order Predictions About Dividends and Debt", Working Paper No. 506, The Center for Research in Security Papers, University of Chicago.

Fama, E. F., & Jensen, M., 1983, "Separation of Ownership and Control", *Journal of Law and Economics*, pp. 301–325.

Fama, E. F., & MacBeth, J. D., 1973, "Risk, Return, and Equilibrium: Empirical Tests", *Journal of Political Economy*, pp. 607–636.

Fama, E. F., & Miller, M., 1972, *Theory of Finance*, New York: Holt, Rinehart and Winston.

Fiegenbaum, A. & Thomas, H., 1988, "Attitudes toward risk and the risk-return paradox: Prospect theory explanations", *Academy of Management Journal*, pp. 85–106.

Findlay, M. C., & Whitmore, G. A., 1974, "Beyond Shareholder Wealth", *Financial Management*, pp. 39–55.

Fisher, I., 1930, *The Theory of Interest*, New York: MacMillan.

French, K., & Roll, R., 1986, "Stock Return Variances: The Arrival of Information and the Reaction of Traders", *Journal of Financial Economics*, pp. 5–26.

Frennberg, P., & Hansson, B., 1993, "Testing the Random Walk Hypothesis on Swedish Stock Prices: 1919–1990", *Journal of Banking and Finance*, pp. 175–191.

Galbraith, J. K., 1961, *The Great Crash* 1929, Harmondsworth, Middlesex: Penguin Books in association with Hamilton.

Galbraith, J. K., 1987, *A History of Economics – The Past as the Present*, London: Penguin Books.

Gebheardt, W., Lee, C., & Swaminathan, B., 1999, "Toward an Ex-Ante Cost of Capital", Woking Paper, Ithaca, NY: Cornell University.

Gitman, L. J., 1992, *Basic Managerial Finance*, 3rd Ed., New York: Harper Collins.

Gitman, L. J., & Maxwell, C. E., 1987, "A Longitudinal Comparison of Capital Budgeting Techniques Used by Major U.S. Firms: 1986 versus 1976", *Journal of Applied Business Research*, pp. 41–50.

Gjesdal, F., & Johnsen, T., 1999, *Kravsetting, lønnsomhetsmåling og verdivurdering*, Oslo: Cappelen Akademisk Forlag.

Gordon, M. J., 1962, *The Investment, Financing and Valuation of the Corporation*, Homewood: Irwin.

Graham, B., & Dodd, D., 1934 (1996), *Security Analysis*, New York: Whittlesey House.

Grant, R. M., 1991, *Contemporary Strategy Analysis – Concepts, Techniques, Applications*, Cambridge, Massachusetts: Blackwell Publishers.

Grinblatt, M., & Titman, S., 1998, *Financial Markets and Corporate Strategy*, Singapore: McGraw-Hill International Editions.

Gujarati, D. N., 1995, *Basic Econometrics*, Singapore: McGraw-Hill International Editions.

Hagnell, H., Holm, L-L., & Larsson, K., 2000, *Contrarian Investment*, Master Thesis, Department of Business Studies, Uppsala University.

Hamberg, M., 2000, *Risk, Uncertainty & Profitability – An Accounting-Based Study of Industrial Firms' Performance*, Department of Business Studies, Uppsala University.

Hamberg, M., & Store, K., 1994, *Mellan Balans och Verklighet – En studie av svenska företags balanserade tillväxt*, Department of Business Studies, Uppsala University.

Hamilton, G., 1996, *Risk Management 2000*, Lund: Studentlitteratur.

Harris, M., & Raviv, A., 1988, "Corporate Governance: Voting Rights and Majority Rules", *Journal of Financial Economics*, pp. 203–235.

Harris, M., & Raviv, A., 1991, "The Theory of Capital Structure", *Journal of Finance*, pp. 297–355.

Hax, A. C., & Majluf, N. S., 1984, "The Corporate Strategic Planning Process", *Interfaces*, pp. 47–60.

Herman, E. S., & Lowenstein, L., 1988, "The Efficiency Effect of Hostile Takeovers", in *Knights, Raiders, and Targets*, (Coffee, J C., Lowenstein, L., & Rose-Ackerman, S.) New York: Oxford University Press.

Higgins, R. C., 1977, "How Much Growth Can a Firm Afford?", *Financial Management*, pp. 7–16.

Hodder, J. E., 1986, "Evaluation of Manufacturing Investments: A Comparison of U.S. and Japanese Practices", *Financial Management*, pp. 17–24.

IASC, 1989, *Framework for the Preparation and Presentation of Financial Statements*, International Accounting Standards Committee.

Isaksson, M., & Skog, R., 1994, "Corporate Governance in Swedish Listed Companies", in *Institutional Investors and Corporate Governance*, (Baums, T., Buxbaum, R. M., & Hopt, K. J.) Berlin: Walter de Gruyter.

Jaffe, J. F., 1974, "Special Information and Insider Trading", *Journal of Business*, pp. 410–428.

Jagannathan, R., & McGrattan, E. R., 1995, "The CAPM Debate", Federal Reserve Bank of Minneapolis Quarterly Review, pp. 2–17.

Jagannathan, R., & Wang, Z., 1996, "The Conditional CAPM and the Cross-section of Expected Returns", *Journal of Finance*, p. 3–54.

Jegadeesh, N., & Titman, S., 1993, "Returns to Buying Winners and Selling Losers: Implications for Stock Market Efficiency", *Journal of Finance*, pp. 65–91.

Jeng, L. A., Metrick, A., & Zeckhauser, R., 1999, *The Myths of Insider Profit*, New York: McGraw-Hill.

Jensen, M. C., 1986, "Agency Costs of Free Cash Flow, Corporate Finance and Takeovers", *American Economic Review*, pp. 323–329.

Jensen, M. C., & Meckling, W. H., 1976, "Theory of the Firm: Managerial Behavior, Agency Costs and Ownership Structure", *Journal of Financial Economics*, pp. 305–360.

Jensen, M. C., & Ruback, R. S., 1983, "The Market for Corporate Control: The Scientific Evidence", *Journal of Financial Economics*, pp. 5–50.

Jonsson, T., 1995, *Value Creation in Mergers and Acquisitions: A Study of Swedish Domestic and Foreign Takeovers*, Department of Business Studies, Uppsala University.

Jorion, P., & Goetzman, W., 1999, "Global Stock Markets in the Twentieth Century", Working Paper, New Haven, CT: Yale School of Management.

Kahneman, D., & Tversky, A., 1979, "Prospect Theory: An Analysis of Decisions Under Risk", *Econometrica*, pp. 262–291.

Kaplan, S. N., 1997, "Corporate Governance and Corporate Performance: A Comparison of Germany, Japan, and the U.S.", *Journal of Applied Corporate Finance*, pp. 86–93.

Keim, D. B., 1983, "Size-Related Anomalies and Stock Return Seasonality", *Journal of Financial Economics*, pp. 13–32.
Keim, D. B., 1988, "Stock Market Regularities: A Synthesis of the Evidence and Explanations", in *Stock Market Anomalies*, (Dimson, E.,) Cambridge, UK: Cambridge University Press.
Kendall, M. G., 1953, "The Analysis of Economic Time Series. I", *Journal of the Royal Statistical Society*, pp. 11–25.
Keynes, J. M., 1921, *A Treatise on Probability*, London: MacMillan & Co.
Kjellman, A., & Hansén, S., 1995, "Determinants of Capital Structure: Theory vs. Practice", *Scandinavian Journal of Management*, pp. 91–102.
Knight, F., 1921, *Risk, Uncertainty and Profit*, Boston: Houghton-Mifflin.
Kothari, S., Shanken, J., & Sloan, R., 1995, "Another Look at the Cross-section of Expected Stock Returns", *Journal of Finance*, pp. 185–224
Lakonishok, J., Shleifer, A., & Vishny, R., 1994, "Contrarian Investment, Extrapolation, and Risk", *Journal of Finance*, pp. 1541–1578.
Landström, J., 2001, "Drömmen Om Evigt Liv – Eller Hur Förvärvad Goodwill Bör Avskrivas", Department of Business Studies, Uppsala University.
Lefevre, E., 1923, *Reminiscences of a Stock Operator*, Greenville: Traders Press.
Levin, J., 1998, Essays in Company Valuation, Doctoral thesis, Stockholm School of Economics, EFI, Stockholm: Elanders Gotab.
Lin, W. L., Engle, R. F., & Ito, T., 1994, "Do Bulls and Bears Move Across Borders? Transmission of International Stock Returns and Volatility", *Journal of International Money and Finance*, pp. 507–538.
Lintner, J., 1956, "Distribution of Incomes of Corporations Among Dividends, Retained Earnings, and Taxes", *American Economic Review*, pp. 97–113.
Lintner, J., 1965, "Security Prices, Risk and Maximal Gains from Diversification", *Journal of Finance*, pp. 587–616.
Lo, A. W., & MacKinlay, C. A., 1988, "Stock Market Prices do not Follow Random Walks: Evidence From a Simple Specification Test", *Review of Financial Studies*, pp. 41–66.
Longin, F., & Solnik, B., 1995, "Is the Correlation in International Stock Returns Constant: 1960–1990?", *Journal of International Money and Finance*, pp. 3–26.
Loughran, T., & Ritter, J. R., 1995, "The New Issues Puzzle", *Journal of Finance*, pp. 23–51.
Lundholm, R., & O'Keefe, T., 2001, "Reconciling Value Estimates from the Discounted Cash Flow Model and the Residual Income Model", forthcoming in *Contemporary Accounting Research*.
MacCrimmon, K. R., & Wehrung, D. A., 1986, *Taking Risks: The Management of Uncertainty*, New York: The Free Press.
Magenheim, E. B., & Mueller, D. C., 1988, "Are Acquiring-Firm Shareholders Better Off After an Acquisition?", in *Knights, Raiders, and Targets*, (Coffee, J C., Lowenstein, L., & Rose-Ackerman, S.) New York: Oxford University Press.
Mandelker, G. N., & Rhee, S. G., 1984, "The Impact of the Degrees of Operating and Financial Leverage on Systematic Risk of Common Stock", *Journal of Financial and Quantitative Analysis*, pp. 45–57.
Mann, M. H., 1966, "Seller Concentration, Barriers to Entry, and Rates of Return in Thirty Industries, 1950–60", *Review of Economics and Statistics*, pp. 296–307.

March, J. G., 1994, *A Primer on Decision Making – How Decisions Happen*, New York: The Free Press.
March, J. G., & Shapira, Z., 1987, "Managerial Perspectives on Risk and Risk Taking", *Management Science*, pp. 1404–1418.
Markowitz, H., 1952, "Portfolio Selection", *Journal of Finance*, pp. 77–91.
Markowitz, H., 1959, *Portfolio Selection*, New York: John Wiley & Sons.
Marshall, A., 1890, *Principles of Economics*, New York: MacMillan.
Mayer, C., 1996, "Corporate Governance, Competition and Performance", Working Paper, School of Management Studies, University of Oxford.
McConnell, J. J., & Muscarella, C. J., 1985, "Corporate Capital Expenditure Decisions and the Market Value of the Firm", *Journal of Financial Economics*, pp. 399–422.
McWilliams, A., & Siegel, D., 1997, "Event Studies in Management Research: Theoretical and Empirical Issues, I", *Academy of Management Journal*, pp. 626–657.
Megginson, W. L., 1997, *Corporate Finance Theory*, Massachusetts: Addison-Wesley, Reading.
Megginson, W. L., Nash, R. C., & van Randenborgh, M., 1994, "The Financial and Operating Performance of Newly-Privatized Firms: An International Empirical Analysis", *Journal of Finance*, pp. 403–452.
Merton, R. C., 1973, "An Intertemporal Capital Asset Pricing Model", *Econometrica*, pp. 867–887.
Michaely, R., Thaler, R. H., & Womack, K. L., 1995, "Price Reactions to Dividend Initiations and Omissions: Overreaction or Drift", *Journal of Finance*, pp. 573–608.
Miller, K. D., & Bromiley, P., 1996, "Strategic risk and corporate performance: An analysis of alternative risk measures", *Academy of Management Journal*, pp. 756–779.
Miller, M. H., & Modigliani, F., 1958, "The Cost of Capital, Corporation Finance, and the Theory of Investment", *American Economic Review*, pp. 261–297.
Miller, M. H., & Modigliani, F., 1961, "Dividend Policy, Growth, and the Valuation of Shares", *Journal of Business*, pp. 411–433.
Miller, M. H., & Modigliani, F., 1963, "Corporate Income Taxes and the Cost of Capital: A Correction", *American Economic Review*, pp. 433–443.
Miller, M. H., & Rock, K., 1985, "Dividend Policy Under Asymmetric Information", *Journal of Finance*, pp. 1031–1051.
Mossin, J., 1966, "Equilibrium in a Capital Asset Market", *Econometrica*, pp. 768–783.
Mueller, D. C., 1977, "The Persistence of Profits Above the Norm", *Economica*, pp. 369–380.
Mueller, D. C., 1985, "Mergers and Market Share", *Review of Economics and Statistics*, pp. 259–267.
Mueller, D. C., 1990, *The Dynamics of Company Profits – An International Comparison*, Cambridge, UK: Cambridge University Press.
Myers, S. C., 1974, "Interactions of Corporate Financing and Investment Decisions – Implications for Capital Budgeting", *Journal of Finance*, pp. 1–25.
Myers, S. C., 1977, "Determinants of Corporate Borrowing", *Journal of Financial Economics*, pp. 147–175.

Myers, S. C., 1984, "The Capital Structure Puzzle", *Journal of Finance*, pp. 575–592.

Myers, S. C., & Majluf, N. S., 1984, "Corporate Financing and Investment When Firms Have Information Investors Do Not Have", *Journal of Financial Economics*, pp. 187–221.

Neill, J. D., Schaefer, T. F., Banson, P. R., & Bradbury M, E., 1991, "The Usefulness of Cash Flow Data: A Review and Synthesis", *Journal of Accounting Literature*, pp. 117–150.

Nissim, D., & Penman, S. H., 1999, "Ratio Analysis and Equity Valuation", Working Paper, Graduate School of Business, Columbia University.

O'Byrne, S., 1996, "EVA, and Market Value", *Journal of Applied Corporate Finance*, pp. 116–125.

Odean, T., 1998, "Are Investors Reluctant to Realize Losses?", *Journal of Finance*, pp. 1775–1798.

Opler, T., & Titman, S., 1993, "The Determinants of Leveraged Buyout Activity: Free Cash Flows vs. Financial Distress Costs", *Journal of Finance*, pp. 1985–1999.

Penman, 2001, *Financial Statement Analysis and Security Valuation*, New York: McGraw-Hill.

Phillips, G. M., "Increased Debt and Industry Product Markets: An Empirical Analysis", *Journal of Financial Economics*, pp. 189–238.

Pilotte, E., 1992, "Growth Opportunities and the Stock Price Response to New Financing", *Journal of Business*, pp. 371–394.

Pinegar, M. J., & Wilbricht, L., 1989, "What Managers Think of Capital Structure Theory: A Survey", *Financial Management*, pp. 82–91.

Pohlman, R. A., Santiago, E. S., & Markel, F. L., 1988, "Cash Flow Estimation Practices of Large Firms", *Financial Management*, pp. 71–79.

Porter, M. E., 1980, *Competitive Strategy: Techniques for Analyzing Industries and Competitors*, New York: Free Press.

Poterba, J. M., & Summers, L. H., 1988, "Mean Reversion in Stock Prices: Evidence and Implications", *Journal of Financial Economics*, pp. 27–59.

Pound, J., & Zeckhauser, R., 1990, "Clearly Heard on the Street: The Effects of Takeover Rumours on Stock Prices", *Journal of Business*, pp. 291–308.

Pruitt, S. W., & Gitman, L. J., 1987, "Capital Budgeting Forecast Biases: Evidence From the Fortune 500", *Financial Management*, pp. 46–51.

Rajan, R. G., & Zingales, L., 1995, "What Do We Know About Capital Structure? Some Evidence From International Data", *Journal of Finance*, pp. 1421–1460.

Rajan, R. G., & Zingales, L., 1998, "Debt, Folklore, and Cross-country Differences in Financial Structure", *Journal of Applied Corporate Finance*, pp. 102–107.

Roberts, H. V., 1959, "Stock Market 'Patterns' and Financial Analysis: Methodological Suggestions", *Journal of Finance*, pp. 1–10.

Roll, R., 1977, "A Critique of the Asset Pricing Theory's Tests – Part I: On Past and Potential Testability of the Theory", *Journal of Financial Economics*, pp. 129–176.

Roll, R., 1983, "On Computing Mean Returns and the Small Firm Premium", *Journal of Financial Economics*, pp. 371–386.

Roll, R., 1988, "R-Squared", *Journal of Finance*, pp. 541–566.

Roll, R., & Ross, S. A., 1980, "An Empirical Investigation of the Arbitrage Pricing Theory", *Journal of Finance*, pp. 1073–1103.

Ross, S. A., 1976, "The Arbitrage Theory of Capital Asset Pricing", *Journal of Economic Theory*, pp. 343–362.

Rouwenhorst, K. G., 1998, "International Momentum Strategies", *Journal of Finance*, pp. 267–284.

Rozeff, M., 1982, "Growth, Beta and Agency Costs as Determinants of Dividend Payout Ratios", *Journal of Financial Research*, pp. 249–259.

Rubinstein, M. E., 1973, "A Mean-Variance Synthesis of Corporate Financial Theory", *Journal of Finance*, pp. 167–181.

Rubinstein, M. E., 2001, Efficient Markets: Yes or No? The Affirmative Case, *Financial Analysts Journal*, p. 15–29.

Samuelson, P. A., 1965, "Proof That Properly Anticipated Prices Fluctuate Randomly", *Industrial Management Review*, pp. 41–49.

Savage, L. J., 1954, *The Foundations of Statistics*, New York: Wiley Publications.

Schiereck, D., De Bondt, W., & Weber, M., 1999, "Contrarian and Momentum Strategies in Germany", *Financial Analysts Journal*, pp. 104–116.

Schwert, G. W., 1983, "Size and Stock Returns, and Other Empirical Regularities", *Journal of Financial Economics*, pp. 3–12.

Segelod, E., 1986, *Kalkylering och Avvikelser: Empiriska Studier av Stora Projekt i Kommuner och Industri*, Malmö: LiberFörlag.

Segelod, E., 1991, *Capital Investment Appraisal – Toward a Contingency Theory*, Lund: Studentlitteratur.

Seyhun, H. N., 1986, "Insiders' Profits, Cost of Trading, and Market Efficiency", *Journal of Financial Economics*, pp. 189–212.

Seyhun, H. N., 1998, "The Information Content of Aggregate Insider Trading", *Journal of Business*, pp. 1–24.

Shapira, Z., 1995, *Risk Taking: A Managerial Perspective*, New York: Russell Sage Foundation.

Sharpe, W. F., 1964, "Capital Asset Prices: A Theory of Market Equilibrium under Conditions of Risk", *Journal of Finance,* pp. 425–442.

Shefrin, H., & Statman, M., 1984, "Explaining Investor Preference for Cash Dividends", *Journal of Financial Economics*, pp. 253–282.

Sherden, W. A., 1998, *The Fortune Sellers – The Big Business of Buying and Selling Predictions*, New York: John Wiley & Sons.

Shiller, R. J., 1981, "Do Stock Prices Move Too Much to Be Justified by Subsequent Changes in Dividends?", *American Economic Review*, pp. 421–436.

Shiller, R. J., 2000, *Irrational Exuberance*, Princeton: Princeton University Press.

Shleifer, A., & Vishny R. W., 1998, "A Survey of Corporate Governance", *Journal of Finance*, pp. 737–775.

Shyam-Sunder, L., & Myers, S. C., 1999, "Testing Static Tradeoff Against Pecking Order Models of Capital Structure", *Journal of Financial Economics*, pp. 219–244.

Simon, H. A., 1978, "Rationality as Process and as Product of Thought", *American Economic Association*, pp. 1–16.

Sirower, M. L., 1997, *The Synergy Trap – How Companies Lose the Acquisition Game*, New York: Free Press.

Smith, A., 1776, *An Inquiry into the Nature and Causes of the Wealth of Nations*, New York: Cannan Edition.

Statman, M., 1995, "Behavioral Finance versus Standard Finance", *In Behavioral Finance and Decision Theory in Investment Management*, Edited by Arnold S. Wood, Charlotteville, VA: AIMR.

Statman, M., 1999, "Behaviorial Finance: Past Battles and Future Engagements", *Financial Analysts Journal*, pp. 18–27.

Stein, J., 1996, "Rational Capital Budgeting in an Irrational World", *Journal of Business*, pp. 429–456.

Stern, J. M., Stewart, G. B., III, & Chew, D. H., Jr, 1995, "The EVA Financial Management System", *Journal of Applied Corporate Finance*, pp. 32–46.

Stewart, G. B., III, 1991, *The Quest for Value*, New York, Harper Business.

Stewart, G. B., III, 1994, "EVA: Fact or Fantasy?", *Journal of Applied Corporate Finance*, pp. 71–84.

Stigler, G. J., 1964, "A Theory of Oligopoly", *Journal of Political Economy*, pp. 44–61.

Solomons, D., 1965, "Division Performance: Measurement and Control", *Financial Executives Research Foundation*, New York.

Sundqvist, S-I., 1982–1996, *Ägarna och Makten*, DNs Ägarservice, Stockholm: DN.

Thaler, R., 1999, "The End of Behavioral Finance", *Financial Analysts Journal*, pp. 12–17.

Thunholm, L-E., 1995, *Ivar Kreuger*, Stockholm: Fischer.

Tobin, J., 1958, "Liquidity Preference as a Behavior Towards Risk", *Review of Economic Studies*, pp. 65–86.

Tversky, A., 1995, "The Psychology of Decision Making", in *Behavioral Finance and Decision Theory in Investment Management*, edited by Arnold S. Wood, Charlotteville, VA: AIMR.

von Neumann, J., & Morgenstern, O., 1944, *The Theory of Games and Economic Behavior*, Princeton, New Jersey: Princeton University Press.

Walker, E. W., & Petty, J. W., 1978, "Financial Differences Between Large and Small Firms", *Financial Management*, pp. 61–68.

Wallace, J. S., 1997, "Adopting Residual Income-Based Compensation Plans: Do You Get What You Pay For?", *Journal of Accounting and Economics*, pp. 275–300.

Warner, J. B., 1977, "Bankruptcy Costs: Some Evidence", *Journal of Finance*, pp. 337–347.

White, G. I., Sondhi, A. C., & Fried, D., 1994, *The Analysis and Use of Financial Statements*, New York: John Wiley & Sons.

Williams, J. B., 1938, *The Theory of Investment Value*, Cambridge: Harvard University Press.

Working, H., 1934, "A Random-Difference Series for Use in the Analysis of Time Series", *Journal of American Statistical Association*, p. 11.

Zakon, A. G., 1976, "Capital-Structure Optimization", in *The Treasurer's Handbook*, (Weston, J. F., & Goudzwaard, M. B.) Illinois: Irwin.

Åkerblom, M., 1996, *Compendium: Corporate Finance and Capital Budgeting*, Företagsekonomiska institutionen, Uppsala University.

Åkerblom, M., 2001, Evaluating and Financing Company Projects, Uppsala: Företagsekonomiska institutionen.